Visual Perception of Music Notation: On-Line and Off-Line Recognition

Susan E. George
University of South Australia, Australia

IRM Press
Publisher of innovative scholarly and professional information technology titles in the cyberage

Hershey • London • Melbourne • Singapore

Acquisitions Editor: Mehdi Khosrow-Pour
Senior Managing Editor: Jan Travers
Managing Editor: Amanda Appicello
Development Editor: Michele Rossi
Copy Editor: Michelle Wilgenburg
Typesetter: Amanda Appicello
Cover Design: Lisa Tosheff
Printed at: Integrated Book Technology

Published in the United States of America by
IRM Press (an imprint of Idea Group Inc.)
701 E. Chocolate Avenue, Suite 200
Hershey PA 17033-1240
Tel: 717-533-8845
Fax: 717-533-8661
E-mail: cust@idea-group.com
Web site: http://www.irm-press.com

and in the United Kingdom by
IRM Press (an imprint of Idea Group Inc.)
3 Henrietta Street
Covent Garden
London WC2E 8LU
Tel: 44 20 7240 0856
Fax: 44 20 7379 3313
Web site: http://www.eurospan.co.uk

Library of Congress Cataloging-in-Publication Data

George, Susan Ella.
Visual perception of music notation : on-line and off-line recognition / Susan Ella George.
p. cm.
Includes bibliographical references and index.
ISBN 1-931777-94-2 (pbk.) -- ISBN 1-931777-95-0 (ebook)
1. Musical notation--Data processing. 2. Artificial intelligence--Musical applications. I. Title.
ML73.G46 2005
780'.1'48028564--dc21

2003008875

ISBN 1-59140-298-0 (h/c)

British Cataloguing in Publication Data
A Cataloguing in Publication record for this book is available from the British Library.

Visual Perception of Music Notation: On-Line and Off-Line Recognition

Table of Contents

Preface

Overview of Subject Matter and Topic Context

The computer recognition of music notation, its interpretation and use within various applications, raises many challenges and questions with regards to the appropriate algorithms, techniques and methods with which to automatically understand music notation. Modern day music notation is one of the most widely recognised international languages of all time. It has developed over many years as requirements of consistency and precision led to the development of both music theory and representation. Graphic forms of notation are first known from the 7th Century, with the modern system for notes developed in Europe during the 14th Century. This volume consolidates the successes, challenges and questions raised by the computer perception of this music notation language.

The computer perception of music notation began with the field of Optical Music Recognition (OMR) as researchers tackled the problem of recognising and interpreting the symbols of printed music notation from a scanned image. More recently, interest in automatic perception has extended to all components of song lyric, melody and other symbols, even broadening to multi-lingual handwritten components. With the advent of pen-based input systems, automatic recognition of notation has also extended into the on-line context — moving away from processing static scanned images, to recognising dynamically constructed pen strokes. New applications, including concert-planning systems sensitive to the emotional content of music, have placed new demands upon description, representation and recognition.

Summary of Sections and Chapters

This special volume consists of both invited chapters and open-solicited chapters written by leading researchers in the field. All papers were peer reviewed by at least two recognised reviewers. This book contains 10 chapters divided into five sections:

Section 1 is concerned with the processing of music images, or Optical Music Recognition (OMR). A focus is made upon recognising printed typeset music from a scanned image of music score. Section 2 extends the recognition of music notation to handwritten rather than printed typeset music, and also moves into the on-line context with a consideration of dynamic pen-based input. Section 3 focuses upon lyric recognition and the identification and representation of conventional lyric text combined with the symbols of music notation. Section 4 considers the importance of music description languages with emerging applications, including the context of Web-based multi-media and concert planning systems sensitive to the emotional content of music. Finally, Section 5 considers the difficulty of evaluating automatic perceptive systems, discussing the issues and providing some benchmark test data.

Section 1: Off-Line Music Processing

- Chapter 1: Staff Detection and Removal, Ichiro Fujinaga
- Chapter 2: An Off-line Optical Music Sheet Recognition, Pierfrancesco Bellini, Ivan Bruno, Paolo Nesi
- Chapter 3: Wavelets for Dealing with Super-Imposed Objects in Recognition of Music Notation, Susan E. George

Section 2: Handwritten Music Recognition

- Chapter 4: Optical Music Analysis for Printed Music Score and Handwritten Music Manuscript, Kia Ng
- Chapter 5: Pen-Based Input for On-Line Handwritten Music Notation, Susan E. George

Section 3: Lyric Recognition

- Chapter 6: Multilingual Lyric Modeling and Management, Pierfrancesco Bellini, Ivan Bruno, Paolo Nesi
- Chapter 7: Lyric Recognition and Christian Music, Susan E. George

Section 4: Music Description and its Applications

- Chapter 8: Towards Constructing Emotional Landscapes with Music, Dave Billinge, Tom Addis
- Chapter 9: Modeling Music Notation in the Internet Multimedia Age, Pierfrancesco Bellini, Paolo Nesi

Section 5: Evaluation

- Chapter 10: Evaluation in the Visual Perception of Music, Susan E. George

Description of Each Chapter

In Chapter 1, Dr. Ichiro Fujinaga describes the issues involved in the detection and removal of stafflines of musical scores. This removal process is an important step for many optical music recognition systems and facilitates the segmentation and recognition of musical symbols. The process is complicated by the fact that most music symbols are placed on top of stafflines and these lines are often neither straight nor parallel to each other. The challenge here is to remove as much of the stafflines as possible while preserving the shapes of the musical symbols, which are superimposed on stafflines. Various problematic examples are illustrated and a detailed explanation of an algorithm is presented. Image processing techniques used in the algorithm include: run-length coding, connected-component analysis, and projections.

In Chapter 2, Professor Pierfrancesco Bellini, Mr. Ivan Bruno and Professor Paolo Nesi compare OMR with OCR and discuss the O^3MR system. An overview of the main issues and a survey of the main related works are discussed. The O^3MR system (Object Oriented Optical Music Recognition) system is also described. The used approach in such system is based on the adoption of projections for the extraction of basic symbols that constitute graphic elements of the music notation. Algorithms and a set of examples are also included to better focus concepts and adopted solutions.

In Chapter 3, Dr. Susan E. George investigates a problem that arises in OMR when notes and other music notation symbols are super-imposed upon stavelines in the music image. A general purpose knowledge-free method of image filtering using two-dimensional wavelets is investigated to separate the super-imposed objects. The filtering provides a unified theory of staveline removal/symbol segmentation, and practically is a useful pre-processing method for OMR.

In Chapter 4, Dr. Kia Ng examines a method of recognising printed music — both handwritten and typeset. The chapter presents a brief background of the field, discusses the main obstacles, and presents the processes involved for printed music scores processing; using a divide-and-conquer approach to sub-segment compound musical symbols (e.g., chords) and inter-connected groups (e.g., beamed quavers) into lower-level graphical primitives such as lines and ellipses before recognition and reconstruction. This is followed by discussions on the developments of a handwritten manuscripts prototype with a segmentation approach to separate handwritten musical primitives. Issues and approaches for recognition, reconstruction and revalidation using basic music syntax and high-level domain knowledge, and data representation are also presented.

In Chapter 5, Dr. Susan E. George concentrates upon the recognition of handwritten music entered in a dynamic editing context with use of pen-based input. The chapter makes a survey of the current scope of on-line (or dynamic) handwritten input of music notation, presenting the outstanding problems in recognition. A solution using the multi-layer perception artificial neural network is presented, explaining experiments in music symbol recognition from a study involving notation writing from some 25 people using a pressure-sensitive digitiser for input. Results suggest that a voting system among networks trained to recognize individual symbols produces the best recognition rate.

In Chapter 6, Professor Pierfrancesco Bellini, Mr. Ivan Bruno and Professor Paolo Nesi present an object-oriented language capable of modelling music notation and lyrics. This new model makes it possible to "plug" on the symbolic score different lyrics depending on the language. This is done by keeping separate the music notation model and the lyrics model. An object-oriented model of music notation and lyrics are presented with many examples. These models have been implemented in the music editor produced within the WEDELMUSIC IST project. A specific language has been developed to associate the lyrics with the score. The most important music notation formats are reviewed focusing on their representation of multilingual lyrics.

In Chapter 7, Dr. Susan E. George presents a consideration of lyric recognition in OMR in the context of Christian music. Lyrics are obviously found in other music contexts, but they are of primary importance in Christian music — where the words are as integral as the notation. This chapter (i) identifies the inseparability of notation and word in Christian music, (ii) isolates the challenges of lyric recognition in OMR providing some examples of lyric recognition achieved by current OMR software and (iii) considers some solutions outlining page segmentation and character/word recognition approaches, particularly focusing upon the target of recognition, as a high level representation language, that integrates the music with lyrics.

In Chapter 8, Dr. Dave Billinge and Professor Tom Addis investigate language to describe the emotional and perceptual content of music in linguistic terms. They aim for a new paradigm in human-computer interaction that they call tropic mediation and describe the origins of the research in a wish to provide a concert planner with an expert system. Some consideration is given to how music might have arisen within human culture and in particular why it presents unique problems of verbal description. An initial investigation into a discrete, stable lexicon of musical effect is summarised and the authors explain how and why they reached their current work on a computable model of word connotation rather than reference. It is concluded that machines, in order to communicate with people, will need to work with a model of emotional implication to approach the "human" sense of words.

In Chapter 9, Professor Pierfrancesco Bellini and Professor Paolo Nesi describe emerging applications in the new multimedia Internet age. For these innovative applications several aspects have to be integrated with the model of music notation, such as: automatic formatting, music notation navigation, synchronization of music notation with real audio, etc. In this chapter, the WEDELMUSIC XML format for multimedia music applications of music notation is presented. It includes a music notation format in XML and a format for modelling multimedia elements, their relationships and synchronization with a support for digital right management (DRM). In addition, a comparison of this new model with the most important and emerging models is reported. The taxonomy used can be useful for assessing and comparing suitability of music notation models and formats for their adoption in new emerging applications and for their usage in classical music editors.

In Chapter 10, Dr. Susan E. George considers the problem of evaluating the recognition music notation in both the on-line and off-line (traditional OMR) contexts. The chapter presents a summary of reviews that have been performed for commercial OMR systems and addresses some of the issues in evaluation that must be taken into account to enable adequate comparison of recognition performance. A representation language (HEART) is suggested, such that the semantics of music is captured (including the dynamics of handwritten music) and hence a target representation provided for recognition processes. Initial consideration of the range of test data that is needed (MusicBase I and II) is also made.

Conclusion

This book will be useful to researchers and students in the field of pattern recognition, document analysis and pen-based computing, as well as potential users and vendors in the specific field of music recognition systems.

Acknowledgments

We would like to acknowledge the help of all involved in the collation and the review process of this book, without whose support the project could not have been satisfactorily completed. Thanks go to all who provided constructive and comprehensive reviews and comments. Most of the authors also served as referees for articles written by other authors and a special thanks is due to them.

The staff at Idea Group Inc. have also made significant contributions to this final publication, especially Michele Rossi — who never failed to address my many e-mails — Jan Travers, and Mehdi Khosrow-Pour; without their input this work would not have been possible.

The support of the School of Computer and Information Science, University of South Australia was also particularly valuable, since the editing work was initiated and finalized within this context.

Finally, thanks to my husband David F. J. George, who enabled the completion of this volume, with his loving support — before, during and after the birth of our beautiful twins, Joanna and Abigail; received with much joy during the course of this project!

Susan E. George
Editor

Section 1: Off-Line Music Processing

Staff Detection and Removal

Ichiro Fujinaga
McGill University, Canada

Abstract

This chapter describes the issues involved in the detection and removal of stavelines of musical scores. This removal process is an important step for many Optical Music Recognition systems and facilitates the segmentation and recognition of musical symbols. The process is complicated by the fact that most music symbols are placed on top of stavelines and these lines are often neither straight nor parallel to each other. The challenge here is to remove as much of stavelines as possible while preserving the shapes of the musical symbols, which are superimposed on stavelines. Various problematic examples are illustrated and a detailed explanation of an algorithm is presented. Image processing techniques used in the algorithm include: run-length coding, connected-component analysis, and projections.

Introduction

One of the initial challenges in any Optical Music Recognition (OMR) system is the treatment of the staves. For musicians, stavelines are required to facilitate reading the notes. For the machine, however, it becomes an obstacle for making the segmentation of the symbols very difficult. The task of separating background from foreground figures is an unsolved problem in many machine pattern recognition systems in general.

There are two approaches to this problem in OMR systems. One way is to try to remove the stavelines without removing the parts of the music symbols that are superimposed. The other method is to leave the stavelines untouched and devise a method to segment the symbols (Bellini, Bruno & Nesi, 2001; Carter, 1989; Fujinaga, 1988; Itagaki, Isogai, Hashimoto & Ohteru, 1992; Modayur, Ramesh, Haralick & Shapiro, 1993).

In the OMR system described here, which is part of a large document analysis system, the former approach is taken; that is, the stavelines are carefully removed, without removing too much from the music symbols. This decision was taken basically for three reasons:

(1) Symbols such as ties are very difficult to locate when they are placed right over the stavelines (see Figure 1).

(2) One of the hazards of removing stavelines is that parts of music symbols may be removed in the process. But due to printing imperfection or due to damage to the punches that were used for printing (Fujinaga, 1988), the music symbols are often already fragmented, without removing the stavelines. In other words, there should be a mechanism to deal with broken symbols whether one removes the stavelines or not.

(3) Removing the stavelines simplifies many of the consequent steps in the recognition process.

Figure 1: Tie Superimposed Over Staff

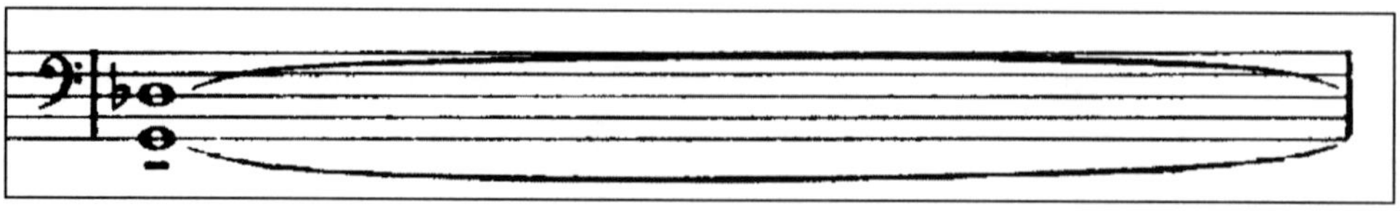

Overview of OMR Research

The OMR research began with two MIT doctoral dissertations (Prusslin, 1966, 1970). With the availability of inexpensive optical scanners, much research began in the 1980s. Excellent historical reviews of OMR systems are given in Blostein and Baird (1992) and in Bainbridge and Carter (1997). After Prusslin and Prerau, doctoral dissertations describing OMR systems have been completed by Bainbridge (1997), Carter (1989), Coüasnon (1996), Fujinaga (1997), and Ng (1995). Many commercial OMR software exists today, such as capella-scan, OMeR, PhotoScore, SharpEye, and SmartScore.

Background

The following procedure for detecting and removing staves may seem overly complex, but it was found necessary in order to deal with the variety of staff configurations and distortions such as skewing.

The detection of staves is complicated by the variety of staves that are used. The five-line staff is most common today, yet the "four-line staff was widely used from the eleventh to the 13th century and the five-line staff did not become standard until mid-17th century, (some keyboard music of the 16th and 17th centuries employed staves of as many as 15 lines)" (Read, 1979, p. 28). Today, percussion parts may have one to several numbers of lines. The placement and the size of staves may vary on a given page because of an auxiliary staff, which is an alternate or correction in modern editions (Figure 2); an ornaments staff (Figure 3); ossia passages (Figure 4), which are technically simplified versions of difficult sections; or more innovative placements of staves (Figure 5). In addition, due to various reasons, the stavelines are rarely straight and horizontal, and are not parallel to each other. For example, some staves may be tilted one way or another on the same page or they maybe curved.

Figure 2: An Example of an Auxiliary Staff

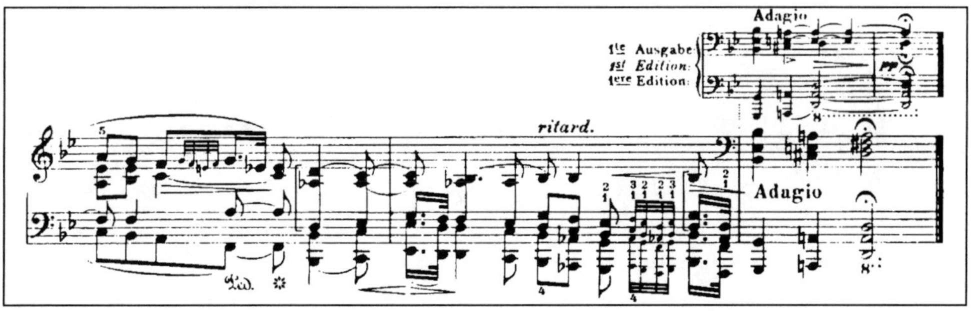

Figure 3: An Example of Ornament Staves

Figure 4: An Example of an Ossia Staff

Figure 5: An Example of Innovative Staff Layout

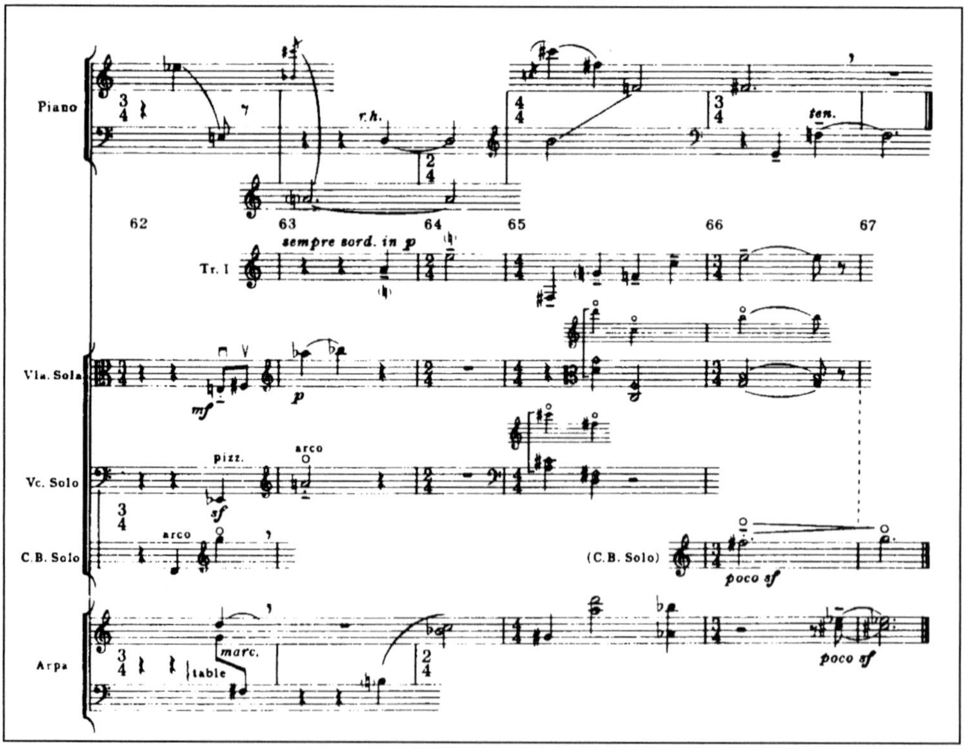

The Reliability of Staffline_Height and Staffspace_Height

In order to design a robust staff detector that can process a variety of input, one must proceed carefully, not making too many assumptions. There are, fortunately, some reliable factors that can aid in the detection process.

The thickness of stavelines, the **staffline_height**, on a page is more or less consistent. The space between the stavelines, the **staffspace_height**, also has small variance within a staff. This is important, for this information can greatly facilitate the detection and removal of stavelines. Furthermore, there is an image processing technique to reliably estimate these values. The technique is the vertical run-lengths representation of the image.

Run-length coding is a simple data compression method where a sequence of identical numbers is represented by the number and the length of the run. For example, the sequence {3 3 3 3 5 5 9 9 9 9 9 9 9 9 9 9 9 9 6 6 6 6 6} can be coded as {(3, 4) (5, 2) (9, 12) (6, 5)}. In a binary image, used as input for the recognition process here, there are only two values: one and zero. In such a case, the run-length coding is even more compact, because only the lengths of the runs are needed. For example, the sequence {1 1 1 1 1 1 1 0 0 0 0 1 1 1 1 1 1 1 1 1 1 1 1 1 0 0 0 0 0 0 0 0 1 1} can be coded as {7, 4, 13, 8, 2}, assuming 1 starts a sequence (if a sequence starts with a 0, the length of zero would be used). By encoding each row or column of a digitized score the image can be compressed to about one tenth of the original size. Furthermore, by writing programs that are based on run-length coding, dramatic reduction in processing time can be achieved.

Vertical run-lengths coding is, therefore, a compact representation of the binary image matrix column by column.

If a bit-mapped page of music is converted to vertical run-lengths coding, the most common black-runs represents the staffline_height (Figure 6) and the most common white-runs represents the staffspace_height (Figure 7). Even in music with different staff sizes, there will be prominent peaks at the most frequent staffspaces (Figure 8). These estimates are also immune to severe rotation of the image. Figure 9 shows the results of white vertical run-lengths of the music used in Figure 8 rotated intentionally 15 degrees. It is very useful and crucial, at this very early stage, to have a good approximation of what is on the page. Further processing can be performed based on these values and not be dependent on some predetermined magic numbers. The use of fixed threshold numbers, as found in other OMR systems, makes systems inflexible and difficult to adapt to new and unexpected situations.

Figure 6: Estimating Staffline_Height by Vertical Black Runs (the graph shows that the staffline_height of 4 pixels is most prominent)

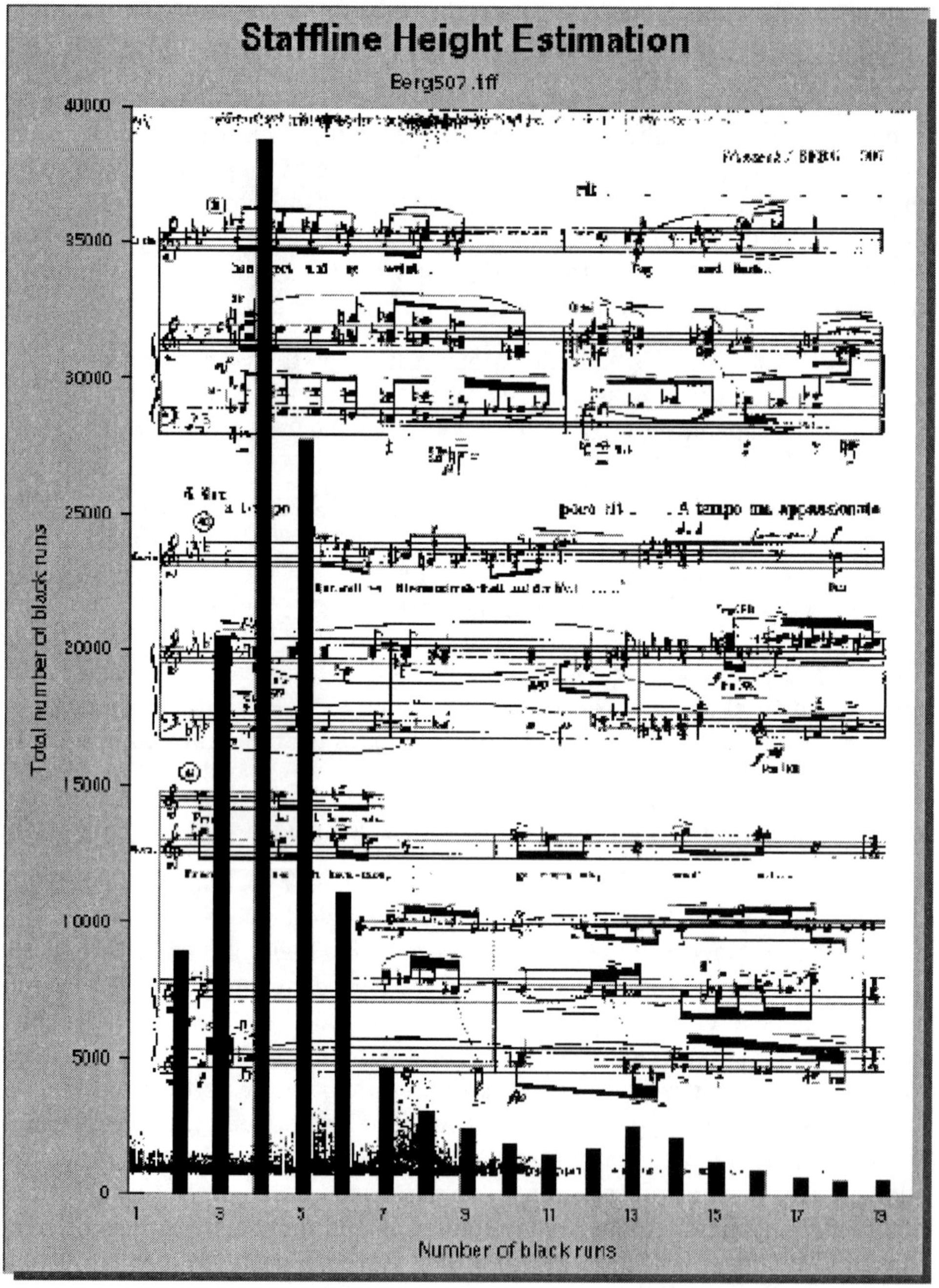

Figure 7: Estimating Staffspace_Height by Vertical White Runs (the graph shows that the staffspace_height of 14 pixels is most prominent)

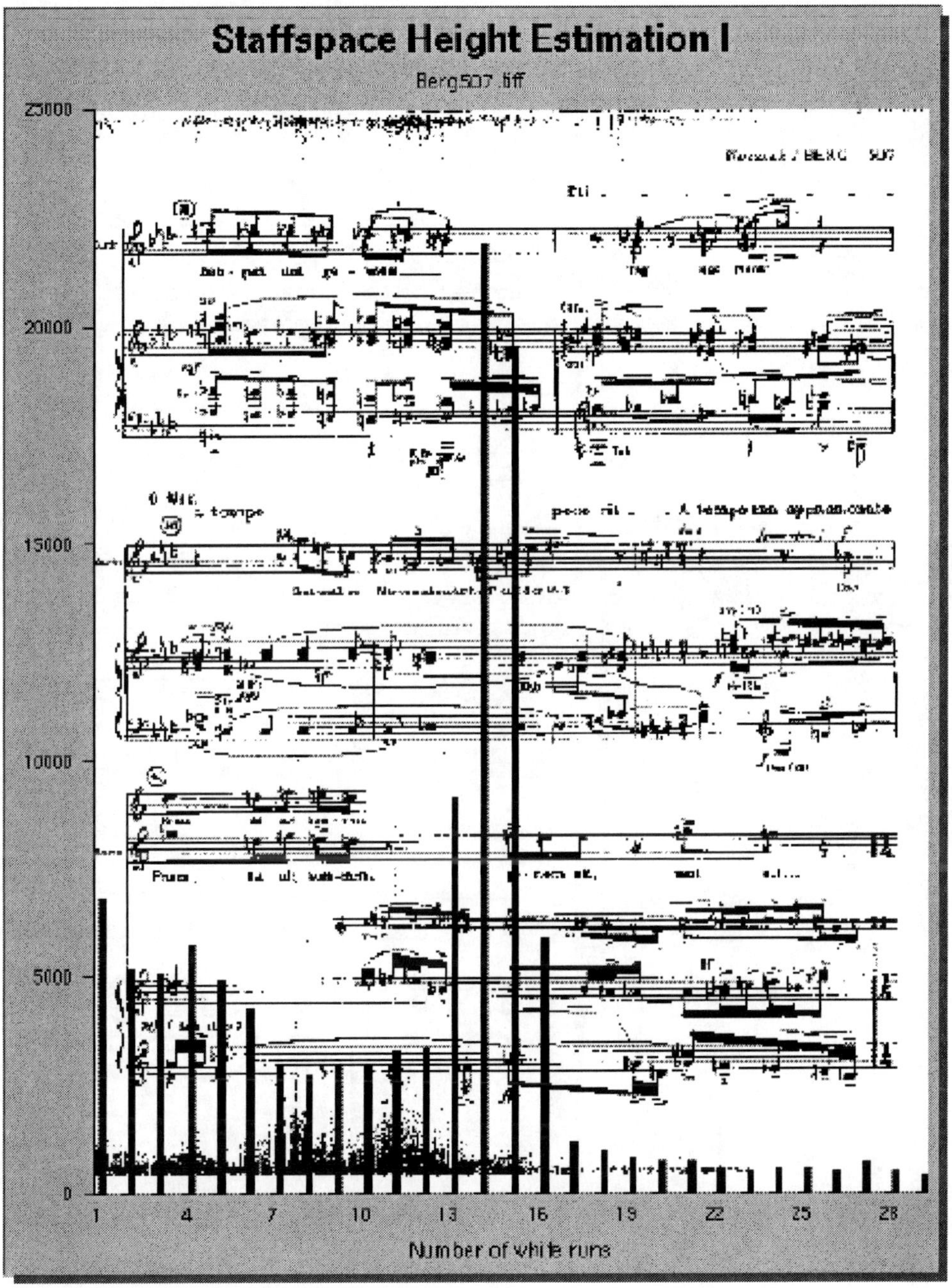

Figure 8: Estimating Staffspace_Height by Vertical White Runs with Multiple-Size Staves

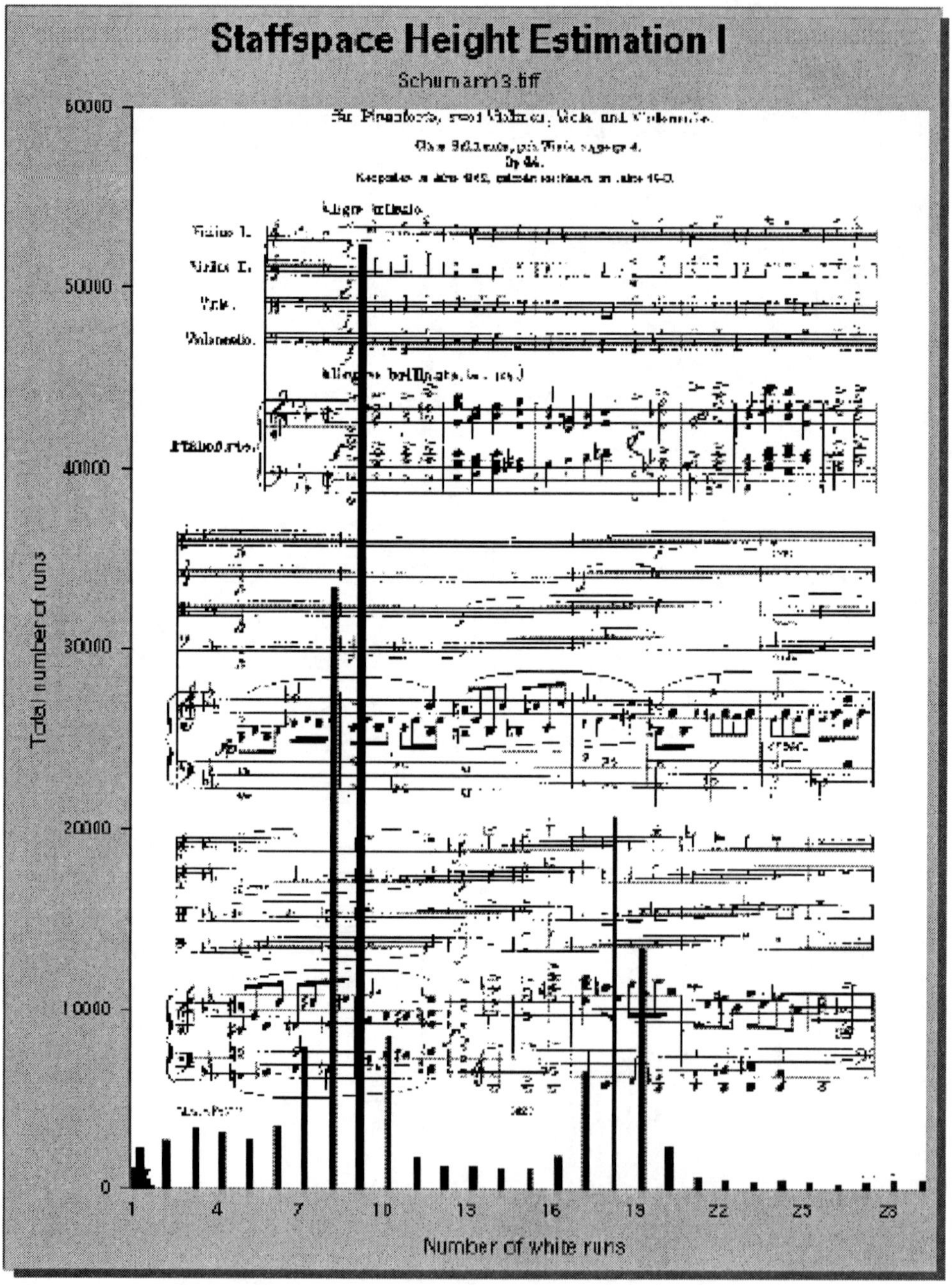

Figure 9: Estimating Staffspace_Height by Vertical White Runs of a Skewed Image (the music used in Figure 8 is rotated 15 degrees)

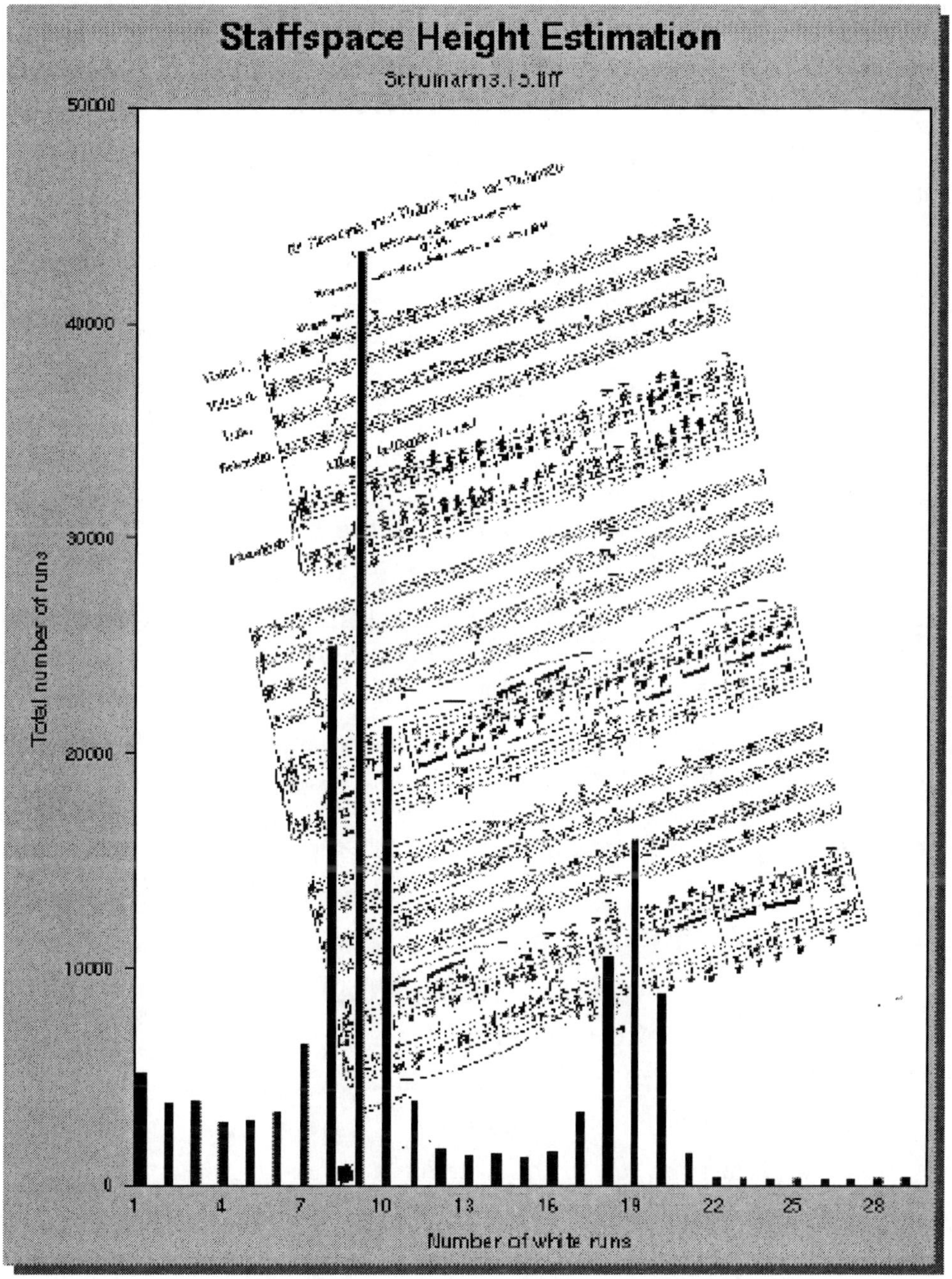

The Connected Component Analysis

Once the initial estimates of the size of the staves have been obtained, the process of finding the stavelines, deskewing them if necessary, then finally removing them can be performed. In this process an image processing technique called the connected component analysis is deployed.

The connected component analysis is an important concept in image segmentation when determining if a group of pixels is considered to be an object. A connected set is one in which all the pixels are adjacent or touching. The formal definition of connectedness is as follows: "Between any two pixels in a connected set, there exists a connected path wholly within a set." Thus, in a connected set, one can trace a connected path between any two pixels without ever leaving the set.

Point P of value 1 (in a binary image) is said to be 4-connected if at least one of the immediate vertical or horizontal neighbours also has the value of 1. Similarly, point P is said to be 8-connected if at least one of the immediate vertical, horizontal, or diagonal neighbors has the value of 1. The 8-connected components are used here.

Since the entire page is already converted to vertical run-length representation, a very efficient single-pass algorithm to find connected components using this representation was developed.

The goal of this analysis is to label each pixel of a connected component with a unique number. This is usually a time-consuming task involving visiting each pixel twice, for labeling and re-labeling. By using graph theory (depth-first tree traversal) and the vertical black run-length representation of the image, the processing time for finding connected components can be greatly reduced.

Here is the overall algorithm:

(1) All vertical runs are first labeled, UNLABLED.

(2) Start at the leftmost column.

(3) Start at the first run in this column.

(4) If the run is UNLABLED, do a depth-first search.

(5) If not last run, go to the next run and repeat Step 4.

(6) If not last column, go to next column and repeat Step 3.

The basic idea, of traversing the tree structure is to find all runs that are connected and label them with a same number. A run X on column *n* is a father to another run Y, if Y is on the next column (*n + 1*) and X and Y are connected. Y is called a child of X. In a depth-first search, all children of a given father are searched first recursively, before finding other relatives such as grandfathers. Note that a father can have any number of sons and each son may have any number of fathers. Also, by definition of run-length coding, no two runs in the same column can be connected directly. The result is a representation of the image that is run-length coded and connected-component labeled, providing an extremely compact, convenient, and efficient structure for subsequent processing.

The Staffline Detection, Deskewing, and Removal

The locations of the staves must be determined before they can be removed. The first task is to isolate stavelines from other symbols to find the location of the staves. Any vertical black runs that are more than twice the staffline height are removed from the original (see Figure 11, Figure 10 is the original). A connected component analysis is then performed on the filtered image and any component whose width is less than staffspace_height is removed (Figure 12). These steps remove most objects from the page except for slurs, ties, dynamics wedges, stavelines, and other thin and long objects.

The difference between stavelines and other thin objects is the height of the connected component; in other words, the minimal bounding box that contain slurs and dynamics wedges are typically much taller than the minimal bounding box that contain a staffline segment. Removing components that are taller than staffline_height, at this stage, will potentially remove stavelines because if the page is skewed, the bounding boxes of stavelines will also have a height taller than the staffline height. Therefore, an initial de-skewing of the entire page is attempted. This would hopefully correct any gross skewing of the image. Finer local de-skewing will be performed on each staff later. The de-skewing, here, is a shearing action; that is, the part of the image is shifted up or down by some amount. This is much simpler and a lot less time-consuming than true rotation of the image, but the results seem satisfactory. Here is the algorithm:

(1) Take the narrow strip (currently set at 32 pixels wide) at the center of the page and take a y-projection. Make this the reference y-projection.

(2) Take a y-projection of an adjacent vertical strip to the right of the center strip. Shift this strip up and down to find out the offset that results in the best match to the reference y-

projection. The best match is defined as the largest correlation coefficient, which is calculated by multiplying the two y-projections.

(3) Given the best-correlated offset, add the two projections together and make this the new reference y-projection. The offset is stored in an array to be used later.

(4) If not at the end (right-side) of the staff, go back to Step 2.

(5) If the right side of the page is reached, go back to Step 2, but this time move from the center to the left side of the page.

(6) Once the offsets for the strips of the entire page are calculated, these offsets are used to shear the entire image (see Figures 13 and 14).

Figure 10: The Original

Figure 11: Vertical Black Runs More Than 2x Staffline_Height Removed

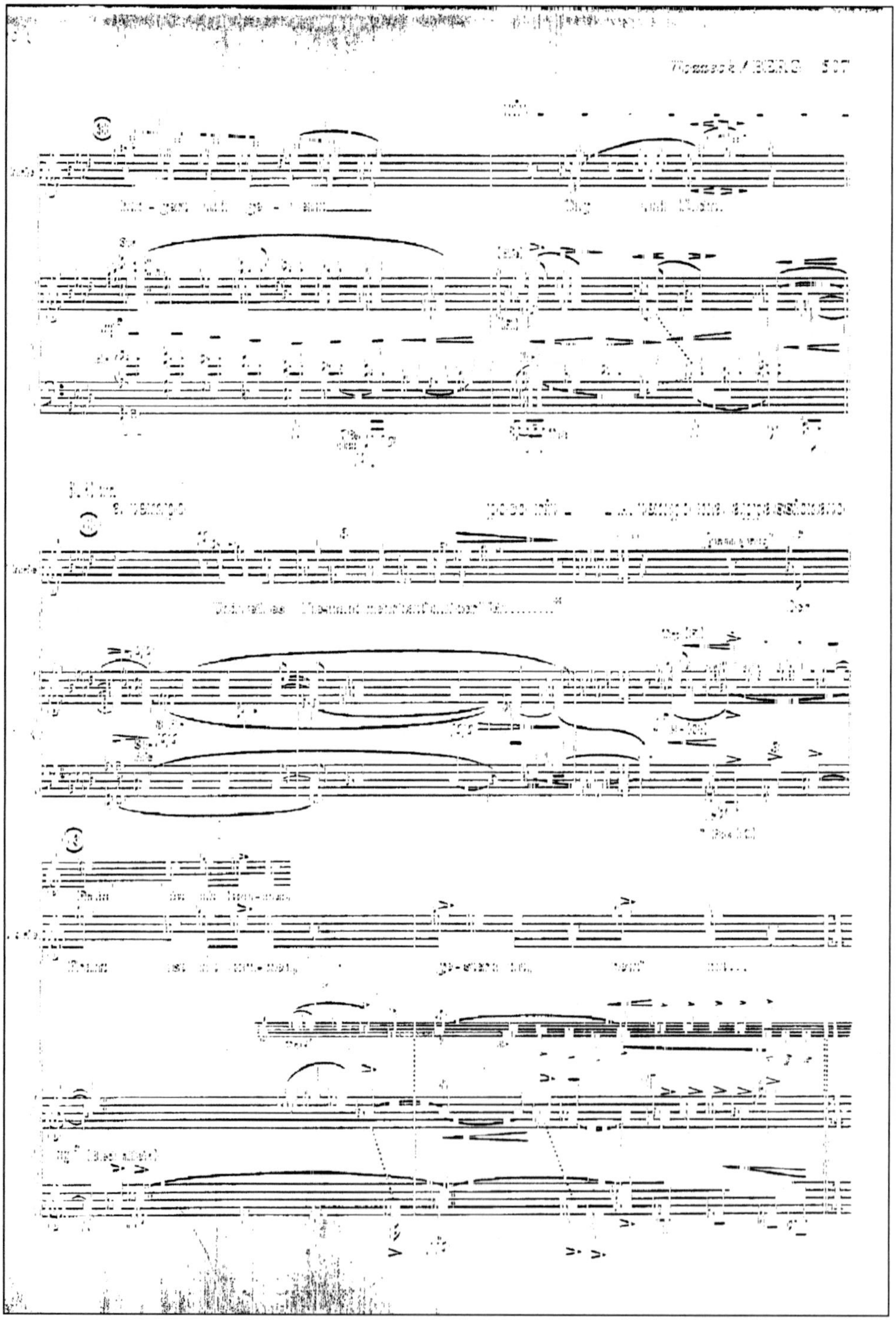

Figure 12: Connected-Components Narrower Than Staffspace_Height Removed

Figure 13: An Example of a Skewed Page

Figure 14: De-Skewed Image of Figure 13 by Shearing (note that because the run-length coded version of the image is used for shearing, only one operation per column is needed, making the operation extremely efficient)

Assuming now that the image is relatively level, i.e., stavelines are horizontal, taller components, such as slurs and dynamic wedges, are removed. The filter here is still rather conservative, since if a long staff line is still skewed, as a component, it may have a considerable height (Figure 15). This precaution is needed because staves on a page are often distorted in different ways.

The result now consists of mostly staffline segments, some flat slurs, and flat beams. At this point y-projection of the entire image is taken again (Figure 16). The derivative of the y-projection is used to locate the maxima in the projection (Figure 17). Using this information along with the known staffspace height, the possible candidates for the staves are selected. For each of these candidates, x-projection is taken to determine if there is more than one staff by searching for any blank areas in the projection. Also, a rough idea of the left and the right edges of the staff can be determined from the x-projection (see Figures 18 and 19).

At this point, the run lengths of the region bounding a staff are calculated in order to obtain a more precise estimate of the staffline height and staffspace height of this particular staff. Also, a shearing operation is performed again to make the staff as horizontal as possible.

Using the y-projections employed during the shearing process, the vertical positions of the stavelines can be ascertained. By taking an x-projection of the region defined by the stavelines, the horizontal extents of the staff are determined.

Figure 15: Tall Connected Components Removed from Figure 12

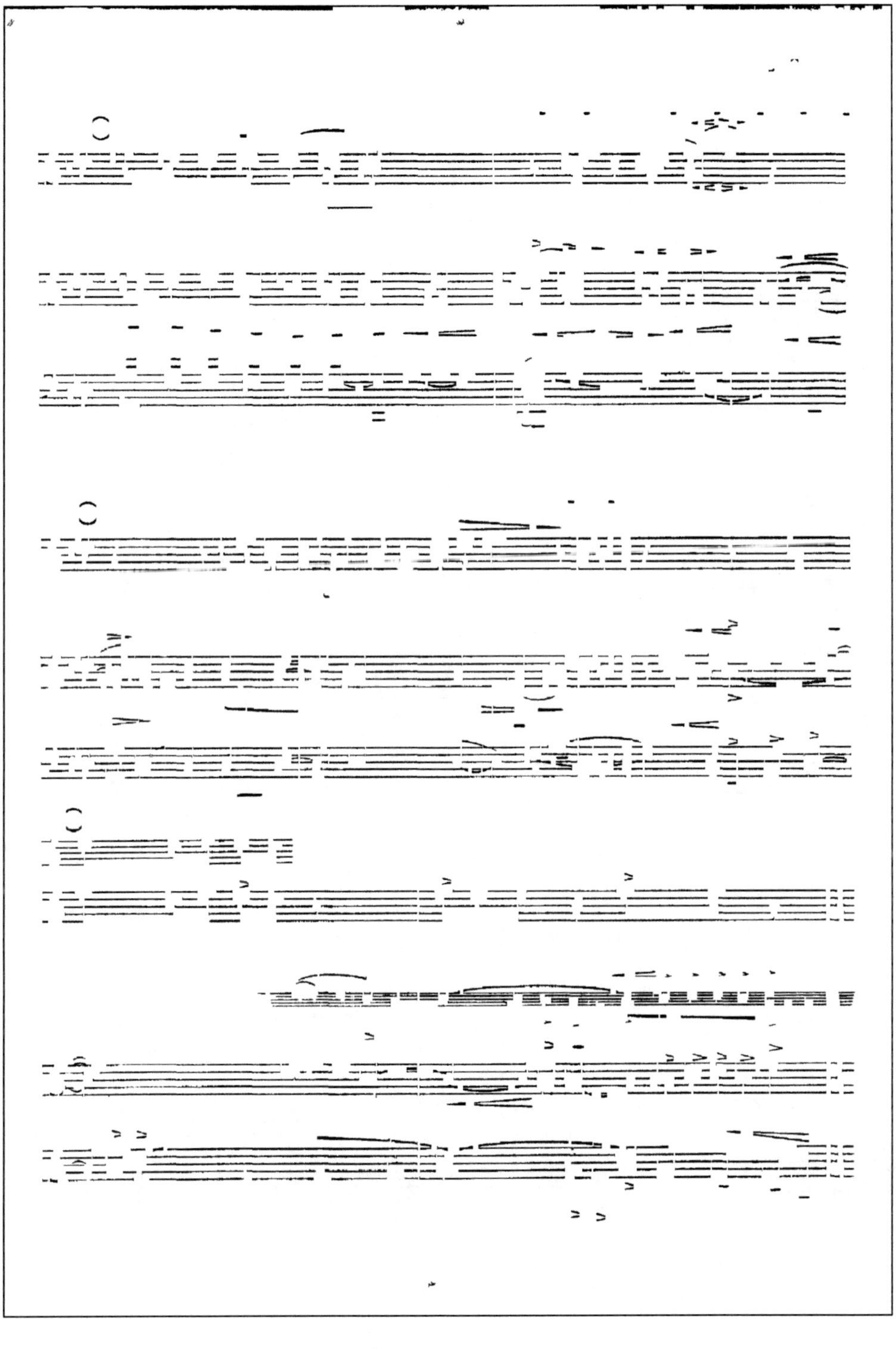

Figure 16: Y-Projection of Figure 15

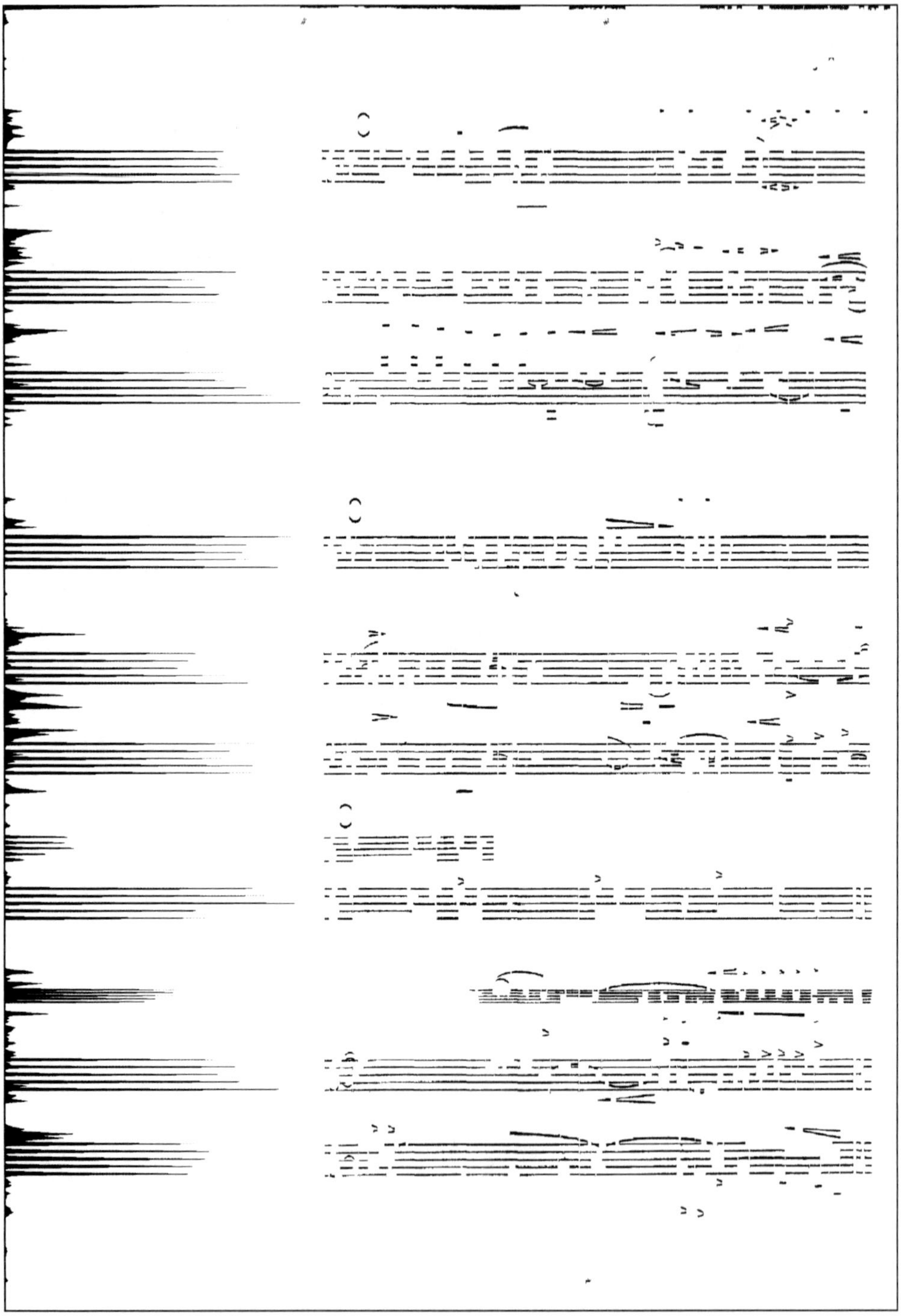

Figure 17: Y-Projection (maxima only) of Figure 15

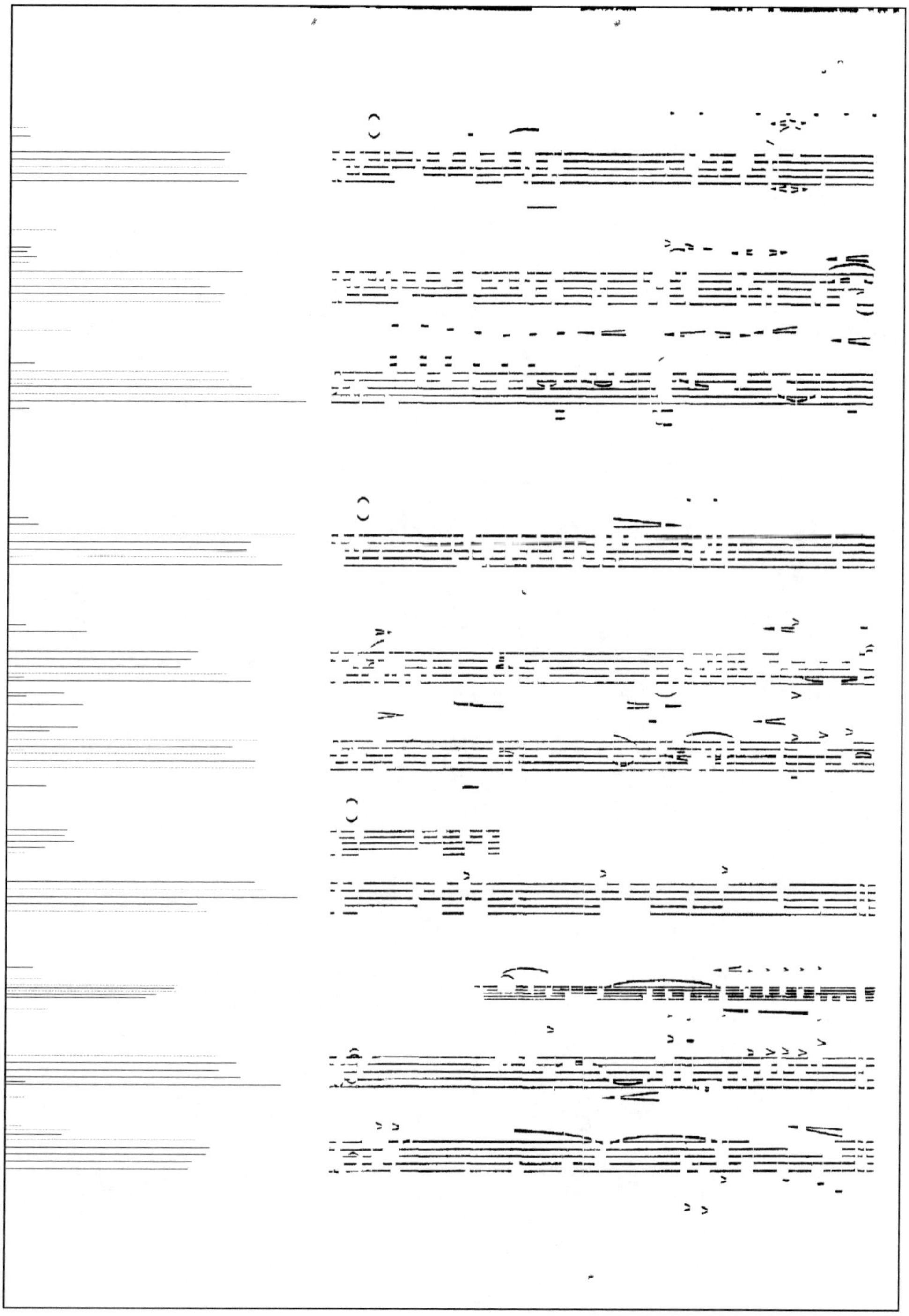

Figure 18: An Example of Staves Placed Side-By-Side

Figure 19: X-Projection of the Top Staves of the Second System in Figure 18

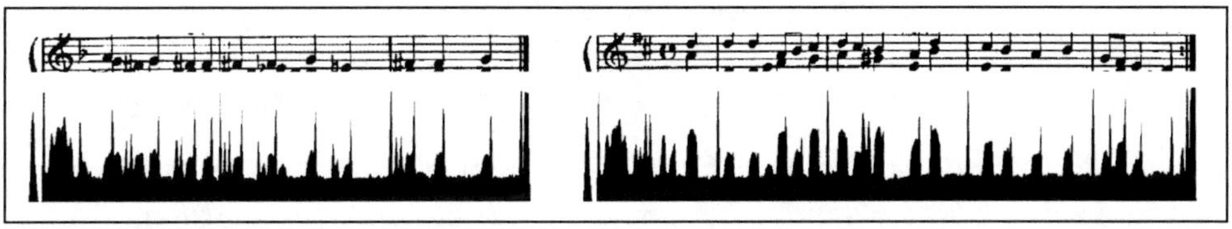

The next step, after knowing the positions of the stavelines, is to remove them. Since the image now consists mainly of staffline segments (Figure 20), the strategy is to delete everything but the stavelines; then the image can be XORed with the original image so that, in effect, the stavelines are removed.

Figure 20: Isolated Staff, from Sixth Staff of Figure 15

At this point, the stavelines are assumed to be flat, so any components taller than the stavelines can be removed (Figure 21). This operation differs from the similar operation performed on the entire image, since the more accurate staffline height that applies to this particular staff is now available.

Figure 21: Tall Connected Components Removed

Also, given the exact positions of the stavelines, components that are between the stavelines are removed (Figure 22).

The result is XORed with the original image. Given two bit-mapped images A and A′, where A′ is a subset of A′ (A′ is derived from A), an XOR operation has the following important property: All black pixels in A′ are removed from A. For example, Figure 22 and Figure 23 are XORed resulting in Figure 24.

The final x- and y-coordinates of each stavelines grouped in staves are stored and forwarded to the symbol recognition step (not described here) and for the final output of the entire score.

Figure 22: Objects Between the Stavelines Removed

Figure 23: The Original Sixth Staff of Figure 10

Figure 24: The Result of XORing Figures 22 and 23

Performance Evaluation

Several examples of the staffline removal are shown in Figures 25 to 35 (located at the end of this chapter). The time the program took to remove the stavelines (including reading the input image and writing the resultant image) of 32 pages of different types of music was approximately 20 minutes, or less than 40 seconds per page on a 550Mhz G4 PowerBook. All of these image processings, such as filtering and XORing, are performed either on the run-length codes or connected components and not directly on the bit-map, thus making computations extremely efficient. Another advantage of this system is its ability to locally deskew the scanned image at the same time as locating the stavelines. Many other types of scores have been successfully tested including some medieval chants (four-line staves), lute tablatures (six-line staves), and keyboard tablatures (seven-line staves). The only time this system fails to detect staves is in orchestral scores with single-line percussion staves.

A Note on Scanning Resolution

The resolution of scanning used here is 300 dpi (dots-per-inch), which seems to be satisfactory for standard piano music or instrumental parts that have eight to ten staves per page. The 300 dpi resolution, however, is not fine enough for orchestral scores or miniature scores. For these types of scores, a recent study (Fujinaga & Riley, 2002) shows that scanning resolution of 600 dpi is needed. Ideally, the thinnest object (usually the stems) should have the thickness of three to five pixels. All of the images used here were converted to binary format before processing.

Related Works

Most of the published literature on OMR uses some combination of projections and run-length coding to detect stavelines and staves. Other techniques for finding stavelines include: use of a piece-wise linear Hough Transforms (Miyao et al., 1990), application of mathematical morphology algorithms (Modayur et al., 1992; Roth, 1992), rule-based classification of thin horizontal line segments (Mahoney, 1982), and line tracing (Prerau, 1970; Roach & Tatum, 1988).

Perhaps the earliest use of projection is by Aoyama and Tojo (1982) where they used y-projections to locate the approximate positions of staves and then vertical run-lengths to precisely locate the stavelines.

Because y-projection of the entire page is affected greatly when the scanned page is skewed, many improvements have been made. One method is to calculate the vertical run-lengths at selected columns of the page beforehand (Kato & Inokuchi, 1992; Kobayakawa, 1993; Reed, 1995). This gives the researcher some information about the page, such as the approximate values of staffline height and staffspace height, potential locations of the staves, and the amount of skew of the page.

The vertical run-length coding has been used without the use of y-projections. Carter (1989) uses a graph structure called line adjacency graph (Pavlidis, 1982, pp. 116-120), which is built from vertical run-length coding. Carter then searches for parts of the graph (filaments) that meet certain characteristics for potential segments of stavelines, then selects these segments that may be part of a staff. Leplumey, Camillerapp, and Lorette (1993) and Coüasnon (1996) also find stavelines by tracing vertical run-length version of the scanned score.

Martin Roth's treatment of staff removal is very similar to the one presented here except that he assumes that the size of the staves are the same on the page and that there is only one staff occupying most of the horizontal space (Roth, 1992). Bainbridge (1997) presents a very sophisticated use of a combination of projection techniques incorporating flood-fill algorithms. The most impressive feature is its ability to detect staves with single-line stavelines.

Conclusions

A robust algorithm for detecting and removing stavelines was presented. This method works for a variety of scores found in the common music practice period. The future challenge is to experiment with more scores from other historical periods and types of music, such as medieval music and lute tablature. The results from initial experiments with these other formats are promising.

References

Aoyama, H., & Tojo, A. (1982). Automatic recognition of music score (in Japanese). *Electronic Image Conference Journal,* 11(5), 427-435.

Bainbridge, D. (1997). *Extensible optical music recognition.* Ph.D. Dissertation. University of Canterbury.

Bainbridge, D., & Carter, N. (1997). Automatic reading of music notation. In H. Bunke, & P. Wang (Eds.), *Handbook of Character Recognition and Document Image Analysis* (pp. 583-603). Singapore: World Scientific.

Bellini, I., Bruno, I., & Nesi, P. (2001). Optical music sheet segmentation. *Proceedings of First International Conference on WEB Delivering of Music*, (pp. 183-190).

Blostein, D., & Baird, H. (1992). A critical survey of music image analysis. In H. S. Baird, H. Bunke, & K. Yamamoto (Eds.), *Structured Document Image Analysis* (pp. 444-455). Berlin: Springer-Verlag.

Carter, N. P. (1989). *Automatic recognition of printed music in the context of electronic publishing.* Ph.D. Thesis. University of Surrey.

Coüasnon, B. (1996). *Segmentation et reconnaissance de documents guidées par la connaissance a priori: application aux partitions musicales.* Ph.D. dissertation. Université de Rennes.

Fujinaga, I. (1988). *Optical music recognition using projections.* M.A. Thesis. McGill University.

Fujinaga, I. (1997). *Adaptive optical music recognition.* Ph.D. Dissertation. McGill University.

Fujinaga, I., & Riley, J. (2002). Best practices for image capture of musical scores. *Proceedings of the International Conference on Music Information Retrieval,* (pp. 261-263).

Itagaki, T., Isogai, M., Hashimoto, S., & Ohteru, S. (1992). Automatic recognition of several types of musical notation. In H. S. Baird, H. Bunke, & K. Yamamoto (Eds.), *Structured Document Image Analysis* (pp. 466-476). Berlin: Springer-Verlag.

Kato, H., & Inokuchi, S. (1992). A recognition system for printed piano music. In H. S. Baird, H. Bunke, & K. Yamamoto (Eds.), *Structured Document Image Analysis* (pp. 444-455). Berlin: Springer-Verlag.

Kobayakawa, T. (1993). Auto music score recognition system. *Proceedings SPIE: Character Recognition Technologies*, (pp. 112-123).

Leplumey, I., Camillerapp, J., & Lorette, G. (1993). A robust detector of music staves. *Proceedings of the International Conference on Document Analysis and Recognition,* (pp. 902-905).

Mahoney, J. V. (1982). *Automatic Analysis of Musical Score Images.* BS Thesis. Department of Computer Science and Engineering, MIT.

Miyao, H., Ejima, T., Miyahara, M., Kotani, K., & Miyahara, M. (1990). Recognition for printed piano scores (in Japanese). *NLC90–34, PRU90–74,* (pp. 39-46).

Modayur, B., Ramesh, V., Haralick, R., & Shapiro, L. (1993). MUSER — A prototype musical recognition system using mathematical morphology. *Machine Vision and Applications,* 6, 140-150.

Ng, K. C. (1995). *Automated computer recognition of music score.* Ph.D. Dissertation. University of Leeds.

Pavlidis, T. (1982). *Algorithms for Graphics and Image Processing.* Rockville, MD: Computer Science Press.

Prerau, D. (1970). *Computer pattern recognition of standard engraved music notation.* Ph.D. Dissertation. MIT.

Pruslin, D. (1966). *Automatic recognition of sheet music.* Sc.D. Dissertation. MIT.

Read, G. (1979). *Music Notation: A Manual of Modern Practice* (2nd ed.). New York: Taplinger.

Reed, T. (1995). *Optical music recognition*. M.Sc. Thesis. University of Calgary.

Roach, J.W. & Tatum, J.E. (1988). Using domain knowledge in low-level visual processing to interpret handwritten music: An experiment. *Pattern Recognition,* 21(1), 333-344.

Roth, M. (1992). *OMR-optical music recognition.* Diploma Thesis. Swiss Federal Institute of Technology.

Figure 25: Stavelines Removed from Figure 10

Figure 26: Stavelines Removed from Figure 14

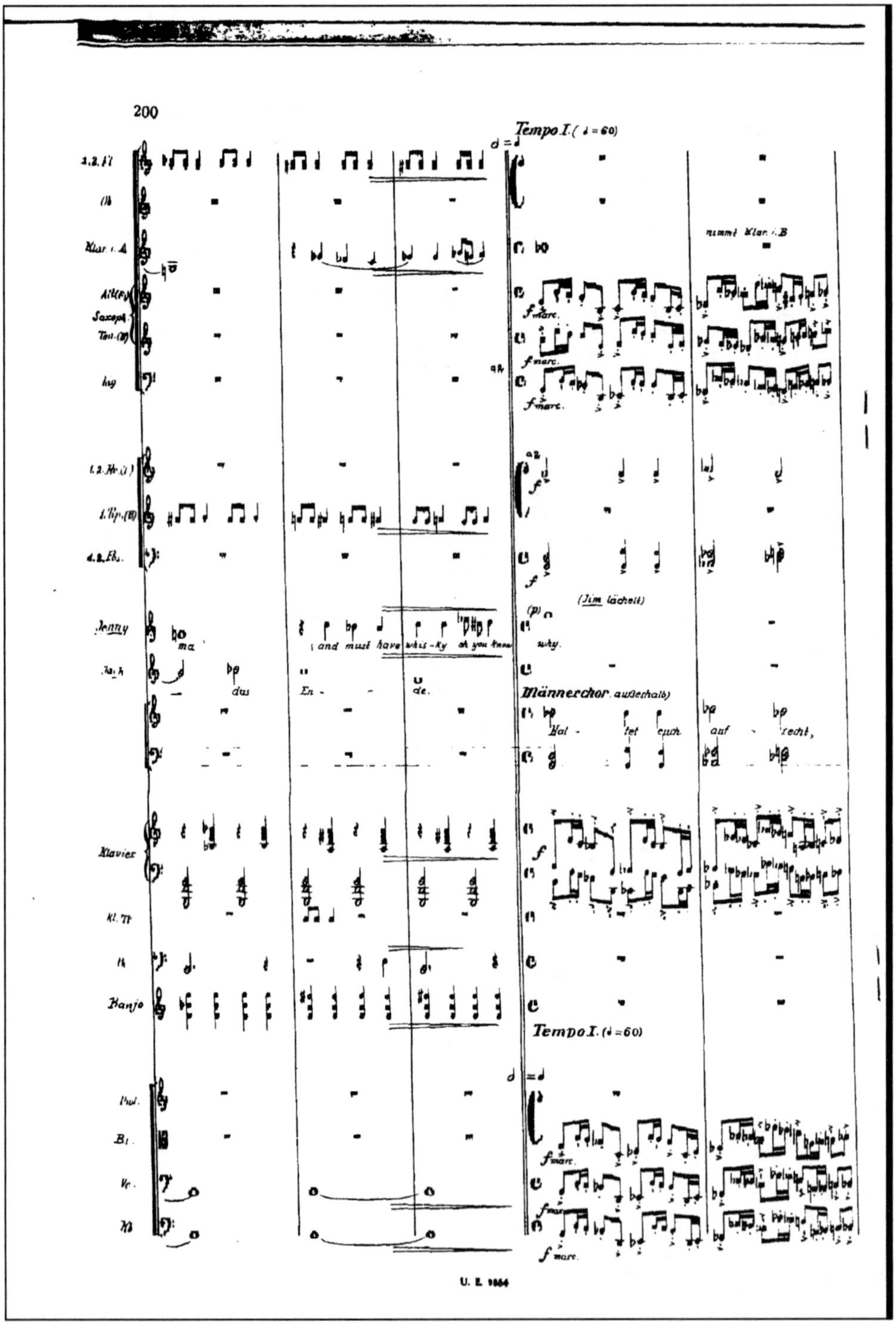

Figure 27: Stavelines Removed from Figure 18

Figure 28: The Original

Figure 29: Stavelines Removed from Figure 28

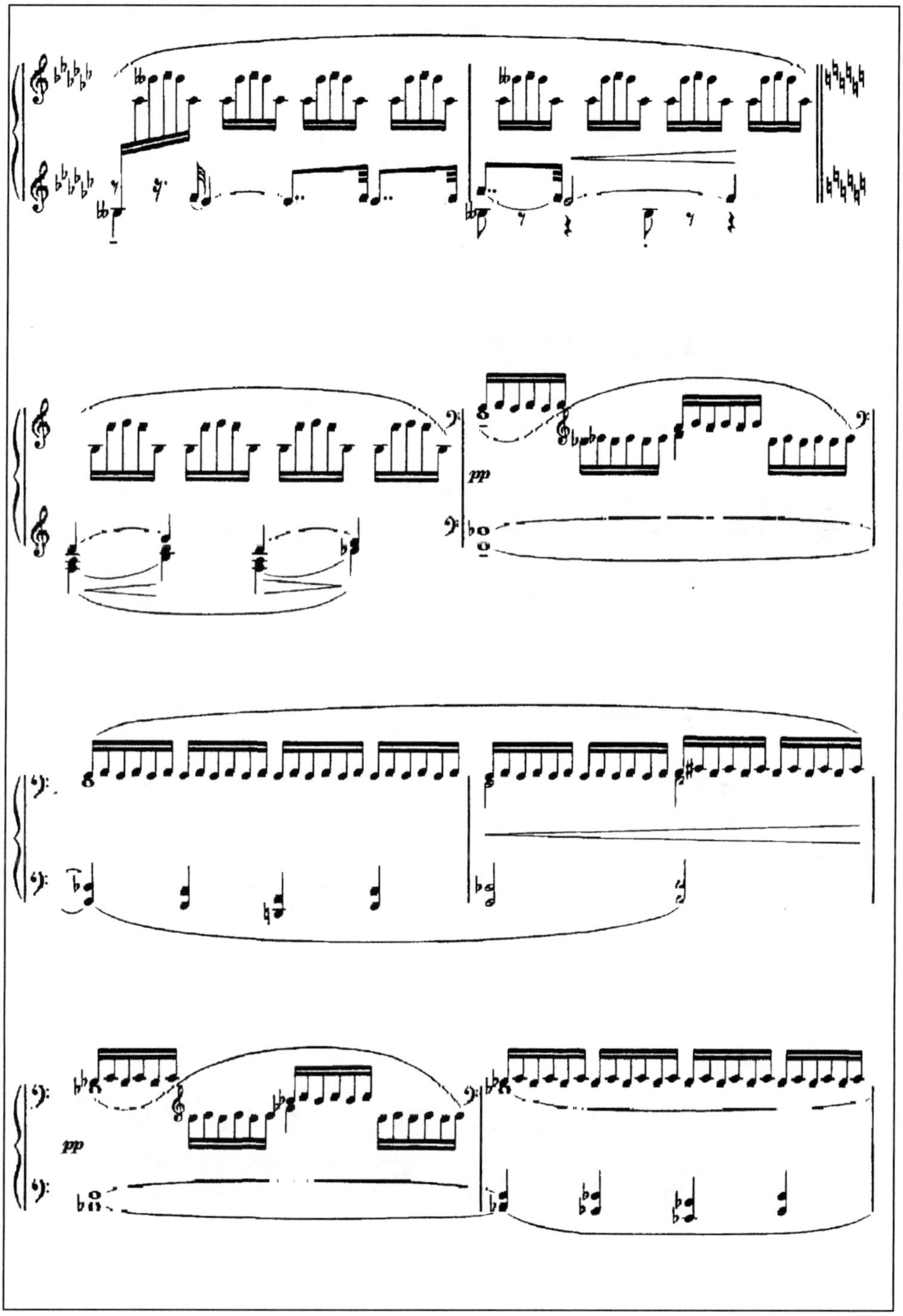

Figure 30: The Original

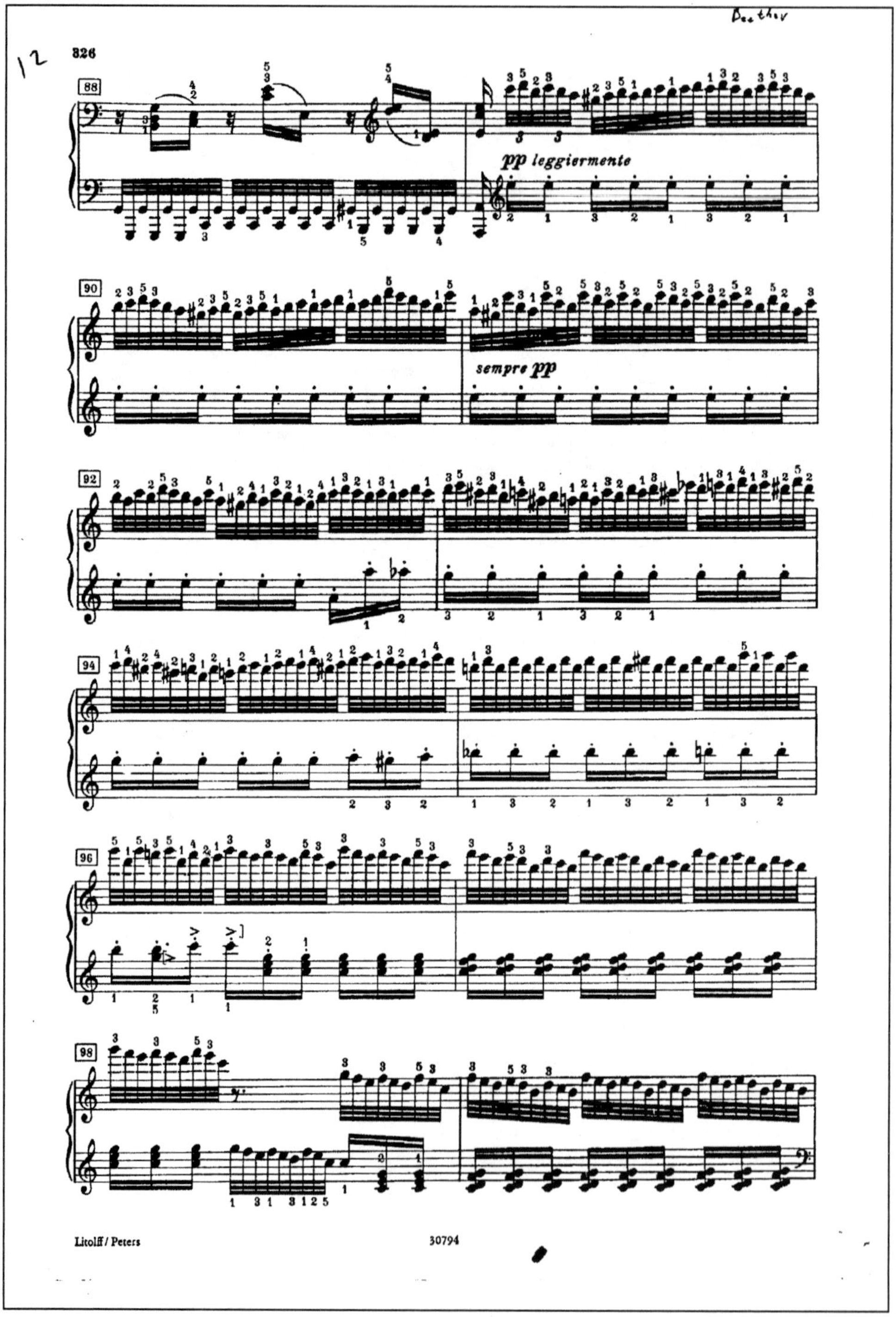

Figure 31: Stavelines Removed from Figure 30

Figure 32: The Original

Figure 33. Stavelines Removed from Figure 32

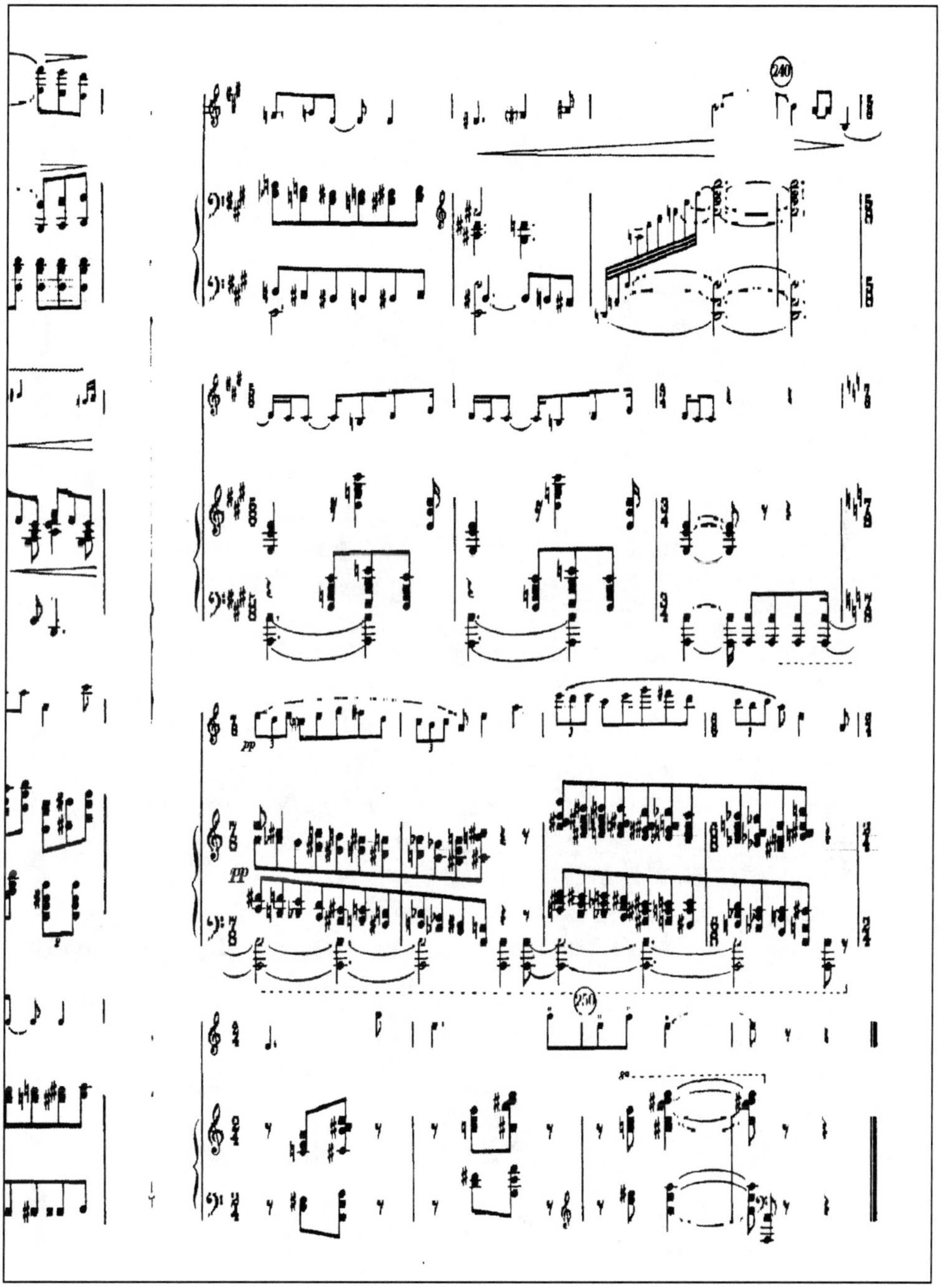

Figure 34: The Original

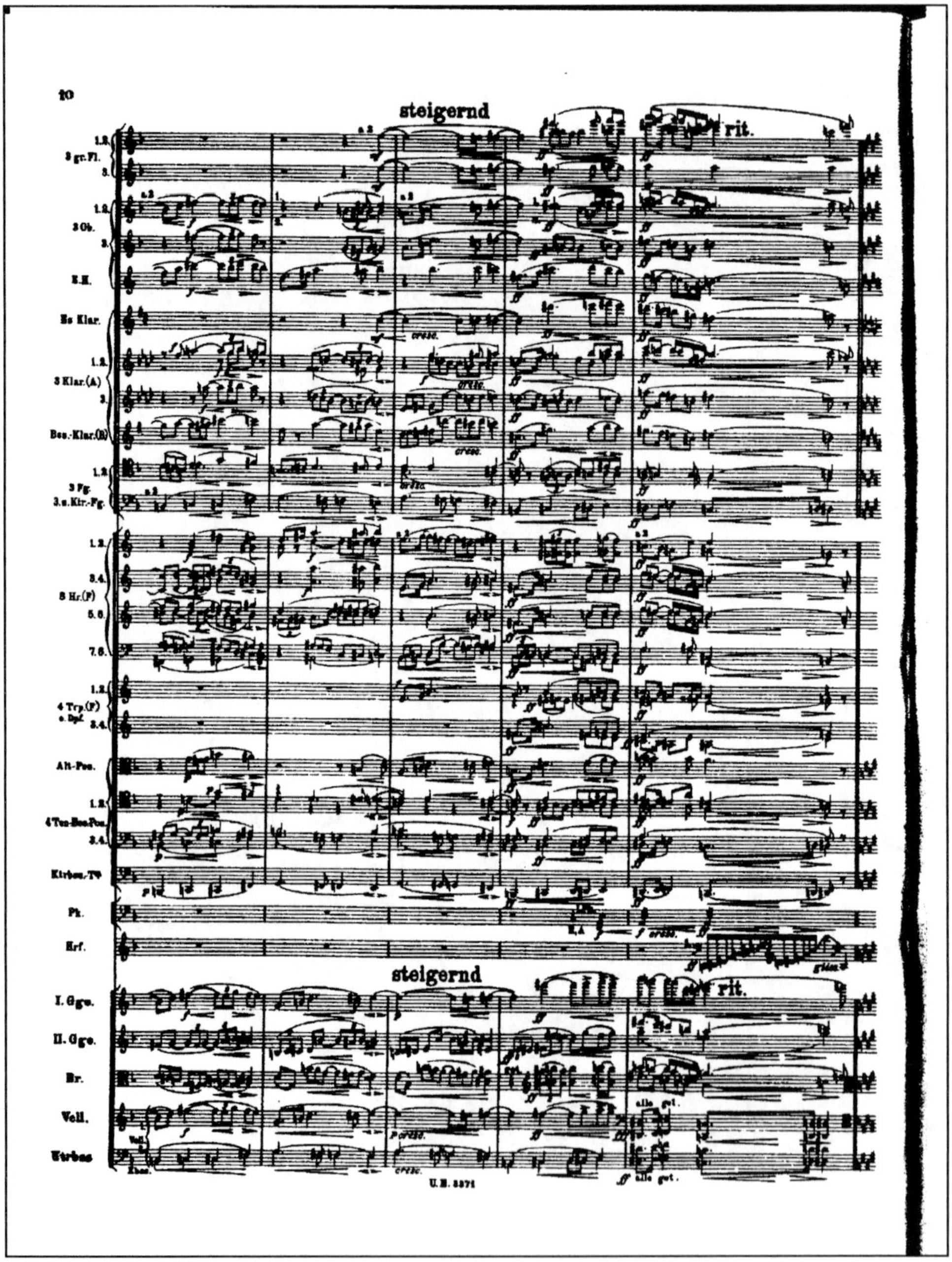

Figure 35: Stavelines Removed from Figure 34

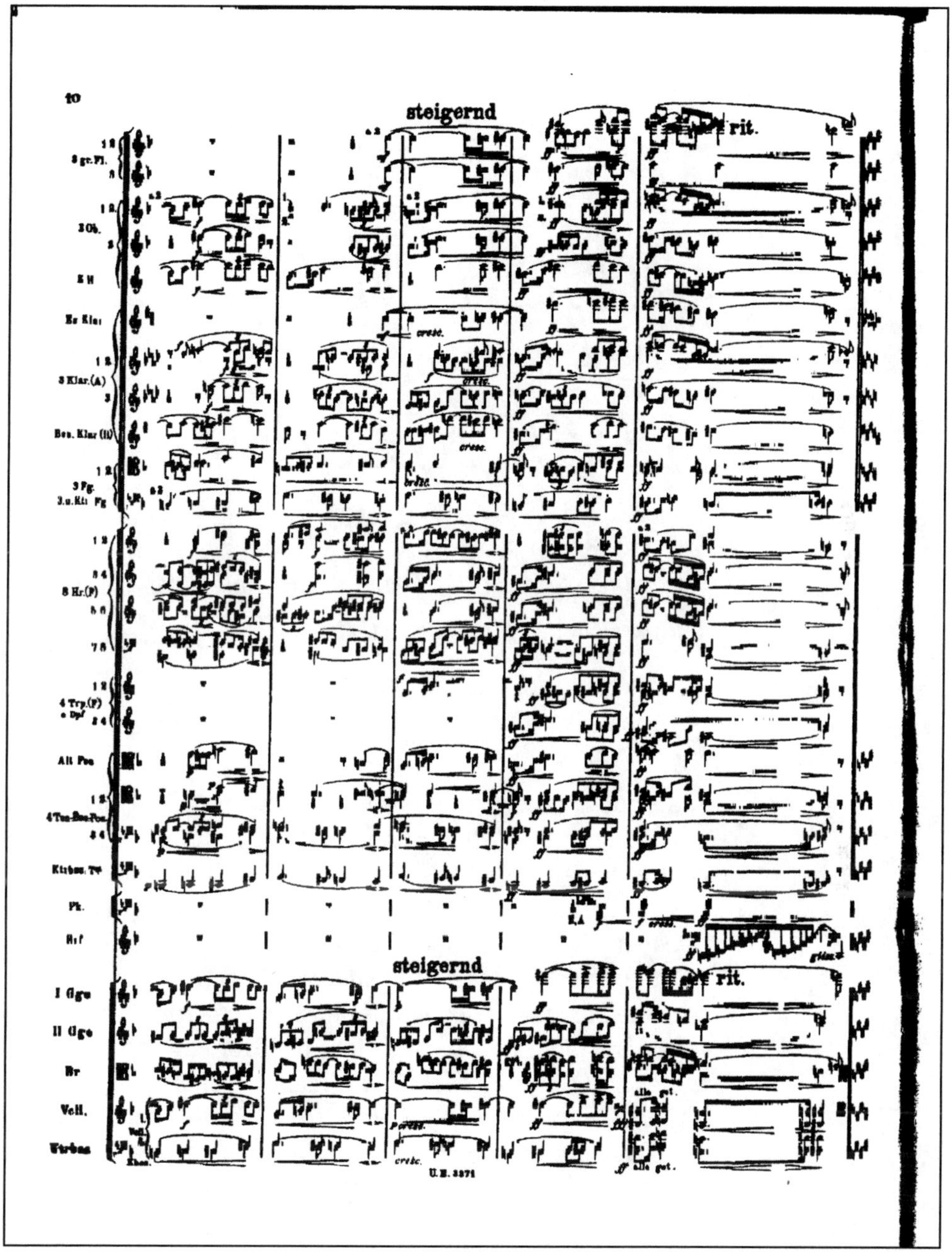

An Off-Line Optical Music Sheet Recognition

2

Pierfrancesco Bellini, Ivan Bruno and Paolo Nesi
University of Florence, Italy

Abstract

The optical music recognition is a key problem for coding music sheets of western music in the digital world. The most critical phase of the optical music recognition process is the first analysis of the image sheet. In optical processing of music or documents, the first analysis consists of segmenting the acquired sheet into smaller parts in order to recognize the basic symbols that allow reconstructing the original music symbol. In this chapter, an overview of the main issues and a survey of the main related works are discussed. The O^{3}MR system (Object Oriented Optical Music Recognition) system is also described. The used approach in such system is based on the adoption of projections for the extraction of basic symbols that constitute graphic elements of the music notation. Algorithms and a set of examples are also included to better focus concepts and adopted solutions.

Introduction

Systems for music score recognition are traditionally called *OMR (Optical Music Recognition) systems*. This term is tightly linked to *OCR (Optical Character Recognition) systems* that are used for reading textual documents. Strictly speaking, *OCR* refers to systems that are based on the segmentation and recognition of single characters. Typically, OCR techniques can not be used in music score recognition since music notation presents a two-dimensional structure. In a staff the horizontal position denotes different duration for notes and the vertical position defines the height of the note (Roth, 1994). Several symbols are placed along these two directions.

OMR is quite a complex problem since several composite symbols are typically arranged around the note heads. Despite the availability of several commercial OMR systems: MIDISCAN, PIANOSCAN, NOTESCAN in Nightingale, SightReader in FINALE, PhotoScore in Sibelius, etc., none of these is completely satisfactory in terms of precision and reliability. This justifies the research work concerned with building reliable OMR systems and tools.

OMR systems can be classified on the basis of the granulation chosen to recognise symbols of the music score. There are two main approaches to define basic symbols. They can be considered as: (1) the connected components remaining after stavelines removal (chord, beam with notes, etc.), or (2) the elementary graphic symbols such as note heads, rests, hooks, dots, that can be composed to build music notation (Ross, 1970; Blostein & Baird, 1992; Bellini, Fioravanti & Nesi, 1999). With the first approach the symbols can be easily isolated from the music sheet (segmented); however, the number of different symbols is very high. The second approach has to cope with a huge number of different symbols obtained from the composition of the basic symbols. This leads to an explosion of complexity for the recognition tool. A compromise is necessary between complexity and the system capabilities.

The architecture of an OMR system and the definition of basic symbols to be recognised is related to the methods considered for symbol extraction/ segmentation and recognition. Generally, the OMR process can be divided into four main phases: (1) the segmentation, to detect and extract basic symbols from the music sheet image, (2) the recognition of basic symbols from the segmented image of the music sheet, (3) the reconstruction of music information, to build the logic description of music notation, and finally (4) the building of the music notation model for representing the music notation as a symbolic description of the initial music sheet.

Optical Music Recognition (OMR)

OMR is the acronym used to indicate automatic music recognition and reader systems. An OMR system is generically defined as the software that recognises music notation producing a symbolic representation of music. A robust OMR system can provide a convenient and timesaving input method to transform paper-based music scores into a machine representation that can be used by commercial music software; this is just like OCR in text processing applications. Converting music sheets into a machine-readable format allows the development of applications for automatic accompaniment, transposition or part extraction for individual instruments, the performance of automated musicological analysis of the music or conversion, and representation of music in different formats (MIDI, Braille Music, etc.).

It is useful to compare score reading to text recognition. This comparison can suggest strategies for tackling the score reading problem, highlight problems specific to score reading, and produce a better understanding of the capabilities and limitations of current character recognition technology.

Typically, OCR techniques cannot be used in music score recognition since music notation presents a two dimensional structure: in a staff the horizontal position denotes different note duration and the vertical position defines the note height. Several symbols are placed and superimposed along these two directions.

In order to optically recognise text, lines of text are identified by searching for the long horizontal space between lines. Each line is processed in sequence. In each line of text, single characters are handled one at a time, without considering their connection (only at a higher level some correction can be applied). Simple region labelling algorithms can extract characters for individual handling. Similarly shaped characters are often mistaken as, i.e., a 'l' (letter L) for a '1' (number one) even in different contexts. Thus, it is imperative to proof-read the results of any text reading because errors are quite common. In a music page, the first steps used by character recognition programs are not applicable. Isolating glyphs on a page of music is difficult because they overlap and have different sizes. Stavelines overlap with almost every other music notation symbol.

The final representation of music is more complex than text. With text the relevant information is the sequence of characters and the places where the paragraphs break. Even though font information would be desirable, commercial optical character readers supply only limited font information. In terms of data structures, this information is typically represented as a sorted sequence of characters with font and size properties attached. On the front page of a newspaper the relative size and position of text provides information which supplements the meaning of words, gives information about the importance, and highlights the relationship with surrounding pieces of information.

A beam groups the set of notes *attached* to it by means of their stems. A key signature is recognised as a *cluster* of accidentals not *beside* note heads. An accidental modifies the note on the right, a dot the note to the left. A slur modifies the performance of notes it marks. The point of view taken in character recognition is inadequate for reading music. In order to address the problem of music recognition different recognition primitives have to be considered as a basis for the architecture of a recognition system that can handle the diversity of visual relations of music scores.

Automatic music recognition systems can be classified and studied under many points of view since in the literature different approaches have been used.

The identification of the general steps of an ideal music recognition process is not easy; however, it is possible to report a list of the most relevant steps for the OMR process:

- Digitalisation of music score/sheet to obtain an image
- Image processing (e.g., filtering) on the acquired image
- Identification and/or removal of stavelines from the image
- Identification and/or segmentation of elementary music symbols (basic symbols) allowing to build music notation
- Reconstruction and classification of music symbols
- Post-graphic elaboration for classifying music symbols
- Generation of the symbolic representation into a symbolic format for music notation.

The elaboration and filtering of the image is always considered as a necessary operation; the identification and the possible removal of the staff are held as a mandatory step by many authors. The graphic analysis (such as basic symbol identification, segmentation, composition and classification) is the core of OMR systems and it is the most studied in the literature. Several techniques and solutions have been proposed, and many of them are strictly connected with image processing and pattern recognition techniques or methods used in the OCR area. Among reconstruction techniques, the solutions based on the syntactic and semantic knowledge play a fundamental role in the phase of post-graphic elaboration to help classify music symbols. The generation of the symbolic representation in the chosen format is presently an open problem since there is not a standard language able to describe completely the music notation.

On-Line and Off-Line Systems

Before presenting a selection of the main works in the literature, it is interesting to observe the OMR problem from different points of view. The first step is to divide the OMR system into two main categories: on-line and off-line systems.

In the on-line case, the system analyses the music sheet directly and provides a result instantaneously; such system could be combined with a robot or a music electronic device connected to a camera to play the music in real time. In this case, the need of generating the music information coding in real time is the most important requirement for such systems. This implies it is necessary to recognise (from each sub-image) the music score locally in order to avoid using correction methods based on global information. Because of the real-time requirement, these systems typically can not consider all aspects of music; for instance, the interpretation and music effects. Another case of an on-line system is offered by writing music with new user-interface technologies and gesture recognition. These approaches allow the development of pen-based input systems (Anstice, Bell, Cockburn & Setchell, 1996; Ng, Bell & Cockburn, 1998) that aid a user to use a pen in the traditional way to input music to the computer. Such systems consist of a tablet, which is normally a touch device on the LCD screen (of any size), and an electronic pen or stylus, which is used to write on the tablet. The goal of such a system is to minimise the input time for data entry into a computer, but the system must deal with the issues derived from the difficulty of recognising the human writing.

In an off-line system, the music sheet is digitised by means of a scanner and is stored as an image. Later, the image is elaborated and analysed and the music information is then converted to a proper symbolic notation code. Such systems do not have strong temporal bounds in terms of time to produce the output, but only in the requirement of quality in the recognition with a low error percentage. This allows more computational resources to be spent in the global analysis and in the refinement of the identified information.

Systems with Stavelines Identification

The stavelines play an important role in music notation. They mark vertical coordinates for the music symbols' height and provide the horizontal direction for the temporal coordinates. In music image analysis, stavelines also provide a dimensional reference and a quality index for the digitalisation, skew, and rotation degree of the scanned image. Some authors consider the staffline an obstacle during the recognition of music symbols; for this reason some solutions for staff removal have been studied. An alternative solution is to start with the music symbol analysis. This means treating the staff as a graphic symbol like the others and a reference for the position of figures. In any case, the position of the stavelines is relevant for the position identification of music notation symbols.

Use of Music Knowledge

To better understand the evolution of OMR systems, it is useful to know how music knowledge can help the recognition process. The two-dimensional nature of the music notation introduces an important consideration: the music symbols cannot be analysed singularly since the relationships with other symbols may change its nature and interpretation. Relationships among music notation symbols can be expressed using two-dimensional grammars. In this sense, Fujinaga (1997) gave an important contribution: he holds that the music notation can be formalised by means of a *context-free* and LL(k) grammar because it represents the way of reading used by musicians (top-down parser). A syntactic approach is not complete, since it leaves out any consideration of the context; for this reason it is necessary to introduce semantic information in the grammar. In this way, the knowledge of the context, together with the syntactic rules, helps in making corrections and in improving the segmentation and the object-labelling phase. Some solutions present a recognition process entirely based on graphic identification and graphic classification techniques.

Issues in the OMR Systems

The study of automatic recognition of music sheets began in the late sixties when hardware aspects, such as CPU (Control Process Unit) performance, memory capacity, and dimension of storage devices, were strongly limited. Nowadays, fast processors, high-density hard disks, and scanners capable of acquiring images at high resolution (more than 300 dpi) are in common use. Thanks to these devices, the automatic recognition of music sheets has been shifted to a purely algorithmic problem of image processing, information modelling, and artificial intelligence.

In the following, some aspects related to OMR technologies are shortly discussed in order to give the reader a global view of the problems of this area.

Graphic Quality of Digitised Music Score

Issues related to the graphic quality of the digitised music score involve the visual representation, object recognition, and music modelling. Aspects concerning the visual representation are mainly print faults and quality of the paper. These include:

- Stave rotation, thus lines are skewed as to the page margin
- Stave bending, thus lines are not straight (this problem can be found in the original, and can be also caused by using a manual scanner or photocopying machine)
- Staffline thickness variation
- Mistaken position of music symbols (a note covering both a space and a line)

Aspects concerning information loss include:

- Staffline interruption
- Shape incompleteness (a quaver note having white spots in the notehead)

Aspects concerning unnecessary information, include:

- Spots, which could be misunderstood as being any music, shape (dot, accent, etc.)

Even though such issues do not seem so important to the human eye, these kinds of irregularities could seriously affect recognition software. Besides, these flaws are more evident when dealing with ancient music scores, which often occurs in the research field.

Graphic Object Recognition

Most common problems are:

- Change of dimension of the same music notation symbol: for instance, the stem height and the beam width in ancient music scores, or the difference between a grace and a common note, or clef changing within a measure. These represent a problem for recognition approaches focused on fixed-symbol dimension.
- Connectivity and overlapping: for instance slurs could generate problems when they overlap with other symbols such as stems; if they touch a note or overlap a dynamic indication, slurs generate visual shapes which are not associated with any graphical music symbol.

Complexity of the Music Piece

Two aspects concerning the music piece complexity can be considered: one is related to the distinction between a single part and a main score; the other deals with "music architecture."

As to the former, for most instruments the single part is made of a melodic line written on a single staff (except for the piano, the harpsichord, and the harp, which have a double staff and the organ, which has three staves). On the other hand, the main score is structured so as to offer a simultaneous view of all single instrument parts, thus being characterised by a system of staves. It is relatively easy to manage a single part having a staff (or maybe three) compared to dealing with a system of staves. A system of staves brings in other problems related to the method for staff identification and the treatment of topological information (symbol positions, staff numbering, staff domain, etc.).

As to the latter, a distinction needs to be drawn between monophonic and polyphonic music: a monophonic piece has a single voice (layer), whereas the polyphonic one has more than one layer/voice. This distinction affects the semantic recognition and consequently the reconstruction step of music content. In both cases, another important issue is the density of music symbols. In fact, with high density it is hard to obtain a good segmentation. The major difficulty is to isolate fragmented symbols.

Manuscript and Printed Music

To deal with handwritten manuscripts is a different task. Apart from the already described issues, handwritten music recognition brings further difficulties, such as:

- The notation variation from writer to writer
- Simple (but important) and even sometimes brutal changes in notation within the same score
- Staffline perturbations where they are not the same height or even straight
- Symbols written with different sizes, shapes, and intensities with variation between the relative sizes of different components
- More symbols are superimposed in handwritten music than in printed music
- Different symbols can appear connected to each other, and the same musical symbol can appear in separated components
- Paper degradation requires specialised image cleaning algorithms

These aspects impact heavily on the choice of methods to be used in the recognition task and represent the main differences in dealing with the printed and handwritten music. The technology used for printed music recognition is not completely reusable for the handwritten one and, generally, such systems are designed in a different manner.

Evaluation of an OMR System

The lack of a standard terminology and a methodology does not allow an easy and correct evaluation of results produced by an OMR system. Generally the evaluation is based on indexes used for OCR systems. For instance, the error rate among correctly recognised and total symbols is not a valid evaluation index because it is difficult to define (a) when a symbol has been really recognised, (b) its features, (c) relationships with other symbols, and (d) the relevance of the context. Another aspect is the set of music symbols used to represent the music. It is difficult to fix a complete set of symbols; their number depends on either the language or the chosen coding format. To conduct an objective evaluation of a recognition system it is necessary also to build a database of test cases. In the character or face recognition field, there are many ground truth databases that enable recognition results to be evaluated automatically and objectively (for more details see http://www.nist.gov/srd/nistsd12.htm). At the present time (Miyao & Haralick, 2000), no standard database for music score recognition is available. If a new recognition algorithm were proposed, it could not be compared with the other algorithms since the results would have to be traditionally evaluated with different scores and different methods. For this reason, it is indispensable to build a master music score database that can be used to objectively and automatically evaluate the music score recognition system. Since the goal of most music score recognition systems is to make re-printable or playable data, in the first case the shape and position information of each symbol is required — whereas in the second, information that includes note pitch, duration, and timing is required. Consequently, the ground truth data must be defined in order to evaluate:

- the result of symbol extraction: evaluation of whether or not each musical symbol can be correctly extracted;
- the result of music interpretation: evaluation of whether or not the meaning of each piece of music can be interpreted correctly and whether or not the music can be correctly converted to playable data.

The following three data representation models have been proposed in order to construct a suitable database for objectively and automatically evaluating the results of a music score recognition system:

(1) Primitive symbol representation including type, size, and position data of each symbol element.

(2) Musical symbol representation denoted by a combination of primitive symbols.

(3) Hierarchical score representation including music interpretation.

The results based upon the extraction of symbols can be evaluated by the data in systems one and two above, and the results of the music interpretation can be evaluated by the data in system three above. In the overall recognition system, the above data is also useful for making standard patterns and setting various parameters.

Symbolic Representation of Music Notation

One of the fundamental aspects in an OMR system is the generation of a symbolic representation in a coding format that allows music information modelling and saving. This problem is shared by music editor applications. In the literature, many music notation-coding formats are available (Selfridge-Field, 1997). None of these has been accepted as a standard format: Enigma format of Finale, SCORE, CMN (Common Music Notation), Musedata, SMX (Standard Music eXpression). Others have been proposed as interchange formats: NIFF (Notation Interchange File Format), MusicXML by Recordare, while others as Multimedia music formats: SMDL (Standard Music Description Language), WEDELMUSIC (an XML based music language).

Related Works

In this section, some of the most important OMR solutions (Blostein & Baird, 1992; Selfridge-Field, 1994) and more recent works are discussed. Their presentation follows a chronological order and the main aspects and innovative ideas are provided without treating technical details of the implementation. The name of the subsection is that of the main proponent of the solution.

Prerau

In the 1970s, Prerau (1970) introduced the concept of music image segmentation to detect primitive elements of music notation. He used fragmentation and assembling methods to identify the stavelines, to isolate fragments of notation and afterwards rebuild music symbols. The process developed by Prerau can be described as follows:

(1) Staves are scanned to detect parts of music symbols (fragments) lying inside and outside the stavelines. The extraction of detected fragments allows removing staves.

(2) Fragments are recombined to build complete symbols. Overlapping rules drive the assembling phase: two symbol fragments that are separated by a staffline are connected if they have horizontal overlap.

(3) Dimensions of the bounding box are measured for each symbol. Prerau holds that height and width of a symbol are sufficient features for the identification of symbols.

(4) Symbols are classified by comparing dimensions with a table where topologic features for each symbol are collected, considering as many music symbols typologies as possible.

Carter

The contribution provided since 1988 by Carter (1989, 1992a, 1992b 1993, 1994a, 1994b) is very important. Apart from considering specific questions such as the identification of staff, he devoted his efforts to the coordination of existing research with the purpose of defining some reference standards. His more important contribution is with regard to the image segmentation process; it is based on a method that uses the Line Adjacency Graph (LAG). First, the music image is analysed vertically, and then horizontally, to search single vertical paths of black pixels, called segments. Graph nodes correspond to unions of adjacent and vertically overlapped segments (sections), while arcs define the overlapping of different segments in an adjacent column (junctions). The graph so built is analysed to detect the stavelines and symbols lying on it. Using this technique provides interesting results, allowing:

- Identification of empty areas of staff (areas without music symbols); in this way it is possible to detect and label the section containing single music symbols or groups of symbols (beamed notes).
- Identification of staff, even if the image is rotated with an angle up to 10 degrees.
- Identification of staff, even if lines are slightly bent or broken and if the thickness of lines is variable.

The main phases of OMR systems developed by Carter consist of two stages:

(1) Application of the method based on LAG to identify the empty areas of stavelines and to isolate the symbols, groups of overlapped or connected symbols.

(2) Classification of the objects coming from the segmentation. Symbols are classified according to bounding box size and the number and organisation of their constituent sections. In case of overlapped or superimposed symbols, specific algorithms are proposed for objects that are not linked with the staff.

Fujinaga

Fujinaga (1988) proposed in 1988 a new approach to the OMR problem based on an intensive use of projection method, in collaboration with Alphonce and Pennycook. He holds that staff removal is not necessary and it is only necessary to identify its position. In this sense, the projection of the image along the Y-axis is very efficient. The identification of the symbols and their features is conducted by means of the information provided from a sequence of projections; first roughly and then more detailed. He associates the music syntax knowledge with the analysis of projections both in the identification and in the classification of symbols.

Fujinaga also provided an important theoretic contribution: the music notation can be formalised by means of a *context-free* and LL(k) grammar. A pure syntactic approach, where the context is not considered, has many limitations; to solve this aspect he suggests introducing semantic information in the grammar. In the following, main phases of the system are briefly described:

(1) The staff is identified by analysing the Y-projection of the image. Groups of five peaks, giving a graphic consistent contribution, mark the staff presence; this allows the image to be divided into horizontal segments that include the staff (only for monophonic music).

(2) Symbols are identified by using the X-projection. Values greater than the background noise caused by the stavelines show the presence of music symbols. As a support for the detection of symbols, some syntactic rules, mainly based on the position of notation, are used.

(3) The symbol classification is performed by calculating both the X- and the Y-projections for each symbol. Projections are used to extract classification features such as width, height, area, and number of peaks in the X-projection. Together with these pieces of information, Fujinaga suggests considering the first and the second derivative of projection profiles.

Roth

Roth (1994) introduced a totally graphic approach to remove both horizontal and vertical lines and solve the problem of objects touching each other and broken symbols caused by staffline removal.

The system is based on the following steps:

(1) Manual correction of the image rotation.

(2) Statistical analysis of vertical paths. The average length of vertical paths for black and white pixels is used to find and fix the thickness of stavelines and the white space between two lines.

(3) Stavelines removal. The stavelines are identified by searching groups of five peaks in the Y-projection profile. Afterwards, the staff is removed by erasing lines having thickness less than the calculated value in step 2.

(4) Vertical lines detection and removal. The identification of all vertical lines (bar lines, stems, vertical lines in accidental shapes, etc.) is obtained by using X-projection profile and morphologic operations.

(5) Object labelling. Objects are marked on the basis of graphic features such as: dimensions, number of pixels, and centre of mass.

(6) Symbol recognition. Symbols are recognised by using the information provided by the labelling step and graphic rules.

(7) Information saving. The result of recognition is stored in a proprietary format.

The first version of the system provided modest results and worked with a limited set of symbols. An improvement of the system has been reached introducing a feedback based on the semantic control. The feedback has been used both to correct results and to establish which zones are not correctly recognised. This last case allows repeating the graphic analysis with more careful methods and it allows changing threshold levels that control the process.

Couasnon and Camillerapp

Couasnon and Camillerapp (1995) in their research affirm that the music knowledge is very important in the recognition process. In addition, they hold that the information coming from knowledge should not be used only as a verifying instrument to correct errors; rather, it should also be used to control the whole process.

They formalise the music knowledge by defining a grammar. The grammar describes syntactic rules and represents both the musical and graphical context. The immediate advantage makes it possible to separate the elaboration part of the system from the definition of music rules. In this way if the document shows a different structure, only the grammar needs to be redefined, while using the same parser. In this approach, the segmentation and labelling phases of basic symbols are controlled by the set-up grammar: basic symbols are not labelled during the extraction phase since the labelling phase depends on the verification of syntactic rule consistency.

The proposed system can be divided into the following main phases:

(1) Segmentation and labelling of primitives. These operations are driven by the music knowledge in order to control the correspondence of detected graphic elements with syntactic rules.

(2) Reconstruction and classification of music symbols. This phase is immediate since the consistency of position and the sequence of primitives have already been tested.

(3) Verification and correction of results and control of note values and figures alignment.

Using the music knowledge to control the whole process allows the evolution of the system and then the recognition of more complex scores (scaling up), since it is always possible to define new grammars formalising music notation with different complexity. The system provided good results with polyphonic music score (two voices).

Bainbridge

Bainbridge (1991, 1996a, 1996b, 1997) focuses his study on the problem of automatic comprehension of music with particular attention to human cognitive process. The wealth of music notations, their evolution, the presence of different sets of symbols and the personalisation by musicians and publishers highlight the dynamic nature of the OMR problem.

In the natural process of music comprehension two main phases can be detected: the recognition of graphic shapes and the application of music knowledge to deduce the meaning. Thus, an optimal OMR system should be constituted by a Drawing Package, where the elementary graphic shapes defining the music symbology are described, together with a Specially Designed Music Language, providing a structure to describe the abstract knowledge of music notation. Both modules should have properties of flexibility and dynamism so as to be easy to fit new music notations or new interpretations of symbols. For this reason, Bainbridge introduces the Primela language that allows defining acceptable configurations of primitive music symbols and to couch the music semantic. A Primela description is written for each type of primitive music shape to be recognised with the pattern recognition routine most appropriate for the task selected. In the Primela language elements such as spatial relationships among primitive symbols, spatial restrictions, graphical rules, and Boolean expressions are used. Once the primitive objects on the page have been identified, they must be assembled into the larger objects they are a part of. For example, note-heads and stems combine to form notes, and a sequence of sharps in a particular context can form a key signature. The CANTOR system was designed for this reason and to be adaptable so that such alternative forms could also be recognised.

The assembly phase in CANTOR is implemented using Definite Clause Grammars (DCGs). DCGs are similar to BNF (Backus Naur Form), but use a slightly different notation, which makes them amenable to implementation in a Prolog environment.

Ng and Boyle

In 1994, Ng and Boyle (1992, 1994, 1996, 2002) developed the *Automatic Music Score Recogniser (AMSR)* at the University of Leeds (Great Britain). The system works on Unix platforms. The input of the system is an image in bitmap format that is visualised on the screen and the output is coded in Standard Midi File. The approach is based on the reverse process of writing music: a composer normally writes at first the note head and then the stem or the beam, as last he adds slur and tie. The system selects first the horizontal and thick elements, such as the slur, and subsequently the beams and stems. In this way composite and complex music symbols are decomposed into primitive symbols. The system is divided into different sub-systems as follows:

(1) The pre-processing sub-system consists of a list of automated processes including:

- Thresholding, to convert the input grey image into a binary image.
- Deskewing. The image is rotated whether any correction of the skew, usually introduced during the digitisation, is needed or not. This step is necessary because the orienta-

tion of the input image affects any further process where the projection method is used.

- Staffline detection and definition of a constant value obtained by adding the average height of a staff's black line with the distance between two lines. The constant value so calculated is used as fundamental unit in further processes and as a general normalisation factor.

(2) In the sub-segmentation process, the composite music symbols are divided into lower-level graphical primitives such as note heads, vertical and horizontal lines, curves, and ellipses. From the initial segmentation, each block of connected features is passed into the classification module. If the object is not classified confidently, and it is too large as a feature, it is passed into the sub-segmentation module to be broken into two or more objects.

(3) In the classification process, primitives are classified using a k-Nearest-Neighbour (kNN) classifier based on simple features such as the aspect ratio and normalised width and height. After recognition, sub-segmented primitives are reconstructed and contextual information is used to resolve any ambiguities. To enhance the recognition process, basic musical syntax and high level musical analysis techniques are employed — for instance, automatic tonality detection and harmonic and rhythmic analysis.

The default output format is set to *Exp*Midi (Expressive Midi) (Cooper, Ng & Boyle, 1997), which is compatible with the standard Midi File format, and it is capable of storing expressive symbols such as accents, phrase markings and others.

The pre-processing task for the recognition of printed music has been re-used for handwritten manuscript analysis in Ng (2002). The sub-segmentation approach relies on the vertical orientation of the musical features and performs unsatisfactorily for handwritten music due to the characteristically slant and curve line segments. For handwritten manuscript, the sub-segmentation module adopts a mathematical morphology approach (Suen & Wang, 1994), using skeletonisation and junction points to guide the decomposition of composite features. They are disassembled into lower-level graphical primitives, such as vertical and horizontal lines, curves and ellipses.

Adaptive Optical Music Recognition

In 1996, Fujinaga (1997, 2001) started to work to the *Adaptive Optical Music Recognition* system. This version enables learning new music symbols and handwritten notation. The adaptive feature allows different copies of the system to evolve in different ways, since each of them is influenced by the experience of different users. The system consists of a database of symbols and three inter-dependent processes: a recogniser detects, extracts and classifies music symbols using a kNN classifier. The recognition is based on an incremental learning of examples and it classifies unknown symbols by finding the most similar object that the system has in its database. An editor for music notation allows the user to make corrections and a learning process improves the performance and the accuracy of any further recognition sessions, updating continuously the database and optimising the classification strategies.

The whole system is divided into the following main sections:

(1) The staff line removal is performed without removing music symbols. To determine the height of lines and white spaces between two lines, the *vertical run-length* is used. All black vertical lines, having a thickness twice as great as the staffline and less than the height of the white space, are erased. To correct the skew of the page, parts of the image are shifted either on the top or the bottom. Objects such as slur and dynamic indications are removed if they have a height similar to the black line thickness and a minimal bounding box comparable with the bounding box containing the line. Stavelines are selected by means of a projection along the vertical axis; the presence of more than one staff and the left and right margin of the page are established by projecting the page along the horizontal axis.

(2) The text location and removal tasks are performed by using heuristics. OCR allows recognising the word; letters as dynamic symbols are not removed since they are not inside a word. This task fails, for instance, when letters are connected to each other or touch the stavelines; a note touching the staff could be recognised as a letter.

(3) In the segmentation task, the image is decomposed in disjoined image segments; each segment contains an object to be classified. For each symbol, measurable features (height, width, area, etc.) are extracted and the *feature vector* is calculated by means of *genetic algorithms*.

(4) The classification is performed using a kNN. The classifier decides the class the symbol belongs to using its feature vector. The kNN does not require the knowledge a priori of the symbol distribution in the space of features; this property allows learning new class of symbols.

(5) Reconstruction of the score is performed by using a Prolog-based grammar.

This system was chosen as the basis for the Levy OMR system, called Gamera, and expanded with an Optical Music Interpretation system (Droettboom & Fujinaga, 2002; Droettboom et al., 2002).

Luth

The work conducted by Luth (2002) is focussed on the recognition of handwritten music manuscripts. It is based on image processing algorithm like edge detection, skeletonisation, run-length. The automated identification begins with the digitising of the manuscript and continues with the following main steps:

(1) Image Processing — The aim of this step is the extraction of a binary image with minimal disturbances and maximal relevant structures. The proposed approach for this task is to conduct an adaptive thresholding in small regions by automatic estimation of optimal threshold value for each region. In this way a good-quality conformity between the binary and the original notation graphics is achieved.

(2) Image Analysis — The binary image is decomposed into five layers and each layer corresponds to special structures: (1) horizontal lines (staff), (2) vertical lines (bar, stems), (3) small, circular, filled structures (note heads), (4) line structures (clefs, note flags or accidentals) and (5) other structures (textual information).

(3) Object Recognition — This step is based on a priori knowledge and structuring rules of abstract models (stavelines, note stem, note heads). It assigns contextual meanings to the extracted structures. This task also generates a special Notation Graph. It involves a syntactic level of handwriting for the description of relationships among structures in terms of geometry, metrical and features.

(4) Identification — A tree of features is built and collects two different forms of structural descriptions: the structure of the abstract object features and the appearance of the features as primitives in the image. Once object features are given in the form of structural descriptions, a graph-matching algorithm determines which image primitives belong to the same object feature, the identity of structure, and the correct object features to each image primitive.

The O³MR

In this section, results of the Object Oriented Optical Music Recognition System (O³MR) are described. This system is under development at the Department of System and Informatics of the University of Florence (Italy) and it is inserted in the context of the Interactive Music Tuition System (IMUTUS) and Web Delivery of Music Scores (WEDELMUSIC) (www.wedelmusic.org) IST (Information Society Technologies) projects. In particular, aspects and adopted solutions related to the off-line printed music sheet segmentation problem are shown in this section (Bellini, Bruno & Nesi, 2001).

The general architecture of the O³MR is based on four main components (see Figure 1).

Figure 1: O³MR Architecture

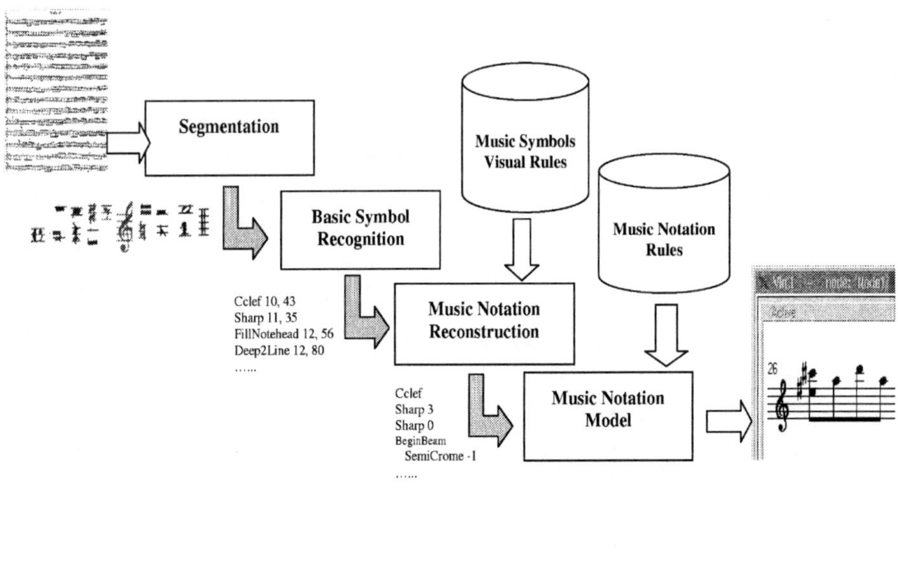

Segmentation — the music sheet is processed with the aim of extracting basic symbols and their positions. A basic symbol is an elementary symbol that can be used for building the music-notation symbols. For example: the filled note head; the deep lines representing beams, rests, sharps, flats; the empty note head; the accidentals; the thin lines used for drawing the staff, stem, slur, tie, wedges, etc. This means that each basic symbol can be used for building more music notation symbols. The exact identification is performed in the third block of O^3MR architecture.

Basic Symbol Recognition — the module performs the recognition of basic symbols by using a neural network. It takes in input image segments of the basic symbols. On the basis of the set of basic symbols a feed–forward neural network has been set and trained to perform the recognition. The output of this module is mainly symbolic. For each recognised basic symbol, the image segment coordinates and the confidence value of recognition are produced. When bar lines are recognised, the corresponding image segment is further elaborated in order to estimate the position of stavelines.

Music Notation Reconstruction — The recognised basic symbols are mapped into the elementary components of music notation symbols. For example, a deep line may be a part of a beam as well as part of a rest, etc. The decision criteria is based on the recognition context: the position of the basic symbols with respect to the position of stavelines, the confidence level of the first phase of recognition, etc. In order to make simple the identification of elementary symbols, on the basis of their possible relationships, the **Visual Rules of the Music Symbols** have been formalised and used during the recognition. According to this process, for each basic symbol a set of probable elementary symbols is assigned. These elementary notation symbols estimate the probability of being basic symbols on the basis of the context. This module may request some additional evaluations when the decision cannot be taken with the current knowledge — for example when two music-notation symbols are similarly probable.

Music Notation Model — once the basic notation symbols are identified they are composed on the basis of a set of **Music**

Notation Rules. Thus, the music model is reconstructed by refining the recognition performed in the previous phase.

Segmentation

The segmentation is the most critical phase of an OMR process. It has to guarantee that *the segmentation of basic symbols is independent of the music score style, size and of the music processed, whether simple (sequence of single notes) or complex (chords in beams with grace notes and several alterations, markers, slurs, expression, ornaments, etc.)*.

The first problem addressed in music score segmentation is the management of stavelines that touch the elementary symbols. The removal of overlapping lines requires a complex process of reconstruction for the involved symbols, with corresponding loss of information. As a consequence some authors preferred to recognise symbols without removing the portion of lines crossing them. For these purposes, the use of projection profiles is very common.

The second problem to be considered is that music notation may present very complex constructs and several styles. Music notation symbols are various and can be combined in different manners to realise several and complex configurations, sometimes using not well-defined formatting rules (Ross, 1970). This aspect impacts on the complexity of the segmentation problem. A method to cope with the complexity is to regard the music notation as a set of basic symbols whose combination can produce the entire set of music notation symbols and their combinations.

Figure 2: Basic Symbols Decomposition

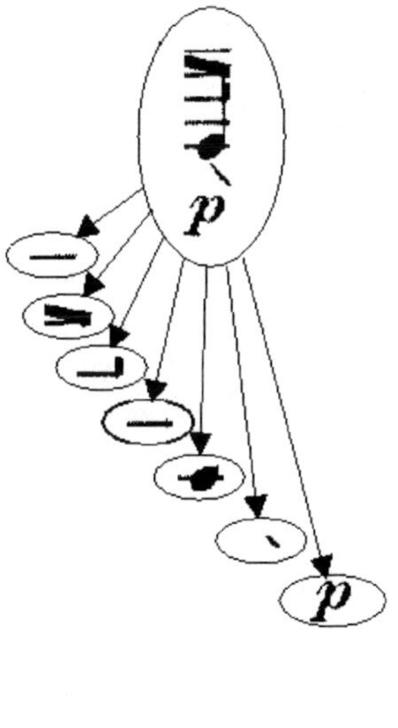

An image of a music score page grabbed with a scanner is the starting point of the segmentation process. The music sheet image is analysed and recursively split into smaller blocks by defining a set of horizontal and vertical cut lines that allow isolating/extracting basic symbols (see Figure 2).

Stavelines are graphic symbols that are independent of the music content. They give important information about music sheet features, since thickness of stavelines, n, and the distance between stavelines, d, are useful to tune the segmentation process. In fact, they allow defining thresholds, tolerance values for measurements and segmentation of basic symbols of the music score. With the thickness of lines and the distance be-

Figure 3: Tuning

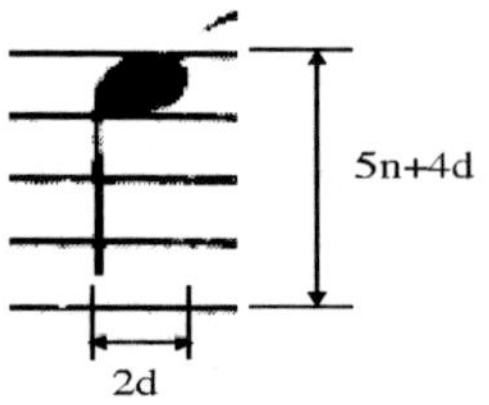

tween two lines, it is possible to describe the graphic features of a note head or to estimate the height of a single staff, as shown in Figure 3.

For these reasons, stavelines are not removed since they are used in the segmentation process. This avoids the introduction of elaboration phases to fix symbols partially cancelled by the staff-lines removal. The knowledge of staff-lines position allows detecting the right pitch of notes in the reconstruction phase.

In more detail, the procedure is based on the three elaboration levels as follows:

Level 0: the music sheet is segmented to extract sub-images, including the single music staff. In addition, a set of image-score parameters are estimated for tuning the next processing phases.

Level 1: the image segment of each staff is processed to extract image segments that include music symbols having a width close to that of note heads. This level is performed in three steps: (1) extraction of beams (e.g., group of beamed notes) and isolated symbols (e.g., clefs, rest, bar line), (2) detection and labelling of note heads, (3) detection of other music symbols or parts of them.

Level 2: music symbols, detected at level 1, are decomposed into basic symbols. In this phase, two decomposition methods are used: one for image segments containing note heads and one for those in which they are missing. In this last case, the image segment may contain other symbols.

Level 0

The main stages of Level 0 are the (1) tuning of the segmentation process by the identification of a set of graphic parameters and (2) detection of image segments in which staves are included. According to the idea of a hierarchical structure, the image is decomposed into a set of sub-images, each of which includes a staff.

Tuning Process — The tuning process is performed to estimate the music sheet parameters from the scanned image: (1) the thickness, *n,* of stavelines, and (2) the distance, *d*, between staves. To estimate these values, the score image is processed column by column, counting sequences of black and white pixels. The values of most frequent occurrence fix the number of pixels for the thickness of the staffline (n) and the space between two lines (d). In order to manage variability and noise on the values of these parameters, two intervals have been adopted as follows:

- n_1 and n_2: the minimum and the maximum values for the staff-line thickness, respectively
- d_1 and d_2: the minimum and the maximum values for the distance between two stavelines, respectively

The above parameters are used in the next steps of the segmentation process.

Staves Detection and Isolation — The staff detection is the first real segmentation phase of the O³MR system. The goal is to identify a rectangular area in which the staff is located in order to process that image segment to extract the contained basic music symbols. The algorithm for detecting the staves is based on the recognition of the staffline profile. The profile, obtained by applying the Y-projection to a portion of stavelines image, presents a regular pattern in terms of structure, whereas other projections have a variable pattern. In Figure 4 the stavelines are zoomed and reported in black on the left. In order to distinguish the projection of lines from the other graphic elements, a transformation of profiles has been introduced.

Figure 4: T-transformation of Staff Lines Profile

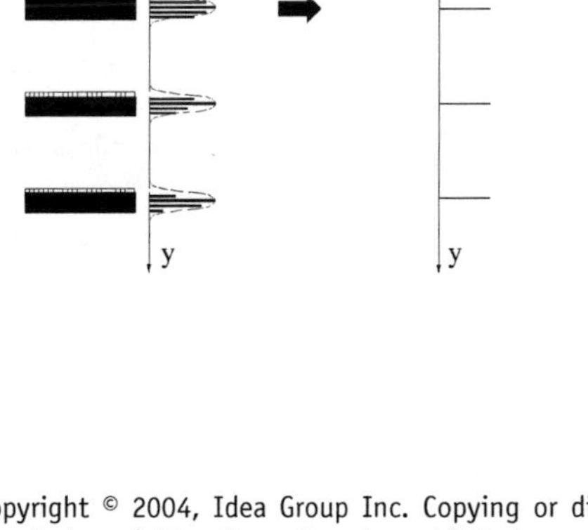

The transformation, T, works on the Y-projection of a vertical image segment. The Y-projection is constituted by a set of groups/peaks, each of which is associated with a staffline. When the width is comparable to values defined by $[n_1, n_2]$, then the position of the mean position for the peak is estimated, otherwise it is not considered. The position of the mean value defines the lines in the T-Profile of Figure 4, and allows characterising the staff in the identification phase. The analysis of the distance between lines in the T-profile is used to understand if the profile is due to the presence of a staff. The distance between lines of the T-domain is strictly related to the values of the above-mentioned parameters. In fact, given the $[n_1, n_2]$ range for the thickness of stavelines and the $[d_1, d_2]$ range for the distance between two lines, the distance between mean values expressed in term of tolerance range $[\alpha, \beta]$ is defined as:

$$[6.1] \quad \begin{cases} \alpha = d_1 \\ \beta = d_2 + 2(n_2-(n_2-n_1)/2) \,. \end{cases}$$

The staff-detection algorithm looks for the structure of "five equidistant" lines. This is performed by analysing thin slices of the image sheet. Each slice has a vertical size equal to the whole image score size and width equal to a few pixels (dx). The slices are processed by performing the T-transformation. On each slice, a window probe with height $I = 5n_2+4d_2$ looks for the five-lines pattern. The probe is applied on a sub-section of the slice and analyses it from top to bottom. The probe looks for the starting coordinate of the five stavelines.

In order to cope with eventual staff deformations, the above value of I has been increased by 20%. The staff detection by means of the probe is performed in two phases: (1) discovering and (2) centring the staff. In the discovering phase, the probe window is used to detect the stavelines and store the starting coordinates of segment in which the staves are present. In the centring phase, a couple of staff coordinates (y_{sup}, y_{inf}) are obtained. These are defined in order to fix the cut lines for extracting the staves contained in the score image. If n is the number of staves, then each new couple of coordinates has been evaluated as:

$$[6.2] \quad \begin{cases} \hat{y}_{\mathrm{sup}}^{(1)} = 0 \\ \hat{y}_{\mathrm{inf}}^{(1)} = \dfrac{y_{\mathrm{sup}}^{(2)} + y_{\mathrm{inf}}^{(1)}}{2} + \varepsilon \end{cases} \qquad \begin{cases} \hat{y}_{\mathrm{sup}}^{(n)} = \dfrac{y_{\mathrm{sup}}^{(n)} + y_{\mathrm{inf}}^{(n-1)}}{2} - \varepsilon \\ \hat{y}_{\mathrm{inf}}^{(n)} = Y\max \end{cases}$$

Where: $i = 2, \ldots n\text{-}1$, and $>= 0$ (a tolerance value to increase robustness). The introduction of ε tolerance allows getting adjacent or partially overlapped image segments containing the staff. In the above definition, the coordinates of the first and last staff are excluded.

An example of staff detection is provided by Figures 5a and 5b to better clarify the described method. The considered image has been acquired at 300 dpi with 256 grey levels. The tuning parameters for this image are n = 4 and d = 17, and they determine the following ranges for the stavelines description:

- [3,5] pixels used for the thickness of black lines
- [16,17] pixels for the distance between two black lines
- [16, 25] pixels for the distance among black lines to be considered after the T transform
- I = (25+68)+20% = 112 pixels for the window probe

Figure 5a: Staff Detection

Figure 5b: Staff Area Extension After the Application of Equations 6.2 with $\varepsilon = 0$

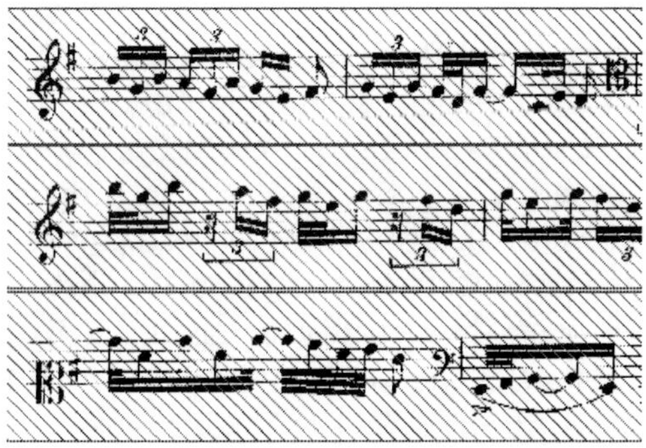

Level 1

Level 1 works on the image segments produced from Level 0 that contain one staff. The aim of this level is to extract the vertical image segments containing music symbols and to produce the lower-level sub-image segments in three phases.

Groups and Isolated Symbols Detection — In this phase, groups of figures and single symbols (e.g., clefs, rest, bar line) are detected. To this end, the staff detection algorithm is applied to produce the value of the binary function, *F*. The detection process has been realised by considering a running image window. This has the height of the image segment coming from level 0, and width, dx_1, equal to three to four pixels. The analysis of the image segment is performed by moving the running window from left to right one pixel at a time.

Figure 6: Symbol Segment Detection, Function F

The result of staff detection sets the values of binary function, *F* (see Figure 6). The 0 value is associated with the presence of an empty staff and 1 otherwise. In this phase, the stand-alone music symbols (clef, bar line, time signature, whole notes, etc.) are detected, whereas non-stand-alone music symbols and all groups of figures have to be processed in the next phase in order to proceed at their decomposition in smaller image segments.

The identification of an empty staff allows processing of the corresponding image segment in order to estimate the coordinates of stavelines. This information is used in Level 2.

Note-Head Detection and Labelling — The goal of this phase is to slice the complex image segments produced by the previous phase and marked as F = 1. In the slices produced by this phase one or more single note heads have to be present along the y-axes. The proposed approach is based on searching the presence of a single note head. In western notation, note heads may present at least a diameter equal to the distance between two stavelines. To consider the note-head width equal to $2d_1$ is a reasonable approximation. For these reasons, image segments coming from the previous phase are processed on the basis of their width. In this case, only image segments larger than $2d_1$ are considered. In the X-projection, we have: (1) spikes due to note stems and vertical symbols, (2) offsets due to horizontal symbols like stavelines, beams, slurs, crescendos, etc., (3) smoothed dense profile due to note head. In order to extract the note heads the dense profile contribution has to be extracted from the X-projection. This means it is necessary to eliminate the other two contributions. To this end, a thin running window is considered on the image segment containing the staff with symbols (see Figure 7). The running window scans the image with a step equal to 1 pixel. For each step/pixel the Y-projection is calculated. In the projection, the presence of a note head can be detected on the basis of its width, H, which is in the range $[2n_2, 2n_2+d_1]$. Since the objective of the process is to detect the location of note heads, only the maximum value of H along the projection of the running window is considered (Hy6). This value is reported in the final X-projection shown in Figures 7 and 8a. The note heads produce higher peaks since they are deeper than beam lines. On the other hand, when note heads are missing the maximum value produced from the beam is reported in the X-projection of maximum Y-projection. The

Figure 7: Building of X-Projection

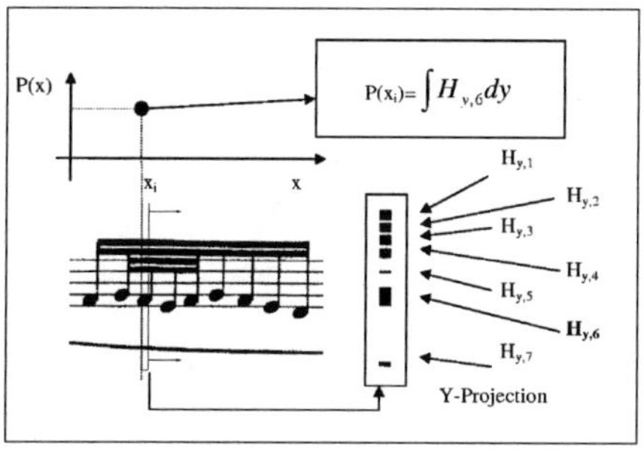

Figure 8: a) X-Projection Before Thresholds Application; b) X-Projection After Thresholds Application and Ready for Extracting Image Segments with Note Heads

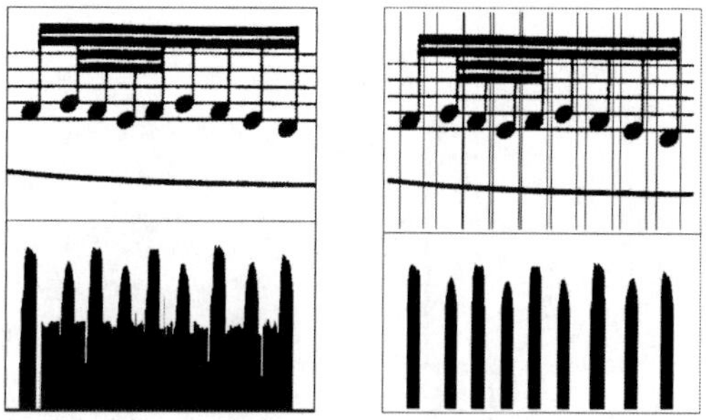

evident difference in the value of the two cases is amplified by the adoption of a running window that considers several overlapped thin windows of the same note head. The final step consists of isolating the note heads. This is performed by using a double-threshold mechanism to obtain the results shown in Figure 8b. The first threshold is defined as the compromise between the dimension of the note head and that of the beams. The second filtering is performed on the width of the remaining peaks that are considered only if their width is larger than $d_1/2$. For each peak of the X-projection the mean position of the peak along the X-projection is estimated. If C is the x coordinate of the mean value, the couple of points is defined as follows: $(C-d_1, C+d_1)$. Each couple of points defines the width of the image segment that includes the note. In particular, the width is equivalent to that of the note head (see Figure 8b).

In this process, each image segment containing a note head is labelled. This information is used by Level 2. The above process for labelling segments that contains note heads is also performed on the image segments marked with F = 1. Please note that with the presented approach, also chords having notes on the same side are managed (see next section). Image segments that do not contain note heads are non-sliced by the described process.

Other Symbols Detection — Image segments that have to be processed typically include groups of symbols very close to each other. In most cases, these symbols are separated by small spaces generating local minima in the X-projection profile, such as in Figure 9. Thus, detecting these points means it is necessary to slice the image segment and thus to extract the basic symbols. To this end, an iterative method has been developed. As a first step, a low-pass

Figure 9: Isolation Points and Minimums of X-Projection

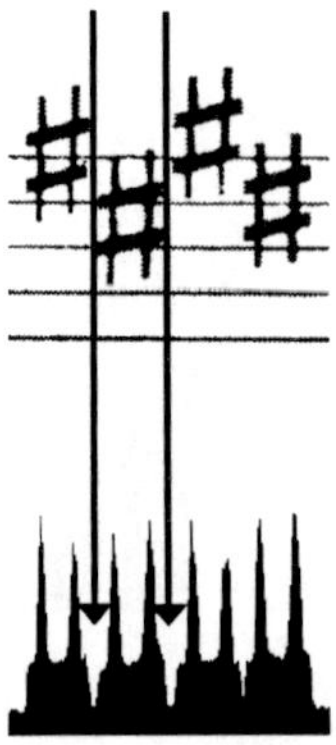

filter is applied to smooth the profile. The smoothed profile is analysed in order to find the position of the minima. Its position is used to divide the image segment into two new sub-images. The same procedure is applied at the two sub-images when their width is greater or equal than $d_1/2$. The process stops when the maximum width of the processed image segments is lower than $(5/2)\ d_1$. The last operation is sorting the vertical image segment points in order to define image segments.

In presence of a "constant" profile the segmentation process produces image segments with a width comparable to that of note heads, $d_1/2$. Image segments having a width lower than the staff-line thickness are not considered in the next segmentation level. This process is capable of coping with key signatures and accidentals, since it allows decomposing the image segments non-decomposed in the previous step.

Level 2

Level 2 is the last phase of the segmentation process. In this phase the images coming from the previous Level 1 are decomposed into a set of basic symbols. This phase covers an important role since the recognition and reconstruction are strictly connected to it. The produced image segments must include graphic details: (1) belonging to the set of defined basic symbols in repeatable manner, (2) additional information needed for their recognition. The first aspect impacts on the reliability of the recognition phase, while the second on the application of the rules of the reconstruction phase.

The previous segmentation phase produced different results depending on the presence or not of the note head. In this process, two different segmentation methods are applied to the received image segments: (1) including, and (2) non-including note heads. This distinction is made possible by using the information given from the labels defined in the note-head detection phase. Both segmentation methods are based on the Y/X-projection and produce couples of vertical coordinates to extract basic symbols. The result of this level is provided in Figure 10.

Images with Note Heads — In image segments containing a note head, this symbol can also be connected to other basic symbols. This implies that a specific process for their division is needed. Ornament (turn, mordent, trill, etc.) and horizontal (slurs, crescendo, etc.) symbols can be more easily identified since they are not connected or strongly close to the note head. The graphic components of the note are mainly: (1) the note head, and (2) beams or hooks. In the Y-projection of notes, the stem contributes. It adds an offset to the projection profile linking the profile of the note head with beams and hooks. In the case of a quarter and whole note, it is only an offset. In both cases, the contribution of the stem is used as the lower value for the threshold applied to the extraction of basic symbols. The proposed approach is based on the result obtained in Marinai and Nesi (1999); it consists of the following steps:

(1) **Stavelines removal from Y-projection.** According to the processing of the last segment containing an empty staff, the position of the stavelines is known (see Level 1). The contribution of the stavelines is removed by masking lines with a contribution width of n_2.

(2) **High-pass filtering.** This filtering phase allows the elimination of the low-frequency components and removal of the offset due to the stem.

(3) **Extraction points computation.** It is based on the computation of extraction points by means of a threshold mechanism (Marinai & Nesi, 1999). When two successive segments are closer than n_2 they are fused into a unique segment.

Figure 10: Decomposition in Basic Symbols: Output of Level 2

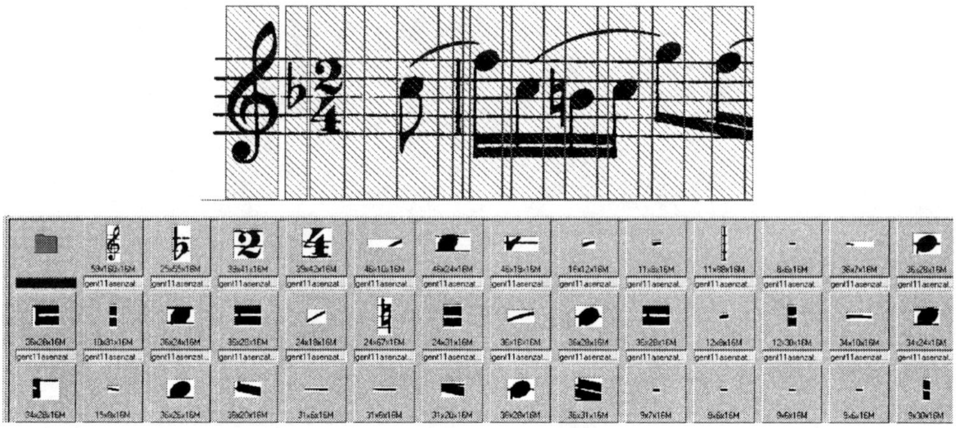

Recognition of Basic Symbols

To perform the recognition and classification of basic symbols (see Figures 10 and 11) an MLP- (Multi-Layer Perceptions) Backpropagation neural network is used (Rumelhart & McClelland, 1986). It takes in input the simple normalised image segments (8x16 pixels) of the basic symbols and provides the class and the confidence of classification (goodness percentage) as output. More than 20.000 basic symbols have been collected and distributed into a database constituted by 54 classes of elementary shapes.

This set is suitable for classical music scores. On this set of basic symbols a feed–forward neural network has been set and trained to perform the recognition.

The MLP network structure consists of 128 inputs, a hidden layer of 256 neurones and 54 output neurones; the neuronal activation function is sigmoidal with output values in the [0,1] range. The normalised image is vectorised and provided as input (see Figure 11). The percentage range of classified symbols oscillates between 80% to 90%; this oscillation depends on the different kinds of font and on the likeness among different basic symbols (i.e., the augmentation dots and black note heads, beam and part of slur, etc.).

For this reason, a confusion table has been defined in order to consider the mistakes introduced by the network. By means of the table and the confidence value associated to the classification, corrections can be done considering the

Figure 11: The MLP Classifier Structure and the Database of Basic

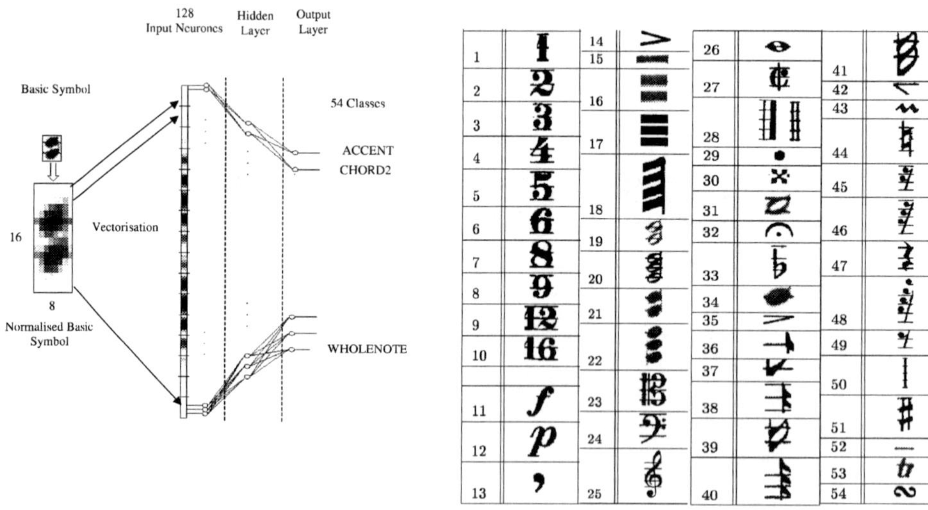

position that the confused symbol occupies in the staff. The error recovery is performed in the reconstruction phase.

The output of this module is mainly a symbolic description. For each recognised basic symbol, the image segment coordinates, dimensions of bounding box, and the confidence value of recognition are produced:

Table 1: Output Format and Textual Description

Class	X	Y	Width	Height	Confidence
CLEFTREBLE	55	48	57	153	0.99

Moreover, when bar lines are recognised, the corresponding image segment is further elaborated in order to estimate the position of stavelines. This information is extracted and communicated to the successive module to be considered as reference lines (STAFF5 line).

In the presence of note groups such as beamed notes, the segmentation task provides the start and the end point of groups. This information is useful since it reduces the context analysis and provides a way to control the reliability of results.

In Figure 12, an excerpt of the symbolic description and the related image are shown.

Figure 12: Classification and Symbolic Description

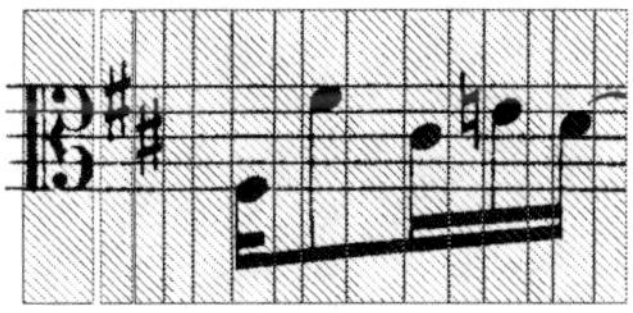

Output

```
STAFF5 48 57 75 94 113 133
CLEFALTO 49 54 54 84 0.31
STAFF5 107 57 76 95 114 134
SHARP 108 37 25 63 0.99
STAFF5 131 57 76 95 114 134
SHARP 134 65 23 61 0.90
STAFF5 207 57 76 95 114 133
BEGIN
FNOTEHEAD 208 123 32 23 0.99
BIGLINE1 208 165 32 14 0.55
BIGLINE1 208 180 32 15 0.81
BIGLINE1 240 178 21 14 0.97
FNOTEHEAD 261 56 34 23 0.99
BIGLINE1 261 174 34 16 0.50
THINLINE 295 170 44 16 0.36
FNOTEHEAD 339 83 34 25 0.98
BIGLINE1 339 152 34 14 0.80
BIGLINE1 339 168 34 14 0.61
NATURAL 373 46 26 61 0.50
BIGLINE1 373 150 26 14 0.51
BIGLINE1 373 166 26 14 0.66
FNOTEHEAD 399 64 34 25 0.99
BIGLINE1 399 145 34 15 0.68
BIGLINE1 399 163 34 15 0.46
BIGLINE1 433 144 19 13 0.95
BIGLINE1 433 160 19 15 0.76
FNOTEHEAD 452 75 31 23 0.99
THINLINE 452 143 31 14 0.97
THINLINE 452 159 31 14 0.97
END
........
```

Music Notation Reconstruction

In this section, the music reconstruction module foreseen in the O^3MR will be briefly described. Referring to Figure 13, the module consists of three main components:

Inputs Elaboration — The basic symbols recognised by the previous step are assembled in strips according to the image segments produced during the segmentation. In this phase, by means of the confusion table of the MLP neural network and a set of rules based on the probability that a symbol can occupy that position in the score (positional grammar), it is possible to perform the recovery of recognition mistakes. At the same time, if a symbol can assume different meanings related to its position (i.e., bass clef or baritone clef), by using the position rules it is possible to establish the right assumption.

Aggregation Module — Symbols are aggregated in order to rebuild music notation symbols. A rule-based music grammar describes the relationships among music symbols. Rules are strictly connected to the way of writing music and take into account how basic symbols have to be configured in order to obtain music symbols and how each music symbol is affected by adjacent symbols. The aggregation is conducted in two steps: (1) vertical aggregation and (2) horizontal aggregation. In the first step, if for instance the strip contains a black note head and a beam, the aggregated music symbol is a one-

Figure 13: Music Notation Reconstruction Module

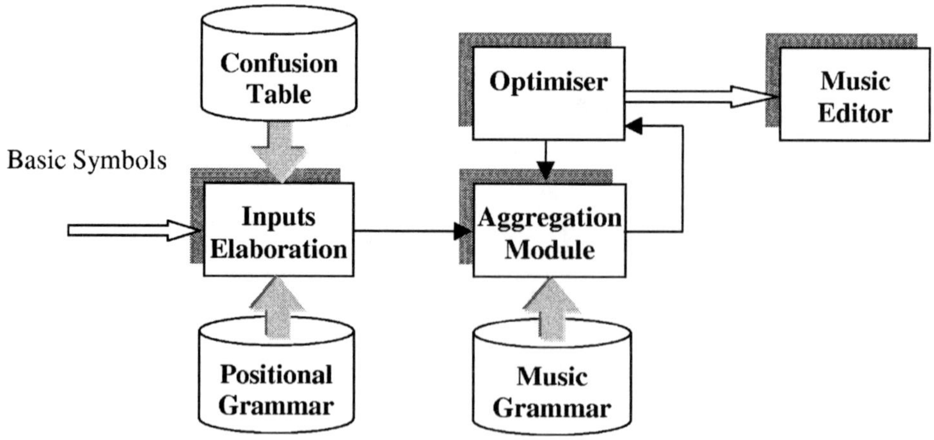

beamed eighth note. In the second step, if the aggregated music symbol is adjacent to an accidental symbol and this symbol stays on the left of the note, then the two symbols are fused together, defining an eighth note with accidental and beamed. In this way it is possible to consider the music context that the music symbol is in. During this phase, a single measure is rebuilt considering the duration of assembled music symbols and indications of start measure and end measure given by the recognition of bar lines.

Optimiser — The input of the optimiser is a music measure assembled by the Aggregation Module. If the measure is already the optimal measure, then it is ready to be converted into the symbolic notation model, else it needs to be elaborated again by the Aggregation Module. The goal of this feedback is to identify the strip that generated the incorrect music symbol. The Aggregation Module reconsiders and modifies the strip. The new strip and the grammar rules will produce a new music symbol that will be considered again in the evaluation of measure correctness. The goal is to determine the "best" strips in order to minimise a cost function that takes into account the duration of measure and the number of recognised basic symbols involved in the aggregation step.

Future Trends and Conclusions

The OMR problem is a wide research field and presents many open problems. Several music recognition systems have been implemented, but it is difficult to compare them because of different sets of data used and judging how much each system is tuned to particular examples for which results are reported. This problem is due to the lack of standard evaluation metrics. To cover this lack, one of the tasks of the MUSICNETWORK IST project (http://www.interactivemusicnetwork.org) is to define the guidelines for evaluating the capabilities and the performance of OMR systems. The main goal of the task is to set up different music scores with different levels of complexity as test cases and a set of rules and to use in the validation of OMR systems.

In music reading, as in other applications, it is difficult to scale up a small working prototype into a large and complete system. A system based on syntactic methods with a grammar could be easily manageable if it uses, for example, 30 production rules; but if this number is elevated to hundreds of production rules it is possible that the system would become difficult to manage. Another example is found in passing from a system that manages monophonic music to another one managing polyphonic music. In order to realise that, one of the possible requirement may be to redesign the whole system.

The high diversity of scores stemming from the possibility of combining the music notation impacts deeply on the project and on the possibility of creating an architecture that can be scaled up.

Finally, another important open problem is how to solve the problem of image noise — for example, when a primitive is expected to be connected for extraction purposes but it is actually broken into more fragments of image, or two objects that touch each other creating a unique unknown symbol.

References

Anstice, J., Bell, T., Cockburn, A., & Setchell, M. (1996). The design of a pen-based musical input system. OzCHI'96: *The Sixth Australian Conference on Computer-human Interaction* (November 24-27, pp. 260-267). Hamilton, New Zealand: IEEE Press.

Bainbridge, D. (1991). Preliminary experiments in musical score recognition. Edinburgh, UK: University of Edinburgh.

Bainbridge, D. (1996a). An extensible optical music recognition system. *The Australasian Computer Science Conference*, (pp. 308-317). Melbourne, Australia.

Bainbridge, D. (1996b). Optical music recognition: A generalised approach. Second New Zealand Computer Science Graduate Conference.

Bainbridge, D. (1997). Extensible optical music recognition. Christchurch, New Zealand: University of Canterbury.

Bellini, P., Bruno, I., & Nesi, P. (2001). Optical music sheet segmentation. *Proceedings of the 1st International Conference of Web Delivering of Music*. Florence: IEEE Press.

Bellini, P., Fioravanti, F., & Nesi, P. (1999). Managing music in orchestras. *IEEE Computer*, (September), 26-34.

Blostein, D., & Baird, H. S. (1992). A critical survey of music image analysis. In H. S. Baird, H. Bunke & K. Yamamoto (Eds.), *Structured Document Image Analysis* (pp. 405-434). Berlin: Springer-Verlag.

Carter, N. P. (1989, February). Automatic recognition of printed music in context electronic publishing. Ph.D Thesis. University of Surrey.

Carter, N. P. (1992a). A new edition of Walton's Façade using automatic score recognition. In H. Bunke (Ed.), *Advances in*

Structural and Syntactic Pattern Recognition, (pp. 352-362). World Scientific, Singapore.

Carter, N. P. (1992b). Segmentation and preliminary recognition of madrigals notated in white mensural notation. *Machine Vision and Applications,* 5(3), 223-230.

Carter, N. P. (1993). A generalized approach to automatic recognition of music scores. Stanford University.

Carter, N. P. (1994a). Conversion of the Haydn symphonies into electronic form using automatic score recognition: A pilot study. *Proceedings of SPIE 2181,* (pp. 279-290).

Carter, N. P. (1994b). Music score recognition: Problems and prospects. Computing in Musicology, 9, 152-8.

Carter, N. P. & Bacon, R.A. (1990). Automatic recognition of music notation. *Proceedings of the International Association for Pattern Recognition Workshop on Syntactic and Structural Pattern Recognition,* (p. 482). Murray Hill, NJ.

Choi, J. (1991). Optical recognition of the printed musical score. M.S. Thesis. University of Illinois at Chicago, USA.

Cooper, D., Ng, K. C., & Boyle, R. D. (1997). MIDI extensions for musical notation: expressive MIDI. In E. Selfridge-Field (Ed.), *Beyond MIDI — The Handbook of Musical Codes* (pp. 402-447). London: MIT Press.

Coüasnon, B. & Camillerapp, J. (1995). A way to separate knowledge from program in structured document analysis: Application to optical music recognition. *International Conference on Document Analysis and Recognition,* (pp. 1092-1097).

Droettboom, M., Fujinaga, I. & MacMillan, K. (2002). Optical music interpretation. *Proceedings of the Statistical, Structural and Syntactic Pattern Recognition Conference.*

Droettboom, M. et al. (2002). Using Gamera framework for the recognition of cultural heritage materials. *Proceedings of the Joint Conference on Digital Libraries,* (pp. 11-17). Portland, OR, USA

Fujinaga, I. (1988). Optical music recognition using projections. M.A. Thesis. McGill University, Montreal, Canada.

Fujinaga, I. (1997). Adaptive optical music recognition. Ph.D Dissertion. McGill University, Montreal, Canada.

Fujinaga, I. (2001). Adaptive optical music recognition. In D. Greer (Ed.), Musicology and Sister Disciplines: Past, Present, Future: Proceedings of the *16th International Congress of the International Musicological Society (1997)*. London, Oxford: Oxford University Press.

Luth, N. (2002). Automatic identification of music notation. In C. Busch, M. Arnold, P. Nesi & M. Schmucker (Eds), *Proceedings of the 2nd International Conference of Web Delivering of Music,* (pp. 203-210). Darmstadt, Germany: IEEE Press.

Marinai, S. & Nesi, P. (1999). Projection-based segmentation of musical sheet. *Proceedings of the 5th International Conference on Document Analysis and Recognition,* (September 20-22, pp. 515-518). IAPR (International Association on Pattern Recognition), Bangalore, India. ICDAR'99: IEEE Press.

Miyao, H. & Haralick, R.M. (2000). Format of ground truth data used in the evaluation of the results of an optical music recognition system. IAPR Workshop on Document Analysis Systems. Rio de Janeiro, Brazil.

Ng, E., Bell, T. & Cockburn, A. (1998). *Improvements to a pen-based musical input system*, (November 29-December 4, pp. 239-252). OzCHI'98: The Australian Conference on Computer-Human Interaction. Adelaide, Australia: IEEE Press.

Ng, K. C. (2002a). *Document imaging for music manuscript*. 6th World Multiconference on Sytemics, Cybernetics and Informatics. Florida, USA.

Ng, K. C. (2002b). *Optical music analysis: A reverse engineering approach*. Florence, Italy: EVA 2002.

Ng, K. C. & Boyle, R.D. (1992). *Segmentation of music primitives.* BMVC92. *Proceedings of the British Machine Vision Conference,* (pp. 472-480). Leeds, UK.

Ng, K. C. & Boyle, R.D. (1994). Reconstruction of music scores from primitive sub-segmentation. School of Computer Studies, University of Leeds.

Ng, K. C. & Boyle, R.D. (1996). Recognition and reconstruction of primitives in music scores. *Image and Vision Computing*, 14(1), 39-46.

Prerau, D. S. (1970). *Computer pattern recognition of standard engraved music notation*. Ph.D. Dissertation. Massachusetts Institute of Technology, MA, USA.

Ross, T. (1970). *The art of music engraving and processing*. Miami, FL: Hansen Books.

Roth, M. (1994). *An approach to recognition of printed music*, tech. rep. ETH Zurich, Switzerland: Swiss Federal Institute of Technology.

Rumelhart, D. E. & McClelland, J.L. (1986). Parallel distributed processing: Exploration in the microstructure of cognition (vol. 1). Cambridge, MA: Cambridge University Press.

Selfridge-Field, E. (1994). Optical recognition of musical notation: A survey of current work. *Computing in Musicology*, 9, 109-145.

Selfridge-Field, E. (ed.). (1997). *Beyond MIDI — The Handbook of Musical Codes*. London: MIT Press.

Suen, C.Y. & Wang, P.S.P. (1994). Thinning methodologies for pattern recognition. Series in Machine Perception and Artificial Intelligence (vol. 8). World Scientific.

Wavelets for Dealing with Super-Imposed Objects in Recognition of Music Notation

3

Susan E. George
University of South Australia, Australia

Abstract

This chapter is concerned with a problem that arises in Optical Music Recognition (OMR) when notes and other music notation symbols are super-imposed upon stavelines in the music image. We investigate a general-purpose, knowledge-free method of image filtering using two-dimensional wavelets to separate the super-imposed objects. Some background is given to the area of wavelets and a demonstration of how stavelines can be located in a wavelet-filtered image. We also explore the separation of foreground objects (notes) from the background (stavelines) over a variety of image resolutions, in binary and greyscale images using a pixel-based truth representation of the image to evaluate the accuracy with which symbols are identified. We find that the Coifmann family of wavelets appear most suitable for vertical image components, and the Daubechies for the horizontal. The motivation for this chapter stems from the desire to (i) make an original wavelet application in image processing, (ii) provide a fresh (theoretical) perspective on the problem of super-imposed objects in music notation, recognising the duality of the segregation task that exists with staveline removal/symbol extraction and (iii) evaluate how beneficial wavelet image filtering might be to the OMR process.

Introduction

The aim of Optical Music Recognition (OMR) is to "recognise" images of music notation and capture the "meaning" of the music. When OMR is successful it will be able to automatically extract a logical representation of printed or handwritten music. There are a variety of reasons why OMR is required. Chiefly it is useful for swift input. Once music is input to a computer it may be performed, edited, used to search a music archive, transposed, typeset for printing, or other. Musicologists and copyright enforcers, educators and concert managers may all have an interest in OMR. This chapter assumes that there is enough motivation for OMR and addresses the difficulties that it presents — focusing upon the problem of super-imposed objects. Music notation symbols are super-imposed upon stavelines, and symbols and lines must be dis-entangled to interpret the music. This chapter develops a fresh theoretical perspective that has practical consequences to dealing with super-imposed objects in OMR.

In this section we consider the super-imposed object that is created by a music symbol(s) placed upon staffline. We note that the OMR field has taken two basic approaches to dealing with super-imposed objects. These approaches are (i) the removal of stavelines and (ii) the recognition/segmentation of music symbols, and we briefly review some of the approaches that have been taken since OMR began in the 1960s. The chapter then moves on to introduce the wavelet as a general image processing technique that is capable of filtering an image into its component parts. The wavelet provides a fresh theoretical perspective on the problem of super-imposed objects in music notation and we describe some experiments where the wavelet is applied to music images to isolate stavelines and segment the symbols from the image. We also evaluate its practical contribution as a general-purpose, knowledge-free stage of image pre-processing in OMR using a pixel-based measure.

The remainder of this introduction motivates the chapter firstly by considering the application of wavelets in image processing. We note that isolating image components for OMR is a novel application of wavelets. Wavelets are most commonly applied to filter the noise from an image or perhaps compress an image for storage purposes. While they are used in many different fields (not just image processing) for many different purposes, dealing with the symbols of music and the stavelines as components of an image presents a challenge to (i) identify whether the super-imposed components can indeed be segregated by a general purpose filtering method, (ii) identify the wavelet family that is most suited to (a) staffline removal and (b) symbol segmentation and (iii) evaluate the wavelet contribution as a pre-processing method in OMR — given the general difficulties of OMR evaluation. Thus some motivation for this chapter comes from investigating wavelets in the context of OMR as a novel application for them.

This chapter is also motivated by the fresh perspective that wavelet filtering presents to OMR. Currently there are two approaches to super-imposed objects in OMR that focus upon either (a) staffline removal or (b) symbol recognition (and subsequent symbol segmentation from the staffline) using very different methods for each approach. The wavelet, as a general-purpose, knowledge-free image processing method, is able to present a unified method of dealing with the image — whether stavelines are removed or symbols segmented — and hence a fresh theoretical perspective to dealing with super-imposed objects in OMR. The filtering that wavelets perform captures the duality of the staffline removal/symbol identification task, since different components of wavelet decomposition are just the stavelines and symbols that must be isolated. Theoretically, with the right wavelet and right decomposition, the respective staves and symbols could be identified and extracted from the image signal. Thus another motivation for this chapter is to investigate this unified theoretical perspective and determine whether wavelet filtering has any practical benefit to OMR.

Super-Imposed Objects

Super-imposed objects pervade music notation. Super-imposition arises when notes and other music symbols are placed upon the staffline (or staff), making "ink" of the symbol overlap with "ink" of the staffline. The overlapping elements are a way of representing music pitch and rhythm and there have been a variety of music notations. Even medieval notations contain the super-imposed object and the prevalent Common Music Notation of today has inherited the foreground/background aspect of notated music. Dealing with super-imposed objects in OMR has been tackled in two main ways: removing stavelines or segmenting music symbols from the staff. Both methods have proved a challenge. There are various reasons why isolating the super-imposed object is so difficult within OMR.

First, the music document is created by image capture, typically a scanning process, and the image is rarely perfect. It may be skewed or degraded by other noise. The stavelines are generally not exactly parallel, horizontal, equidistant, of constant thickness, or even straight. Any image perturbation introduces an added practical complexity to the recognition task. Second, even on an image corrected for skew and other perturbations, other symbols within the music (such as beams, phrase marks and other) can be mistaken for stavelines and, hence, lines mis-located. Third, and perhaps most importantly, once a line has been identified it cannot simply be removed from the image without also removing part of any music symbol that touches it; there is only one piece of 'ink' for objects that are super-imposed upon the lines. The stavelines have to be extracted leaving the symbol intact — or conversely the symbol has to be segmented from the staffline having identified its location within the staff.

When focusing upon the segmentation of symbols from a staffline there are difficulties specific to music notation that make some forms of pattern recognition inapplicable. First, music symbols may be variant in size (e.g., phrase markings, slurs) and the scope for variant sized symbols renders any form of template matching inappropriate. Rather a more sophisticated form of feature extraction would have to be undertaken. Second, a given piece of music may be expressed, or typeset, in various ways. For example, a note of two beats may be represented by two tied single-beat notes, or a single two-beat note; a run of four half-beat notes may be represented by two groups of two half-beats, four single half-beats, or a group of beamed half-beats. The number of ways of typesetting a particular musical sound is potentially infinite and, again, template matching would not suffice for all the possibilities, making more sophisticated recognition methods necessary. In short, it is not simple to either locate and remove the stavelines, or to identify and extract the music symbols.

Approaches to Super-Imposed Objects in Music

Since the 1960s there have been various approaches to dealing with super-imposed objects. All of these approaches are knowledge-based techniques, in that they are assuming some information is known about the format of music images in order to locate the stave-lines or isolate symbols. As we mentioned previously, dealing with super-imposed objects in OMR has been tackled in two main ways: removing stavelines or segmenting music symbols from the staff. Blostein and Baird (1992) present a critical survey of problems and approaches to music image analysis. Here we summarise some of the approaches to OMR from the initial attempts in the 1960s.

- Pruslin (1967) — remove thin horizontal lines (by thresholding the length of continuous vertical runs of pixels, assuming that a figure for "line thickness" was known).
- Prerau (1975) — remove stavelines and restore those parts that coincide with symbols (using a contour trace from the edge of each staffline to locate the start of symbols that might be placed on those lines).
- Nakamura, Shindo and Inokuchi (1979) — remove stavelines using line tracker calculating a least-squares fit for stavelines computing threshold to erase the stavelines and achieve segmentation.
- Andronico and Ciampa (1982) — remove just the exposed stavelines.
- Aoyama and Tojo (1982) — detect stavelines by using the horizontal histogram of black pixels within each block of low-resolution scan lines and use a threshold to find sets of five peaks. Coarse segmentation was then undertaken, removing obvious, exposed sections of staffline by examining the vertical run-lengths involved. Fine segmentation detected black and white noteheads by searching for overlapping pixel runs.
- Mahoney (1982) — isolate symbols from stavelines interpolating between end-points where there were "gaps."
- Matsushima et al. (1985) — detect stavelines by a short bar-like filter, which operated down equi-spaced columns in the image simultaneously with the scanning process.
- Roach and Tatem (1988) — detect stavelines with a line-tracking algorithm calculating line direction and thickness at each pixel in a grey-scale image by passing a window of

appropriate proportions over the image. They have also considered the specific challenges of handwritten music.

- Bainbridge and Bell (1997) — determine presence of stavelines by following the wobble in groups of pixels and remove with heuristics.
- Lin and Bell (2000) — propose colour printing and scanning technology to help deal with the issue of super-imposed objects.
- Choudhury and Lauro (2001) — remove staff lines using projection profiles, remove text by heuristics, vertical components of stems and barlines and horizontal components of note heads, recognizing the remaining symbols with k-Nearest Neighbor (kNN) classifier combining the glyphs again.
- Droettboom et al. (2002) — describes the use of classifiers for symbols recognition providing tools for the creation of a simple heuristic classifier, a template-based image matching and a kNN learning classifier.

All these approaches have met with some success and various limitations. Perhaps the biggest limitation is that they are knowledge-based, requiring specific knowledge about music to isolate the symbols or to follow stave-lines. Implicitly, knowledge-based techniques are constrained by the knowledge that they may draw upon. For example, a symbol-finding algorithm can only find symbols that it knows about, and should new symbol be encountered within the music notation the recognition is likely to fail. Similarly, a staffline tracking algorithm is constrained by heuristics about how stavelines generally appear, or in what ways they may be corrupted. When knowledge is explicitly utilised, at some point, a novel input will be encountered that falls outside the scope of the knowledge-based method (this is especially the case when dealing not with "printed" documents, but with handwritten ones). Hence the importance and appeal of general-purpose, knowledge-free methods.

Introduction to Wavelets for OMR

In this section we introduce the wavelet transform. Wavelets are a relatively recent mathematical approach extending some of the principles of Fourier analysis. Fourier techniques are suitable for the study of periodic signals, while wavelet theory is well suited for complex signals, where the frequency structure changes throughout the signal (i.e., non-periodic signals). Since very few signals or images are truly periodic, wavelet techniques are ideal. Wavelets are basically a way of decomposing a signal into its component parts. We consider a little of the way that a signal may be decomposed, explaining the importance of "coefficients" in the wavelet expansion, outlining how wavelets can be used for two-dimensional image processing in OMR.

Wavelet Background

Wavelets are basically an ideal tool for decomposing a signal — either a one-dimensional temporal signal (such as a radio transmission) or two-dimensional spatial signal (such as an image) — into its component parts. Wavelets permit the signal to be viewed so that the large-scale fluctuations are emphasised (with the small detail as noise), or such that the small fluctuations are emphasised (with the larger scale fluctuations as background). Disentangling the signal into its component parts (at various levels or scales) is the main principle of wavelets. Taking a wavelet transform simplifies the signal that has to be stored (enabling compression), and from this information it is possible to reconstruct an approximation of the original signal (often with remarkable accuracy).

Interest in wavelets is fueled by the wide range of applications that have been made, including: (a) time-frequency analysis, (b) noise removal — smoothing, (c) image compression and (d) reducing dimensionality of data for computation speed. They are particularly useful for representing signals that have localized features (Fourier methods assume a continuous infinite feature). Interest is also stimulated by the fact that some wavelets may be implemented in an extremely computationally efficient manner by means of multi-resolution analysis. Just as Fast Fourier Transform algorithms made the Fourier Transform a practical tool for spectral analysis, the multi-resolution analysis has made the Discrete Wavelet Transform a viable tool.

Mathematical Definition

The wavelet is defined by the "mother wavelet" from which other wavelets in the "family" can be generated. All members of a particular family share the same basic wavelet shape that is shifted or dilated (i.e., they are made tall and skinny or short and fat). The specific parameters are translation ("b") and contraction ("a"). Members of an individual wavelet family $y^{a,b}(x)$ can be defined by (1):

$$\psi^{a,b}(x) = |a|^{-1/2}\,\psi\left(\frac{x-b}{a}\right) \qquad (1)$$

Equation 1 generates a one-dimensional function that can be plotted. There are a number of families of wavelets including Haar, Daubechies, Coifmanns, Mexican Hat, Meyer and Morlet. The Daubechies-1 wavelet is identical in shape to the Haar wavelet, while Daubechies-10 is a far more complex function as illustrated in Figure 1, which plots the Coifmann-1, Haar and Daubechies-10 wavelets. Wavelet functions are admissible, meaning that the area above and below the curve must cancel out when a line is drawn at y = 0. There are other properties that a wavelet function may possess, including orthogonality.

Figure 1: Examples of Wavelet Functions

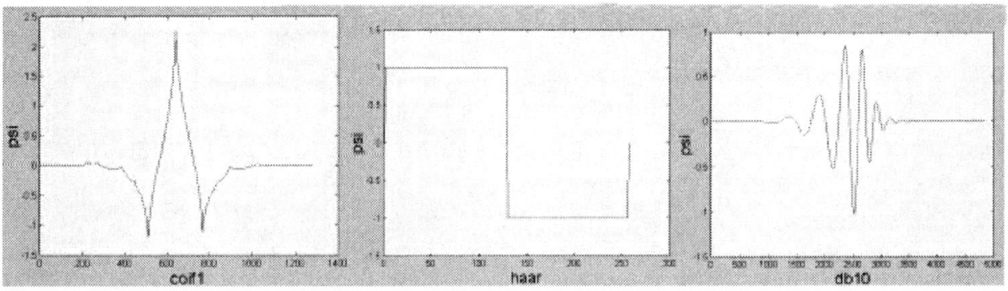

The coefficients in the wavelet transform are an important part of the wavelet expression since (combined with the generating mother wavelet) they compact the signal and can be used to approximate a function. Instead of having to store every value of the function, it is only necessary to store the coefficients, perhaps at various levels of decomposition, and from these the signal can be obtained. For example, suppose we want to represent the data vector (4,2) using a wavelet basis. We may represent this by the standard (orthogonal) cartesian basis vectors (1,0) and (0,1) when we have (4,2) = 4* (1,0) + 2 * (0,1). The (coefficient) number in front each basis vector (e.g., 4*(1,0)) is derived from the orthogonal (i.e., perpendicular) projection of the data vector, (4,2), onto the basis vector. For a good tutorial on wavelets see Polikar (1996).

Wavelets in Image Processing

Two-dimensional wavelets can be applied to two-dimensional signals, that is, images. A typical application of wavelets in image processing is noise removal achieved by filtering (combing the image with the filter in some way). Filters traditionally smooth the data to reduce the noise, but, in the process, also blur the data. Wavelets can remove the noise more effectively while preserving the edges in the data (Vidakovic, 1999). Wavelets have also been used to compress images (Saha, 2001) and this OMR application proposes wavelets are utilised to locate particular components of the image, so aiding the task of separating super-imposed objects in music notation.

Wavelets decompose images into their high- and low-pass components in row- and column-wise directions. There are four combinations of low-pass filters (H1 and H2) and high-pass filters (G1 and G2) in the vertical (H1 and G1) and horizontal (H2 and G2) directions, summarised by: H1 = low-pass filter, column-wise; H2 = low-pass filter, row-wise; G1 = high-pass filter, column-wise; and G2 = high-pass filter, row-wise. When a two-dimensional decomposition of an image is made, these low- and high-frequency components can be isolated. In Figures 2a and 2b we provide an example of a wavelet decomposition into respective components using Matlab (Mathworks, 1994). Figure 2a shows the original greyscale image. Figure 2b shows the wavelet decomposition using the Coifmann-5 wavelet. The top left quadrant contains an approximation of the original image; the top right contains the horizontal components; the bottom left the vertical components; and the bottom right the diagonal components.

When considering wavelet image decomposition, it is worth observing that the music image possesses certain properties including: (i) the music staffline —

Figure 2a: Original Image

Figure 2b: Coifman-5 Wavelet Decompositions

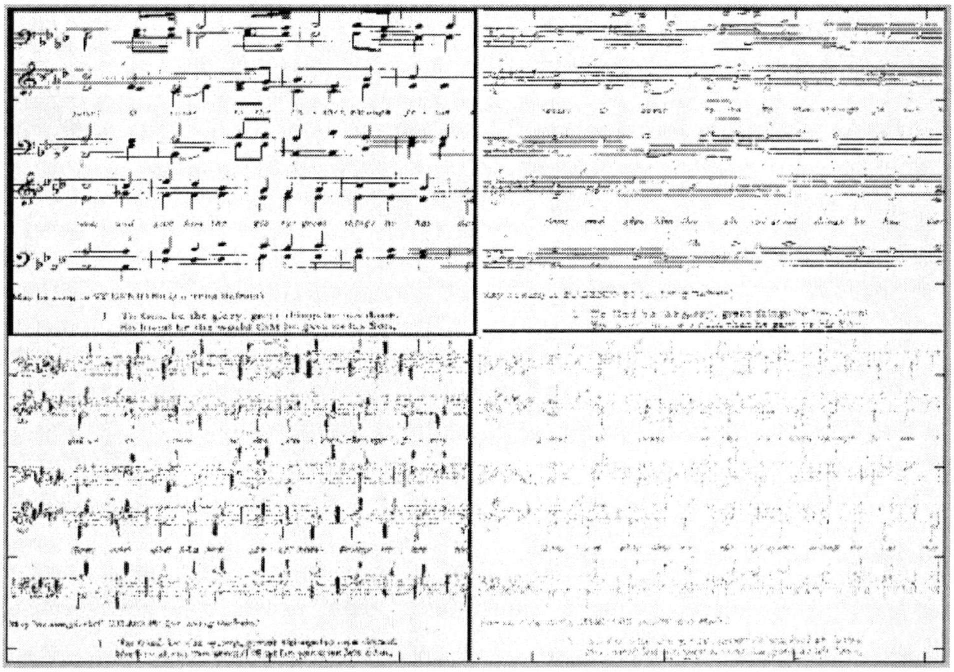

which present a strong horizontal component to the image signal and which are (generally) regular across the image page, and (ii) other music notation symbols — which present a more vertical component and are more local perturbations within the image; wavelets are particularly useful for such local irregularities within an image, and some wavelets may be more suitable than others for the regular/irregular patterns that occur within a music image.

Wavelets and Super-Imposed Objects in OMR

This section considers the wavelet and super-imposed objects in OMR. We describe some of the issues from image capture to how the wavelets filter the image. We then present some experimental work that specifically considers how wavelets can be used to contribute a knowledge-free, pre-processing method that moves towards isolating superimposed objects. Specifically we break this task into (i) identifying staffline occurrence (regardless of where they appear on the page) and (ii) segmentation of images to isolate the stavelines from the symbols.

Parameters of Image Capture

Image capture is achieved by some scanning device or digital camera. It produces a computer-compatible digital representation that can be interpreted in visual terms. There are various choices that can be made when capturing an image — such as whether we retain colour or not, the resolution (in dots per inch (dpi)) to use, and other. What we wish to do with the captured image affects the choices we make when we capture it.

The biggest distinction in image capture is whether we have a binary, greyscale or, indeed, colour image. Greyscale images can distinguish up to 256 greyscale levels, meaning eight bits are required to store every pixel (picture element), while binary images distinguish just two levels (meaning one bit can store each pixel). The next biggest distinction is the resolution of the image. This refers to the dimensions of the image. Generally a scanning device is capable of capturing images represented in printed form on paper up to the size of standard A4/letter size. The dimensions of such a page are approximately 1200 by 900. Within the dimension of the image we may further select how many dpi we devote to each portion of the image. This parameter generally starts at about 75dpi and increases up to about 600dpi (that which can be represented on most quality printers) and beyond to almost 20000dpi.

Figure 3 illustrates some differences between binary and greyscale images scanned at 100dpi resolution. Both images are 210 by 136 pixels. The main difference is in image quality. Some detail is lost with the binary image, including stavelines and beam stems (important horizontal and vertical components of the music notation!). Yet, the binary image may indeed suffice (or be better than greyscale) for some OMR image recognition algorithms since the notation symbols are clear enough.

Figure 3: Illustration of Binary and Greyscale Image Capture at 100dpi

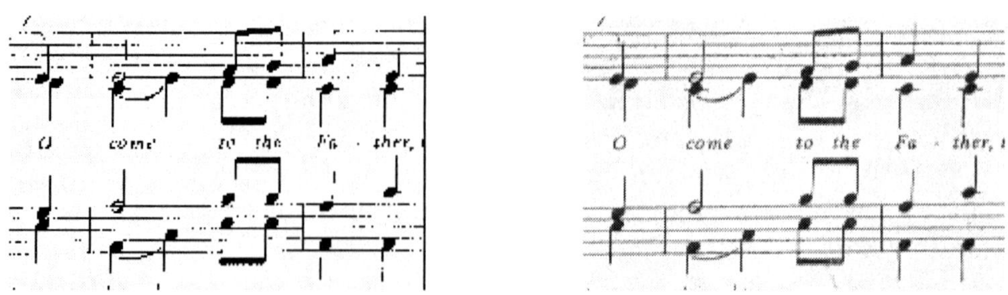

Image Filtering for Super-Imposed Objects

The wavelet provides a unified theoretical framework within which to deal with super-imposed objects in OMR. Rather than taking a staffline-removal or a symbol-segmentation approach, the principle of filtering can be used for both. The principle of using wavelets for OMR image filtering is to decompose the image into component parts — horizontal, vertical and diagonal — and then utilise the image breakdown. The image components can be re-combined with themselves and the original in various ways and/or thresholded to produce new images with some details removed or enhanced.

Figure 4 illustrates some wavelet filtering. The original 256 by 256 image is in the top left. It was filtered with a Daubechies wavelet transform and the resulting image (top right) has been blurred in the horizontal direction, making the stavelines and other horizontal components less distinct. The

Figure 4: Examples of Wavelet Filtering

bottom left quadrant contains the thresholded transformed image, showing how the cut-off has removed the lighter, blurred pixels from the image. These are precisely the stavelines, leaving chiefly the notes in the filtered image. The bottom right quadrant illustrates the difference between the original and the thresholded transformed image. Removing the notes from the original image has essentially left the stavelines, beams, phrase marks and horizontal components — together, with the edges of the other symbols.

Evaluating Wavelet Image Filtering

One of the first questions that arises with the application of wavelet transforms to super-imposed objects within music is the question of evaluation. That is, the question of "how can we know whether a wavelet transform has been of any benefit to OMR?" We may also be interested in comparing different wavelet transforms. This question of evaluation must be faced by both the complete OMR system and any sub-processes, such as wavelet filtering, that are used en-route to a full recognition. The issue of evaluation in OMR has been dealt with elsewhere in this volume. It is necessary to consider what is being evaluated (accuracy, efficiency or other) in a particular context of use. Fundamental to evaluating accuracy is some target of "truth representation."

In the context of filtered images we suggest that the target representation is another image, and evaluation is a pixel-based measure that compares the "black ink" on the filtered image with the "black ink" ideally present in the "truth representation." For greyscale images we would choose a cut-off that divided pixels into "black" or "white" pixels, enabling the comparison. A pixel-based measure could be the percentage of correctly recognised black/white pixels, or as we suggest, a sensitivity/specificity-based measure.

Sensitivity/specificity are commonly used to determine the accuracy of a method in detecting the presence/absence of a disease. We will use these measures to detect the correct presence/absence of a black pixel. When comparing the pixels in the truth representation with the pixels in the filtered image there are basically four possibilities after comparison — either the pixels match exactly (whether black or white) or there is a mismatch (black expected and white found or vice versa). We shall call these events true positives/negatives and false positives/negatives: true positive (TP) where a black pixel is correctly recognised as black, true negative (TN) where a white pixel is correctly recognised as black, false positive (FP) where a while pixel is incorrectly recognised as black and false negative (FN) where a black pixel is incorrectly recognised as white. These measures can be used to provide the sensitivity/specificity of the image filtering.

The sensitivity of the system is the true positive ratio and is defined as TP/(TP + FN). It measures the extent to which the system is capable of diagnosing positive instances (e.g., of a black pixel). It is in fact the likelihood that an event will be detected given that it is present. The specificity of the system is the true negative ratio and is defined as TN/(FP + TN). The false positive ratio is FP/(FP + TN) and is the same as (1 - specificity). It is the likelihood that the absence of an event will be detected, given that it is absent. Ideally, we would have a sensitivity of 1 and a specificity of 1, but typically in practice we must accept a less than maximum value for both measures. Often we may adjust some parameter of the classifier (in this case this might be the threshold cut-off for a black/white pixel) to maximise the sensitivity (at the expense of specificity) or vice versa. Ideally, any classifier would perform better than chance alone (that is 0.5) in both measures.

Experiment 1: Locating Stavelines

Aim: We aim to determine whether stavelines can better be detected in the original image or in a wavelet-filtered version, where the horizontal components are isolated. We consider a range of music notation cases including: empty stavelines (Image 0), stavelines interspersed with text (Image 3), small font inserted staves (Images 1 and 2), incomplete staves (Image 2) and skewed staves (Image 4). These examples are designed to present special challenges to staveline finding methods.

Method: All images are scanned at 350 dpi, greyscale with a resolution of 256 by 256 pixels. Image 1 is taken from "English Country Garden," by Percy Grainger, Schott and Co., 1919. Image 2 is taken from Rhapsodies Hongroises (Rhapsodie 2), Liszt, Augener Ltd. Image 3 is taken from "Pilgrim," Michael Hurd, Novello and Company, 1978. Image 4 is taken from "Songs of Fellowship," Book 2, Kingsway Publications, Eastborne, 1985. The Daubechies-3 wavelet is applied to the images and the two-dimensional signal decomposed into the component high- and low-pass components. The horizontal component is isolated and visually displayed, together with the original image. Figure 5 illustrates the original and wavelet transform for the five images.

Stavelines are located in the original image and the wavelet transform using a simple pixel histogram along the rows to locate where the "peaks" and "troughs" of black pixels are. The peaks in the distribution are caused by a staffline that runs the whole length of a page (as opposed to a portion of the script that has notes or vocals or other directives). The pixel histograms of the original and transformed image are compared.

Figure 5: Examples of Stavelines and their Wavelet Transform

(a) Image 0

(b) Transform Image 0

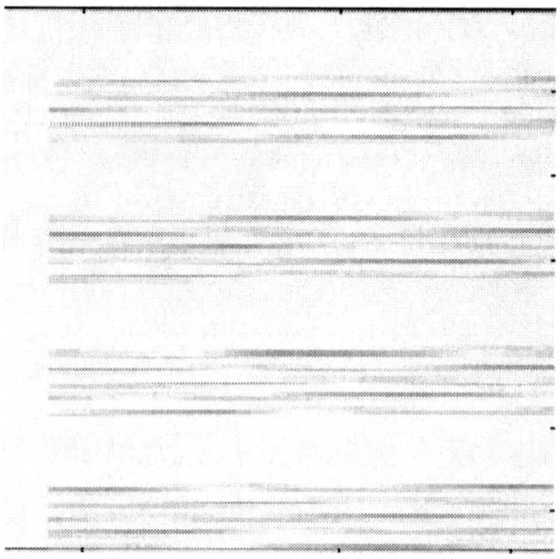

(c) Image 1

(d) Transform Image 1

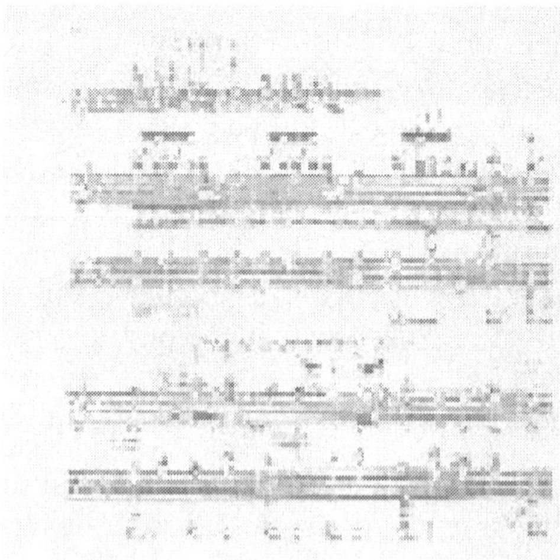

Figure 5: Examples of Stavelines and their Wavelet Transform (continued)

(e) Image 2

(f) Transform Image 2

(g) Image 3

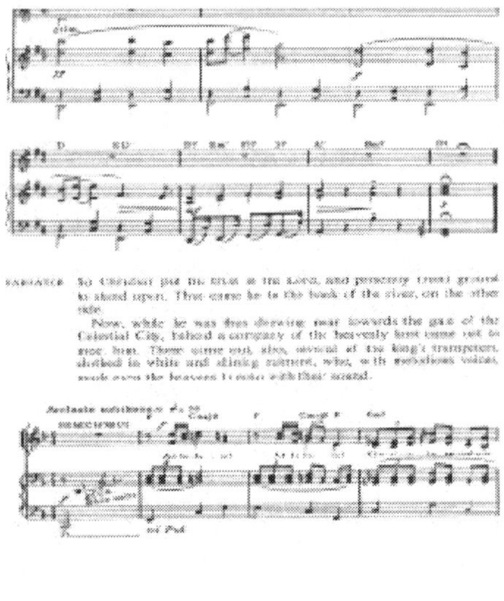

(h) Transform Image 3

Figure 5: Examples of Stavelines and their Wavelet Transform (continued)

(i) Image 4 (j) Transform Image 4

Results: Figure 6 illustrates the frequency plots for the wavelets (left) and original image (right). The peaks in the plots correspond to the presence of a number of black pixels (i.e., a horizontal line).

Figure 6: Frequency Plots for the Presence of Black Pixels (showing staffline occurrence)

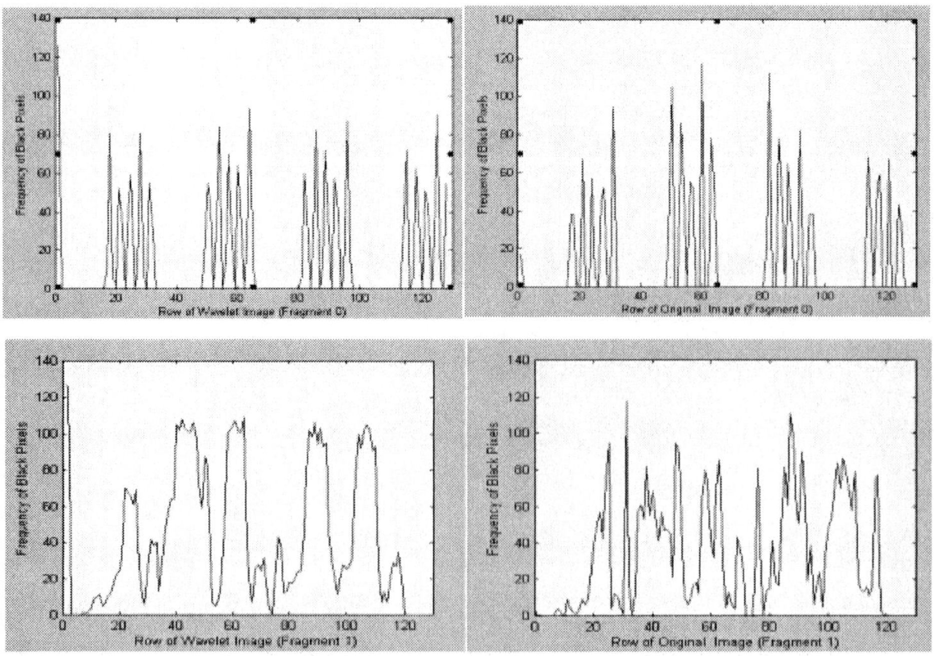

Figure 6: Frequency Plots for the Presence of Black Pixels (showing staffline occurrence) (continued)

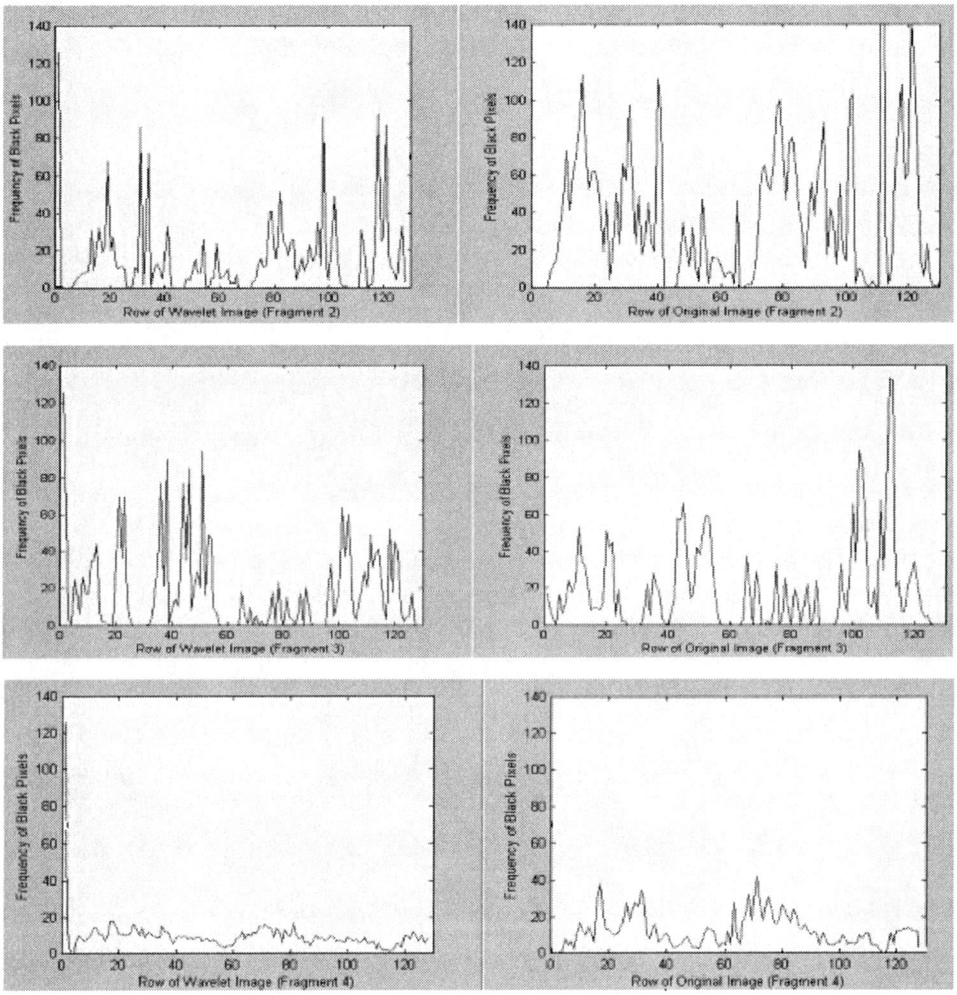

The presence of peaks in the plots of Figure 6 indicates where there is a strong horizontal signal in the image. Ideally, for locating stavelines there will be five such peaks close together. This can most easily be seen in Fragment from Image 0 where the empty stave produces a clear horizontal signal in both the original image and the wavelet transform. The signal is more regular in the wavelet transform, having a more consistent value for the maximum peak, while the histogram for the original image demonstrates some variation with the middle two stavelines showing a stronger signal than the top or bottom group of five lines.

Fragment 1 shows the clearest improvement between wavelet transform and original image, having four main peaks that correspond to the main portions of music staveline and one smaller peak corresponding to the smaller inserted lines. This distinction is not so obvious in the histogram from the original image. Fragments 2 and 3 are both similar in that there are horizontal signals interspersed between the stavelines. For Fragment 2 there is a mid-image confusion (around row 50) where there is a small staveline insertion. This similarity can be seen in both the original image and the wavelet decomposition. The text does achieve a fairly strong horizontal signal in the wavelet transform (occurring just after row 60). This pattern also appears in the original at the same point. However the anticipated six peaks before this block of text does not stand out especially clearly in either the wavelet or the original image. The skewed image (Fragment 4) does not give a strong horizontal signal in either the original image or the wavelet transform.

Conclusion: In general the peaks and troughs of the horizontal pixel histograms are easier to detect in the wavelet decompositions rather than the original image for each of the image fragments. In OMR, when trying to locate stavelines, there is some benefit in using wavelets to filter the image and emphasise the horizontal components in order to make it easier to locate the stavelines. While other staffline-finding methods may also be useful, the wavelet transform does provide some advantage over the original image, and we may consider applying these line finding algorithms to the filtered image to see whether the pre-processing has emphasised the horizontal signal to any advantage.

Experiment 2: Segmentation of Images to Isolate the Stavelines from the Symbols

Aim: We aim to determine whether the wavelet can help isolate the symbols superimposed upon the lines. We also wish to determine the image-capture parameters (dpi and greyscale/binary) that lead to optimal separation of superimposed objects from the stavelines.

Method: Three music fragments were selected. Fragment 1 is from Liszt Rhapsodies Hongroises (Rhapsodie 8), Fragment 2 is from The Potter's Hand, Hillsong's Australia, and Fragment 3 is from Chopin complete piano works (PolonaiseFantaise op 61). In these samples some variety was provided in terms of "resolution" of music upon the image; Fragment 2 contains just a few bars of music while there are lines in the other cases. Fragment 3 includes examples of the most intricate superimposed objects. Figure 7 illustrates these music fragments (using the 350dpi greyscale representation of the image).

Figure 7: The Music Fragments Used (in 350dpi greyscale representation)

(a) Fragment 1 (b) Fragment 2 (c) Fragment 3

From these music fragments six images were generated, capturing the image at 150, 250 and 350dpi in binary and greyscale modes. For each of these images a truth representation was constructed by hand, separating the stavelines from the music symbols that appear upon them.

The Daubechies-3 wavelet transform was applied to each of the images in turn isolating the horizontal and vertical components of the image. There are a variety of ways that the components of the transform can be used to isolate the symbols; the horizontal or vertical components may be subtracted from the original image, or some combination of them to leave the symbols. We removed all components other than the horizontal and sought to compare the wavelet transform filtered image with the staffline truth representation on a pixel-by-pixel basis. As described above the accuracy of the image filtering was evaluated using a crude pixel-based measure of accuracy. Sensitivity and specificity measures were computed for each of the images and these are reported in Table 1.

Results: Considering the individual music fragments, the results suggest that Image 2 (containing just a few bars) was the easiest image to deal with since the average sensitivity was 0.65 and specificity was 0.75 over all the image capture parameters. The hardest image was Image 3 with average sensitivity of 0.31 and specificity of 0.78 over the image capture parameters, and Image 2 achieved on average 0.65 for sensitivity and 0.78 for specificity across the image parameters.

Table 1: Sensitivity/Specificity of the Wavelet Transform Applied to Remove Stavelines

	Binary (256x256)			Greyscale (256x256)		
Image 1	150dpi	250dpi	350dpi	150dpi	250dpi	350dpi
Sensitivity	0.52	0.50	0.48	0.59	0.45	0.47
Specificity	0.76	0.23	0.75	0.67	0.24	0.74
Image 2	Binary (256x256)			Greyscale (256x256)		
Sensitivity	0.83	0.76	0.82	0.24	0.57	0.67
Specificity	0.79	0.85	0.81	0.73	0.74	0.73
Image 3	Binary (256x256)			Greyscale (256x256)		
Sensitivity	0.43	0.36	0.43	0.23	0.23	0.17
Specificity	0.79	0.83	0.84	0.71	0.76	0.77

Considering next the different image capture parameters, Figure 8 plots the average sensitivity/specificity for the three images across the different images, illustrating how in general the greyscale images all produce worse measures than the binary images. Not surprisingly the sensitivity measure is always poorer (since correctly recognising a black pixel is a more difficult task than recognising a white pixel — and there are more white pixels within an image than there are black pixels). In terms of absolute sensitivity/specificity measures, there is no clear difference between the 150dpi and 350dpi case, suggesting that no one level is better/worse than another.

Figure 8: Average Sensitivity and Specificity Across all Images

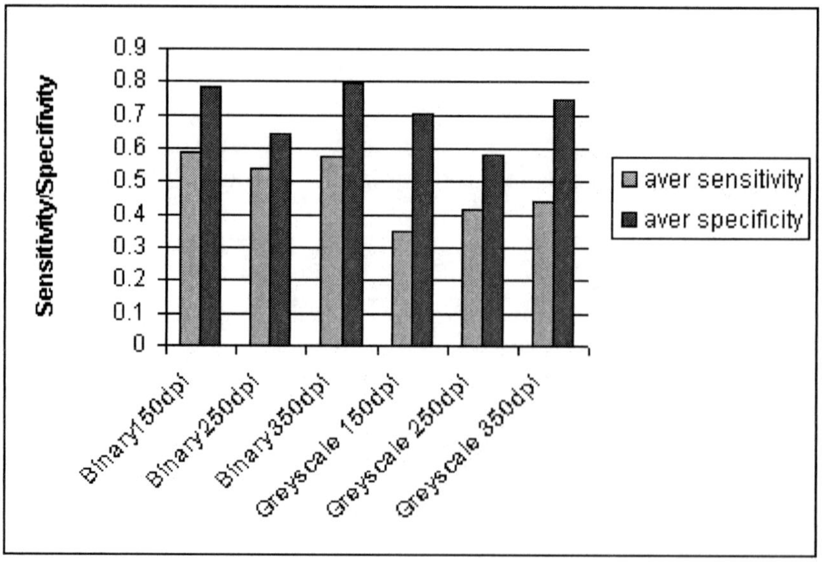

Discussion: While the results appear to suggest that a binary image is the best type of image capture to use this may be misleading. If we look at the 150dpi binary representation of the music fragments, we find that the clarity of the resolution is extremely poor and indeed information seems to have been lost — it would be hard for a human musician to recognise the content of the images. Figure 9 illustrates the same music fragments captured at the lower binary resolution. Both stavelines and symbols are poorly represented and information has indeed been lost. Thus while binary images may appear to give a good level of performance in terms of accuracy (when evaluated with the pixel-based measure) we cannot conclude that using binary images will contribute to the overall recognition of the music fragment.

Figure 9: The Music Fragments Used (in 150dpi binary representation)

(a) Fragment 1 (b) Fragment 2 (c) Fragment 3

We may find that the lowest resolution binary image produces the best results simply because it is artificially the "easier" problem (as measured by this means of evaluation); and even better results may be achieved by images consisting almost entirely of white space (e.g., certain drum notations, captured in low resolution binary mode, may appear to give the most promising results simply because there is less "ink" on the page to recognise!). Thus we may be better off simply inspecting the images that result after wavelet image filtering to see how well superimposed objects have been isolated. Figure 10 illustrates the vertical components of music Fragment 2. It is likely that some symbol-finding algorithm will have to be applied to the image to completely isolate the individual symbols and move to a symbol-based recognition and evaluation of the transform process.

Figure 10: The Vertical Components from the Wavelet Transforms for Fragment 2

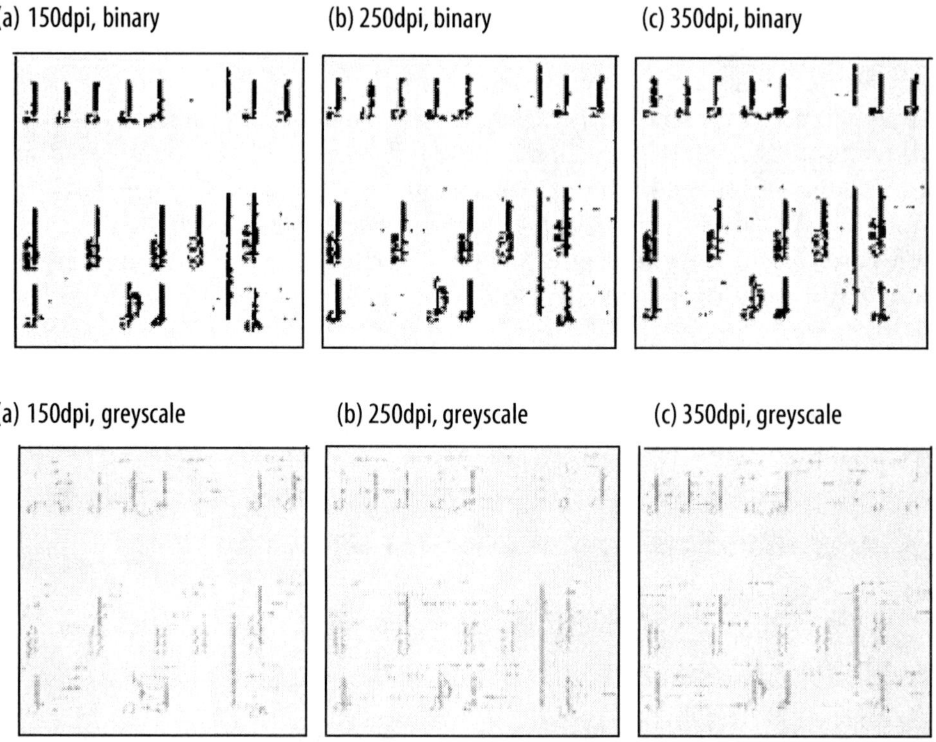

Conclusion: To fully answer the question of whether the wavelet can isolate symbols we must have a criteria for evaluation linked to the actual symbols on the page. A pixel-based evaluation may be misleading — there may be many pixels in common between the wavelet transform and the truth representation, but this does not mean it is possible to re-construct the symbols within the original image (additionally there may be much noise where pixels are simply shifted left or right, implying a poor match with the truth representation when in reality the information is present). The experiments here in fact suggested that binary images of low dpi are sufficient for a good sensitivity to identify the non-staffline components, but the success can be attributed to the fact that images captured at this resolution simply have less "ink" detail to recognise. Informally visualising the results of the wavelet transform may be more useful than trying to quantify the accuracy of the transform with a pixel-based measure.

Experiment 3: Visualising the Wavelet Transform

Aim: The aim of these final experiments is simply to visualise different wavelet transforms of a variety of music images (containing printed music notation samples of various complexity). We propose to use the Daubechies-3, 4 and 10 transform and Coifmann-1, 2 and 5 transform, illustrating the range of symbol isolation that can be achieved with each transform in order to determine whether the most appropriate wavelet transform can be identified by informal visual inspection.

Method: Two image samples were selected. The first contained a few lines of music and was originally sampled at 350 dpi greyscale using a resolution of 1633x1283. It was rescaled to 256 by 256. The second contained just a single bar of music and was originally sampled at 350dpi greyscale using a resolution of 758x443. It was rescaled to 256 by 256. The re-sized images are illustrated in Figure 11.

Figure 11: Images Re-sized to 256 by 256, 350 dpi Greyscale from the Original a) 1633 by 1283 and b) 758 by 443

(a) Image 1

(b) Image 2

The six wavelet transforms (Daubechies 3, 4 and 10 and Coifmann 1, 2 and 5) were applied to the image and the horizontal and vertical components isolated and displayed.

Results: Figure 12 illustrates the wavelet transforms for Image 1 showing the horizontal components to the left of each image pair and the vertical components to the right of each image pair.

Figure 12: Horizontal and Vertical Components of the Wavelet Transforms for Image 1

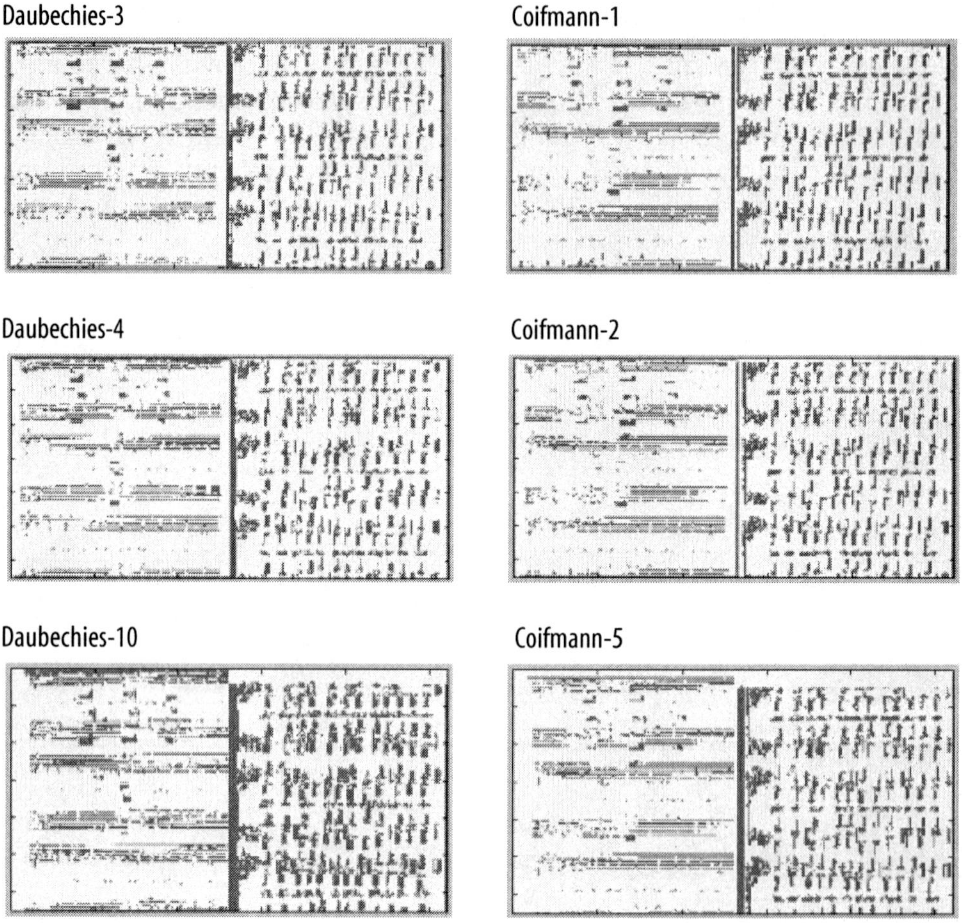

With Image 1 the Coifmann family of wavelets has done a better job with the vertical components — especially identifying the final barlines, which are particularly clear with the Coifmann-1 filter, compared to Daubechies-4 or 10. However, the horizontal components are clearest with the Daubechies-3 transform where the beams of the quaver notes are most strongly visible in between the actual stavelines. Figure 13 illustrates the wavelet transforms for

Image 2 showing the horizontal components to the left of each image pair and the vertical components to the right of each image pair.

Figure 13: Horizontal and Vertical Components of the Wavelet Transforms for Image 2

Daubechies-3

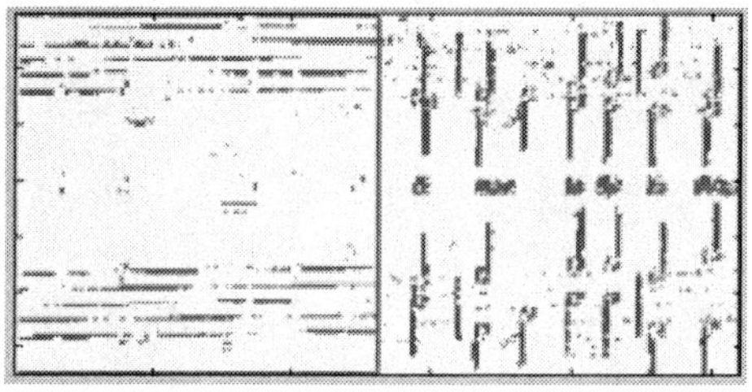

Coifmann1

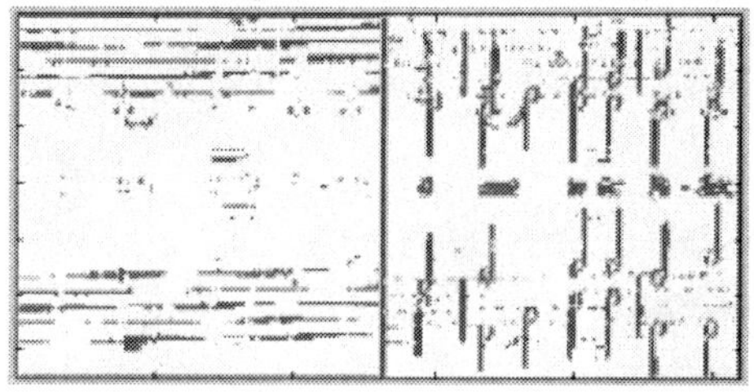

Daubechies-4

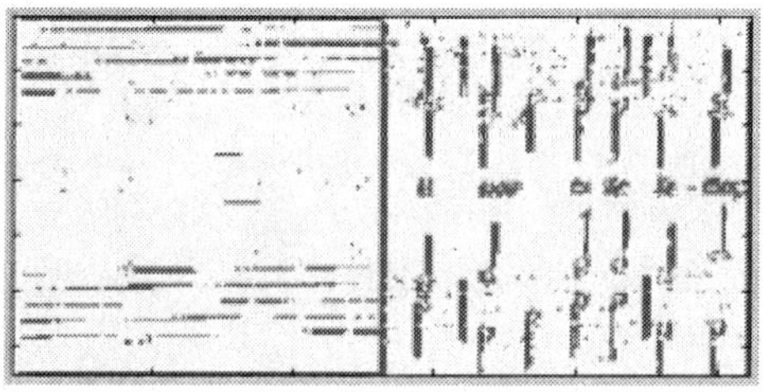

Coifmann-2

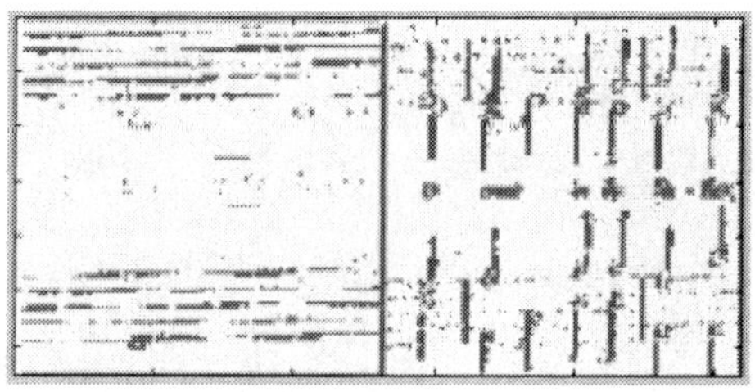

Daubechies-10

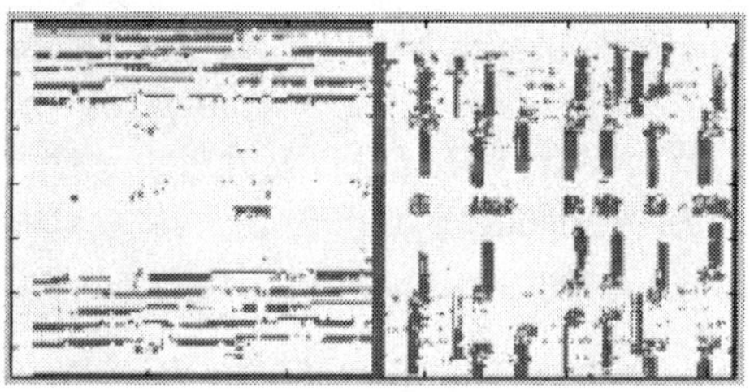

Coifmann-5

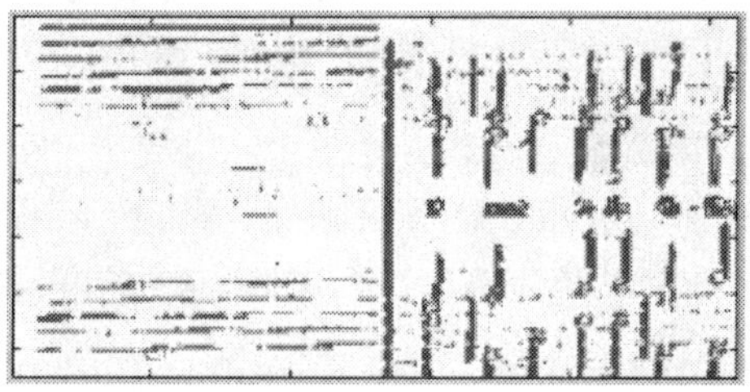

With Image 2 the Coifmann family of wavelets appears to have done a better job, particularly with the vertical components of Coifmann-1 being especially clear compared to the vertical components of Daubechies-10. However, there is no clear improvement in the horizontal component with the Daubechies as there was for Image 1. The Coifmann family have identified the beams in between the stavelines, while the Daubechies-3 and 10 have had trouble.

Conclusion: Visual inspection is a subjective criteria for evaluation, and it does not address the final symbol level criteria for accuracy (i.e., are the high level music symbols correctly recognised). However, inspection of the horizontal and vertical components of six wavelet transforms for two images has suggested that there are differences, and hence some transforms may be more suitable than others for particular tasks. In particular it appears that the Coifmann family are suitable for vertical components, and the Daubechies for the horizontal components in images of different complexity.

Conclusion

We have found that it is possible to provide a unified theory for dealing with super-imposed objects in OMR, since both staffline location and symbol segmentation can be addressed by the same technique — that of wavelet filtering. As a knowledge-free, general-purpose image processing technique, wavelet filtering makes it possible to emphasise certain features of the image using the image decompositions. We observed that (i) the horizontal pixel histograms made stavelines easier to detect in the filtered image. Staveline-finding algorithms may want to use the filtered image rather than the original to improve upon their results, (ii) the accuracy of detection for segmented music symbols appeared better in low-resolution binary images, but this was mainly due to the amount of 'ink' involved in the pixel-based accuracy evaluation (which was made between the "truth representation" and the filtered image). Nevertheless, filtering the image to isolate the non-staffline components emphasised a feature that was not so obvious in the original image and (iii) different wavelet transforms may be more or less suitable for the regularities/irregularities within a music image. In particular it appears that the Coifmann family is most suitable for vertical components, and the Daubechies for the horizontal components in images of different complexity.

At present wavelet filtering is likely to be most practically useful as a pre-processing method to emphasise certain features of the images for conventional OMR methods. However, there is scope that it may be used in isolation as a knowledge-free OMR procedure for super-imposed objects that can isolate notation symbols from stavelines. We consider that further work is required to continue the investigation of the wavelet as a knowledge-free, general-purpose image processing technique for OMR that is able to provide a unified theory for super-imposed objects.

Acknowledgments

Original discussions of wavelets applied to OMR were made with Dr. Li Hua Yang, visiting scientist of the Centre for Pattern Recognition and Machine Intelligence (CENPARMI) lab, Montreal. Initial experiments were similarly conducted at the CENPARMI lab thanks to Dr. Ching Suen. Subsequent developments and interpretations are entirely the author's responsibility.

References

Andronico, A. & Ciampa, A. (1982). On automatic pattern recognition and acquisition of printed music. *Proceedings of the International Computer Music Conference,* (pp. 245-270). Venice, Italy.

Aoyama, H. & Tojo, A. (1982). Automatic recognition of printed music. *IECE (Japan) Technical Report*, PRL 82-85, 33-40. (Translated from the original Japanese).

Bainbridge, D. & Bell, T.C. (1997). Dealing with superimposed objects in optical music recognition. *6th International Conference on Image Processing and its Applications.*

Blostein, D. & Baird, H.S. (1992). A critical survey of music image analysis. In H.S. Baird, H. Bunke & K. Yamamoto (Eds.), *Structure Document Image Analysis* (pp. 405-434). Berlin, Heidelberg: Springer-Verlag.

Choudhury, G. S. & DiLauro, T. (2001, February). Deriving searchable and playable digital formats from sheet music. D-Lib Magazine, 7(2).

Droettboom, M. et al. (2002). *Using Gamera for the recognition of cultural heritage materials.* Submitted for consideration to Joint Conference on Digital Libraries.

Lin & Bell (2000). *Integrating paper and digital music information systems.* International Symposium on Music Information Retrieval. Retrieved March 20, 2002: http://ciir.cs.umass.edu/music2000/papers.html.

Mahoney, J. V. (1982, May). Automatic analysis of music score images. B.Sc. Dissertation. Massachusetts Institute of Technology, MA, USA.

MathWorks. (1994). MATLAB Reference Guide. MA: The MathWorks Inc.

Matsushima, T. et al. (1985). Automated recognition system for musical score. Bulletin of Science and Engineering Research Laboratory, Waseda University, 112, 25-52.

Nakamura, Y., Shindo, M., & Inokuchi, S. (1979). Input method of musical note and realization of folk-music database. *IECE (Japan) Technical Report,* PRL 78-73, 41-50. (Translated from the original Japanese).

Polikar, R. (1996). *The wavelet tutorial part 1, fundamental concepts & an overview of the wavelet theory*. Retrieved February 8, 2003: http://www.public.iastate.edu/~rpolikar/WAVELETS/WTpart1.html.

Prerau, D. S. (1975, January). DO-RE-MI: A program that recognizes music notation. *Computers and the Humanities,* 9(1), 25-29.

Pruslin, D. H. (1967, January). *Automatic recognition of sheet music.* Sc.D. Dissertation. Massachusetts Institute of Technology, MA, USA.

Roach, J. W. & Tatem, J. E. (1988). Using domain knowledge in low-level visual processing to interpret handwritten music: An experiment. *Pattern Recognition,* 21, 33-44.

Saha, S. (2001). Image compression — from DCT to wavelets: a review. ACM Crossroads *Student Magazine.* Retrieved February 8, 2003: http://www.acm.org/crossroads/xrds6-3/sahaimgcoding.html.

Vidakovic, B. (1999). Statistical modeling by wavelets. Wiley Series in Probability and Statistics. New York.

Section 2: Handwritten Music Recognition

4

Optical Music Analysis for Printed Music Score and Handwritten Music Manuscript

Kia Ng
University of Leeds, United Kingdom

Abstract

This chapter describes an optical document imaging system to transform paper-based music scores and manuscripts into machine-readable format and a restoration system to touch-up small imperfections (for example broken stave lines and stems), to restore deteriorated master copy for reprinting. The chapter presents a brief background of this field, discusses the main obstacles, and presents the processes involved for printed music scores processing; using a divide-and-conquer approach to sub-segment compound musical symbols (e.g., chords) and inter-connected groups (e.g., beamed quavers) into lower-level graphical primitives (e.g., lines and ellipses) before recognition and reconstruction. This is followed by discussions on the developments of a handwritten manuscripts prototype with a segmentation approach to separate handwritten musical primitives. Issues and approaches for recognition, reconstruction and revalidation using basic music syntax and high-level domain knowledge, and data representation are also presented.

Introduction

There is a vast amount of invaluable paper-based heritage, including printed music scores and handwritten manuscripts, that are deteriorating over time due to natural decaying of paper and chemical reaction (e.g., between printing ink and paper), similar to many other paper-based items in library and museum archives. Various efforts have been focused on this issue in order to preserve the record of our heritage. For example, the paper-splitting technique used (Porck & Teygeler, 2000; Wächter, Liers & Becker, 1996) to conserve Bach's manuscripts. This is a skillful technique, physically splitting each page of the manuscripts in two in order to add a new thin core for reinforcement.

Digitisation has been commonly used as a possible tool for preservation. Although the digital copy may not conserve the original document, it can preserve the data in the document, with the advantage of easy duplications, distribution, and digital processing.

This chapter describes the development of an Optical Music Recognition (OMR) system to transform paper-based music scores and manuscripts into a machine-readable symbolic format, and an optical music restoration system to reconstruct small discontinuities and imperfection in the musical writings, including broken stems and stavelines.

Optical Character Recognition (OCR) is perhaps the best-known related document image processing problem, but OMR can be critically different (Bainbridge & Bell, 2001). The visual problem might seem simple since writing is normally black on white paper. However, OMR introduces an additional layer of complexity due to the wide range of possible shape variations resulted from inter-connections and groupings of symbols. For example, two or more notes could be grouped together depending on certain conventions to reflect the rhythmical context and time-signature; consider the different visual appearances of (see Figure 1):

(a) two individual semi-quavers (or sixteenth note),
(b) three groups of two beamed semi-quavers, and
(c) two group of four beamed semi-quavers.

Figure 1: Different Visual Appearances of a Note Type

(a) two individual semi-quavers

(b) three groups of two beamed semi-quavers

(c) two group of four beamed semi-quavers

Besides horizontal grouping, notes can also be grouped vertically (e.g., chords). Furthermore, there may be other symbols (e.g., expressive signs, fingerings, bowing, texts, etc.) that are positioned around and sometime overlaid on parts of other music symbols — for example, a tie (curve line) crossing a stem or touching a note-head.

Direct recognition of musical symbols is difficult due to the design of the notation. This project uses a divide-and-conquer approach to sub-segment compound musical symbols and inter-connected groups (e.g., beamed quavers) into lower-level graphical primitives, such as lines and ellipses, before recognition. The processing involves disassembling the musical printing (or writing), which reverses the process of writing. A composer or copyist would normally write a note head followed by a connected stem and beams, as necessary, and lastly other articulation markings such as ties and slurs; in contrast, this approach would first detect long and thin features (e.g., slurs and ties), followed by beams, and then separate note-head from their stem, before recognition.

This chapter presents a brief background of OMR and describes an earlier OMR prototype for printed music scores, followed by a discussion on its limitations for handwritten manuscripts processing, which led to the development of a stroke-based segmentation approach using mathematical morphology. Developments in optical music restoration and graphical music score representation are also reported.

Background

Generally, the first process in a document analysis system is to threshold a given grey input image into a binary image. Some systems used binary input images produced by the digitiser. Typical scan resolution used is 300d.p.i. (Selfridge-Field, 1994). More recent literature on archiving and preserving music scores recommends higher resolution at 600d.p.i. Fujinaga and Riley (2002) reported that 600d.p.i. is a sufficient resolution for all significant details. The paper suggested that further increase in resolution is not necessary for OMR.

OMR was first attempted more than 30 years ago (Pruslin, 1966). It has received much attention over the last 15 years (Bainbridge & Wijaya, 1999; Bellini, Bruno & Nesi, 2001; Ng & Boyle, 1992; Ng, 1995; Ng, Cooper, Stefani, Boyle & Bailey, 1999; Ng, 2001; Ng, 2002), and there are currently a number of commercially available packages, such as capella-scan (capella-scan), Optical Music easy Reader (OMeR), PhotoScore (PhotoScore), SharpEye (SharpEye), SmartScore (SmartScore) and Vivaldi Scan (Vivaldi Scan). However there is still much room for improvements in many aspects. Reviews and background on the development of various OMR systems can be found in Bainbridge and Carter (1997), Blostein and Baird (1992) and Selfridge-Field (1994). An online bibliography on OMR can be found at the Interactive MUSICNETWORK website (http://www.interactivemusicnetwork.org) and http://www.kcng.org/omrbib.

Pruslin (1966) mainly focuses on note-head recognition. A pre-processing process was used to locate and remove all thin horizontal and vertical lines. The resulting image consists of only note-heads and beams, and these are recognised with contour-tracing approaches. Chords, with a limit of four notes per cluster, were supported. From the combination of four (or fewer) note heads, 23 geometrically distinct forms were illustrated and much effort has been concentrated on this problem.

In 1985, Waseda University, Japan, presented a robotic organist at the International Exposition (Matsushima et al., 1985; Roads, 1986). The robot plays music on the electronic organ and "reads" sheet music using a CCD (Charge Coupled Device) camera. Nearly real-time recognition on simple sheet music was achieved by using dedicated hardware (x17 16-bit computers and x50 8-bit computers with fiber-optic links). A line filter was used as the basis of the staffline detection circuitry. In order to compensate for skew angle introduced by the positioning of the sheet music, the hardware was designed to detect short horizontal lines across the page, and then logically connect the detected lines to determine the possible skew angle and separation of stavelines. Using the results from the stavelines detection hardware, the input image was rotated and normalised.

The pre-processing process does not remove the stavelines. A template-matching method, performed by a hardware implementation of correlation, is used to locate the note heads and bar lines. After that, a slicing technique is applied to recognise the remaining objects, where a slice is taken through an object at a predetermined position and orientation, and the number of transitions from foreground black pixels to background white pixels is counted. Carefully chosen slices can provide different number of transition counts and, hence, recognition of symbols.

Carter (1992, 1994; Carter & Bacon, 1990) presents a segmentation approach based on a Line Adjacency Graph (LAG). LAG is obtained from a vertical run-length encoding of a binary image where a segment is an individual vertical run of pixels. A transformed LAG is obtained by linking neighbouring segments into sections, and sections are formed using linked neighbouring segments that are vertically overlapped. This approach is capable of supporting small amounts of skew without deskew pre-processing.

The transformed LAG is searched for staffline sections (referred to as filaments) using aspect ratio, angle, and connectedness. After that, filaments are concatenated logically and a histogram of filament thickness is used to determine the threshold of staffline thinness, which is used to identify any long beams that may have been classified as filaments. After staffline detection, further merging of broken features is performed to connect sections to symbols. For recognition, normalised bounding box sizes are used to divide larger symbols, e.g., beamed groups and stemmed notes. Vertical lines within an object are detected using run-length encoding and note heads are searched for near the detected vertical lines.

Roth (1994) presents an OMR system with rule-based classification. Staffline thickness and inter-staffline space is estimated by the vertical-run-length of foreground and background pixels over the input image [binary input image in PBM (Portable Bitmap) format is used]. The median of a foreground vertical run provides the staffline thickness and the median of a background vertical run provides the inter-stage space. The sum of the two medians (which is referred to as "dis") is used as the basic unit of symbol size. Similar to most other system, the staffline detection assumes near-horizontal stage orientation and a rotation process is included. Stavelines are located by locating groups of five peaks which form a horizontal projection of the image. Vertical lines (e.g., stems, bar lines and vertical-line parts of other features such as sharps) are detected and removed. Two methods are attempted:

(1) projection-based approach,
(2) Mathematical Morphology operations.

Syntactical rules, such as neighbouring features and relative location, and normalised geometry information are used for recognition.

Fujinaga (1988) proposes an approach based on projection techniques. A horizontal project of the whole input image is used for staff detection. The mean of the projection is used as the threshold to locate possible group of five peaks. The system uses the k-Nearest Neighbour (kNN) scheme for classification and classification features include width, maximum height, area, and a measure of rectangularity. It uses syntactical rules and includes an interactive manual correction tool. Later works (Fujinaga, 2001; Fujinaga, 1996; Choudhury et al., 2000) include adaptive functionality for the system to learn to recognise different or new symbols by combining kNN classifier and genetic algorithm.

The direct and effective projection-based approach has also inspired a number of other works including O^3MR (Object Oriented Optical Music Recognition System). The O^3MR system (Bellini, Bruno & Nesi, 2001; Bruno & Nesi, 2002) uses neural network for low-level symbol recognition and an object-orientated model of music for high-level analysis of the score. This system is output in WEDELMUSIC format (Bellini & Nesi, 2001).

Besides common music notation, OMR-related developments for other music notations include Greek Byzantine Music (Gezerlis & Theodoridis, 2000) and ancient music (Pinto et al., 2000).

Similar to other optical document imaging developments such as OCR, higher-level domain knowledge can offer various enhancements using syntactical rules, statistical characteristics, and conversions.

Fahmy and Blostein (1994, 1998) propose a graph-rewriting approach for OMR enhancement. Stückelberg, Pellegrini and Hilario (1997) propose an architecture for OMR with high-level domain knowledge, and Stückelberg and Doermann (1999) explore probabilistic reasoning for musical score recognition. Coüasnon (2002) comments that existing OMR software is not suitable for industrial context due to time-consuming and tedious manual proof-reading, and proposes a system that is capable of self diagnostics to detect error (Coüasnon & Rétif, 1995). The paper discusses the application of musical knowledge of music writing to enhance OMR processing and recognition using DMOS (Description of MOdification of Segmentation), a generic recognition approach for structured document analysis with grammatical formalism EPF (Enhanced Position Formalism). The application of tonality and rhythmical structures are discussed later in the section on Recognition and Reconstruction.

The potential benefits of such a system have been widely recognised. With an effective and robust OMR system, it can provide an automated and time-saving input method to transform paper-based music scores into a machine readable representation for a wide range of music software, in the same way as OCR is useful for text-processing applications. Besides direct applications, such as playback, musical analysis, reprinting, editing, and digital archiving, OMR would enable efficient translations, for example, to Braille notations (Dancing dots) or other non-Western musical notations. It could provide better access and widen participation of music and, at the same time, provide digital preservation of this invaluable paper-based cultural heritage.

Pre-Processing

This section describes an OMR prototype for printed music scores. The prototype takes a digitised music-score grey image (300 d.p.i. with 256 grey) as input. The pre-processing sub-systems consist of a list of automated processes, including:

- thresholding,
    - To convert the input grey image into a binary image.
- deskewing,
    - The skew of the input image is usually introduced during digitisation, as it is not easy to position the score with the staves perfectly horizontal in a scanner. Using the binary image, the skew can be automatically detected by reference to the music-typographical feature of the roughly

parallel stavelines, and the image is deskewed by rotation. This process is necessary because the orientation of the input image affects further processing due to the projection method used.

- staff detection and general layout analysis,
    - o Detecting staves, coverage, positions and groupings, and general layout analysis.

The staffline is the fundamental element of the Common Music Notation. It forms a grid system for musical symbols. Hence, most of the sizes of the musical symbols that are printed or written on this grid system are related to the geometry of the staves. For example, the height of a note head normally approximates the distance between two stavelines plus the thickness of the two stavelines.

Hence, it is important to detect the staffline and measure its geometrical positions and sizes accurately. The sum of the average distance between two stavelines and the average staffline thickness forms the fundamental unit used by the classification process and serves as the general normalisation factors.

Most systems rely on a horizontal orientation of the input image to detect stavelines. Some approaches claim to support slight skew (Carter, 1994), while others provide automatic or manual deskew processes (Roth, 1994).

In practice, the stavelines are not found to be completely straight or of even thickness, even on printed manuscript papers. Hence, the left- and right-most coordinates and the minimum or maximum point of each staffline are recorded. Once the stavelines have been located, a line-tracing algorithm with a local vertical projection window is used to detect the average staffline thickness and electively mark the pixels that belong to each staffline, thereby removing the stavelines to isolate the musical features for further processing (Ng & Boyle, 1992, 1996).

Sub-Segmentation

After an initial segmentation using an image-labelling method, a rule-based classifier recognises primitives that are isolated (e.g., dots and bar lines), and symbols that are normally located at certain positions with respect to their staff (e.g., clefs and rests).

To deal with the problem of the interconnected and overlapping features of musical symbols, composite music objects are disassembled into lower-level graphical primitives, such as vertical and horizontal lines, curves, and ellipses at this stage. From the initial segmentation, each block of connected features is passed to the classification module (described in a later section). If the object is not classified confidently, and it is too large as a feature (typically in low density and with a normalised width and height > 1.5 of the fundamental unit), it is passed to the sub-segmentation module to be broken into two or more objects, and the process continues.

There are three sub-segmentation approaches:

- horizontal tracking,
- vertical tracking,
- horizontal cuts.

Figure 2: Sub-Segmentation

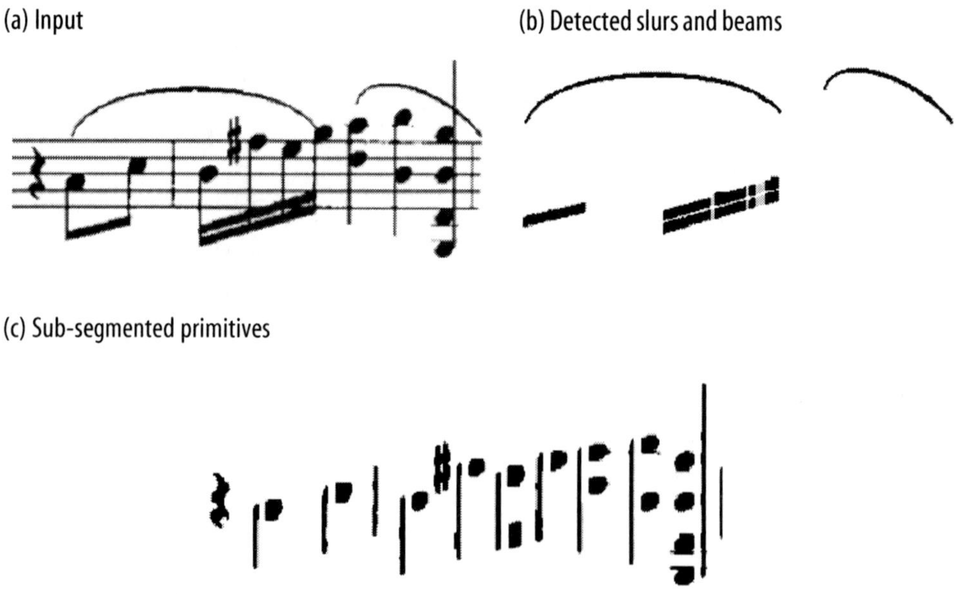

The criteria for the appropriate choice of sub-segmentation methods are based on the normalised width and height, and density of the object. The best break point is measured by the highest *sudden change* in vertical projection histogram (V_x), estimated by

$$(V_{x-1} - 2V_x + V_{x+1}) / V_x.$$

Figure 2 illustrates the separation of detected slurs and beams features and sub-segmented primitives.

Handwritten Manuscript Processing

The pre-processing processes for the recognition of printed music are reusable for handwritten manuscript analysis (see Figure 3).

Figure 3: Handwritten Manuscript Pre-processing and Staff Line Detection (Manuscript courtesy of the Music Division, The New York Public Library for the Performing Arts, Astor, Lenox and Tilden Foundations)

(a) Example input manuscript

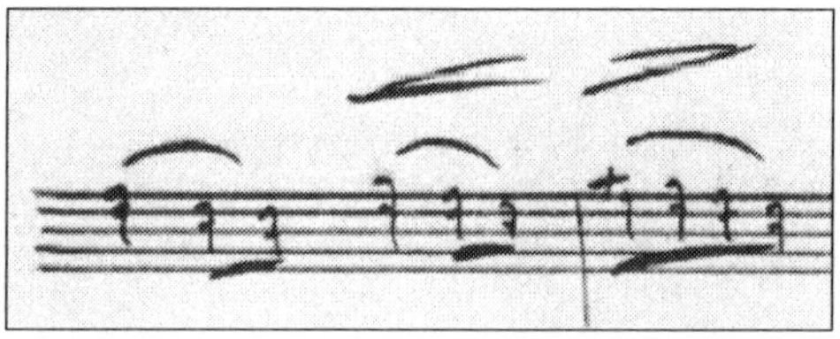

(b) Thresholded binary image

(c) Staffline removal

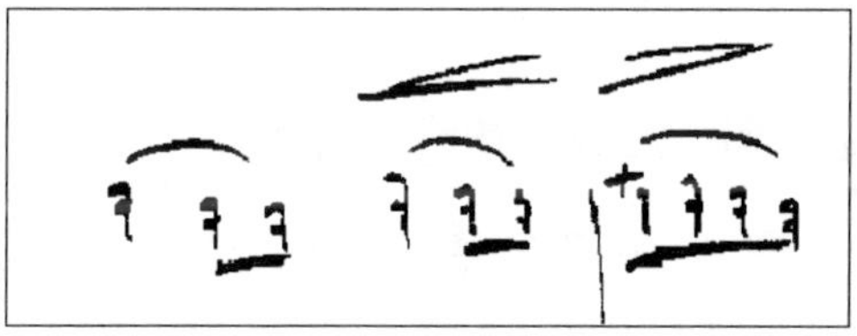

However, the sub-segmentation approach relies on the vertical orientation of the musical features and performs unsatisfactorily for handwritten music due to the characteristically slanted and curved line segments. For handwritten manuscript, the sub-segmentation module adopts a mathematical morphology approach (Suen & Wang, 1994), using skeletonisation and junction points to guide the decomposition of composite features, and disassembles them into lower-level graphical primitives, such as vertical and horizontal lines, curves and ellipses. Figure 4 illustrates the pre-processing and skeletonisation and junction points.

Figure 4: Example Input, Pre-processing (thresholding, deskewing, and staff line detection), and Detected Junction and Termination Points

(a) Example input

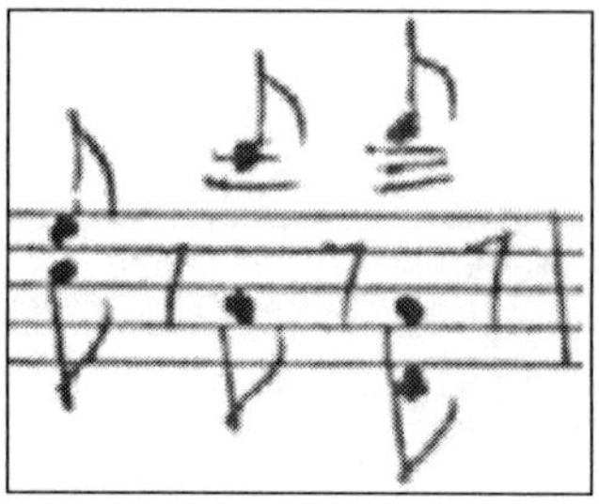

(b) Staff line removal

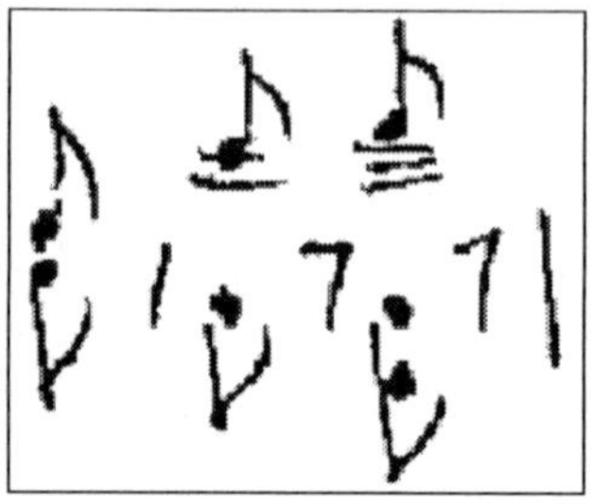

(c) Skeletonisation

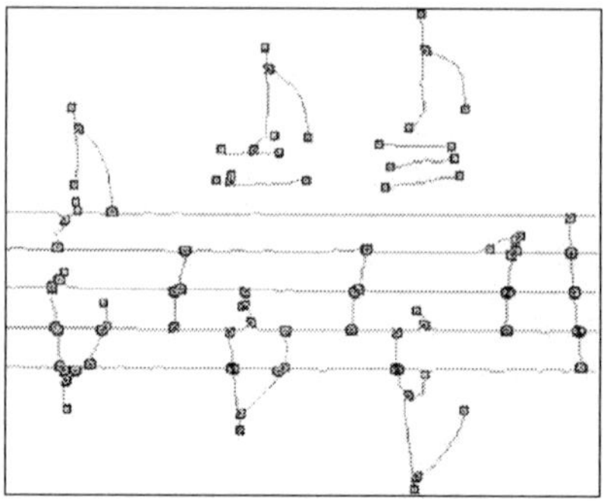

Recognition and Reconstruction

These primitives are classified using a kNN classifier with simple features such as the aspect ratio and normalised width and height, since at this level the graphical features of the primitives are relatively simple.

After recognition, these sub-segmented primitives need to be reconstructed. To resolve any ambiguities, contextual information is used; for example, a dot classified by the kNN classifier could be an expression sign or a duration modifier depending on its relative position with respect to a note head nearby.

After classification and reconstruction, basic musical syntax and a number of high-level musical analysis techniques are employed to enhance the recognition. The reconstructed results are re-examined in light of the analysis and corrections and enhanced guesses are made if necessary. These include automatic local tonality detection and harmonic and rhythmic analysis (Ng,

Boyle & Cooper, 1996; Ng & Cooper, 2000; Ng & Boyle, 1996). The application of domain knowledge is particularly important in handwritten manuscript recognition since it takes years of experience for a trained copyist or engraver to intelligently decipher poorly or inconsistently written scores.

Although there are syntactic rules and conventions that could be applied to accurately resolve many ambiguities, this subject remains complex since composers may use conflicting meters — for example, the apparently conflicting 3/4 and 6/8 meters in Beethoven's Piano Sonata Op.10 No.2, 2nd movement. Sometimes, composers could also rely on conventions such as the omission of the triplet sign, which could introduce additional confusion.

Output and Data Representation

Many factors in the input source, for example resolution, contrast, and other inherent complexities, could influence the performance of the automatic recognition and transcription process. To provide flexible and efficient transcriptions, a graphical user-interface editor with built-in basic musical syntax and some contextual intelligence to assist the transcription and output is required. The default output format is currently set to *Exp*MIDI (Cooper, Ng & Boyle, 1997), which is compatible with the standard MIDI file format, and is capable of storing expressive symbols such as accents, phrase markings, and others.

There have been active developments on musical file formats, for example:

- Notation Information File Format (NIFF),
- MusicXML (Good, 2001, 2002),
- GUIDO (Hoos, Hamel, Renz & Kilian, 1998),
- Score,
- WEDELMUSIC (Bellini & Nesi, 2001),
- and many others.

It is intended to include output filters for some of these musical file formats.

Informative and consistent evaluation of OMR systems is non-trivial due to the complexities and diverse range of music notation. In order to provide a coherent comparative study of OMR systems, a set of ground-truth dataset is required. Ideally this dataset should include a wide range of sample music scores from all major music publishers, containing a representative range of fonts used, layout styles, page sizes and many other variations. Different recognition systems work at different levels (musical symbols or its graphical primitives) and, hence, a precise and clear definition of musical features is necessary in order to allow meaningful comparative analysis. Miyao and Haralick (2000) and Bruno and Nesi (2002) discussed OMR system evaluation with a multi-level approach, recommending an assessment matrix for three levels:

- low-level graphical primitives (e.g., stem, dot, etc.),
- musical symbols (e.g., crotchet, quaver, etc.), and
- score representation.

These issues are currently being investigated by a new initiative called Interactive MUSICNETWORK supported by the European Commission (http://www.interactivemusicnetwork.org), with a specialist working-group on music imaging. The music imaging working-group is primarily focused on imaging and processing of music sheets, scores, and manuscripts, including digitisation, restoration, preservation, OMR, and related topics.

Graphical Restoration and Preservation

Besides recognition and translation into machine-readable symbolic representation, I am also working on graphical representation of music scores and manuscripts. The idea is to digitise, extract, and encode the music graphically, reusing the pre-processing modules as discussed earlier to extract the layout and other features of the scores to preserve the look and feel of the original image from the paper-based input.

This is particularly important for handwritten music manuscripts, since this approach preserves the writing style and enables scalable reconstruction and visualisation. Currently we are using SVG (Scalable Vector Graphics), which is an XML-based vector graphics file format.

Typical enhancement and restoration processes include reconstructing broken stavelines and stems and removing ink spillage and noise (see Figure 5). The last row of Figure 5 illustrates a layout alteration of an isolated symbol, typically required by publishers. In this case, the forte symbol has been moved to the right manually. Working at this level allows minor alterations such as this. However, this is not an effective approach for modifications involving larger interconnected features or alterations affecting multiple staves.

The advantage of optical music restoration is that the processes do not jeopardise the original layout of the scores, which have been optimised by the engravers, and normally represents the ideal visual configurations. Since the original spacing of the music is untouched, there are no large modification and, hence, it does not require extensive proofreading. However, the process is only concerned with small and local modifications. Larger adjustments, for example insertions or deletions of a group of symbols, cannot be fully automated without altering the original layout. No full recognition is necessary for this process and, hence, it does not provide multimedia functionalities such as playback or search. This process is robust and it can improve the visual qualities of the scores and manuscript for reprinting and archiving.

Figure 5: Typical Restoration (Example images courtesy of Music Imaging Ltd., UK)

(a) Example inputs (b) After processing

Conclusion

This chapter presented an overview of OMR and discussed a system for printed music- score recognition and a prototype for handwritten-manuscript analysis. Besides processes and issues on recognition and translation from paper-based music to symbolic representation, ongoing works on optical music restoration and graphical music representation are also reported.

The proposed system uses the simplest possible features to assist recognition and avoid unresolvable ambiguities by deploying syntactic musical knowledge.

In order to take full advantage of syntactical musical knowledge, the approach seeks to commence with sub-feature primitives, working bottom-up, and to deploy top-down domain knowledge to constrain the reconstructions.

In this process, basic musical syntax is very useful and important for the reconstruction and to resolve ambiguous recognition. To further enhance the recognition and translation, higher-level domain knowledge could be applied to model the reading process of music scores. Works in hand include automatic tonality detection based on note distributions and rhythmical analysis. With this high-level information, a more reliable solution could be provided to cope with imperfect or incomplete input. Recognition errors may be detected and plausible corrections deduced based on the higher-level domain knowledge.

Besides direct applications of OMR to convert paper-based scores and manuscripts into a machine-readable format, I am also interested in extending the recognition system to process other musical notations beyond the Western Common Music Notation, and making use of this technology to enable conversion of music across cultural boundaries.

Acknowledgments

Thanks to the Arts and Humanities Research Board (AHRB) and EC Interactive MUSICNETWORK for financial assistance. Thanks to Music Imaging Ltd. (UK) for sample illustration of the music restoration process, and thanks to the Music Division, The New York Public Library for the Performing Arts, Astor, Lenox and Tilden Foundations for the test data (Brahms's Alto Rhapsody, Op. 53).

References

Bainbridge, D. & Bell, T. (2001). The challenge of optical music recognition. *Computers and the Humanities*, 35, 95-121.

Bainbridge, D. & Carter, N. (1997). Automatic recognition of music notation. In H. Bunke & P. Wang (Eds.), *Handbook of Optical Character Recognition and Document Image Analysis* (pp. 557-603). Singapore: World Scientific.

Bainbridge, D. & Wijaya, K. (1999). Bulk processing of optically scanned music. *Proceedings of the 7th International Conference on Image Processing and Its Applications*, (pp. 474-478). Manchester, UK.

Bellini, P. & Nesi, P. (2001). Wedelmusic format: An XML music notation format for emerging applications. *Proceedings of the First International Conference on WEB Delivering of MUSIC*, (pp. 79-86). Florence, Italy.

Bellini, P., Bruno, I., & Nesi, P. (2001). Optical music sheet segmentation. *Proceedings of the First International Conference on WEB Delivering of MUSIC*, (pp. 183-190). Florence, Italy.

Blostein, D. & Baird, H. S. (1992). A critical survey of music image analysis. In H.S. Baird, H. Bunke & K. Yamamoto (Eds.), *Structured Document Image Analysis* (pp. 405-434). Berlin: Springer-Verlag.

Bruno, I. & Nesi, P. (2002). Multimedia music imaging: Digitisation, restoration, recognition and preservation of music scores and music manuscripts. 1st MUSICNETWORK Open Workshop. Darmstadt, Germany.

capella-scan. (n.d.). capella Software. Retrieved February 9, 2003: http://www.whc.de/.

Carter, N.P. (1992). Segmentation and preliminary recognition of madrigals notated in white mensural notation. *Machine Vision and Applications*, 5(3), 223-30.

Carter, N.P. (1994). Conversion of the Haydn symphonies into electronic form using automatic score recognition: A pilot study. In L.M. Vincent & T. Pavlidis (Eds.), *Proceedings of the SPIE – Document Recognition*, 2181, (pp. 279-290). San Jose, CA. See http://www.spie.org/web/abstracts/2100/2181.html.

Carter, N.P. & Bacon, R.A. (1990). Automatic recognition of music notation. *Proceedings of the International Association for Pattern Recognition Workshop on Syntactic and Structural Pattern Recognition*, (p. 482). Murray Hill, NJ.

Choudhury, G.S., DiLauro, T., Droettboom, M., Fujinaga, I., Harrington, B. & MacMillan, K. (2000). Optical music recognition system within a large-scale digitization project. International Conference on Music Information Retrieval. Plymouth, MA.

Cooper, D., Ng, K.C. & Boyle, R.D. (1997). An extension of the MIDI file format: expressive MIDI – expMIDI. In E. Selfridge-Field (Ed.), *Beyond MIDI: The Handbook of Musical Codes* (pp. 80-98). Cambridge, MA: MIT Press.

Coüasnon, B. (2002). Improving optical music recognition. Position paper, First MusicNetwork Open Workshop. Darmstadt, Germany.

Coüasnon, B. & Rétif, B. (1995). Using a grammar for a reliable full score recognition system. *Proceedings of the International Computer Music Conference (ICMC)*, (pp. 187-194). Banff, Canada.

Dancing dots. (n.d.). Goodfeel Braille music translator. Retrieved August 8, 2002: http://www.dancingdots.com.

Fahmy, H. & Blostein, D. (1994). A graph-rewriting approach to discrete relaxation: Application to music recognition. *Proceedings of the SPIE*, 2181, (pp. 291-302). San Jose, CA. See http://www.spie.org/web/abstracts/2100/2181.html.

Fahmy, H. & Blostein, D. (1998). A graph-rewriting paradigm for discrete relaxation: Application to sheet-music recognition. *International Journal of Pattern Recognition and Artificial Intelligence*, 12(6), 763-99.

Fujinaga, I. (1988). Optical music recognition using projections. Master Thesis. McGill University, Montreal, Canada.

Fujinaga, I. (1996). Exemplar-based learning in adaptive optical music recognition system. *Proceedings of the International Computer Music Conference*, (pp. 55-56). Hong Kong.

Fujinaga, I. (2001). An adaptive optical music recognition system. In D. Greer (Ed.), Musicology and Sister Disciplines: Past, Present, Future. *Proceedings of the 16th International Congress of the International Musicological Society*. (p. 666). Oxford: Oxford University Press.

Fujinaga, I. & Riley, J. (2002). Digital image capture of musical scores. *Proceedings of the 3rd International Conference on Music Information Retrieval (ISMIR 2002)*. IRCAM – Centre Pompidou, Paris, France.

Fujinaga, I., Alphonce, B. & Pennycook, B. (1992). Interactive optical music tecognition. *Proceedings of the International Computer Music Conference*, (pp. 117-120). San Jose, CA.

Gezerlis, V.G. & Theodoridis, S. (2000). An optical music recognition system for the notation of the Orthodox Hellenic Byzantine music. International Conference of Pattern Recognition (ICPR-2000). Barcelona, Spain.

Good, M. (2001). MusicXML for notation and analysis. In W.B Hewlett & E. Selfridge-Field (Eds.), *The Virtual Score: Representation, Retrieval, Restoration* (pp. 113-124). Computing in Musicology (vol. 12). Cambridge, MA: MIT Press.

Good, M. (2002). MusicXML in practice: Issues in translation and analysis. *Proceedings of the 1st International Conference MAX 2002: Musical Application Using XML*, (pp. 47—54). Milan.

Hoos, H.H., Hamel, K.A., Renz, K., & Kilian, J. (1998). The GUIDO music notation format — a novel approach for adequately representing score-level music. *Proceedings of the International Computer Music Conference*, (pp. 451-454). Ann Arbor, Michigan, USA.

Matsushima, T. et al. (1985). Automated recognition system for musical score: The vision system of WABOT-2. Bulletin of Science and Engineering Research Laboratory. Waseda University.

Miyao, H., & Haralick, R. M. (2000). Format of ground truth data used in the evaluation of the results of an optical music recognition system. IAPR Workshop on Document Analysis Systems. Rio de Janeiro, Brazil.

Ng, K.C. (1995). Automated computer recognition of music scores. Ph.D. Thesis. University of Leeds, UK.

Ng, K.C. (2001). Music manuscript tracing. *Proceedings of the 4th IAPR International Workshop on Graphics Recognition (GREC 2001)*, (pp. 470-481). Canada.

Ng, K. C. (2002). Document imaging for music manuscript. *Proceedings of the 6th World Multiconference on Systemics, Cybernetics and Informatics (SCI 2002), XVIII*, (pp. 546-549). Orlando, FL, USA.

Ng, K.C., & Boyle, R.D. (1992). Segmentation of music primitives. *Proceedings of the British Machine Vision Conference*, (pp. 472-480). Leeds, UK.

Ng, K.C., & Boyle, R.D. (1996). Reconstruction of music scores from primitives subsegmentation. *Image and Vision Computing*, 14, 39-46.

Ng, K.C., & Cooper D. (2000). Enhancement of optical music recognition using metric analysis. *Proceedings of the XIII CIM 2000 – Colloquium on Musical Informatics*. Italy.

Ng, K.C., Boyle, R.D., & Cooper, D. (1996). Automatic detection of tonality using note distribution. *Journal of New Music Research*, 25(4), 369-381.

Ng, K.C., Cooper, D., Stefani, E., Boyle, R.D., & Bailey, N. (1999). Embracing the composer: Optical recognition of hand-written manuscripts. *Proceedings of the International Computer Music Conference (ICMC'99) – Embracing Mankind*, (pp. 500-503). Tsinghua University, Beijing, China.

OmeR. (n.d.). Optical Music easy Reader. Myriad Software. Retrieved February 8, 2003: http://www.myriad-online.com/omer.htm.

PhotoScore. (n.d.). Neuratron. Retrieved February 8, 2003: http://www.neuratron.com/photoscore.htm.

Pinto, J., Vieira, P., Ramalho, M., Mengucci, M., Pina, P., & Muge, F. (2000). Ancient music recovery for digital libraries. Fourth European Conference on Research and Advanced Technology for Digital Libraries (ECDL 2000). Lisbon.

Porck, H. J., & Teygeler, R. (2000). Preservation science survey: An overview of recent developments in research on the conservation of selected analogue library and archival materials. Council on Library and Information Resources. Washington, D.C., USA.

Pruslin, D.H. (1966). *Automated recognition of sheet music*. D.Sc. Dissertation. MIT.

Roads, C. (1986). The Tsukuba musical robot. *Computer Music Journal*, 10(2), 39-43.

Roth, M. (1994). An approach to recognition of printed music. Extended Diploma Thesis. Swiss Federal Institute of Technology, Zürich, Switzerland.

Scorscan. (n.d.). npc Imaging. Retrieved August 8, 2002: http://www.npcimaging.com.

Selfridge-Field, E. (1994). Optical recognition of music notation: A survey of current work. In W.B. Hewlett & E. Selfridge-Field (Eds.), *Computing in Musicology: An International Directory of Applications* (vol. 9, pp. 109-145). Menlo Park, CA: CCARH.

SharpEye. (n.d.). visiv. Retrieved August 8, 2002: http://www.visiv.co.uk.

SmartScore. (n.d.). Musitek. Retrieved February 8, 2002: http://www.musitek.com/.

Stückelberg, M.V. & Doermann, D. (1999). On musical score recognition using probabilistic reasoning. *Proceedings of the Fifth International Conference on Document Analysis and Recognition*. Bangolore, India.

Stückelberg, M.V., Pellegrini, C. & Hilario, M. (1997). An architecture for musical score recognition using high-level domain knowledge. *Proceedings of the Fourth International Conference on Document Analysis and Recognition*, (vol. 2, pp. 813-818).

Suen, C.Y., & Wang, P.S.P. (1994). Thinning methodologies for pattern recognition. Series in Machine Perception and Artificial Intelligence (vol. 8). Singapore: World Scientific.

Vivaldi Scan (n.d.). VivaldiStudio. Retrieved February 8, 2003: from http://www.vivaldistudio.com/Eng/VivaldiScan.asp.

Wächter, W., Liers, J., & Becker, E. (1996). Paper splitting at the German library in Leipzig. Development from Craftsmanship to Full Mechanisation. *Restaurator*, 17, 32-42.

Chapter 5

Pen-Based Input for On-Line Handwritten Music Notation

Susan E. George
University of South Australia, Australia

Abstract

This chapter is concerned with a novel pen-based interface for (handwritten) music notation. The chapter makes a survey of the current scope of on-line (or dynamic) handwritten input of music notation, presenting the outstanding problems in recognition. A solution using the multi-layer perceptron artificial neural network is presented explaining experiments in music symbol recognition from a study involving notation writing from some 25 people using a pressure-sensitive digitiser for input. Results suggest that a voting system among networks trained to recognize individual symbols produces the best recognition rate in the order of 92% for correctly recognising a positive example of a symbol and 98% in correctly rejecting a negative example of the symbol. A discussion is made of how this approach can be used in an interface for a pen-based music editor. The motivation for this chapter includes (i) the practical need for a pen-based interface capable of recognizing unconstrained handwritten music notation, (ii) the theoretical challenges that such a task presents for pattern recognition and (iii) the outstanding neglect of this topic in both academic and commercial respects.

Introduction

This chapter addresses the issues surrounding the development of a pen-based interface for music notation; an interface that might be used by music editing and composing software, educational resources, audio search engines and others. Various methods exist to input music to a computer, although a pen-based interface to recognise unconstrained handwritten music notation is notably absent from academic literature and commercial products. This chapter goes someway toward rectifying this situation.

First we place the work in context by (i) surveying the various non-notation based means by which music might be input to a computer (e.g., directly playing electronic instruments) and (ii) contrasting on-line recognition with conventional off-line Optical Music Recognition (OMR). We then make a particular focus upon pen-based interfaces reviewing the different types of pen-based input devices and the three basic approaches that might be taken (point and click, gesture-based, and symbol recognition) towards recognising input from those devices. We then focus upon a symbol recognition technique, the artificial neural network (ANN), describing how ANNs have been applied to music notation recognition (in both on-line and off-line contexts). We also present our own experiments in using the multi-layer perceptron (MLP) ANN to recognise dynamically constructed music notation symbols. Finally we consider the development of a pen-based music editor and identify the requirements of such a system. The remainder of this introduction considers some of the motivation for pen-based interfaces for music notation.

There are many different reasons why we might want to input music notation into a computer. These range from editing and composing tasks, to more educational applications of teaching music theory, to sophisticated searches of music archives based upon a melodic fragment supplied as search criteria or simply producing transposed arrangements appropriately typeset for given groups of performers. Musicologists may be interested in analysing the style of a collection of composer works and draw upon computer techniques to analyse the music, or copyright enforcers may be interested in detecting legal infringements of new works that are based too heavily on existing compositions. In all these instances it may be more convenient to input notation rather than some performed version of the music.

Given that it is useful to input music notation to a computer (rather than some performed version of the music) we can also ask under what circumstances is it desirable to use a pen-based interface rather than a mouse or keyboard-based one. The use of a pen immediately suggests an on-line context where symbols are dynamically constructed (as opposed to read from a scanned page). There are a number of application contexts where a dynamic input of notation symbols is required — not least of which is a music-editing environment, which might form a front-end to composing software or a search engine of a music database. The pen-based interface would be particularly useful in those contexts where a few notation symbols must be entered, or perhaps an educational environment where dynamic feedback is required on the music that is input. A formal study assessing convenience and usability of a pen-based versus mouse-based interface for input of music notation would in itself be a useful piece of work — assessing and comparing aspects such as data input speed, interface acceptability, efficiency and accuracy — but that is not the focus of this research (and a pen-based interface for music notation recognition would have to be in existence first!).

Aside from the practical instances where dynamic recognition of handwritten music might be necessary there is the theoretical question of whether it is possible and how. We observe that the ANN is frequently utilized in many symbol recognition contexts. The ANN is a non-parametric statistical method that has been identified as robust, flexible and often particularly good for recognition problems that are closely aligned to human perception tasks. For this reason we would consider the ANN as a pattern-recognition method for handwritten music symbols and seek to explore its applicability as a recognition method for symbols in this domain.

In almost every other domain where there are written symbols there are methods (and often products) that are capable of recognizing those handwritten symbols. Whether these symbols are Roman letters, signatures, oriental characters, mathematical formulae, postcodes or other. We may ask why the recognition of handwritten music symbols is so blatantly absent from the list of domain areas to which symbol recognition techniques have been applied for notation recognition. This omission further motivates a study into the recognition of pen-based, dynamically constructed, handwritten music notation.

Background

In this section we place the work in context by providing some background to the area of music input to a computer. Firstly we consider the various non-notation-based means by which music might be input to a computer (e.g., directly playing electronic instruments) and then contrast on-line recognition with conventional off-line OMR.

Approaches to Music Input

At present musical information is most often entered onto the computer using (a) the computer keyboard, (b) computer mouse, (c) piano keyboard (or some other electronic instrument) attached to the computer, or (d) scanning device for a sheet of printed music. In many instances these methods have disadvantages, including being frustratingly slow, difficult to use, inaccurate, or being dependent upon bulky equipment. We briefly consider these input mechanisms now.

With the computer keyboard or mouse the prevailing technology is "point and click" where various musical symbols are selected from a menu and meticulously placed on a staff. A constant movement between menu and the staff is necessary; a parallel (in the context of word processing a text document) would be to individually select the alphabetical characters and place them on the page to compose a sentence. The point-and-click paradigm is slow and difficult to use, although the principles are very general and no non-standard computing equipment is necessary. The setup is also compatible with a portable computing environment, with all the advantages and convenience of a transportable platform. The stylus of many handheld computers can also utilise the point-and-click approach (using the pen as a selector rather than a generator of handwritten symbols).

The input from an electronic instrument in the MIDI interface standard is particularly useful in that enables music to be transcribed directly from an electronic instrument to a computer. Such an input mechanism often requires great care in the musical performance for accurate data entry and also presupposes the user has skills with that particular instrument. The requirement for music equipment additional to the computer means this may not be universally accessible, nor is the setup particularly portable. However, for some experienced musicians MIDI input may be the preferred mode of data entry.

Finally, input may be obtained from a scanned music image. There are many commercially available music-scanning programs that can perform remarkably well with a wide range of music complexities (now including text lyrics and performance markup notations). However, these products are not 100% accurate on every possible variation in notation that may be found and it is usual that a post-editing stage is necessary, for which conventional point-and-click input (or a pen-based alternative) is preferable to MIDI. Additionally, music scanning programs are primarily designed for printed music, and do not cope so well with handwritten notation. Recognition rates for handwritten music are, in fact, very low for commercial products. Although Roach et al. report some image-processing techniques that have been explored for dealing with handwritten scanned music inputs (Roach & Tatem, 1988).

On-Line versus Off-Line Recognition

We observe that one of the biggest points of distinction between off-line and on-line recognition of music notation is that the on-line instance is dealing with handwritten (or scribed) music (and the off-line instance may be dealing with either printed or handwritten — typically printed music). Handwritten music presents many challenges. There are going to be stylistic differences between writing symbols such as clefs, as well as the normal variation between and within people's writing. If recognition is extended to identification of lyrics, or marks of musical expression, then we face the general unconstrained on-line handwriting recognition problem.

Additionally, with a pen-based interface we face the situation where this handwritten music is dynamically expressed and is built up over time periods. This means that there is a sophisticated spatio-temporal relation between components. Not everyone will necessarily enter music in the same way — some people may leave note fragments incomplete (subsequently beaming and dotting them as needed in different orders), others may insert barlines after the event, others insert them before and "fill-in" the intervening symbols. Accidentals and ornaments may be added to the music at any point and, in short, two spatially related "inputs" may not be "temporally" related at all. This has implications for the recognition methods that are applied.

With the on-line dynamic input of music symbols there is also the possibility of needing to deal with the "delete" function. Many pens have an eraser as one end of the pen. Exactly how this delete operation might be organised is an important question. We would have to consider what fragment of page, line, symbol or other could be removed; whether every part of "ink" had to be removed or just part of it. Pen devices may not have a physical delete and so a software delete button may have to be activated to change the function of the nib. We may generate lengthy "histories" for just how a document was built up, since it is likely that a pen movement would be recorded and a delete signal would have to "undo" that movement, but not necessarily erase it from the record. Such a delete function has no counterpart in off-line recognition.

Finally, one other point of difference between on-line and off-line recognition of music notation is that there is the possibility of knowing in advance the location of the stavelines. One scenario for input is that the user writes music notation on an already existing staff, as opposed to drawing the staff freehand (which would certainly be an option). In most situations it is likely that the staff would be completely under control in a pen-based, although there may be situations when this was one of the "free-forms" that was written.

Pen-Based Recognition of Music Notation

In this section we consider the pen-based interface, reviewing the different types of pen styluses that might be utilised within a pen-based interface — ranging from a handheld device to a digitiser complete with LCD display, or from a mouse replacement pen-tablet to a smart pen. We also review the research that has been conducted into recognition of inputs made from a pen device, noting the ways that pen-based devices have been applied to the input task — and how, so far, they have largely avoided recognising completely unconstrained handwritten music notation. Instead they use the pen as a stylus to select music symbols from a menu bar, or require that the user learn a special sequence of movements to input a given musical symbol.

Range of Pen-Based Input Devices

In a PC-based context one of the biggest distinctions between pen-based devices is whether they are (mouse-replacement) pen tablets or part of more sophisticated digitising equipment. In the former, the pen is a stylus that replaces the mouse. The user interacts with a conventional computer monitor and uses the stylus to select or write on a mouse-pad. Earlier technology used a "light-pen" to directly write upon the screen, but there were serious ergonomic issues with this arrangement that made it unsuitable for routine use. Thus, the simplest (and cheapest) arrangement is to write on a mouse pad and have some software mirror the pen movements on the screen. The alternative is to have a special (more expensive) piece of digitising equipment that is actually a computer monitor display itself lying flat (or angled) on the desktop, next to the actual monitor. The user writes on a display and "sees" the result of pen movements directly under the pen as if writing on paper. There are options to have special paper inserted between the display and the pen such that a hardcopy is directly obtained.

This distinction between digitiser and pen-tablet disappears in smaller handheld devices since the stylus for such a device requires that they are directly impressed upon the display. There is no display isolated from pen movements. In this instance we have a greatly reduced display area compared with a standard PC monitor, and we note that this may make editing in some musical contexts difficult. But the device is highly portable and there is the "advantage" that the user writes and "sees" the display directly on the surface. One final class of pen-input devices that deserves mention is the smart-pen. This is a device that is able to detect pen movements as the pen is moved across regular paper. The movements can be transmitted to a computer and reproduced there, leaving the user with a regular paper copy as well as an electronic version of the pen movements that can be subsequently interpreted. This approach is perhaps the most natural, as the smart pen is hardly any different to a regular scribing method.

All the pen-based methods have the distinction of being able to capture spatio-temporal events. That is, there is a time-stamp associated with every location of the pen. It is possible to retrieve how symbols are built up, and isolate them from the background. Most pens make it possible to retrieve pressure information as well, so there is some measure of how firmly the pen was applied — which is useful in some handwriting and signature recognition contexts. Many pens also offer a "delete" function where it is possible to "undo" certain pen-movements. Naturally this can be implemented in software, although many do have a delete function built into the non-nib end of the pen. Catering for such a delete mechanism poses additional interesting possibilities for pen-based interfaces.

Pen-Based "Point and Click"

With pen-based point and click, we are essentially building up a musical work symbol by symbol. This looses the naturalness that is possible with a pen-based interface that could recognise handwritten input notation. The advantage is that a person is able to point with a slightly more "natural" pointing device, i.e. the pen. As an example of pen-based point and click, we can consider the work of the IBM, Thomas J. Watson Research Center, which has devised a pen-based computer system for writing and editing music (Silberger, 1996). It is known as the Pen-based Music Editor, and reporters tell how it is simpler and more natural to use than currently available systems since it does not rely heavily on pull-down menus nor require its users to learn complicated commands. Rather, an interface was designed in which the notes and other symbols were arranged along the border of the screen. A composer could then use the pen to grab a symbol and place it on the score in the middle of the screen. In a later approach, the user begins simply by touching the location on the screen where he or she wants to put a note. This pen-based augmented point-and-click approach is based on the observation that handwriting recognition software is limited to 85% or 90% accuracy, and so a music input system based on interpreting the handwritten form did not seem feasible.

Gesture-Based Input

With gesture-based input the user must learn a special set of symbols for interacting with the computer rather than utilising the conventional musical notation symbols. While this might enable more accurate recognition, it does not comply with the naturalness of actually writing musical notation symbols. Nor would it ever be possible to use such an approach to learn to write music symbols in an educational context, which is one important application of on-line music. We may even question whether this is still "handwritten music." Examples of gesture-based input include the research group at the University of Canterbury, New Zealand, take a different approach again to the recognition of handwritten forms. They report the design of a pen-based input system called Presto that uses easily learned gestures to facilitate fast input. Researchers Jamie Anstice, Tim Bell, and Martin Setchell are primarily concerned with the efficiency of the input and find that a gesture-based system is approximately three times as fast as other methods of music data entry reported in the literature (Anstice, Bell, Cockburn & Setchell, 1996). Also, Brown University has developed the music notepad using a similar gesture-based approach where researchers Forsberg, Dieterich and Zeleznik (1998) have demonstrated a pen-based interface. There are four modes corresponding to buttons of the stylus including (a) marking gestures leaving a trace on the display, (b) moving symbols about, (c) sheet manipulation, and (d) interactive playback.

Also, the IBM, Thomas J. Watson Research Center has devised a pen-based computer system for writing and editing music. Known as the Pen-based Music Editor, it is simpler and more natural to use than currently available systems. It does not rely heavily on pull-down menus nor require its users to learn complicated commands. Researchers observe that handwriting recognition software is limited to 85% or 90% accuracy, and a system based solely on writing all the notes did not seem feasible. Beigi designed an interface in which the notes and other symbols were arranged along the border of the screen. A composer could then use the pen to grab a symbol and place it on the score in the middle of the screen. In a later approach, the user begins simply by touching the location on the screen where he or she wants to put a note.

Andy Brown at the Queensland University of Technology presents empirical exploration of a simplified gesture-based system (Brown, 1998). The results indicate that whilst there appear to be many benefits to such an approach, particularly the flexible placement and actuate editing of symbols, the implementation employed is considered overly error prone to be compelling. In addition, the absence of audible feedback and performance capture were considered significant disadvantages by the users. Despite this, for music-notation entry, pen input may be preferable to mouse input and gesture recognition may be quicker than the pallet-selection techniques most often employed in current music systems.

Symbol Recognition

The final approach to pen-based input that we consider is that of symbol recognition, where an attempt is made to actually recognise the written music symbols. There has been surprisingly little work done in this area. One of the big challenges is that there are likely to be stylistic differences between writing styles of different people. Recognition must use sophisticated methods in order to isolate the salient signal from a symbol. If recognition is extended to identification of lyrics, or marks of musical expression, then we face the general unconstrained on-line handwriting recognition problem. Another challenge is that symbols are constructed temporally and built up (possibly in an *ad hoc* fashion) over time. Writers may vary greatly in how symbols are constructed; for example, whether notes are immediately beamed or not, whether accidentals are inserted immediately as a note symbol is written, and even when bar lines are inserted. There may be a "delay" in the construction of complete symbols that presents an additional challenge to a recognition system. Recognition in other contexts (e.g., handwritten Chinese) typically includes a "time-out" after which a symbol is deemed complete. This may or may not be appropriate for a dynamically constructed score. There are also potentially huge semantic complexities in the music created by the potential for editing — as notes are deleted or added or changed in some way to make a meaningful manuscript.

In on-line recognition in other contexts there are a variety of different approaches to classification that might be made — based on statistical pattern recognition, structural analysis of symbol components, template matching, neural networks and other. The approach presented in the remainder of this paper proposes the use of a neural network classifier for identifying symbols obtained from an on-line, pen-based input mechanism.

Neural Network Approaches to Music Notation Recognition

This section reviews neural network-based (ANN) approaches to music notation recognition. We provide some background to the ANN as a non-parametric statistical method of pattern recognition that must "learn" to recognise patterns through a training process. It is thus appropriate for both handwritten and printed notation forms. We review how they have been used in off-line contexts to recognise printed symbols and discuss how they might also be used in an on-line context — suggesting pattern recognition based on clustering (with an unsupervised learning paradigm) and classification (with a supervised learning paradigm).

Neural Networks

ANNs are a non-parametric pattern recognition approach that was born with the field of Artificial Intelligence (AI) in the 1950s. They are non-parametric since they do not require assumptions (such as normality or presence of a certain mean value) to be made about data distributions to which they are applied to analyse. Neural networks represent the "sub-symbolic" approach to enabling computers to "do things that would require intelligence if people did them" (e.g., visual perception, recognition of language, planning and problem solving). They contrast to the "symbolic" approach of AI that uses rule-based expert systems and the like that are reliant upon complex if-then rules, and other formalisms of domain-specific knowledge. Neural networks are unique to sub-symbolic AI because they "learn." The parameters of the system, expressed in terms of "weights" between network nodes, are adjusted during the training phase. Once trained, the networks can be presented new data which they will be able to process, even though they may have never seen anything exactly like it before.

There is an analogy made with the human neural processing system that is itself a network of simple biological neurons that are able to "learn" and come to complex recognition capabilities in language, vision and so on. Artificial neural architectures all involve the same basic framework — that of a collection of simple processing elements (or nodes) connected by weighted links. The nodes are very simple computing devices that take an input and make an output. There are a variety of architectures for artificial neural systems. One of the most widely used forms of ANN is the multi-layer perceptron (MLP). Multi-layer perceptrons typically consist of an input layer, an output layer, and one or more hidden layers (where a layer contains nodes or processing elements). Adjacent layers are fully interconnected by weighted links with a connection between every node of adjacent layers. The connections have associated weight values that are set during the learning phase. In a single-layer perceptron the weights can be regarded as the "coefficients" (m1, ..., mn) in a series of equations of the form y = m.x1 + m2.x2 + ... + mn.xn where y is the value output by a given output neuron where the network receives an input vector (x1, ... , xn).

There are many different ways of adapting the weights, but learning mechanisms fall into two main categories: supervised learning and unsupervised learning. Supervised learning involves making a network learn an input and corresponding output mapping. The output mapping guides the change of weights (hence supervised learning). Once trained the network can perform classification tasks identifying which pre-defined class a new input item belongs to. Unsupervised learning involves the network identifying categories within the data. In this sense it is performing clustering rather than classification, and groups of similar items are established, based solely on the input data (hence unsupervised). The most famous type of supervised learning algorithm is back-propagation training (Rulmelhart, Hinton & Williams, 1986), which is used to train a MLP. In structure this network has an input layer, one or more hidden layers, and an output layer. Unsupervised learning is dominated by applications of the self-organising feature map (Kohonen, 1982). In structure this map has a two-dimensional grid of output neurons that are connected to the input neurons.

Use of Neural Networks in Off-Line Recognition

The use of neural networks has been demonstrated in the off-line context in various ways. Miyao and Nakano (1995, 1996) describe the use of a supervised learning-based neural network for the recognition of printed music. They extract noteheads and identify candidates based on the stem positions. A couple of three-layer neural networks are used. The networks are trained using position information and reliability factors of candidates. They report an extraction rate of more than 99% for 13 printed piano scores on an A4 sheet, which have various difficulties. The efficiency of the music recognition system achieves average processing times of about 90 seconds (on a SPARC Station 10).

Kiernan (2000) describes a musicological application where a neural network was used to establish compositional authenticity. The self-organising feature map learned to cluster musical compositions from Frederick, Quantz and Bach. Tested music was similar in nature, style, and structure (i.e., common time allegro movements). Frequency of note-distribution statistics were collected and other data, which formed input to the network and was the basis upon which the clustering was made.

The Neume Notation Project for medieval music has also employed neural networks demonstrating a proof-of-concept OCR programme that recognizes individual neume forms by means of neural networks (http://scribe.fas.harvard.edu/medieval/). Neumes are the symbols that were used in medieval Europe for writing down chant melodies for the Christian liturgy. They are the precursors of modern-day musical symbols. There were a wide variety of regional styles of notation in medieval Europe; these are all grouped together under the general category of neume notation. The neural networks used were additionally optimised by genetic algorithms since a difficulty noted was how to arrive at an optimal specification of the network configuration. Genetic algorithms "evolve" programmes automatically and select solutions according to their fitness for a specified task.

Use of Neural Networks in On-Line Recognition

There are many ways that a neural network could conceivably be utilised to assist with the recognition of on-line handwritten music. When dealing with handwritten music it is very likely that the symbols will be formed differently for different people. The ability of a network to "learn" will be very useful, since it can be trained to learn the different styles of different people — just as it does in domains such as handwriting recognition where individualistic characteristics of writing are present. We discuss some of the ways that neural networks could be applied to on-line recognition of handwriting now, identifying it either as a symbol classifier or clusterer.

Symbol classifier: We could use a MLP to learn crucial music symbols (such as notes, rests, clefs) taking as input the "ink" used to create the symbol, or some feature extracted from this ink (such as number and direction of line ends in the symbol, number of crossed components etc.). The disadvantages of this approach include: (a) that "new symbols" (those not present in training) would not have a class, (b) training data is required — perhaps several samples of each different note so that the network has adequate data upon which to base the classifications, and (c) a fair amount of writer consistency would be required in how symbols were written (and often this varies with fatigue, mood, etc.). The advantages include: (a) individual differences between people in the style of writing music symbols can be accommodated and (b) we achieve a pen-based input of handwritten music that does not require learning a set of pen-gestures.

Symbol clustering: We could use the self-organising map to cluster the written symbols and provide a visual map of the different symbols that were written. We could base this on the "ink" or some feature and would have a class, or group of classes, to represent all the different symbols that were written. We may then impose a correct "interpretation" upon these symbols. The disadvantages of this approach include: (a) recognition must wait until all the symbols have been written, and (b) the boundaries on the "map" and what symbol they represent must be decided by the writer. The advantages include: (a) the writer would not need to provide an exhaustive set of training data for each symbol (fixing in advance those symbols that would be recognised) and (b) it would probably be more possible to cope with "variations" in how the symbol was written (e.g., due to fatigue) since this would just form a related (but distinct) class to the more "perfectly" formed symbols.

Experiments in On-line Handwritten Music Notation Recognition

This section presents some experimental work that was performed in on-line handwritten music symbol recognition using ANNs. We provide background to the data collection that involved obtaining samples of written music from some 25 people using a LCD digitising tablet. We analysed the data that was collected in four different ways, seeking to investigate the recognition of isolated handwritten symbols using (i) a single MLP for all symbols from all people, (ii) a separate MLP to recognise all the symbols written by each person, (iii) a separate MLP for each different symbol, and (iv) a separate MLP for each different symbol with a voting system among networks. We find the voting system the most useful in accurately recognising the handwritten symbols.

Background to Data Collection

We utilised a fairly sophisticated pen-based interface in a Wacom PL-400 digitising tablet with LCD display (screen resolution 1024x768) with the UP

811E pressure-sensitive pen (256 pressure levels) recording pen location and pressure at a sampling rate of 20 samples per second (sampling period of 50ms). The tablet was connected to a computer and data was recorded and written to a file using appropriately designed software capturing one symbol sample per screen. Symbols could be cleared using an erase feature of the software. Writers wrote directly onto the LCD display surface and had an image of pen movements echoed as they wrote.

We were primarily interested in investigating the recognition potential for some of the most common music symbols: (a) notes (semi-breve, minim, crotchet, quaver and semi-quaver) with rising and falling stems and (b) sharps, flats and naturals, (c) clefs (treble and bass), (d) rests (quaver, crotchet, minim, semi-breve and breve) all in isolation of the music staff save from the clefs. There were a total of 20 unique symbols (four notes stem up, four notes stem down, one note no stem, two clefs, six rests, a sharp, a flat and a natural) as illustrated in Figure 1.

Figure 1: Illustration of the 20 Symbols to be Recognised

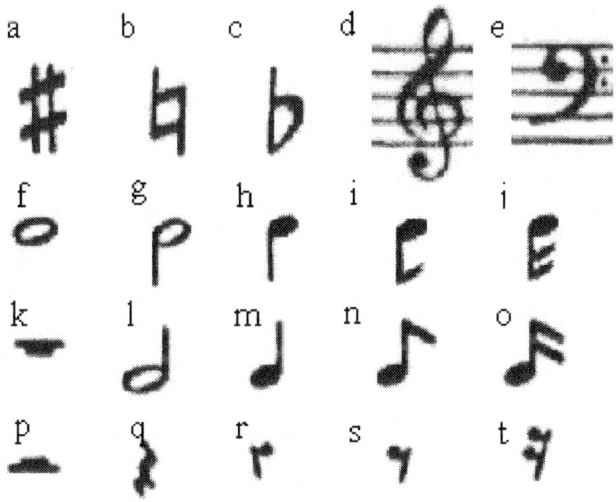

Volunteers were recruited to take part in a short exercise where they repeatedly copied these symbols onto the digitising tablet. Some 25 people were included in the data input, with approximately half of these people having some familiarity with music and the remaining ones being unfamiliar. Each person was asked to repeatedly copy each symbol in turn and most provided in the order of 10 samples of each (starting with symbol a and ending with symbol t). There was a delete facility that enabled people to remove symbols if they made an error in constructing them. Table 1 summarises the data revealing that there were some 10 people who supplied repeat examples of all symbols, with the remaining people only producing examples of some of the symbols. In total there were 4,188 symbols drawn from the 25 people.

Table 1: Summary of the Amount of Data Collected for Each Symbol

	Symbol Identifier																			
person	a	b	c	d	e	f	g	h	i	j	k	l	m	n	o	p	q	r	s	t
1	12	14	11	11	11	11	12	11	11	2										
2	11	2																		
3	12	18	16	13	11	11	17	15	12	12	13	13	4							
4	9																			
5	8	6	8	9	11	11	12	10	8	6	11	11	11	11	9	2				
6	11	11	11	11	11	11	11	11	11	15	6	11	11	11						
7	11	12	9	11	11	12	11	11	11	11	11	11	11	11	9					
8	11	11	11	11	11	11	11	11	11	11	11	11	11	12	10	3				
9	11	11	11	11	11	11	8	6	11	11	8	8	11	11	11	11				
10	11	11	11	10	11	11	11	11	11	10	11	11	11	11	11	11	7			
11	11	11	11	11	10	11	11	11	11	10	9	11	11	11	11	11	11	7	10	11
12	11	11	11	11	11	11	11	11	11	10	10	11	11	11	11	11	11	11	18	
13	11	11	11	11	11	11	11	11	11	11	11	11	11	2						
14	11	11	11	11	11	11	11	11	11	11	11	7	3	9	11	11	11	12		
15	11	11	11	11	11	11	11	11	11	11	11	11	11	11	11	11	11	11	11	11
16	11	11	11	11	11	11	11	11	11	11	11	11	11	11	11	11	11	11	11	11
17	10	10	10	10	10	11	10	10	11	11	11	14	6							
18	11	11	11	11	11	11	11	11	11	11	11	11	11	11	11	11	11	11	11	2
19	11	11	11	11	11	11	11	11	11	11	11	11	11	11	11	11	11	11	11	11
20	11	12	11	10	11	11	11	11	11	10	11	10	10	10	11	12	11	11	10	10
21	11	11	14	10	11	11	11	12	10	12	12	11	10	11	13	13	11	15	15	17
22	11	11	11	11	11	11	11	11	11	11	11	11	11	11	11	13	11	13	9	5
23	11	11	11	11	11	11	11	11	11	11	11	11	11	11	11	11	11	11	11	11
24	11	11	11	11	5															
25	11	11	11	11	11	11	11	11	11	11	11	11	11	11	11	12	11	11	11	11

Figure 2 illustrates the range of variations in writing these symbols for 10 people who completed at least one sample of all 20 symbols. The variations between people's writing include errors (e.g., person 19 treble clef), size differences (e.g., person 22 and 15, sharp symbol), style differences (e.g., person 15 and 16, upward stem semi-quaver), note head size (e.g., person 11 and 15) and many others. Quantifying the variation that was possible within a correctly formed symbol would enable a comparison of consistency between different people writing a given symbol and also an individual repeatedly writing the same symbol. Some symbols, such as the treble clef (symbol d) and crotchet rest (symbol q) intuitively appear to contain the most scope for variation, and symbols such as the semi-breve note (symbol f) informally contain the least. Naturally, one difference between all the symbols that can be eliminated is the differences in size. Thus all symbols were normalised into

Figure 2: Samples of Written Symbols from 10 People

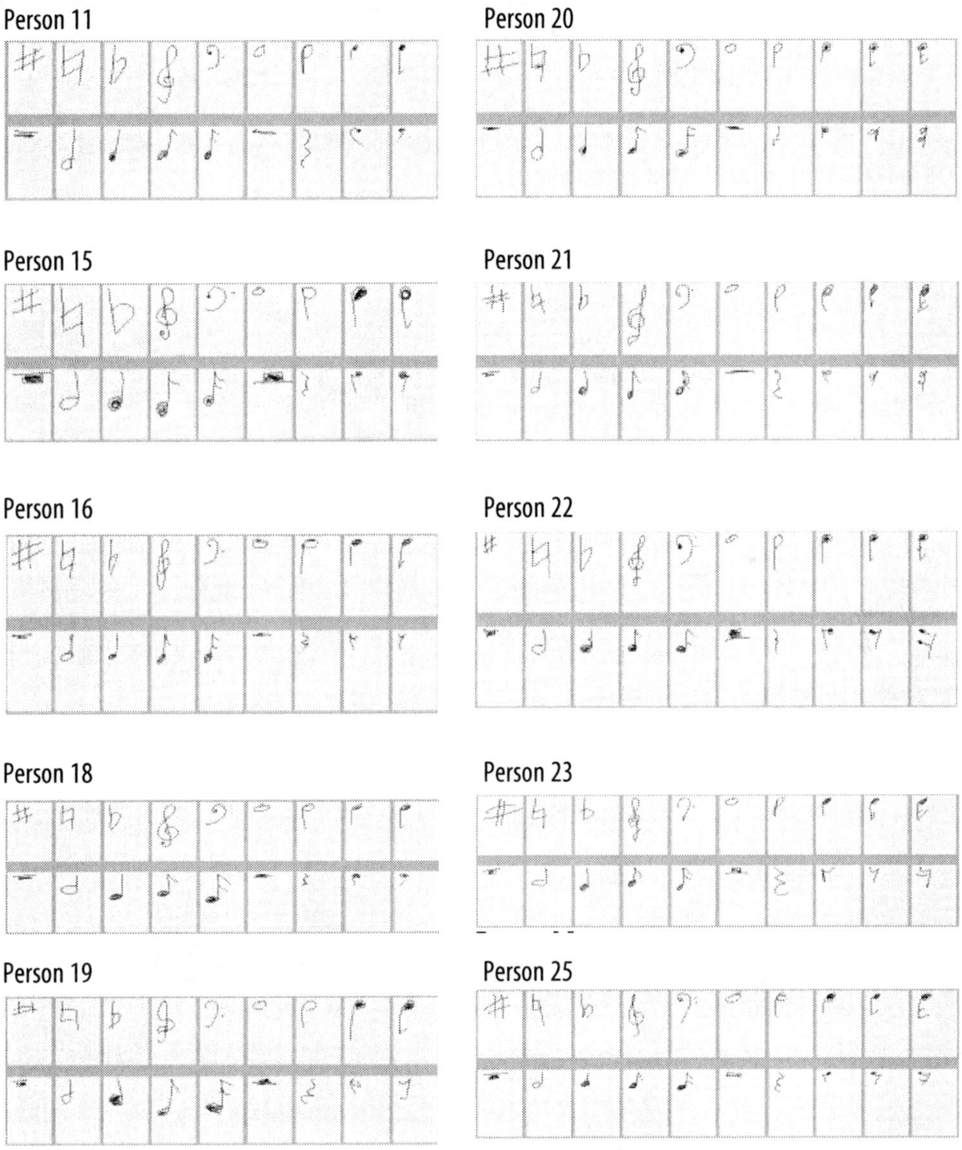

a 100 by 100 pixel square. This can create some real distortions (especially in the minim/semi-breve rest symbols) since a long-thin symbol is stretched out into a unit square accentuating the pen movements that were made.

Experiment 1 – Recognition of Isolated Symbols Using Coordinate Frequency and a Single Network

AIM: The first experiment sought to determine whether x and y coordinate co-occurrence is enough to accurately distinguish the 20 different music notation symbols. We explored the architecture and training parameters for a single MLP trained with back-propagation. The aim was to investigate (i) whether one network was sufficient to recognise all the symbols from all the people, using this x-y coordinate co-occurrence information and (ii) what network parameters achieved the best recognition for symbols.

METHOD: The data was prepared, making some 25 divisions of the 100 by 100 pixel square, taking x coordinate values from one to 20, 21 to 40, etc., and y over the same range. The number of scaled data values within a particular square were counted, importantly removing values with non-zero pressure (since these represented times when the pen was not in contact with the tablet), and a percentage frequency computed (since symbols varied in the number of points of which they were composed). Figure 3 illustrates the raw values and percentage frequency of points within the 25 regions of the pixel square. The symbol was the "#" symbol and concentrations of data points are indicated by three levels of shading (0 < x < = 5, 5 < x < = 10, and x > 10), showing how three of the four corners are blank (as would be expected in this symbol) and the most central point nearly so. Thus each symbol was represented by a 25-element feature vector of the number of data points within each region of the square.

Figure 3: Illustration of the 25 Regions of the Pixel Square

0	9	8	5	0
5	7	6	4	5
0	3	1	3	0
0	4	3	5	3
6	7	0	5	0

0.0	10.1	9.0	5.6	0.0
5.6	7.9	6.7	4.5	5.6
0.0	3.4	1.1	3.4	0.0
0.0	4.5	3.4	5.6	3.4
6.7	7.9	0.0	5.6	0.0

Neural network input consisted of the 25 percentage frequencies scaled to a value between 0 and 1. The neural network output consisted of the 20 possible symbols, represented by a distributed encoding method where all but one output is 1 at any time — the remaining being 0. The MLP thus had 25 input nodes and 20 output nodes. A range of hidden-layer nodes were explored, being five, 10, 30 and 40; and the learning coefficient also varied for networks through 0.25, 0.5, 0.75 and 0.95. All networks were trained for 200,000 iterations making a random pass through the training set.

Five different training and test sets were created from the available 4,188 symbols. The first method of dividing the data split the data between training and test examples by using half the symbols for each person for testing and half for training. The division created 2,100 training examples and 2,088 test examples, including (approximately) equal samples of all symbols from each person in both sets. The next four methods made a random selection from the 4,188 available symbols, taking the same number (2,100) for training and leaving the remainder for testing (2,088). In these sets there was no guarantee that examples of all symbols for each person were included in both training and testing. A random pass through the training data was used during the training.

RESULTS AND DISCUSSION: Table 2 summarises the performance of the networks with different training sets showing the percentage of symbols correctly recognised. Set 0 corresponds to the equally divided training set and the remaining four sets are the randomly selected ones.

Table 2: Percentage of Correct Symbol Classification for the Different Training/Test Set Divisions by the Network Size

Hidden layer nodes	Learning coefficient	Set 0 (train)	Set 0 (test)	Set 1 (train)	Set 1 (test)	Set 2 (train)	Set 2 (test)	Set 3 (train)	Set 3 (test)	Set 4 (train)	Set 4 (test)
5	0.25	40.9	40.1	45.5	43.5	43.7	43.2	42.5	41.7	47.8	45.4
5	0.5	50.9	50.1	54.0	51.5	53.3	50.6	46.6	46.6	48.8	47.4
5	0.75	56.0	53.1	54.1	50.2	52.2	52.1	52.0	50.4	47.9	45.6
5	0.95	51.1	49.7	52.2	51.4	53.8	53.1	54.1	52.1	53.0	49.1
10	0.25	58.2	56.0	56.3	52.9	55.6	55.0	57.7	56.8	55.3	54.7
10	0.5	62.4	59.5	67.0	63.0	69.1	66.5	69.6	66.5	66.0	64.3
10	0.75	72.0	68.2	71.6	67.7	72.4	68.2	71.6	66.1	74.7	70.4
10	0.95	67.0	62.8	69.8	65.0	74.6	69.4	74.4	70.3	70.4	66.5
30	0.25	62.1	58.4	60.4	57.2	60.4	58.9	62.0	60.5	61.1	59.8
30	0.5	78.8	73.3	77.8	73.0	72.6	69.5	78.8	73.8	73.3	70.4
30	0.75	78.4	74.1	77.8	73.8	80.4	76.7	77.3	72.5	80.7	75.0
30	0.95	84.7	78.1	79.9	75.9	84.3	79.4	78.9	74.4	80.2	76.2
40	0.25	62.7	59.9	62.3	59.2	62.5	61.5	60.5	58.8	60.8	59.1
40	0.5	78.5	74.5	74.1	69.5	76.8	73.7	77.9	74.0	75.2	72.0
40	0.75	79.1	73.1	73.2	68.2	80.8	76.2	77.9	73.9	83.1	77.2
40	0.95	83.1	77.4	79.5	72.9	80.7	75.3	79.5	75.0	81.8	77.3

As far as network architecture is concerned the average performance of "fan-in" networks (with fewer hidden-layer nodes than input-layer nodes) is not so good as that for "fan-out" networks (with more hidden-layer nodes than input-layer nodes). The average training set performance for networks with five, 10, 30 and 40 hidden-layer nodes are 50.0, 66.8, 74.5 and 74.5 respectively. The corresponding test set performance is 48.3, 63.5, 70.5 and 70.4 respectively. This suggests that a "fan-out" architecture should be preferred; but there is no definitive benefit over 30 or 40 hidden-layer nodes, since the average training and test results are within a 0.1 difference for networks of either size. However, the standard deviation of performance for percent correct, for each of the networks trained with 30 nodes, shows that the standard deviation (of test results) is most consistent with this size network. The average standard deviations for the network test results are 2.16, 2.24, 1.68 and 2.13 for networks with five, 10, 30 and 40 nodes. Hence, networks with 30 nodes may be more reliable and consistent. As expected for all network sizes the "seen"' training data always produces better results than the "unseen" test data.

As far as the learning coefficient is concerned, the average network "unseen" test set performance generally increases as the value of the learning coefficient is increased. Between a learning coefficient of 0.25 and 0.95, there are improvements of 8.3, 11.7, 17.9 and 15.9 respectively in the percentage of correct symbol classifications, in networks with five, 10, 30 and 40 hidden-layer nodes. The only exception in this data comes with the 10 hidden-layer node network where a slightly better test performance is achieved (68.1) for a learning coefficient of 0.75 compared to the results (66.8) for learning coefficient 0.95.

Considering whether there is any difference between the totally random data sets and the data division for set 0 (with examples of all symbols for all people in the training and test sets), it appears that the random data division is better for the "fan-in" networks. For "fan-in" networks the average test set performance for set 0 is 54.9 and for the data randomly divided it is 56.2; but for the "fan-out" networks the average test set performance for set 0 is 71.1 and for the data randomly divided it is 70.3. This pattern is also seen in the training data with the average performance for set 0 being 57.3 and 75.9 respectively, and for the randomly divided data, 58.7 and 74.1. Thus, for a "fan-out" network a random division of data does not produce the best results.

CONCLUSIONS: It is possible to train a single neural network to recognise the 20 different music notation symbols written by 25 different people. The "fan-out" type network (with more hidden-layer nodes than input-layer nodes) generally achieves better results than a "fan-in" type network, and the percent correct performance suggests that the 30-node hidden-layer architecture can achieve on average 74.5 on training data and 70.5 on test data when trained with 200,000 iterations. The consistency of this size network was better than the consistency of the 40-layer network and a learning coefficient of 0.95 produced the best results. Also, a slightly better average performance is attained with such a "fan-out" network when the training data includes not totally random examples, but samples of every symbol from every person.

Experiment 2 – Recognition Using Multiple Networks for Each Person

AIM: The second experiment sought to determine whether a separate neural network could be trained to learn the symbols written by a particular individual, and that individual alone (again using the x and y coordinate co-occurrence information). The aim was to determine (i) whether recognition performance could be improved by having a specific network learn the writing patterns of given individuals using the optimal network architecture and training parameters suggested in Experiment 1, and (ii) whether there was significant variation among individuals in how successful recognition performance was.

METHOD: The coordinate co-occurrence data prepared for Experiment 1 was again utilised, taking the 25 divisions of the 100 by 100 pixel square and scaling the percentage frequencies to a value between 0 and 1 as neural network input. There were ten individuals (11, 15, 16, 18, 19, 20, 21, 22, 23 and 25) who supplied examples of all symbols and data from these people were used in the experiment. Sets of training and test data were created for each person, including a sample of each symbol written in both the training and test data. On average there were 110 examples in the training set and 109.5 examples in the test set. Networks with 25 input nodes, 30 hidden-layer nodes and 20 output nodes were trained for these people. As suggested by Experiment 1, a learning coefficient of 0.95 was utilised over 200,000 iterations making a random pass through the training data.

RESULTS: Table 3 summarises the network performance for each of the ten people included, using the optimal network training parameters previously selected. The recognition accuracy is greatly improved with it being possible to train a network to attain over 98% accuracy (on training data) for all but one person. There is also an improvement in the accuracy of recognising unseen test data with the average result being 80.2 for recognising unseen symbols, and the writing of two people produced an accuracy of 88.2%.

Table 3: Summary of the Network Performance for Individuals

Person	Training Data Percent Correct	Test Data Percent Correct	Person	Training Data Percent Correct	Test Data Percent Correct
11	98.1	73.3	20	99.1	80.4
15	99.1	88.2	21	95.9	72.5
16	100.0	84.5	22	98.1	81.5
18	98.1	78.1	23	100.0	79.1
19	100.0	76.4	25	98.2	88.2

The biggest discrepancy between training and test data was found for person 11 (24.8%) and the smallest difference (10%) was found for person 25. The distribution of test data percent correct across the people do not include any surprising results. For all people the training data was recognised better than the test data.

CONCLUSIONS: The neural-based recognition performance can be improved by having a specific network learn the writing patterns of individual people. There is no outstanding difference between people, with training and test results including "similar" success levels and patterns with unseen/seen data.

Experiment 3 – Recognition Using Networks to Learn Each Symbol

AIM: The third experiment sought to determine whether a separate neural network could be trained to learn the particular symbols written, including samples of that symbol for all individuals. The aim was to determine (i) recognition performance of a specific network trained to recognise an individual symbol, with a single output node where a high output (1) corresponded to a positive example of the symbol, and a low output (0) corresponded to a negative example of the symbol.

METHOD: The coordinate co-occurrence data prepared for Experiment 1 was again utilised, taking the 25 divisions of the 100 by 100 pixel square and scaling the percentage frequencies to a value between 0 and 1 as neural network input. Sets of training and test data were created for each symbol. The available samples for each symbol were split into training and test data. There are more examples of some symbols than others (for example, there are 271 examples of symbol "a" (the sharp), and only 100 examples of symbol "t" (the semi-quaver rest), with an average of 209.4 samples for each symbol). Having split the data for each symbol into training and test data, a training set was constructed for a given symbol by supplying positive and negative examples of the symbol. The negative examples were selected from the training data of other symbols (and the network asked to learn to produce "0" instead of "1" for these foreign symbol examples).

A network with 25 input-layer nodes, 10 hidden-layer nodes and 1 output-layer node was trained for 200,000 iterations with a learning coefficient of 0.9 (after preliminary investigation revealed that such a "fan-in" network produced slightly better results than other architectures). Once again the cut-off threshold for interpreting the response of an output node was set to 0.5, meaning an output above this threshold was interpreted as recognition of a positive example of the symbol and an output below this threshold was interpreted as a negative example.

Once trained, the networks were tested (a) with the training set containing the seen positive and negative examples of the symbol, (b) with the remaining test data for the symbol containing unseen positive examples of the symbol, and (c) with the remaining test sets from all other symbols containing all negative examples of the symbol. A measure of the network's recognition capability was computed taking into account its ability to correctly recognise positive examples and reject the negative examples. The simple notion of percent correct has to be modified in order to take into account correctly recognising instances of a given symbol *and* rejecting non-instances of that symbol. For this purpose sensitivity and specificity measures were used.

Sensitivity/specificity measures were used drawing upon four basic measures: true positive (tp) — a positive example recognised as such, true negative (tn) — a negative example recognised as such, false positive (fp) — a negative example mistaken for a positive example and false negative (fn) — a positive example mistaken for a negative. In particular sensitivity and specificity were computed using Equation (1)

$$sensitivity = \frac{tp}{tp + fn} \qquad specificity = \frac{tn}{tn + fp} \qquad (1)$$

The measures range between 0 and 1 with a high value corresponding to good recognition performance for both accepting positive examples and rejecting negative examples. Ideally both measures will be 1. Such measures were computed for the training data to produce a measure of how well the network had learned from the available data. The measures were also computed for the "unseen" data. Test (b) contained only positive examples and only permitted a sensitivity measure to be made and test (c) contained all negative examples and only permitted a specificity measure to be made. Such a specificity was computed on a symbol-by-symbol basis and an average computed to represent how well the network rejected all non-symbols. The average specificity was combined with the sensitivity to assess the network's performance on "unseen" test data, and compare that with the performance on "seen" training data.

RESULTS: Table 4 summarises the performance of twenty networks trained to recognised the symbols ("a" to "t" — sharp, natural, flat, treble clef, bass clef, semi-breve note, minim note (stem down), crotchet note (stem down) quaver note (stem down), semi-quaver note (stem down), semi-breve rest, minim note (stem up), crotchet note (stem up), quaver note (stem up), semi-quaver note (stem up), minim rest, crotchet rest x 2, quaver rest and semi-quaver rest).

The performance on training data is given in the first two columns with many networks able to perfectly learn to distinguish the positive and negative examples of a symbol. In particular the most distinct symbols are natural, flat, semi-breve, minim and crotchet (stem up) with all these networks achieving perfect recognition of positive and negative examples.

Table 4: Summary of the Recognition Performance of 20 Networks Trained to Recognise 20 Different Music Notation Symbols

Symbol network trained to recognise	Training sensitivity	Training specificity	Test sensitivity	Average test specificity
a (sharp)	0.97	0.99	0.93	0.91
b (natural)	1.00	1.00	0.99	0.97
c (flat)	1.00	1.00	0.98	0.95
d (treble clef)	0.95	0.96	0.97	0.90
e (bass clef)	0.98	0.97	0.96	0.87
f (semi-breve)	1.00	1.00	0.95	0.93
g (minim st do)	0.99	0.97	0.91	0.90
h (crotch st do)	0.99	0.93	0.96	0.90
i (quaver st do)	0.98	0.93	0.97	0.86
j (semi-q st do)	0.98	0.96	0.97	0.85
k (semi-b rest)	0.99	0.99	0.91	0.89
l (minim st up)	1.00	1.00	1.00	0.96
m (crotch st up)	1.00	1.00	0.95	0.98
n (semi-q st up)	1.00	0.98	0.97	0.88
o (semi-q st up)	1.00	0.95	0.97	0.93
p (minim rest)	0.98	0.98	0.84	0.93
q (crotchet rest)	0.94	1.00	0.71	0.94
r (crotchet rest)	0.94	0.97	0.81	0.94
s (quaver rest)	0.94	0.99	0.77	0.93
t (semi-q rest)	0.96	1.00	0.82	0.93

In the test data only symbol "l", the minim (stem up), achieved a perfect sensitivity. The worst recognition in test set performance was found with symbol "q", the crotchet rest. Figure 4 plots the sensitivity and specificity measures for the test data showing how they vary through symbol, with some symbols apparently being harder to recognise accurately than others. In particular, symbols "m", "p", "q", "r", "s" and "t" have lower sensitivity measures than specificity, suggesting that it is hard to accurately identify positive examples of these symbols — perhaps because these symbols are genuinely ambiguous, perhaps because the amount of training data was not sufficient in these instances.

Figure 4: The Sensitivity and Specificity Measures for Test Data in Networks Trained to Recognise Given Symbols

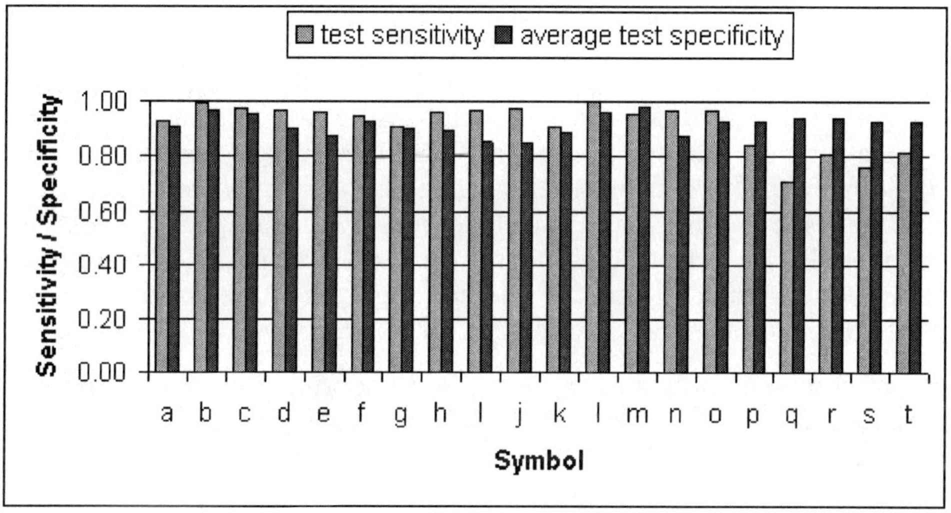

For all symbols the average sensitivity and specificity of training data is 0.98 and for the test data the average sensitivity and specificity is 0.92. These are high and satisfactory measures for the "seen" and "unseen" data suggesting that a recogniser based upon a single network to recognise each symbol is a plausible approach to identifying the written notation symbols from different people.

CONCLUSION: A neural network can be trained to learn a particular symbol, taking training data from all the people who supplied examples of that symbol. The measure of network performance must take into account both its ability to correctly recognise the symbol and reject non-instances of the symbol. The sensitivity and specificity measures for the training and test data indicate that recognition is possible with a high degree of accuracy, and a neural-based recogniser for individual symbols of written music notation is a the most appropriate approach.

Experiment 4 – A Voting System Among Networks

AIM: The fourth experiment sought to determine whether a separate neural network could be trained to learn the particular symbols written, and a voting system among the networks used to produce a final classification of a given symbol. The aim is to determine (i) whether recognition performance can be improved by such a voting system.

METHOD: The coordinate co-occurrence data prepared for Experiment 1 was again utilised, taking the 25 divisions of the 100 by 100 pixel square and scaling the percentage frequencies to a value between 0 and 1 as neural network input. Sets of training and test data were created for each symbol as per Experiment 3. A network with 25 input-layer nodes, 10 hidden-layer nodes and one output-layer node was trained for 200,000 iterations, with a learning coefficient of 0.9 for each of the 20 symbols. Such networks were tested on all available test data from every symbol and sensitivity and specificity measures computed. However, instead of simply applying a 0.5 threshold cut-off to the output of networks to determine whether there was a true positive/negative or false positive/negative a voting system was employed.

The voting system considered the output of all networks in parallel. Essentially a variable threshold value was utilised. Those input examples that produced a network response of <0.5 were checked across all networks to determine what the maximum responding network actually was. If the weak response of the network (<0.5) actually was the best response across all networks, then the threshold was lowered (for that example) and a positive output was ascribed to the input example. Thus, during testing, instead of recording a false negative it was possible to record a true positive and improve the accuracy of results.

Similarly, if a network response of ≥ 0.5 was attained — for what should have been a negative example — a check was made to see whether this was the ultimate maximum response from all the networks. If it was then there was a genuine false positive. If, however, some network was found with a better response, then the threshold was raised (for that example) and a negative output was ascribed to the input example. Instead of recording a false positive, it was possible to record a true negative.

RESULTS: With the voting system improvements were noted in both the sensitivity and specificity of networks during the testing phase (focusing upon the unseen test data). Improvements to the specificity were particularly noted, meaning that a network would correctly reject non-instances of a symbol using the voting system, while an individual network would incline to accept that symbol (in absence of evidence from any other network). Slight improvements were noted in the sensitivity for symbols "a" (sharp), "d" (treble clef), "e" (bass clef), "j" (semi-quaver stem down) and "l" (minim stem up). Specificity was most improved with symbols "f" (semi-breve), "g" (minim stem down), "o' (semi-quaver stem-up), "r" (crotchet rest), "s" (quaver rest) and "t" (semi-quaver rest). These symbols were recognised with an improvement of more than 0.1, with absolute measures going from 0.87 to 0.98, 0.84 to 0.96, 0.88 to 0.98, 0.85 to 0.98, 0.81 to 0.96 and 0.81 to 0.95. The overall average sensitivity was 0.92 and average specificity was 0.98. Without the voting system (for the test data) the average sensitivity and specificity were both 0.92. Figure 5 presents the improvements made for each of the networks (one to 20) trained to represent symbols "a" to "t" respectively.

Figure 5: Improvement in Sensitivity/Specificity When Using a Voting System

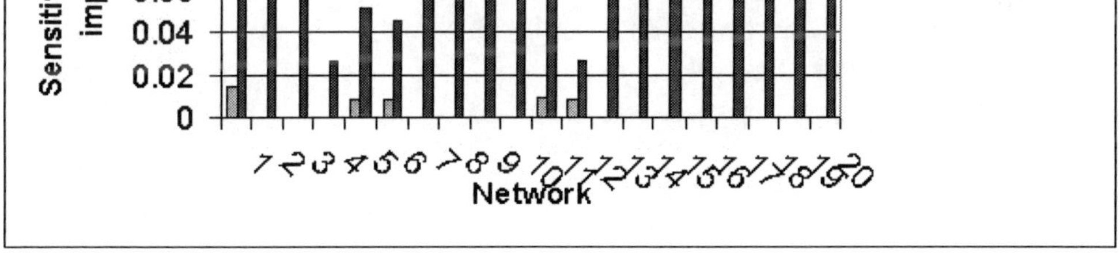

CONCLUSION: A voting system among the neural networks can improve the recognition performance, particularly the specificity of the networks — enabling them to correctly reject the negative instances of a symbol when presented to the network. Thus we have established that it is possible to train neural networks to recognise 20 individual music notation symbols and established that a voting system among the networks attains the best recognition rates for unseen data. This is regarded as good accuracy in the order of 0.92 for correctly recognising a positive example of a symbol and 0.98 in correctly rejecting a negative example of the symbol. Classification had been based upon x and y coordinate co-occurrence information dividing a symbol (normalised into a 100 by 100 pixel region) into 25 areas and using these as input to a MLP with 25 input nodes, 10 hidden-layer nodes and one output node trained with back propagation.

A Pen-Based Recognition System for Handwritten Music Notation

This section considers the development of a pen-based recognition system for handwritten music notation. Having demonstrated that a neural-based recogniser is capable of identifying hand written music notation symbols with good accuracy (0.92 sensitivity and 0.98 specificity), there are a number of complexities that should be addressed including how, and whether, it is possible to generalise from recognising an isolated symbol to recognising one that appears written within a music fragment. This section starts by considering the general requirements of a pen-based interface, before considering the recognition of primitive symbols versus units, and finally the complexities of spatio-temporal construction.

Requirements of a Pen-Based Interface

We believe that, ideally, a pen-based interface for music input would have a certain basic functionality. We consider some of these specifications now in informal terms. Ideally a pen-based interface for a music editor would:

- Recognise the normal scribed version of the whole range of music symbols that are available in common music (and other) notations, including those that are variant in size (e.g., phrase markings) and those that are fixed (e.g., clefs).
- Cope with recognition of other "ink" such as performance directives/lyrics/chord markings for guitar/titles.
- Permit an incremental construction of symbols (e.g., adding beams and stems after note bodies, bar-lines after notes, and other).

- Provide a "delete" function to remove handwritten elements or components of handwritten elements.
- Provide automatically generated stavelines as needed, and facilities to "insert" handwritten stavelines in an already constructed music manuscript.
- Allow the "insertion" of staffline space (lines or bars) after music has already been written, rearranging and keeping components in correct relationship.
- Render the elements recognised in a representation language suitable for performance or typesetting, associating lyrics and other performance directives with the notation elements.
- Highlight "semantic" inconsistencies with symbols and combinations that are written (such as number of beats in a bar and that expected from the time signature).
- Highlight "syntactic" errors in how primitive components are formed (e.g., recognising that a symbol is illegal or ambiguous).
- Be capable of "learning" from user input so that the recognition method gains experience and improves recognition over time with the examples of writing provided from a given writer.

Clearly these and other elements comprise a far more comprehensive system than merely recognising music symbols, but recognition of the music symbol is at the heart of the exercise, and a suitable technique for doing this ultimately must be established if the first requirement cited above can be satisfied. Basic recognition will ideally include (a) the full range of music notation symbols (e.g., notes of all durations, other clefs, bar lines, and time signatures), (b) symbols that are variant in size (e.g., phrase markings, note beams, slurs), (c) symbols constructed incrementally (e.g., adding beams and dots after the main note has been written), (d) permitting symbols with deleted components, (e) handling symbols not specific to music notation (e.g., lyrics and bar numbering), and (f) locating the symbol upon the staffline (for pitch).

Primitive Symbols and Units

One of the biggest difficulties in extending the neural network-based recognition above, is isolating the primitive symbols that the network must learn.

There are many ways that the "primitive" music symbols may be combined to form unique (musical) "utterances" (just as words are combined to form sentences within natural language). While it may be useful to base the music primitive on a given music fragment — for example, pairs of beamed quavers may be a commonly occurring pattern in some music and, hence, considered primitives — it is unlikely that it is possible to identify a complete set of primitives that would cover every possible expression of notation that may be found in a music fragment. Rather there will be composite "units" built from whatever elements are deemed primitives. We are left with the question of how to deal with recognising music, given a limited set of primitives, and the possibility that they are combined into units.

Figure 6 illustrates a music fragment showing how the primitive symbols (used to train the neural networks above) appear (e.g., the clef symbols, the sharp, flat and natural, the rests, and some notes including minim stem up and crotchet stem up), but also variations of those symbols including (a) those that are part of a chord (in stem up and down position), (b) those that are beamed with other notes, and (c) those that are ledger notes. The music contains the information that could be used by a neural-based recogniser, but it is within units and not within primitive elements. Whether the units could easily be isolated from the score is an important question.

Figure 6: Illustration of the Basic Symbols within Music Score and Variations

When seeking "units," or primitives, within the music fragment, there are similarities with the segmentation problem found in on-line handwriting recognition, where characters in writing must be separated. However, it is a more complex task since we are not just identifying the boundary of a group

of pixels, but are aiming to identify a primitive within the unit. This may involve isolating (perhaps overlapping) subsets of points within that unit, to distinguish individual primitive symbols. Thus, a chord unit that contains a single stem and some note heads might be isolated into three individual crotchet primitives, each with note head and stem. Or it might involve simply identifying a primitive crotchet rest symbol within the score. In the most general sense the score is composed of units. Sometimes these units are primitive elements themselves, and sometimes they are composite so that the primitives have to be extracted from the units.

Identifying the units within a music fragment might be possible using (a) spatial information (points are considered "close" according to their coordinate information), or (b) temporal information (points are "close" because they occur within the same "pen-down" movement, or they are created within a particular time frame). Either, or both, of these criteria may be utilised for identifying units, although the possibility of great variation in spatio-temporal construction of handwritten score poses challenges.

Spatio-Temporal Construction

One fundamental difficulty of recognising dynamically constructed symbols is that they are constructed dynamically with pen-up/down movements. Points grouped together by virtue of occurring within one "pen-down" unit may be considered part of the same primitive unit (e.g., a note stem) or indeed the whole unit (e.g., a rest). But it may take several movements to construct a symbol. Similarly, composite symbols (e.g., two note stems and a joining beam) may be constructed within the same "pen-down" movement, although they may properly be regarded as two primitives.

With dynamic writing there is the additional complication that these units may have been composed as distant spatio-temporal events. For example, the stem joining notes of a chord might have been added after the basic note heads were constructed — making it harder to isolate the group of points as coming from the same unit by time information alone. Conversely, spatially close note heads might actually belong to two different unit groupings, making it hard to combine points into the same unit by space information alone.

Figure 7 illustrates the problem of dynamic construction and static segmentation with (a) two beamed notes and the different segments (or primitives) that may be identified (i.e., quaver notes and beam), together with (b) three different ways "pen-up/down" movements may have been used to create the beamed pair.

Figure 7: Illustration of Note Segmentation and Creation

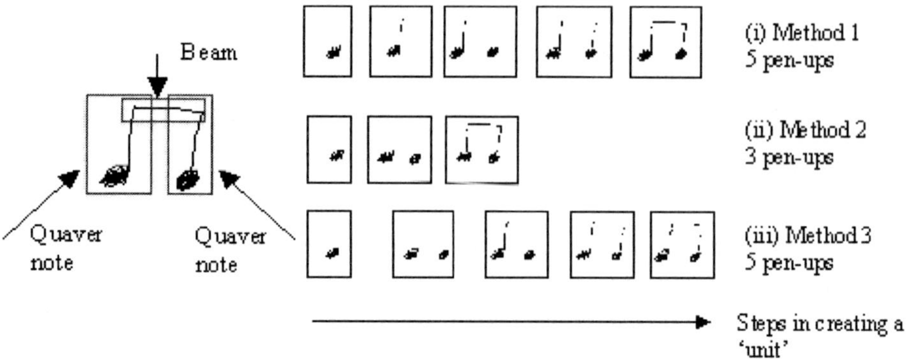

If identification of units (and hence primitives) is essentially spatial, then the "bitmap" representation of the dynamic data (or at least a computation of where dynamically produced points would lie in a bitmap) may be the most useful for isolating units and then primitives for recognition. The spatial interpretation of "connecting" components to define a unit would need some consideration in those symbols that have disjointed parts (e.g., double bar lines and dotted notes), and also for symbols that accidentally overlapped (e.g., a slur touching a note head or crossing a barline). Also, if ever a spatial portion of the image was revisited there would have to be a reinvestigation of the units within the area, since dotting notes, adding stems or beams would potentially modify the unit and primitives that might be found within the unit. Alternatively, if identification of units (and, hence, primitives) is essentially temporal, then the pen-up/down information may be useful to define the unit, especially when combined with the absolute timing of when points were written.

There are a variety of choices and only further experimental work would reveal exactly how the neural-based recogniser might be used in the context of a pen-based editor — with questions of whether there should be primitive units and what these might be, how they could be isolated from the writing, and so on. It is possible that the basic pen-down movement would be the basis for a primitive unit with a higher level grammar expressing how these pen movements could be combined. While there are a variety of ways that symbols might be constructed, the grammar may express the higher level symbol in spatial terms alone to remove the complications of dynamic construction.

Conclusion

This chapter has considered on-line pen-based input for handwritten music notation, placing the work in context of the various ways that music might be entered into a computer and conventional OMR for reading scanned music notation. The nature of pen-based input devices was also surveyed and the ways that input through a stylus has been used to enter notation to a computer. Recognition of genuine unconstrained handwritten music notation was not possible with the existing systems and consideration was given of how the ANN might be used to classify and cluster music symbols. A survey of ANNs applied to music notation recognition revealed that they had been applied in off-line contexts, and mainly the MLP had been utilized.

The chapter then introduced how the MLP was explored as a pattern-recognition method for isolated music symbols, demonstrating how a number of isolated symbols could be successfully recognized using a single artificial neural network. Networks were also capable of recognizing the writing of individual people and individual symbols, with a voting system between networks trained to recognize individual symbols producing the best results.

A discussion of how this approach can be used in a pen-based music editor suggested that the basic pen-down movements would form the "primitive units" that networks were trained to recognize and, after recognition, these primitives would be combined to form the actual music notation symbol written in context of unconstrained, dynamically constructed handwritten notation.

Acknowledgments

Thanks to the School of Computer and Information Science, University of South Australia for equipment funding and financial support necessary for this investigation. Thanks also to the student volunteers who provided samples of music writing.

References

Anstice, J., Bell, T., Cockburn, A., & Setchell, M. (1996). The design of a pen-based musical input system. In *Proceedings of the Sixth Australian Conference on Computer-Human Interaction* (pp. 260-267). Los Alamitos, CA: IEEE Computer Society.

Brown, A.R. (1998). Composing by pen: Exploring the effectiveness of a system for writing music notation on computers via pen input. *Australian Journal of Music Education,* No. 1 ASME, 48-56.

Forsberg, A.S., Dieterich, M.K., & Zeleznik, R.C. (1998). The music notepad. *Proceedings of UIST '98, ACM SIGGRAPH.* New York.

Kiernan, F.J. (2000). Score-based style recognition using artificial neural networks. International Symposium on Music Information Retrieval. Retrieved March 20, 2002: http://ciir.cs.umass.edu/music2000/papers.html.

Kohonen, T. (1982). Self-organized formation of topologically correct feature maps. *Biological Cybernetics,* 43, 59-69.

Miyao, H. & Nakano, Y. (1995). Head and stem extraction from printed music scores using a neural network approach. *Proceedings of the Third International Conference on Document Analysis and Recognition (ICDAR '95).* (August 14-16). Montreal, Canada: IEEE-CS Press.

Miyao, H. & Nakano, Y. (1996). Note symbol extraction for printed piano scores using neural networks. *IEICE Transaction INF. & SYST.,* E79-D, (pp. 548-554).

Roach, J.W. & Tatem, J.E. (1988). Using domain knowledge in low-level visual processing to interpret handwritten music: An experiment. *Pattern Recognition,* 21(1), 33-44.

Rumelhart, D.E., Hinton, G.E., & Williams, R.J. (1986). Learning internal representations by error propagation. In D.E. Rulmehart & J.L. McClelland (Eds.), *Parallel Distributed Processing* (vol. 1, pp. 318-362). Cambridge, MA: MIT Press.

Silberger, K. (1996). Putting composers in control. IBM Think Research, 34(4). Retrieved February 13, 2002: http://domino.research.ibm.com/comm/wwwr_thinkresearch.nsf/pages/musiceditor496.html.

Section 3: Lyric Recognition

Chapter 6

Multilingual Lyric Modeling and Management

Pierfrancesco Bellini, Ivan Bruno and Paolo Nesi
University of Florence, Italy

Abstract

This chapter presents a new way to model multilingual lyrics within symbolic music scores. This new model allows one to "plug" onto the symbolic score different lyrics depending on the language. This is done by keeping separate the music notation model and the lyrics model. An object-oriented model of music notation and for lyrics representation are presented with many examples. These models have been implemented in the music editor produced within the WEDELMUSIC IST project. A specific language has been developed to associate the lyrics with the score; the language is able to represent syllables, melismas (extended syllables), refrains, etc. Moreover, the most important music notation formats are reviewed focusing on their representation of multilingual lyrics.

Introduction

Textual indications have been always present in music scores (rall., cresc., a tempo, allegro, etc.), this kind of text is treated as a sign; it does not have to be translated. Lyrics are a special kind of textual indication within a music score; they should be translated in different languages when needed.

Automatic translation of lyrics is not feasible with current translation technology, which works poorly even with prose texts. The translation of lyrics is a very complex task; specific words have to be identified to match with the number of notes, melody and length. Information technology (IT) can only partially support this process. What can be done to support multilingual lyrics in music scores is to give the possibility to "plug" the appropriate lyric onto the score without creating a new version of the score. This means that in some way the lyric has to be a separate entity from the music connected to it, and dynamically replaceable. This is the solution adopted in the WEDELMUSIC editor for managing multilingual lyrics. One music score and lyrics in several different languages can be selected by the user and joined with the music score. In this chapter, only character-based languages are discussed. Asian languages based on symbols may need a completely different model depending on which kind of alphabet is used for coding the lyric. Some oriental alphabets are oriented to single sounds rather than to concepts and/or words. Frequently only the former type of alphabet is used to allow the assignment of distinct symbols to the music score notes. In that case, the production of lyrics for that language is not really different from the character based one.

In the presence of lyrics several rules for music notation formatting have to be followed:

(1) Tempo, dynamic markers, articulation, wedges, accents, expressions, etc., have to be placed above the staff and the lyric below.

(2) The lyric text must be divided into syllables, with each syllable related to one or more notes.

(3) The note has to indicate the "tone" to be used when singing the syllable.

(4) A syllable can be sung on more than one note (syllable extension or *melisma*) and also two consecutive syllables of different words can be connected to the same note. The punctuation of the lyric has to be attached to the word before the graphic extension or melisma.

(5) When syllables are sung on two or more notes, those notes must be slurred.

(6) The syllables and the single words sung on a single note have to be centered under the note, except for the first of the lyric.

This chapter is not focused on the theory about lyric association to music. Rather it is strongly focused on the lyrics' internal and visual representation. A good internal representation makes it possible to have a good and flexible external visualization. Details on vocal notation can be found in Read (1979) and Ross (1987). Figure 1 reports a sample of lyric notation highlighting some of the above cases.

Figure 1: Lyric Notation Example

Another aspect is connected with refrains. The refrains make it possible to avoid the duplication of the same sequence of measures in the score (music notation). In several cases, when executing the same "music" measure, the lyric text may be different in different refrains; for this reason the lyric is placed on different lines as shown in Figure 2. The refrain configuration can be quite complex in some music pieces.

Figure 2: Lyric Notation Refrain Example

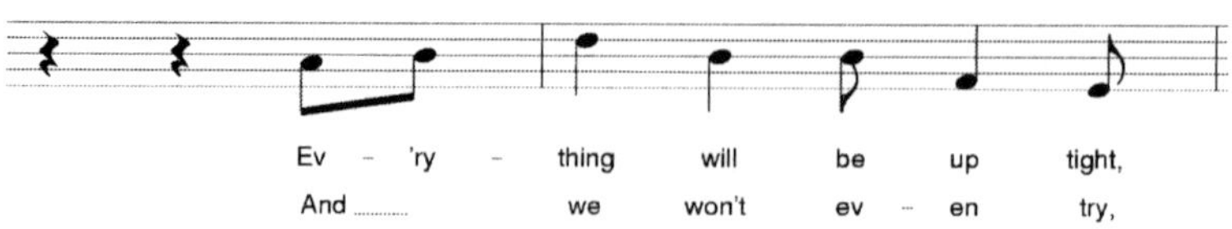

In another situation, more frequent in popular music than in classical music, the music notation on the music sheet is only related to the accompanying instrument (piano, guitar, etc.) and the lyric is merely synchronous with the instrument melody. In those cases, the lyric can be also associated with rests. Most of the tools for music editing do not permit that operation with their lyric model and thus the text is added to the music score by using simple floating text without establishing a format relationship between syllables and notes/ rests.

Another possibility is having different lyrics on the same staff. This may be for two reasons. When the staff presents only one voice, it may be for (i) assigning different words to different singers, or for (ii) presenting several languages of the same lyric at the same time on the same music sheet. When the staff presents more voices, each voice may have its own lyric. For example, a single staff may report two voices, one for the soprano and the other for the alto (both of them are in treble clef). Each of them may have distinct lyric text.

The chapter is structured in the following way: the chapter begins by focusing on background and briefly reports how the lyric is modelled in several formats. The chapter then gives an overview of the WEDELMUSIC object-oriented model of music notation. This is followed by a section that presents the lyric model and the main problems related to lyric representation. Examples and object diagrams are used to show how certain kinds of lyrics are modelled including aspects of multilingual lyrics. The WEDELMUSIC model for lyrics makes it possible to "plug" different sources of lyrics onto the same symbolic music description. A "language" used by the user to enter lyric is presented as well. This language is XML based and it is interpreted in the WEDELMUSIC editor and transformed into the lyric model, which can be seen in the music editor.

Background

Lyrics have been modelled within music notation formats since the beginning. In the following section, some well-known music notation encoding models are presented giving some details on how lyrics are represented. In the following section multilingual lyrics management is considered.

Languages for Modelling Lyric

In **MIDI (Music Instrument Digital Interface)** (Selfridge-Field, 1997; Hewlett & Selfridge-Field, 1997) lyric text meta-events have been introduced to deal with lyrics. This kind of event simply states the time when the syllable has to be sung, despite its duration (it has to be sung within the next lyric event), and it is not explicitly connected to a melodic line.

In **MuseData** (Hewlett, 1997) the syllables are associated with the notes of the melodic line, as in the example extracted from the Telemann Aria:

Figure 3: An Example to Compare Lyric Encodings

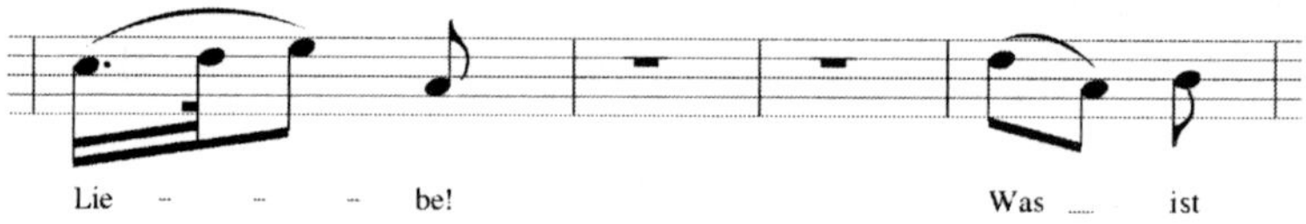


```
...
measure 15
C#5      3      s.     d [[     (        Lie-
D5       1      t      d =]\             -
E5       4      e      d ]      )        -
A4       4      e      u                 be!
measure 16
rest   12
measure 17
rest   12
measure 18
D5       4      e      d [      (        Was_
A4       4      e      d ]      )        _
B5       4      e      d                 ist
...
```

In this encoding, the first column reports the note pitch, the second column the duration (in divisions), the third column the graphical duration (i.e., s. = dotted sixteenth), the fourth column the stem direction, the fifth the beaming information, the sixth the slur start/end and the last reports the lyric syllable associated with the note. In the case where a syllable extends over more notes the characters "-" and "_" are used to state that the preceding syllable is extended at least to the referring note. If more then one lyric line is present the char "|" is used to separate the syllables of the different lines associated with the note (i.e., Deck|See|Fast).

MusicXML (Good, 2001) adapts the *MuseData* and *Humdrum* formats to XML (Bray, Paoli, Sperberg-McQueen & Maler, 2000). For this reason the MusicXML encoding has a similar structure of the MuseData one, although it is much more understandable. The following is the MusicXML (partial) encoding of the Telemann Aria sample:

```
<measure number="15">
   <note>
      <pitch>
         <step>C</step>
         <alter>1</alter>
         <octave>5</octave>
      </pitch>
      <duration>3</duration>
      <type>16th</type>
      <dot/>
      <stem>down</stem>
      ...
      <lyric>
         <syllabic>begin</syllabic>
         <text>Lie</text>
         <extend/>
      </lyric>
   </note>
   <note>
      <pitch>
         <step>D</step>
         <octave>5</octave>
      </pitch>
      <duration>1</duration>
      <type>32th</type>
      <stem>down</stem>
      ...
      <lyric>
         <extend/>
      </lyric>
   </note>
   <note>
      <pitch>
         <step>E</step>
         <octave>5</octave>
      </pitch>
      <duration>4</duration>
      <type>eighth</type>
      <stem>down</stem>
      ...
      <lyric>
         <extend/>
      </lyric>
   </note>
   <note>
      <pitch>
         <step>A</step>
         <octave>4</octave>
      </pitch>
      <duration>4</duration>
      <type>eighth</type>
      <stem>up</stem>
      ...
      <lyric>
         <syllabic>end</syllabic>
         <text>be!</text>
      </lyric>
   </note>
</measure>
```

The **Notation Interchange File Format (NIFF)** (Grande, 1997) (NIFF Consortium, 1995) was designed to allow interchange of music notation data among music-notation editing and publishing programs and music-scanning programs. It is a binary format based on the RIFF (Resource Interchange File Format) specification from Microsoft. The basic entity is the *chunk*, a variable length binary data, whose content type is identified by four chars. A chunk ("note") is used to represent a note head, a chunk ("stem") to represent the stem of a note, a chunk ("lyric") to represent the lyric associated with a note head, etc. Chunks are grouped in lists and lists in other lists; stems, notes, and many other chunks are grouped in a staff list, staffs are grouped in systems, and systems in a page. A chunk contains required data (fixed-length) and optional data (variable-length). The optional data is handled using tags; each tag is identified with a byte, it is variable-length and it contains optional information (i.e., AbsolutePlacement, IDs, etc.). Strings (i.e., the syllable text) are not stored within the chunks; in the chunk there is a reference (an offset) into a specific chunk (String Table) that contains all the strings (zero-terminated). This chunk is stored in the *Setup Section* and it is separated from the music notation data that is stored in the *Data Section*.

The following example is an excerpt of the NIFF encoding of the Telemann Aria translated in an ASCII code to be understandable:

```
////////////////////////////////////////////////////////////////////////////////
// NIFF Form
FORM:'RIFX' ( 'NIFF' // size=2380
////////////////////////////////////////////////////////////////////////////////
// Setup Section
LIST:'setp' size = 676
    ...
    // String Table
    CHUNK:'stbl' size=71
        ...
        // offset == 49
        "Lie-"Z
        // offset == 54
        "-"Z
        // offset == 56
        "-"Z
        // offset == 58
        "be!"Z
        // offset == 62
        "Was_"Z
        // offset == 67
        "ist"Z
        ...
    ENDCHUNK
    ...
ENDLIST
////////////////////////////////////////////////////////////////////////////////
// Data Section
LIST:'data' size = 1684
    LIST:'page' size = 1672
        ...
        LIST:'syst' size = 1002
            ...
```

```
LIST:'staf' size = 968
    ...
    // Time-Slice
    CHUNK:'tmsl' size = 11
         tsMeasureStart  // type
                      0  // start time numerator
                      4  // start time denominator
        TAG:AbsolutePlacement size = 4
                0  // horizontal
              400  // vertical
        ENDTAG
    ENDCHUNK
    CHUNK:'clef' size = 3
         clefshapeGclef  // shape
                      2  // staffStep
        clefoctNoNumber  // octaveNumber
    ENDCHUNK
    CHUNK:'keys' size = 1
                      2  // standardCode
    ENDCHUNK
    CHUNK:'time' size = 2
                      3  // top number
                      8  // bottom number
    ENDCHUNK
    // Time-Slice
    CHUNK:'tmsl' size = 11
                tsEvent  // type
                      0  // start time numerator
                      4  // start time denominator
        ...
    ENDCHUNK
    CHUNK:'stem' size = 6
        TAG:LogicalPlacement size = 3
                logplaceHDefault  // horizontal
                  logplaceVBelow  // vertical
             logplaceProxDefault  // proximity
        ENDTAG
    ENDCHUNK
    CHUNK:'beam' size = 10
              0  // beamPartsToLeft
              2  // beamPartsToRight
        TAG:NumberOfNodes size = 2
                3  // value
        ENDTAG
        TAG:ID size = 2
                0  // value
        ENDTAG
    ENDCHUNK
    CHUNK:'slur' size = 8
        TAG:ID size = 2
                1  // value
        ENDTAG
        TAG:NumberOfNodes size = 2
                2  // value
        ENDTAG
    ENDCHUNK
    // Notehead
    CHUNK:'note' size = 10
             noteshapeFilled  // shape
                           5  // staff step
                           3  // duration numerator
                          32  // duration denominator
        TAG:PartID size = 2
                0  // value
        ENDTAG
```

```
                ENDCHUNK
                CHUNK:'augd' size = 0
                ENDCHUNK
                CHUNK:'lyrc' size = 19
                       49L // text offset into String Table
                        0  // lyricVerseID
                    TAG:FontID size = 2
                        0  // value
                    ENDTAG
                    TAG:PartID size = 2
                        0  // value
                    ENDTAG
                    TAG:Absolute Placement size = 4
                        210  // horizontal
                        580  // vertical
                    ENDTAG
                ENDCHUNK
                ...
                ...
            ENDLIST // Staff
        ENDLIST // System
    ENDLIST  // Page
ENDLIST // Data Section
ENDFORM // NIFF Form End
```

Finale music notation editor and format presents an internal model of lyrics that directly establishes a relationship between the music notation symbol and its corresponding syllable contained in a unique string of characters that represent the whole lyric text. The syllables are simply separated by "-". Special symbols for syllable extension are managed separately and not coded into the string representing the lyric in the music editor.

SMDL (Sloan, 1997; ISO/IEC, 1995) represents the melodic line with a sequence of notes/rests (thread) followed by a sequence of syllables/rests. The syllables are associated with the notes in the melodic line according to the order. The following example reports the encoding in SMDL of the Telemann Aria:

```
<thread id=soprthd nominst="soprano">
       …
       <note>3t4 1 c
       <note>t4 1 d
       <note>t 1 e
       <note>t 0 a
       <rest>6t
       <note>t 1 d
       <note>t 0 a
       <note>t 0 b
       …
</thread>
<lyric id=soprtxt thread=soprthd>
       …
```

```
      <syllable tie>Lie-
      <syllable tie>
      <syllable>
      <syllable>be!
      <rest>6t
      <syllable tie>Was
      <syllable>
      <syllable>ist
      ...
</lyric>
```

The **GUIDO** format (Hoos, Hamel, Renz & Kilian, 2001), in implementation 0.8a, associates the lyric with a sequence of notes binding the syllables to the notes according to the order. In the event of a rest in the melodic line, the sequence has to be broken, giving a fragmented representation of the lyric.

The encoding of the four measures of Telemann Aria is the following:

```
[  \clef<"G"> \key<"+2"> \meter<"3/8">
...
\bar
\lyrics<"Lie---be!">( \slur(\beam(c2*1/16. d2/32 e2/8)) a1 )
\bar
_*3/8
\bar
_*3/8
\bar
\lyrics<"Was_ ist">( \slur(\beam(d2*1/8 a1)) b )
\bar
...
]
```

However, in GUIDO only one lyric line can be specified and thus it is not possible to manage refrains.

Languages and Multi-Lingual Lyrics

In MIDI, the multilingual lyrics may be realised using different tracks for the lyric events of different languages. However, it seems that lyric events have been introduced mainly for karaoke systems.

The **Humdrum** format (Huron, 1997) performs a better work. The melodic line is separated from the lyric text. One column is reserved to the Kern representation of the melodic line, while another column is used for lyric text synchronised with the melodic line, explicitly stating the language, and eventually another column may be used for the IPA (International Phonetic Alphabet) phonetic representation of the lyric text. This organisation allows multilingual lyrics representation since more than one column of lyric text may be present, all sharing the same melodic line.

The following is an excerpt of the encoding of Telemann Aria:

```
**kern      **text       **IPA
*           *LDeutsch    *LDeutsch
!voice      !lyrics      !phonetics

...         ...          ...

=15         =15          =15
(16.cc#     Lie-         'li_
32dd        .            .
8ee)        .            .
8a          -be!         _b@
=16         =16          =16
4.r         .            .
=17         =17          =17
4.r         .            .
=18         =18          =18
(8dd        Was          v&s
8a)         .            .
8b          ist          Ist

...         ...          ...
```

The first column contains the melodic line, the second column the lyric text and the last column the phonetic translation. No encoding seems to be present for multiple line of lyrics.

Formats such as MuseData, NIFF, and MusicXML, as well as Finale and Sibelius commercial music editors, associate the lyric syllables directly with the melodic line notes, which does not fit for multilingual management since the lyric is directly integrated in the melodic line. These formats do not include the possibility of integrating, in a unique music score, several different lyrics associated with the same score. For these, the only solution to cope with the multilinguistic aspects is to produce more versions of the same music score. The representation adopted in SMDL does not deal directly with the multilingual aspects, but it can be simply extended to accomplish this task. The GUIDO format does not deal with multiple lyric lines or multilingual lyrics.

The model adopted in WEDELMUSIC (http://www.wedelmusic.org) is based on an *object-oriented* model of music and presents a *symbolic indexing* of each music notation element. These aspects are discussed in the next two sections. WEDELMUSIC has a native XML music notation model and editor (Bellini & Nesi, 2001). The XML music notation model includes a XML model of lyrics that has been developed to support multiple lyrics. In addition, a specific lyric editor has been also built to support and edit the lyric in an easy manner. It is on this model and format that the rest of the chapter is focused.

WEDELMUSIC Object-Oriented Music Notation Model

WEDELMUSIC is based on an object-oriented model of music notation. The model presents several innovative aspects that have been defined to create a common framework on which to build a set of tools for multimedia music manipulation — including music notation and multilingual lyrics. The object-oriented paradigm was initially developed in the artificial intelligence context and then software engineering. It is useful in modelling situations, where relations among "entities" are complex and the number of entities may be constrained to grow with time to satisfy new aspects and symbols. For these reasons it is frequently used for the implementation of Computer-Aided Design (CAD) tools and for flexible and expandable frameworks. Music notation is certainly a context where relations among music notation entities could be very complex and in continuos evolution.

Notation Used for the Following Diagrams

The notation used in this chapter for representing an object diagram has been proposed by the authors as a working extension of that of Booch (1996). The two diagram types reported in the following are the class diagram (those with the ellipses), that depicts the generalization/specialization relations among classes and aggregations relations, and the object diagram (those with squares) where the aggregation relationships between specific objects instances of a class are depicted just to show an example of the relationships among real data.

Figure 4: Notation for Class Diagrams and Object Diagrams

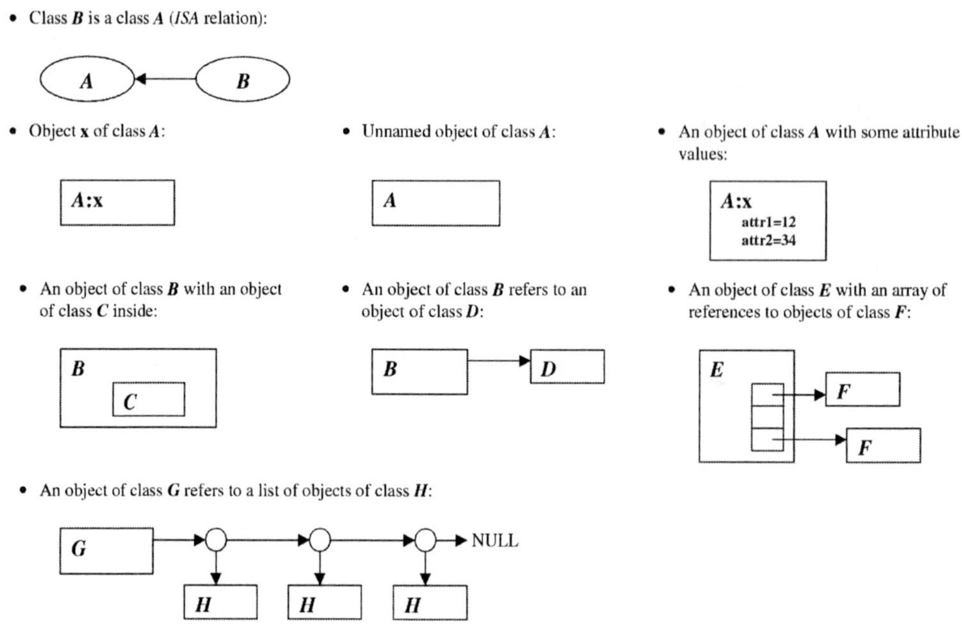

In short, classes are the formal definition of data structure of objects and the implementation of the procedures (called methods, operators, etc.) that can be used to manipulate them. The relationships defined among classes are concretized when the objects are instantiated from the formers. In the object diagrams, the lines represent pointers, while the inclusion of one square into another represents the inclusion of one data structure into another.

Main Relationships among Music Notation Structures

This section provides an overview of the WEDELMUSIC object-oriented music model, which is used for the lyric model presented in the next section. The examples reported show some "real" music notation and the related object diagrams representing them. The description is focused on the structural part of music (measures, notes, rests, beamed notes, multivoice) and fewer details are given on symbols around notes. The model reported is general enough to be considered as formal representation of the music notation.

The main score is modelled as a sequence of parts and each part is made of:

- a sequence of measures,
- a sequence of horizontal symbols (slurs, crescendo/diminuendo),
- a sequence of syllables (for lyric).

Each part can use from one to three staves, depending on the instrument.

Figure 5 depicts how a main score with two parts and two measures is represented. This model is partial; information about horizontal symbols is missing and will be detailed later on:

Figure 5: Main Score Model with Object Relationships

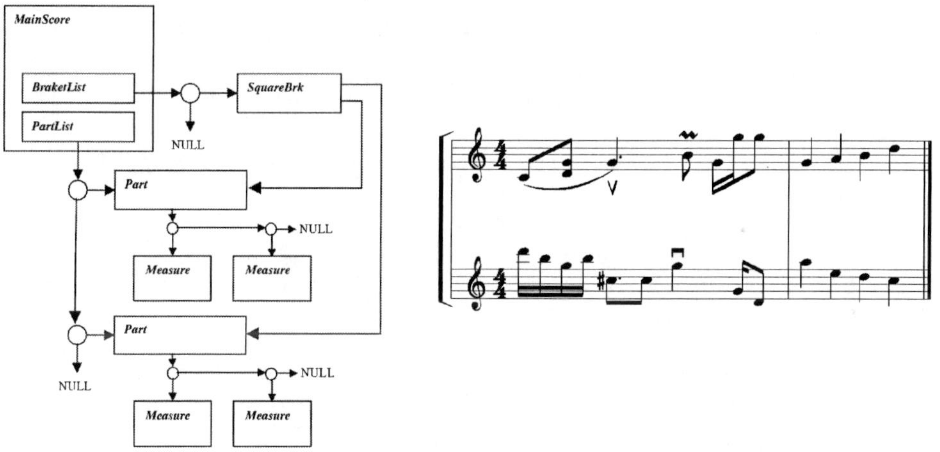

A *Part* object can use one, two or three staves, depending on the instrument (i.e., violin, piano, organ). In the example reported above there are two single staff parts. A *Measure* object can have from one to three headers (depending on the type of part) one for each staff. A measure can manage up to 12 layers, each of which may contain sequences of *figures* (notes/rests/change of clef/ ...). The measure header contains the clef, the key signature and the time, plus additional indications. Each *Measure* object has a full header and whenever the measure is visualised, the information associated with the headers is displayed or omitted according to the music notation rules. In general, according to music notation terminology, the *figures* are notes, rests, chords, beams, etc. The concept of figure in music notation is an abstraction to refer to music notation symbols that are the main symbols sequentially arranged along with a voice.

The *Figure* is an abstract class; it is sub-classed into:

- class *Note* representing a musical note; it is sub-classed in: *Note1*, *Note1_2*, *Note1_4*, *Note1_8*, *Note1_16*, ... depending on the duration,
- class *Rest* representing a rest; similarly it is sub-classed in: *Rest1*, *Rest1_2*, *Rest1_4*, *Rest1_8*,...,
- class *Anchor* representing a point between two figures; it is used as an anchor point for some types of symbols (e.g., *Breath*),
- class *Space* representing a symbol that takes space but has no duration; in this class there are the *Clef*s and the *KeySignatures,*
- class *Chord* that contains a sequence of simple notes with the same duration,
- class *Beam* that contains a sequence of notes/rests/chords/anchors/spaces.

Figure 6 reports the class diagram (ISA, relationship of specialisation of the Object Oriented) of these classes.

The most important *Figure* attributes are:

- the *staff* (1, 2 or 3) where the figure is positioned; staff 1 is the upper one, staff 2 is the middle one and staff 3 is the lower one
- the *height* of the figure, meaning the staff line/space where it is positioned, where 0 is the bottom line of the staff, 1 the first space, 2 the second line, 3 the second space, etc.

This representation makes it possible to model chords spanning between staves and beaming across staves as well as multivoice measures.

Figure 6: Class Diagram - ISA Relationships

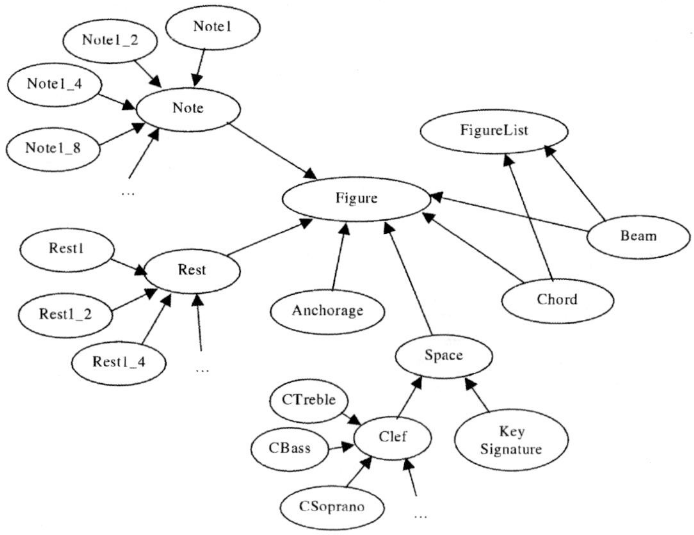

In Figure 7, two examples are reported: a single staff measure with two voices and a measure with two voices on two different staves.

Figure 7: Measure Models

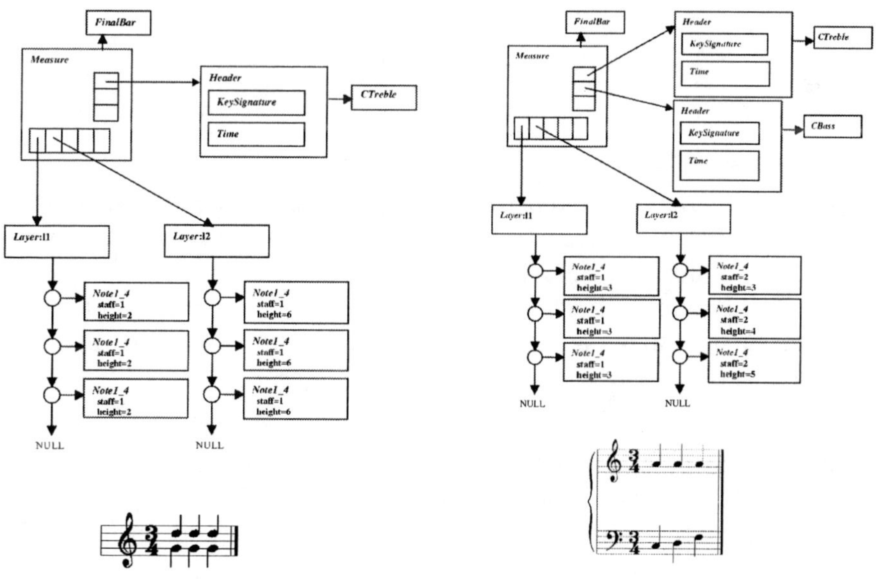

Two voices – one staff measure

Two voices – two staff measure

A chord is modelled using the *Chord* object that can contain more than one *Note* of the same class (i.e., the same duration). Moreover, the notes can belong to different staves as shown in Figure 8.

The *Beam* class is used to model beamed notes (with duration less or equal to 1/8). A *Beam* object can contain *Note, Rest, Chord* and *Space* objects, provided that the first and the last note of the beam have to be a *Note* or a *Chord* object.

Figure 8: Multi Staff Chords and Beams Model

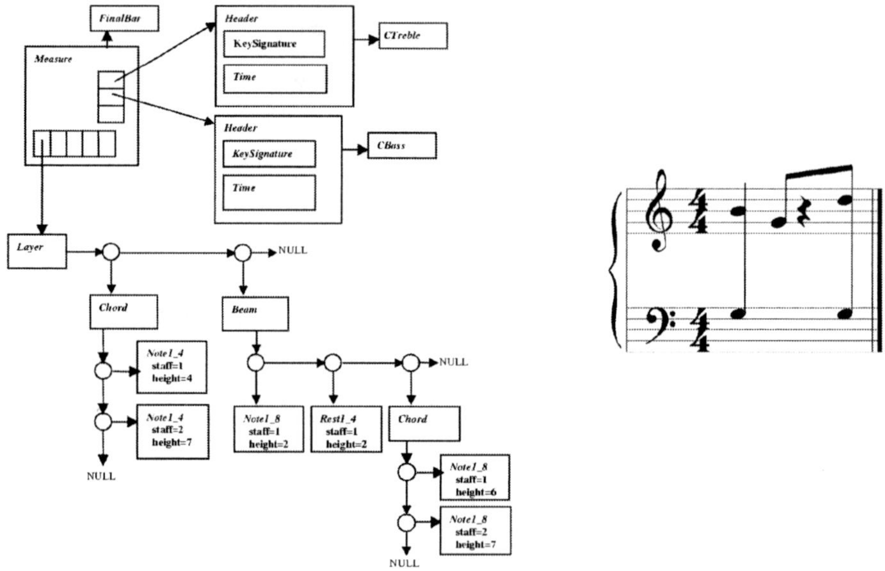

The horizontal symbols (slurs, crescendo, diminuendo, etc.), spanning from one figure of a measure layer to another figure of the same layer and eventually in another measure, are modelled with class *HorizontalSym*. Each horizontal object has a reference to the starting and the ending figure. The HorizontalSym is specialised by classes *Slur, Tie, Crescendo, Diminuendo, Wave, TrillWave, Change8va, Arrow, Tuple,* etc., according to their specific features.

The example reported in Figure 9 shows a *Slur* object connecting two notes of two measures and a crescendo starting from a note and ending on an *Anchor* object. The anchor object represents a point in the middle (dist = 50%) of the space, after the last quarter note. It is just a reference point in the middle of two symbol along a voice.

Figure 9: Horizontal Symbols Model

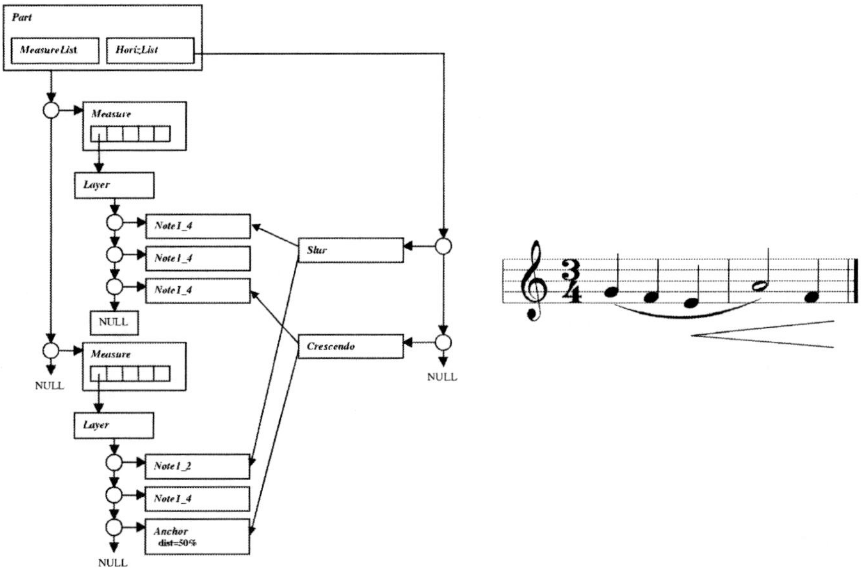

Also tuplets are modelled as horizontal symbols, so as to allow nested tuplets and tuplets across measure boundaries. In Figure 10, an example of nested

Figure 10: Nested Tuplets Model

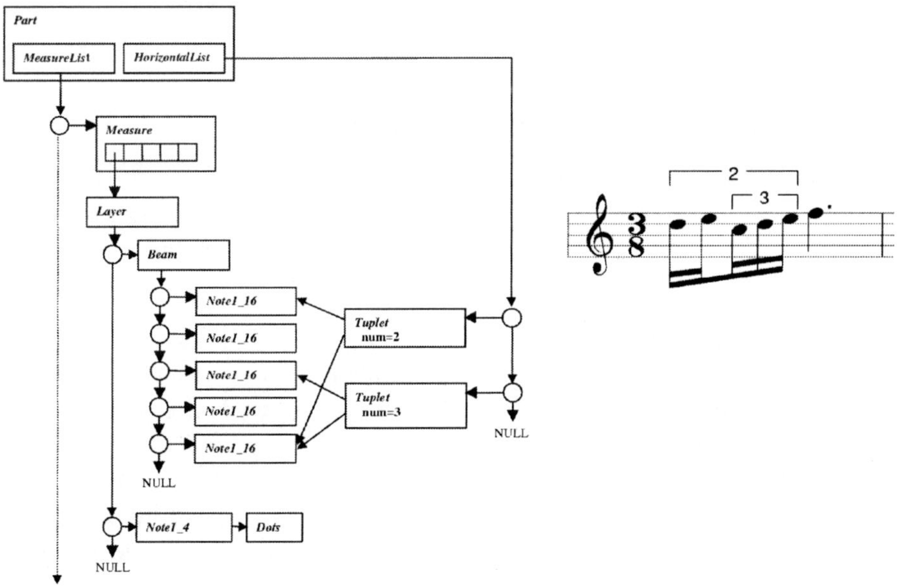

tuplets is presented and Figure 11 displays how the tuplets across a barline are modelled.

Figure 11: Tuplets Across Barlines

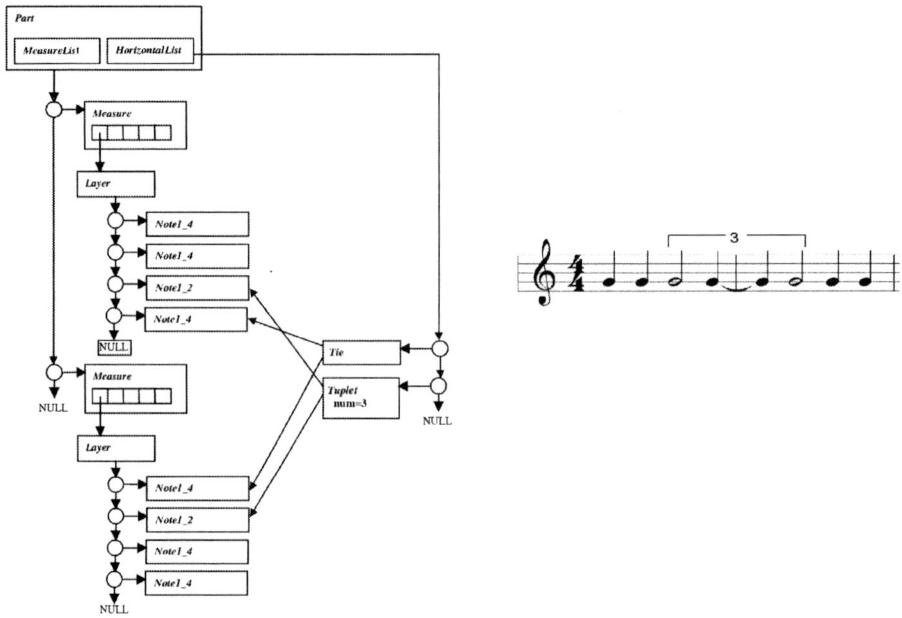

WEDELMUSIC Modelling of Lyric

This section is devoted to present the lyric model used in WEDELMUSIC. It is XML compliant (Bray et al., 2000). The main problems of lyric representation are highlighted and discussed. Examples and object diagrams are used to show how certain kinds of lyrics are modelled.

The lyric text is modelled as a sequence of syllables. Each syllable starts on a certain note and it may be extended to a following one (not necessarily in the same measure). The syllables are to be drawn aligned with the starting figure, all on the same horizontal line, except for refrains where different text is reported in different lines within the same melody. In order to associate lyric to music notation, two different models can be used: (i) each note presents a relationship to one or more syllables, (ii) any associated syllable presents a reference (symbolic or absolute) to the music notation symbol. The first solution is the best solution if only one lyric is associated with the music score. When more lyrics are associated with the same music score, the first solution becomes too complex, since each figure has to refer to all the syllables of the several lyrics. In these cases, the second solution can be better since it might make it possible to realise new lyrics even without modifying the music notation. In WEDELMUSIC, this second solutions has been chosen.

Single Language Lyrics and Refrain Management

Similarly to other symbols, lyric text is handled as horizontal symbols. The *Part* object refers to a list of *Syllable* objects and each syllable has a reference to the starting and ending *Figure* object. The order of the syllables in the list follows the lyric text, so that the text can be reconstructed by following the list.

Syllables are separated by using:

- an empty space when the two consecutive syllables belong to different words,
- a hyphenation mark when the syllables belong to the same word,
- a continuous line if the ending syllable of a word has to be extended on more than one note.

An attribute of the *Syllable* object (*sep*, in the following) is used to indicate which kind of separator has to be used: " " for empty space, "n" for new line, "/" for hyphenation mark, "_" for syllable extension at the end of a word and "-" for syllable extension inside a word.

The relation between separators and start/end figures has to be analysed in a more detailed manner. The *start* figure reference is set always to the *Figure* object under which the syllable has to be positioned; on the other hand, when it comes to the *end* figure, what follows can be applied:

- if the syllable is a single word or is the ending syllable of a word and it is not extended (*sep* = " " or sep = "n"), then the *end* figure is not set (meaning NULL),
- if the syllable is not the last one and it is not extended (*sep* = "/"), then the *end* figure is set to the figure where the next syllable is positioned,

- if the syllable is not the last one and it is extended (*sep* = "-"), then the *end* figure is set to the figure where the next syllable is positioned. The symbol "-" in the text word can be written by using "\-",
- if the syllable is the ending one and it is extended (*sep* = "_"), then the *end* figure is set to the figure under which the extension line has to be drawn; generally it is the previous figure of the next syllable.

Figure 12: The Model of an English Lyric

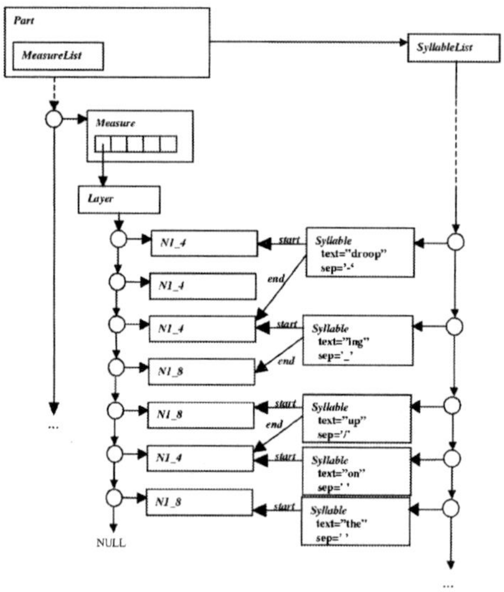

Frederic Delius: from *Sea Drift* (1904)

The example in Figure 12 shows all such events with an English lyric, and Figure 13 reports the same melody with German lyrics.

In vocal parts, the slurs or ties between syllables are used to highlight syllable extension; therefore, they are strictly related to the lyric text. As highlighted in Figure 12 (English lyric), in comparison to Figure 13 (German Lyric), two slurs are met due to the two syllable extensions (*droop*, *ing*); the two slurs are replaced with only one in the German lyric because only one syllable is extended (*sinkt*). In these cases, changing the lyric has also to imply the modification of related slurs/ties. Therefore, to cope with this situation, some slurs/ties should be associated with the lyric by storing the identifier of the

Figure 13: The Model of a German Lyric

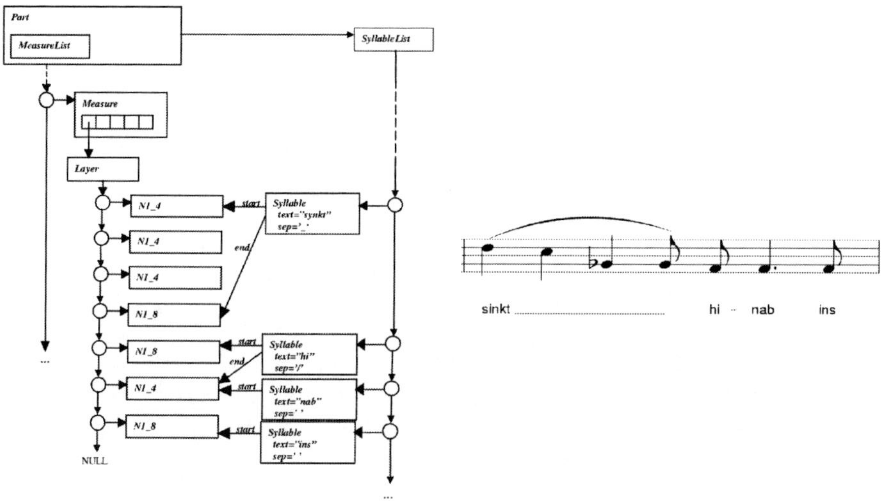

lyric in which they can be applied. In this way, they can be visible only when "plugging" in that specific lyric.

The case should be also considered in which a note has to be split into more tied notes for the total duration, or more tied notes are merged to accommodate the syllables of a translated lyric, as it occurs with the example reported in Figure 14. In these cases, the simplest solution is to use syllable extension and ties producing the equivalent form reported in Figure 15. When the same word contains an odd number of syllables a tuple can be used.

Figure 14: English and German Lyric, Comparison

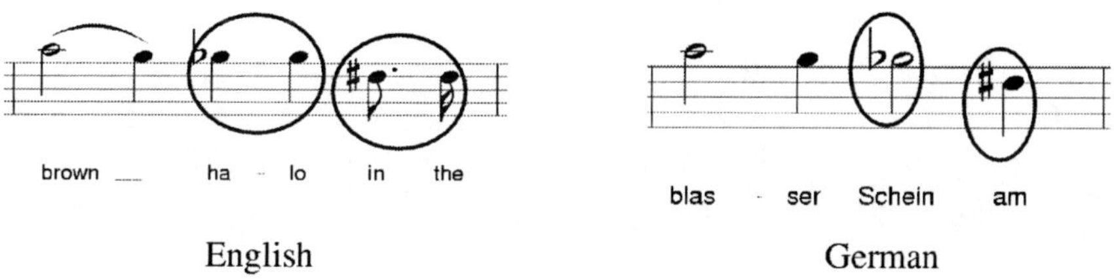

Figure 15: Solution with Syllable Extension

When two consecutive syllables of different words (one starting and the other ending with a vowel) have to be sung on the same note, as in Figure 16, the special character "+" was selected to represent the slur in the syllable text. Therefore, the two highlighted "syllables" are represented through texts "ra+in" and "me+a" in the *Syllable* objects. The drawing/printing engine replaces the + character with a slur when displaying or printing the music.

Figure 16: Consecutive Syllables

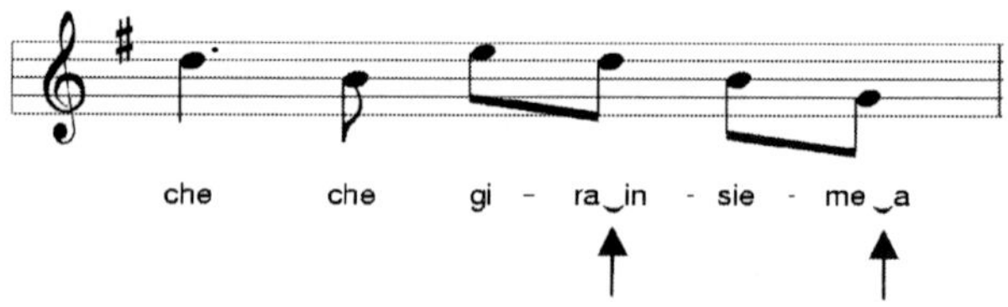

The different lines of lyrics are managed using an attribute (*line*) of the *Syllable* object, pointing out on which line the syllable has to be placed. An example is reported in Figure 17.

Another possibility of the WEDELMUSIC model is to have different lyrics to the same staff. This is possible when the staff presents more voices (for instance the voice of Soprano and of Tenor), each voice may have its own lyric. In this way, it is possible to have on the same staff two or more parts for singers with their related music. With the WEDELMUSIC model, it is also possible to have different lyrics associated to the same voice, as frequently occurs in sacral music that provides under the same staff the same lyric in different languages.

In addition, WEDELMUSIC supports also a real multilingual lyrics representation since different *SyllableLists* can be "plugged" on a *Part* object, depending on the language.

Figure 17: A Model of Multi Line Lyrics

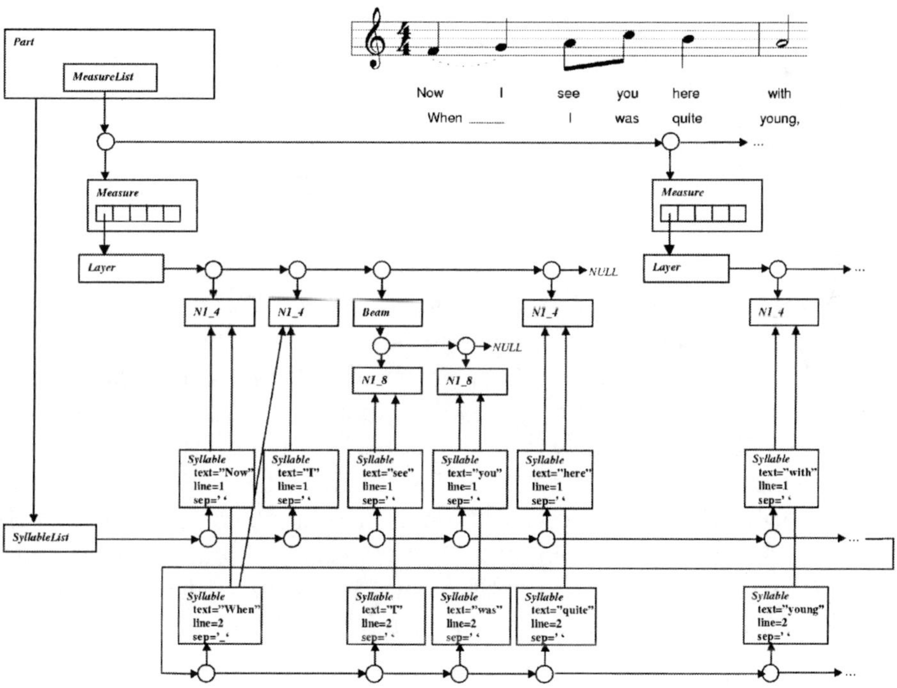

Multilingual Aspects and Lyric Editor

This section deals with the issues related to multilingual lyrics management. Mainly, it explains the language to be adopted by the WEDELMUSIC users to enter lyric text. This language is interpreted in the editor and transformed in the lyric model, which can be seen in the WEDELMUSIC music editor. The example reported in Figure 18 has been produced by using the WEDELMUSIC lyric editor, and presents both English and German lyrics. Please note the different arrangement of slurs and ties.

Figure 18: Example of Multilingual Lyric, English and German Versions

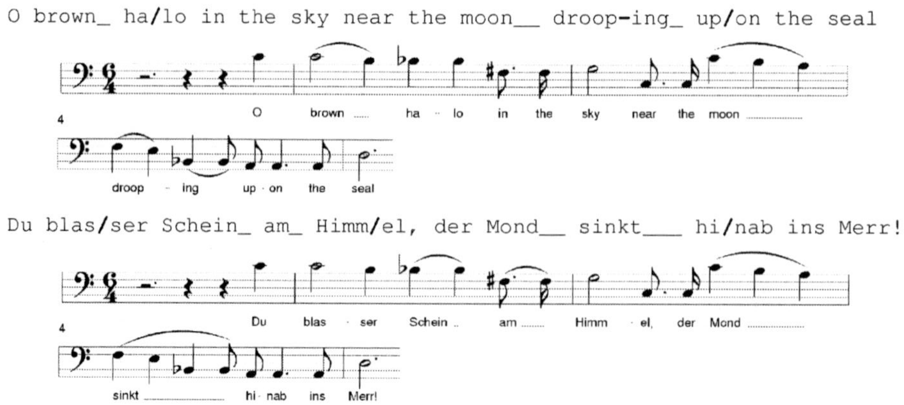

As shown in the examples above, the lyrics text is *augmented* with some special characters: "/", "_" and "-", and also the "@" and "+" characters are possible, as it will be shown later in the complete example. Please note that they are extremely useful in some languages, while in others their usage is marginal. The WEDELMUSIC lyric editor parses the text entered and assigns each syllable to a note, starting from the first note (a particular setting of the editor allows it to assign syllables to both rests and notes). The blank character, the carriage return and the "/", "_", "-", and "@" characters are considered as syllable separators, whereas the "+" character cannot be. When such symbols are part of the lyric to be shown in the score, they have to written as "\/", "_", "\-", and "\@".

Particular situations are met when syllables extensions have to be entered; for this reason separators like "-" and "_" are used at the end of the syllable to state that it is extended. The separator can be repeated to state the number of notes on which the syllable is extended. For example the "moon" syllable in the English lyric is followed by two "_" separators, meaning the syllable is extended to the two following notes. The same occurs with the "sinkt" syllable in the German lyric, where it is followed by three "_" separators to extend the syllable over three notes.

In some particular circumstances avoiding any syllable assignment is necessary; for this reason the "@" separator has been introduced to skip one note during the assignment of the syllables.

As syllables separators, the lyric text includes spaces, returns and tabs used to format the lyric. The idea is to grant the user the possibility to view the lyric text in the editor just as a poem, thus hiding the special separators but viewing the text correctly formatted with spaces and carriage returns. To perform that, the model has to store also this kind of information that is useless for lyric representation in the score, but becomes useful when viewing the lyric text as a poem.

The solution adopted in WEDELMUSIC is to use a *Syllable* object with no figure reference (*start* and *end* attributes are both NULL) and using the *text* attribute to store such kind of information. This special *Syllable* object is skipped during the syllable visualization on the score, not being associated with a figure. Besides, some other textual information like the title, the author, the date of composition, etc., can be found in the lyric; thus, the "{' and '}" characters have been used to mark the beginning and the end of a comment section (which is stored in the model as it is, while it is not associated with the score). The following is an example:

```
{<H1>}{Canto della Terra}{</H1>}
{lyrics by Lucio Quarantotto}
```

← one *Syllable* object contains this text

```
Si lo so a/mo/re che io+e te
for/se stia/mo+in/sie/me so/lo qual/che+i/stan/te
...
{1999}
```

That is viewed in the lyric editor by hiding the special separators as:

```
Canto della Terra
lyrics by Lucio Quarantotto

Si lo so amore che io e te
forse stiamo insieme solo qualche istante
...
1999
```

The "{<" and ">}" sequences are treated in a special way; they are used to embed HTML formatting commands in the text. When viewing the lyric by hiding the special operators, the characters between these two markers are completely hidden, thus removing the HTML commands. On the contrary, these sequences are not removed anymore when exporting the lyric to HTML.

What follows is a clarification on how blank spaces are treated within the model. The first blank character of a sequence of blanks is stored in the *sep* attribute and the following ones in a comment syllable.

The management of refrains is a complex task. The main constraint is that the entered lyric text has to be in reading order, which means first the syllables of the first line then the syllables of the second line, etc. A way to mark the beginning of a refrain is needed and the "[" character was chosen to point out that the note associated with the following syllable has to be considered as the refrain start. The character "%" is used like a RETURN — the assignment returns back to the previous refrain start, thus incrementing the current line. Finally the "]" character is used to end the refrain and decrement the current line.

For example the sequence **"A [B % C] D"** (where A,B,C,D are syllable sequences of any complexity) produce something structured like:

1.	A	B	D
2.		C	

Where 1. and 2. represent the lyric line where the syllables are positioned under the music score staff. The sequence **"A [B % C %D % E] F"** produces a lyric structured as follows under the score:

1.	A	B	F
2.		C	
3.		D	
4.		E	

The above introduced operators can be nested as in **"A [B [C % D] E % F [G % H] I] J"**, thus producing the following complex structure:

1.	A	B	C	E	J
2.			D		
3.		F	G	I	
4.			H		

To avoid inconsistencies, the number of notes used in the assignment of each refrain should be the same; for example in sequence "A [B % C] D", the syllable sequences B and C have to use the same number of notes. A way to avoid multiple assignments due to different numbers of used notes consists in storing the number of notes assigned and the next usable note when "%" is found, and in restoring the assigning position with the maximum number of used notes when the end "]" is found.

On the side of multilingual management, on each score part the user can:

- Create a new lyric and edit it with the WEDELMUSIC Lyric Editor,
- Edit the lyric text with the Lyric Editor and assign the lyric to the score,
- Select the lyric out of those available,
- Hide the lyric currently shown,
- Delete the lyric which will be destroyed,
- Export the lyric into HTML format and visualize it by a browser.

Figure 19: The WEDELMUSIC Editors (Music Editor, Lyric Editor & Viewer)

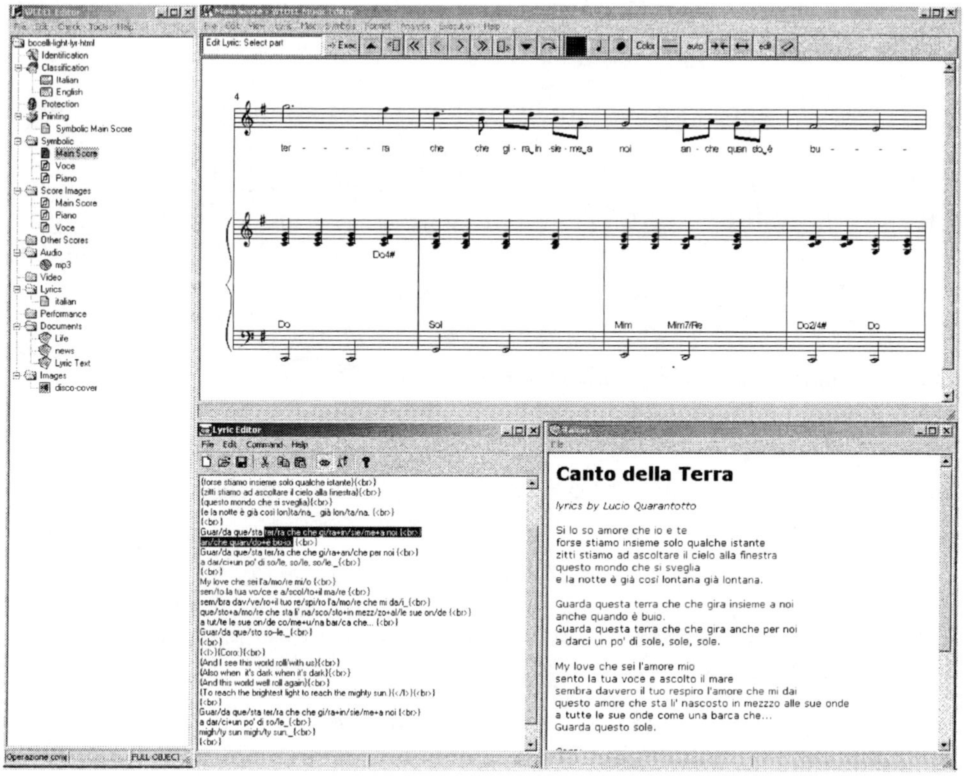

Figure 19 presents the WEDELMUSIC Editor user interface. On the left side, the tree structure is used to show the content of the music object. In this case, "il Canto della Terra" by Andrea Bocelli has been loaded. The Music Editor on the upper-right side shows the main score, while on the bottom-left side the Lyric Editor shows the lyric text (the lyric visible in the Music Editor has been highlighted to better identify it) and on the bottom right side the HTML viewer shows the lyric text formatted with HTML commands. With the Lyric Editor, the user may write the lyric in plain text for augmenting it in order to associate the right syllables to the specific notes.

XML Lyric Format of WEDELMUSIC

In the framework of the WEDELMUSIC project, a XML format for music notation representation has been developed (Bellini & Nesi, 2001). It is mainly structured as depicted in Section 3. Each part is stored in a different XML file (.swf files) and each lyric associated with a part is stored in a different file (.lwf files). The lyric file is practically a "dump" of the *SyllableList* object.

The main problem is to store the *start* and *end* pointers to the *Figure* objects, which are present in the *Syllable* objects. The solution offered is the same used for the *Part* object's horizontal symbols.

This is possible since in WEDELMUSIC each music notation object has a unique identifier (a symbolic index which is comprised of a sequence of numbers greater than 0). More specifically, within its container, each *Measure* object has a unique ID within the *Part*, each *Figure* object has a unique identifier within the Layer, and each *Figure* object has a unique identifier within the *Beam* and *Chord* objects. Using these IDs each leaf *Figure* object is identified by a path. For example:

MeasureID/LayerNumber/BeamID/ChordID/NoteID

Identifies a note in a chord in a beam in a layer of a measure.

This is the longest possible path. For example, other possible configurations are:

MeasureID/LayerNumber/FigureID

Identifies a note/rest/chord/beam/anchorage/clef/keysignature in the layer.

MeasureID/LayerNumber/ChordID/FigureID

Identifies a note in a chord.

MeasureID/LayerNumber/BeamID/NoteID

Identifies a note/rest/chord/anchorage/clef/keysignature in a beam.

Since any lyric is associated to single notes or chords, the longest path turns out to be impossible.

A lyric is represented in WEDELMUSIC XML as follows:

```
<?xml version="1.0" encoding="UTF-8"?>
<LWF ID="1" SCOREID="1">
  ...
  <language>eng</language>
  <text>&#xa;{Frederic Delius: from Sea Drift (1904)}&#xa;&#xa;
 </text>
  <syllable LINE="1" SEP=" ">
     <text>O</text>
     <start MEASURE="5" LAYER="1" FIGURE="4"/>
  </syllable>
  <syllable LINE="1" SEP="_">
     <text>brown</text>
     <start MEASURE="4" LAYER="1" FIGURE="1"/>
     <end MEASURE="4" LAYER="1" FIGURE="2"/>
  </syllable>
  <syllable LINE="1" SEP="/">
     <text>ha</text>
     <start MEASURE="4" LAYER="1" FIGURE="4"/>
     <end MEASURE="4" LAYER="1" FIGURE="5"/>
  </syllable>
  <syllable LINE="1" SEP=" ">
     <text>lo</text>
     <start MEASURE="4" LAYER="1" FIGURE="5"/>
  </syllable>
  <syllable LINE="1" SEP=" ">
     <text>in</text>
     <start MEASURE="4" LAYER="1" FIGURE="6"/>
  </syllable>
  <syllable LINE="1" SEP=" ">
     <text>the</Text>
     <start MEASURE="4" LAYER="1" FIGURE="7"/>
  </syllable>
  ...
</LWF>
```

The *LWF* (Lyric WEDELMUSIC File) tag represents the whole lyric text, the *ID* attribute represents the identifier of the lyric, and the *SCOREID* attribute refers to the score the lyric is related to. The *language* tag is used to state the lyric language; in this case "eng" stands for English. The LWF is composed of a sequence of *syllable* or *text* tags, one for each *Syllable* object being present in the *SyllableList*. *Text*-only tags are used to store comments that are not associated with the score. Attributes of the *syllable* tag are:

- *LINE* indicating the line where the syllable is positioned,
- *SEP* indicating the separator to the next syllable. In case of syllable extension the "_" and "-" are replicated as many times as the number of notes on which the syllable is extended (except for the first),
- *REFRAIN* indicating the refrain management character associated with the syllable ("[", "%" or "]"). The association abides by the following criteria: the start of refrain "[" and the "%" are associated to the following syllable, and the end of refrain "]" is associated to the preceding syllable. For example in **"aa [bb cc % dd ee] ff"**, "[" is associated with syllable "bb", "%" to syllable "dd" and "]" to syllable "ee".

The *text* tag within the *syllable* represents the text of the syllable, and the *start* and the *end* tags store the path to the starting and to the ending figures of the syllable.

The attributes of *start* and *end* tags are:

- *MEASURE*: the measure ID
- *LAYER*: the layer number starting from 1
- *FIGURE*: the first-level figure ID
- *CHORD.OR.BEAM*: the second-level figure ID (a figure in a Chord or a Beam)
- *CHORD.IN.BEAM*: the third-level figure ID (a note in a beamed chord), never used with lyrics.

The last two attributes are optional and have a default value of "0".

The example of Figure 20 has been produced by assigning:

Figure 20: Multiple Lyric and Refrains

```
{A lyric to show refrain management}
aa bb [ cc dd ee ff % gg hh ii jj ] kk ll
```

The WEDELMUSIC XML description of the lyric, stored in a .lwf file, is:


```
<?xml version="1.0" encoding="UTF-8"?>
<LWF ID=1 SCOREID="1">
    ...
    <language>eng</language>
    <text>&#xa;{a lyric to show refrain management}&#xa;&#xa;</text>
    <syllable LINE="1" SEP=" ">
        <text>aa</text>
        <start MEASURE="1" LAYER="1" FIGURE="9" CHORD.OR.BEAM="1"/>
    </syllable>
    <syllable LINE="1" SEP=" ">
        <text>bb</text>
        <start MEASURE="1" LAYER="1" FIGURE="9" CHORD.OR.BEAM="8"/>
    </syllable>
    <syllable LINE="1" REFRAIN="[" SEP=" ">
        <text>cc</text>
        <start MEASURE="1" LAYER="1" FIGURE="10" CHORD.OR.BEAM="7"/>
    </syllable>
    <syllable LINE="1" SEP=" ">
        <text>dd</text>
        <start MEASURE="1" LAYER="1" FIGURE="10" CHORD.OR.BEAM="6"/>
    </syllable>
    <syllable LINE="1" SEP=" ">
        <text>ee</text>
        <start MEASURE="1" LAYER="1" FIGURE="11" CHORD.OR.BEAM="5"/>
    </syllable>
    <syllable LINE="1" SEP=" ">
        <text>ff</text>
        <start MEASURE="1" LAYER="1" FIGURE="11" CHORD.OR.BEAM="4"/>
    </syllable>
    <syllable LINE="2" REFRAIN="%" SEP=" ">
        <text>gg</text>
        <start MEASURE="1" LAYER="1" FIGURE="10" CHORD.OR.BEAM="7"/>
    </syllable>
    <syllable LINE="2" SEP=" ">
        <text>hh</text>
        <start MEASURE="1" LAYER="1" FIGURE="10" CHORD.OR.BEAM="6"/>
    </syllable>
    <syllable LINE="2" SEP=" ">
        <text>ii</text>
        <start MEASURE="1" LAYER="1" FIGURE="11" CHORD.OR.BEAM="5"/>
    </syllable>
    <syllable LINE="2" REFRAIN="]" SEP=" ">
        <text>jj</text>
        <start MEASURE="1" LAYER="1" FIGURE="11" CHORD.OR.BEAM="4"/>
    </syllable>
    <syllable LINE="1" SEP=" ">
        <text>kk</text>
        <start MEASURE="1" LAYER="1" FIGURE="12" CHORD.OR.BEAM="3"/>
    </syllable>
    <syllable LINE="1" SEP=" ">
        <text>ll</text>
        <start MEASURE="1" LAYER="1" FIGURE="12" CHORD.OR.BEAM="2"/>
    </syllable>
</LWF>
```


And the XML description of the part, stored in the .swf file, is:


```
<?xml version="1.0" encoding="UTF-8"?>
<SWF_Part>
    ...
    <score ID="1" TYPE="NORMAL" INSTRUMENT="" LYRIC="1">
        <origin FROM="WEDELED"/>
        <measure PROGRESSIVE="1" ID="1">
          <justification MAINTYPE="LOG" MAINJUST="2.000000"/>
          <header>
                    <clef TYPE="TREBLE"/>
                    <keysignature TYPE="DOM"/>
          </header>
```

```
        <timesignature TYPE="FRACTION" NUMERATOR="4" DENOMINATOR="4"/>
        <layer NUMBER="1">
                <beam ID="9" STEMS="DOWN">
                        <note ID="1" DURATION="D1_8" HEIGHT="4"/>
                        <note ID="8" DURATION="D1_8" HEIGHT="3"/>
                </beam>
                <beam ID="10" STEMS="DOWN">
                        <note ID="7" DURATION="D1_8" HEIGHT="3"/>
                        <note ID="6" DURATION="D1_8" HEIGHT="3"/>
                </beam>
                <beam ID="11" STEMS="DOWN">
                        <note ID="5" DURATION="D1_8" HEIGHT="3"/>
                        <note ID="4" DURATION="D1_8" HEIGHT="3"/>
                </beam>
                <beam ID="12" STEMS="DOWN">
                        <note ID="3" DURATION="D1_8" HEIGHT="5"/>
                        <note ID="2" DURATION="D1_8" HEIGHT="4"/>
                </beam>
        </layer>
        <barline TYPE="END"/>
      </measure>
    </score>
</SWF_Part>
```


Finally a XSL style sheet can be used to translate the XML lyric description into HTML or plain text. For example:

```
{Title}
Aa/bb__ cc/dd
ee/ff gg.
```

Producing something like:

Title
Aabb ccdd
eeff gg.

Conclusions and Future Trends

This chapter has been focussed on the issues related to multilingual lyric modelling and management. In order to highlight the related modelling problems, several examples have been provided and an overview of a fully representative collection of models for lyrics have been presented. From the reported analysis and the presentation of the real needs, it is evident that most of the considered models proposed in the literature are non-satisfactory. For this reason, the WEDELMUSIC object-oriented model has been studied, defined, and used for music notation modelling including lyric. The adoption of the object-oriented paradigm has made it possible to refine the model to arrive at a good representation of the real needs. This has motivated the presentation of an object-oriented model of music notation in this chapter. In addition to the object-oriented model, the symbolic indexing for music notation symbols is one of the most important aspects that permits multilingual lyrics on the same music score. This is a very innovative solution that can be used for building software tools for educational purposes and for creating dynamic karaoke in opera and concerts.

The WEDELMUSIC model for lyrics copes with the issues of multilingual management, giving the possibility to "plug" different lyrics written in different languages on the same melodic line or voice. A language to be used to augment the lyric text for appropriate assignment of syllables to the score has been introduced. Some examples highlighted the use of such language and their translation into the model has been reported. This language is meant to allow the visualization of the lyric as a poem, just by hiding the special operators and permitting the addition of further textual information present in the lyric text but not reported in the score. The corresponding WEDELMUSIC XML format for lyric storing and interchanging has been presented.

As a conclusion we can state that the proposed model is complete for character-based lyrics and that it should be extended to symbolic-based lyrics such as those of oriental languages. In addition, the model proposed can be applied to all other music notation languages, provided the adoption of a symbolic indexing for the main music notation symbols. The symbolic indexing also presents several other advantages since it is a suitable support for implementing versioning mechanisms, selective and nonlinear undo, cooperative editing of music (Bellini, Nesi & Spinu, 2002), etc.

More specifically, it is difficult to say which future trends will appear in lyric representation. Needless to say, in the field of music notation much more effort is needed to develop a standard for music notation (and also for lyric) interchange. The NIFF substantially failed its mission, being too much focused on representing graphic details, and the use of a binary format does not help in developing tools based on it. Now the broad adoption of XML as an interchange meta-format is pushing us towards an age where interoperability, interchange and intercommunication are and will be key aspects of IT applications. Among them there are also applications based on music notation which still have to cover the gap; it is what happens, for example, with audio music applications and multimedia applications in general such as karaoke on video, opera, music sheets, and mobiles applications. At present they are now riding the Internet "wild horse," a horse full of energy and potential and at the same time very difficult to control, in order to go where they want to. In addition, the research in this field has to cope with the problems of automatic translation of lyrics to generate lyrics in other languages and assign the translation to music with syllable decomposition. This process is presently only for poets, due to the complexity of selecting correct words in order to preserve sound, feeling, moods, etc. Frequently, the translation is not literal — word-by-word and several versions exist. In that field, IT will have large difficulties in substituting the human perception. On the other hand, computer-based assistants may be set up to make the process of lyric translation easier.

References

Bellini, P. & Nesi, P. (2001). WEDELMUSIC FORMAT: An XML music notation format for emerging applications. *Proceedings of the 1st International Conference of Web Delivering of Music*. Florence: IEEE press.

Bellini, P., Nesi, P. & Spinu, M. B. (2002, September). Cooperative visual manipulation of music notation. ACM Transactions on Computer-Human Interaction, 9(3), 194-237. Retrieved at http://www.dsi.unifi.it/~moods/.

Booch, G. (1991). *Object-oriented Design with Applications*. Redwood City, CA: The Benjamin/Cummings Publishing Company.

Bray, T., Paoli, J., Sperberg-McQueen, C.M. & Maler, E. (2000). *Extensible Markup Language (XML) 1.0 (2nd ed.)*. (Internet) W3C Consortium. Found at: http://www.w3.org/TR/REC-xml. October 2000.

Good, M. (2001). MusicXML for notation and analysis. In W. B. Hewlett & E. Selfridge-Field (Eds.), *The Virtual Score Representation, Retrieval, Restoration* (pp. 113-124). Cambridge, MA: The MIT Press.

Grande, C. (1997). The notation interchange file format: A windows-compliant approach. In E. Selfridge-Field (Ed.), *Beyond MIDI — The Handbook of Musical Codes* (pp. 491-512). London: The MIT Press.

Hewlett, W.B. (1997). MuseData: Multipurpose representation. In E. Selfridge-Field (Ed.), *Beyond MIDI — The Handbook of Musical Codes* (pp. 402-447). London: The MIT Press.

Hewlett, W.B. & Selfridge-Field, E. (1997). MIDI. In E. Selfridge-Field (Ed.), *Beyond MIDI — The Handbook of Musical Codes* (pp. 469-490). London: The MIT Press.

Hoos, H., Hamel, K., Renz, K., & Kilian, J. (2001). Representing score-level music using the GUIDO music notation format. In W. B. Hewlett & E. Selfridge-Field (Eds.), *The Virtual Score Representation, Retrieval, Restoration* (pp. 113-124). Cambridge, MA: The MIT Press.

Huron, D. (1997). Humdrum and Kern: Selective feature encoding. In E. Selfridge-Field (Ed.), *Beyond MIDI - The Handbook of Musical Codes* (pp. 375-401). London: The MIT Press.

ISO/IEC. (1995). Standard Music Description Language. ISO/IEC DIS 10743.

NIFF Consortium. NIFF 6a: Notation Interchange File Format.

Read, G. (1979). *Music Notation: A Manual of Modern Practice*. New York: Crescendo Publishing.

Ross, T. (1987). *Teach Yourself. The Art of Music Engraving*. Miami, FL: Hansen Books.

Selfridge-Field, E. (Ed.). (1997). *Beyond MIDI - The Handbook of Musical Codes*. London, UK: The MIT Press.

Sloan, D. (1997). HyTime and standard music description language: A document-description approach. In E. Selfridge-Field (Ed.), *Beyond MIDI — The Handbook of Musical Codes* (pp. 469-490). London: The MIT Press.

Lyric Recognition and Christian Music

Susan E. George
University of South Australia, Australia

Abstract

The chapter is about lyric recognition in Optical Music Recognition (OMR). Discussion is made in the context of Christian music where the lyric is definitive of the genre. Lyrics are obviously found in other music contexts, but they are of primary importance in Christian music — where the words are as integral as the notation. This chapter (i) identifies the inseparability of notation and word in Christian music, (ii) isolates the challenges of lyric recognition in OMR providing some examples of lyric recognition achieved by current scanning software and (iii) considers some solutions outlining page segmentation and character/word recognition approaches, particularly focusing upon the target of recognition, as a high level representation language, that integrates the music with lyrics. The motivation for this chapter includes the observation that high quality lyric recognition is largely omitted by OMR research, but in the context of a music genre inseparable from the word, it is vital. Theoretical, practical (typesetting arrangements/singing synthesis) and philosophical reasons motivate a better examination of lyric recognition.

Introduction

Lyric recognition is often considered secondary to Optical Music Recognition (OMR). There is the assumption that the identification of music notation symbols is the primary activity and that the textual elements of the manuscript are secondary both to the music and the OMR process. This chapter observes otherwise, noting that the lyric is definitive of the Christian genre and cannot be isolated from the music, especially in the final representation stage, where capturing notation alone is unsatisfactory. Christian music is always vocal proclaiming a certain message; any music representation language that cannot express this and any OMR process that cannot process this, simply cannot handle Christian music — hence, it is inadequate for a genre that contributes vast proportions to the world of music.

This chapter begins by reviewing the importance of the lyric in Christian music — arguably, without the lyric Christian music would not be Christian music. We consider the development of the genre from its biblical basis to the various choral and hymn forms that developed, including the questionable instrumental music that has been incorporated into the worship context within which Christian music is found.

Second, the chapter highlights some of the challenges that are presented by character and word recognition within the context of music with lyrics. There are a number of complexities including the association of lyrics to various vocal parts (often within the same staff); the spreading of syllables, words and phrases across the page (in a way that is not found within most text contexts); the use of various languages within the lyrics (as exemplified by the music of Taize); the presence of performance directives, guitar chords and other markings that may be confused with lyrics by automatic recognition systems; and the crucial, but implicit, alignment of characters with the music staff indicating their association, and verse text that may be removed from the music line entirely but still needs to be associated with the music (accounting for the rhythm). We continue by illustrating the typical performance that can be expected from a commercial OMR recognition software system (Smartscore) and we see they are limited in the range of phenomena that can be handled.

Thirdly, we consider some solutions to the outstanding difficulties in lyric recognition. We review some approaches to character recognition and page segmentation, where the use of character template matching is actually highly effective and simple for most printed forms once corrections have been made for skew and other distortions in the image. We also identify the outstanding need for a suitable logical representation language that captures the various associations between music and lyric, and make some suggestions for the requirements of such a language.

Before we undertake the review of the nature of Christian music, the challenges of lyric recognition, and suggested solutions, we consider the motivation for lyric recognition and consider the question of why we might need to undertake automated lyric recognition in OMR. Naturally there is the theoretical interest; this is a problem that needs a solution and we may pursue various methods and algorithms to address the task. However, there are also practical reasons for why lyric recognition is necessary, found in applications that perform typesetting and part-arrangement where rearrangement of the score with lyrics can only be done if the lyrics are correctly identified and matched with the notes. Such tasks are needed in fields as diverse as education and management, recreation and law.

Also if we are interested in the entertainment novelty of building the first sight-singing robot (perhaps to accompany the robot that is able to sight-read and play piano music in real time) we would be interested in the questions and issues of this area so that singing could be synthesised from a digitised page of music. DECtalk is one computer karaoke system that is capable of playing music and singing at the same time (Murray, 1999) and the Flinger project, based on a speech synthesis system, was developed at the Centre of Spoken Language Understanding (http://cslu.cse.ogi.edu/tts/flinger) for synthesised singing. The CANTO project also aims to produce a synthetic singing voice from an XML-based language (http://www.computing.edu.au/~stalloj/projects/canto). Finally, at the intersection of artificial intelligence and theology, there are more philosophical questions that may be asked should machines undertake a behaviour (in performing sung Christian worship) that is presently uniquely reserved for the human soul.

Background to Christian Music

With many musical genres there is justification for ignoring the lyrics since the notation symbols are primary; however, there are some genres — notably Christian music — in which it can be argued that the lyric is primary. Some have argued that without the lyric Christian music would not be Christian music. In this section we consider what is Christian music, its biblical basis, its development into various hymn and choral formats and finally address the instrumental form used in certain contexts. While the lyric is obviously not exclusive to Christian music we do find it such an integral component that it cannot be ignored; patterns of "pitch" and "rhythm" alone cannot capture the genre.

What is Christian Music?

When we consider what is Christian music we come to the realisation that there is no distinctive sound, or tonal ingredient, that makes a piece of music Christian. Music cannot be un-Christian because it does not contain the tones from a particular culture, or certain note patterns for certain instruments. This is in contrast to other genres such as jazz, or classical, or modern where there are certain (albeit not formally defined) properties that the music possesses to be music of that genre. With Christian music we cannot analyse the notation symbols to identify the music as Christian or not; there is simply no definitive distinguishing mathematical arrangement between the notes, or within the rhythm, or between instruments. So we may ask what makes music Christian?

Firstly, we may wonder whether Christian music can be defined by its use? That is, can any music used in a worship context be deemed Christian? The Christian church has employed roughly four criteria in order to determine what music is appropriate for Christian worship. These criteria are: (a) instrumentation, (b) style, (c) judgments concerning the results of the music (in the player and the listener) and (d) the lyrics or song text. Using these criteria we still find there are questions about what type of music is appropriate for worship — and we cannot necessarily define music as Christian simply because it is used in worship.

Each criterion has received its own discussion about what is appropriately "Christian." Initially there was much controversy about the use of instrumentation since it was not originally a component of worship, and some people have even made a biblical argument against the use of instruments. The style of music has also been contentious in regards to whether or not it can draw upon contemporary culture. Some may view a style of rock music or heavy metal appropriate (so long as the lyrics are Christian in nature), yet others would consider this music totally alien to Christianity. Some judge music as Christian if it produces a more fervent religious life, or other good result in the listener — yet there are many things that may produce a "good result" and this is not really an adequate definition. Ultimately, we believe it is only through the words — the lyrics — and what they convey, that music can be deemed Christian, or not. Rather than "Christian music" it is in fact necessary to consider what are "Christian lyrics."

The lyrics of all music make some statement: they express the themes of contemporary life, or have a powerful impact upon culture, and people within it. Popular music expresses criticism, commendation, reflection, questioning and rebellion (whether for good or evil). The distinguishing aspect of the Christian lyric would be that it is biblically based, or in accord with Christian doctrine and theology, or that it proclaims the message of salvation (through faith in the death and resurrection of Christ), or glorifies God through the words. Now, the words of the music can also present some very different theological perspectives, and the "truth" of the lyric is integral to such music being acceptable in a particular context of worship. Christians would maintain that the "truth" of the words were important to God who seeks those who will worship in "spirit and in truth."

As well as expressing a culture the lyrics of songs also have power to influence thought and behaviour (as has been demonstrated by studies that have observed behavioural problems in those influenced by the "negative" message conveyed in abusive, anti-social and violent lyrics). The positive message within Christian lyrics also has power to influence that community, although we still maintain that the definitive aspect of it being "Christian" is in the "truth" of what is proclaimed, rather than in the effects it produces or other.

Biblical Instructions for Christian Music

There are a few other references to worship and singing in Christian Scriptures that are necessary to consider in order to obtain an understanding of the deep nature of Christian music — where the lyric is vital. We also see that the spiritual element cannot be ignored ["...the true worshipers will worship the Father in spirit and truth, for they are the kind of worshipers the Father seeks" (John 4:23, NIV)]. In Ephesians 5 and Colossians 3 Christian believers are given instructions of how to worship and use "spiritual" songs. Both passages suggest that singing is done "unto the Lord" that the Lord will be glorified with the heart directed to God a component of the singing. In I Corinthians we again see the spiritual component being advocated — using not only mind, but spirit.

The Corinthians reference is particularly interesting occurring as it does in the context of "tongues" or unintelligible charismatic utterances. The Apostle Paul writes about the meta-physical dimension of the spirit in Christian music when he writes: "For if I pray in a tongue, my spirit prays, but my mind is unfruitful. So what shall I do? I will pray with my spirit, but I will also pray with my mind; I will sing with my spirit, but I will also sing with my mind" (I. Corinthians 14:14 –15, NIV). Clearly the mind and spirit are to be involved in the singing, and what is proclaimed may be in a different "tongue" and not always even be intelligible to human ears!

In Ephesians 5 singing is an expression of the soul toward God, and the emphasis is on the proper attitude of the soul: "Speak to one another with psalms, hymns and spiritual songs. Sing and make music in your heart to the Lord, always giving thanks to God the Father for everything, in the name of our Lord Jesus Christ" (vrs. 19-20, NIV). The word *psallo* is used in the original Greek — and refers to making music in the heart of the believer who is singing (*ado*-ing) and celebrating the praises of God. Hymn actually means "a song of praise to God." Thus the heart directed to God is to be a component of the music.

In Colossians 3, the singing is an expression of doctrine in the soul expressed toward other people who benefit from it via teaching and admonishing: "Let the word of Christ dwell in you richly as you teach and admonish one another with all wisdom, and as you sing psalms, hymns and spiritual songs with gratitude in your hearts to God" (vrs.16, NIV). Again the heart directed to God is to be a component of the music.

Development of Christian Music

We can presume that the original Christian church that composed these Scriptures also followed them! The early church fathers also appear to have affirmed that the word (*logos*) held primacy over the music, unlike the mystery cults that believed in the power of musical incantations. Musicians were admonished to keep the words audible and to avoid excessive musical elaboration. Solo songs and unison chants were preferred features of musical worship. The texts for the songs were based upon Old Testament Scriptures (principally psalms) or drawn from Christian doctrine found in writings comprising the New Testament.

The Christian church of the first two centuries sought to avoid any mixing of pagan musical practices with their own religious experiences. Clement, for instance, banned all instruments from Christian worship due to their association with pagan ceremonies and the low reputation of instrumental musicians. He also forbade the singing of psalms and the reading of Scriptures in profane meetings so that Christians would not be confused with the "wandering minstrels, singers and tellers of tales of high adventure, who perform their art for a mouthful of bread" (http://www.piney.com/FathRecClemBIV.html).

Since then church music changed in several respects. In the 9th Century part-singing contained two melodic lines sung in fifths or fourths. Centuries later independent melodies were sung in counterpoint to the main vocal line. Then instruments were introduced, at first sparingly. One of the first instruments was the organ, used to reinforce the main melodic line, followed by the violin. By the 16th Century instrumental music was fully welcomed and a variety of instruments would often perform with or without soloists or choirs. Toward the end of the Middle Ages there again arose a demand for congregational singing, initially expressed in spiritual songs and carols. In England, the hymns of the congregations were limited almost entirely to Psalms prepared by Thomas Steinhold and John Hopkins from 1549 to 1562.

Evangelical hymnology began at the end of the 17th Century. Luther openly proclaimed his desire to use all available music, including the most obviously secular, for the worship of the church. The use of contrafacta, that is the setting of Christian text or poetry to secular music, was widespread. The common ingredient to all hymns of the Reformation churches was that all hymns were either actual Bible passages or paraphrases of Bible passages. John and Charles Wesley wrote what became some of the most popular hymns in the English language. In the 20th Century music further developed to include the more informal choruses, which are currently popular — choruses that are sometimes regarded as shallow (with respect to the "truth" of their lyrics) compared to more traditional hymns — and that either directly proclaim biblical passages, or contain comprehensive expressions of reformed theology.

Instrumental Worship?

Not only is the lyric vital in Christian music, but there are some who believe that Christian music should not consist of instruments at all. Historically, as we have seen, instrumental music and accompaniments in Christian worship is generally less than 1000 years old. The ancestors of the Christian religion (the Jews) had no instruments in their liturgy since an exile some 500 years BC, although they originally enjoyed the use of instruments in their worship, notably the "psalm;" to *"psallo"* a harp meant to pluck a string. Over time, to *"psallo"* a harp came to mean "to play a harp" and later it came to mean "to sing."

Many protestant theologians were strongly opposed to suggestions that instruments be brought into their churches for worship, including: John Wesley (founder of Methodism), "I have no objections to instruments of music in our chapels provided they are neither heard nor seen"; John Calvin (theologian behind much Baptist and Presbyterian doctrine), "Musical instruments, in celebrating the praises of God would be no more suitable than the burning of incense, the lighting up of lamps, the restoration of the other shadows of the Law"; and Martin Luther (founder of the Lutheran Church) who called instrumental music "an ensign of Baal" (http://www.worship.nu/prcedm/hist_instrument.html). Some churches, such as Greek Orthodox, continue to understand the Bible to prohibit musical instruments in its worship services.

The reasons for not wanting instrumental music are scripturally based. In the previously mentioned Ephesians passage, it has been argued that the Greek words suggest singing without instrumental accompaniment; in Latin this is *"a cappella"* — literally meaning "to sing in the manner of the church." They may also be a distraction. With instruments people tend to listen to the instrument rather than sing; they ignore the words of the song and come away mostly with an appreciation of pretty music. Without instruments people tend to sing better, pay attention to the words better, and generally get more internally from the singing. In summary, musical instruments may aid the time and accuracy of singing, but may even hinder the spiritual character of worship.

Defenders of instrumental music in Christian worship today are, of course, many. Their arguments include: (i) The biblical Scriptures do not specifically forbid it; (ii) Harps are mentioned as being used in the book of Revelation; (iii) Instruments are mentioned in the Old Testament; (iv) The meaning of the Greek word *"psallo"* found in the New Testament might allow instrumental music in Christian worship; (v) Does God really care about such details compared to sincerity? and (vi) Without instruments the church's music would just sound awful.

Instrumentation is a critical issue for many of our churches today. For instance, the *Digest of Regulations and Rubrics of Catholic Church Music* (Hayburn, 1961) written in 1961 states that, "The use of the piano is forbidden in church as also that of all more or less noisy instruments, such as drums of any kind, cymbals, bells, and so on." Similarly, electric guitars and saxophones bear the stigma of popular culture and may be avoided by some congregations. Whether instruments are or are not used within a worship context, the vital and distinguishing element of Christian "music" is the words — the lyrics, the message that is proclaimed.

Challenges of Lyric Recognition in Christian Music

This section considers some of the challenges that are presented in the context of music with lyrics. There are a number of complexities with recognising lyrics that mean it is not just a simple character recognition problem added to an OMR process for recognition of the notation symbols. The issues in page segmentation are non-trivial, and aligning lyrics with the music symbols (especially in the context of different musical parts) is also a challenge given the spreading of syllables, words, and phrases across the page (in a way that is not found within most text contexts). We summarise some of these challenges and present the scope of the problem that lyric recognition must address, providing some illustration of the scope of current recognition software.

Association of Lyrics to Various Vocal Parts

There are a number of complexities in music that contains lyrics, including the association of lyrics to various vocal parts — the basic issue being that different notes are assigned to the same word in different parts. Frequently there are four parts — soprano, alto, tenor and bass — and these voices may sing the same word but at different musical pitches (sometimes according to different rhythms). Associating lyrics to vocal parts is made easier if the parts are arranged on separate staves as illustrated in Figure 1, where there are three verses and four voices on separate staves. Clearly, each voice has a single staff and different music notes within that staff corresponding to the same lyric.

Figure 1: Part Arrangements on Separate Staves, "O Come, O Come, Emmanuel," Arranged by Stefan Karpiniec

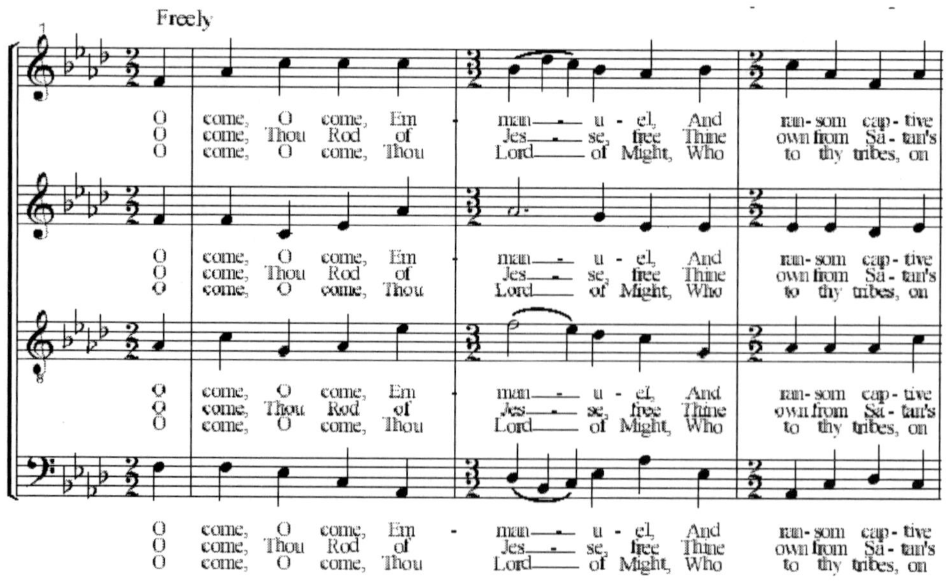

However, this information is often included together on one staff in four-part harmony (as illustrated in Figure 3) and isolating this information from one staff would be an even harder task, since it is necessary to disentangle the parts before matching them with lyrics.

The Spreading of Syllables, Words and Phrases Across the Page

Associated with the different voice in music is the spreading of syllables across notes. This frequently occurs in four-part harmonies, although it can be found in isolation. Figure 2 illustrates the spreading of syllables across notes. Multiple syllables are mapped to more than one note (e.g., "Fa-ther") or one syllable mapped to multiple notes (e.g., "I" and "too").

Figure 2: Syllable Arrangement Across Multiple Notes, "Father I place into your hands," Songs of Fellowship

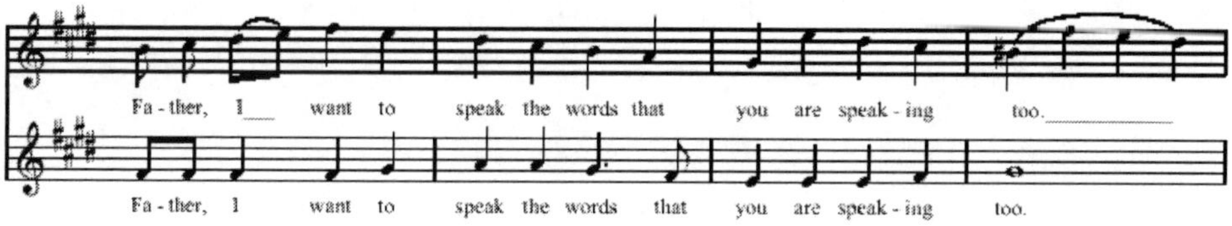

We can also see the splitting of words (e.g., "Father" and "speaking") in a way that would be most unusual in conventional character-recognition contexts.

The Use of Various Languages within the Lyrics

Another challenge in lyric recognition is the presence, not only of different fonts (e.g., italic and regular), but also of different languages! The music of Taize exemplifies the use of language variety within the lyrics where there may be several different (typically European) languages within one manuscript and it would be impossible to know in advance which languages might be expected. This is perhaps one of the most extreme cases where languages are mixed, as illustrated in Figure 3, and we have the complexities of different "symbols" to recognise from the different languages, including Greek. The same words are represented in various European languages.

Figure 3: Lyrics from Multiple Languages, "Bless the Lord, my Soul," Taize

Occasionally we may encounter the same lyrics in languages with two vastly different character sets, as Figure 4 illustrates with the mixture of Chinese and Latin script. Obviously, the text recognition would have to be prepared for whether there was a single script, or mixed, or embedded (as may be found when the lyrics genuinely call upon words from different languages — this can be found in many Catholic songs, especially with the use of Latin invocations).

Figure 4: Lyrics from Chinese and Latin Scripts, "How I love you, O Lord," LambMusic

The Presence of Other Markings/Distant Verse Text

One important task is to separate, or segment, those text markings that are lyrics from those that are performance directives or other. Other textual-based markings may include, among other things, voice annotations (such as solo/choir), initial performance directives (such as tempo and mood), guitar chords (either annotated with a single letter or with a chord diagram — possibly showing alternatives depending whether the "capo" is used), bar numbering, and title/composer information.

Figure 5: Examples of Page-Segmentation Problems

(a) Choir directives/bar numbers/initial directives

(b) Guitar chords

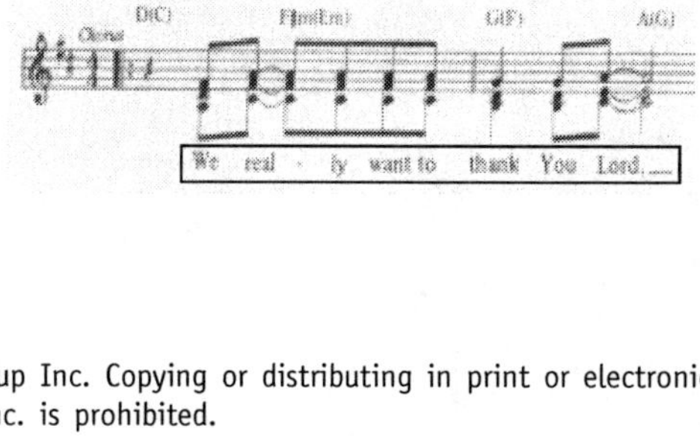

(c) Lyrics above and below (No 560)

(d) Lyrics and verse directions (No 558)

(e) Distance verse text

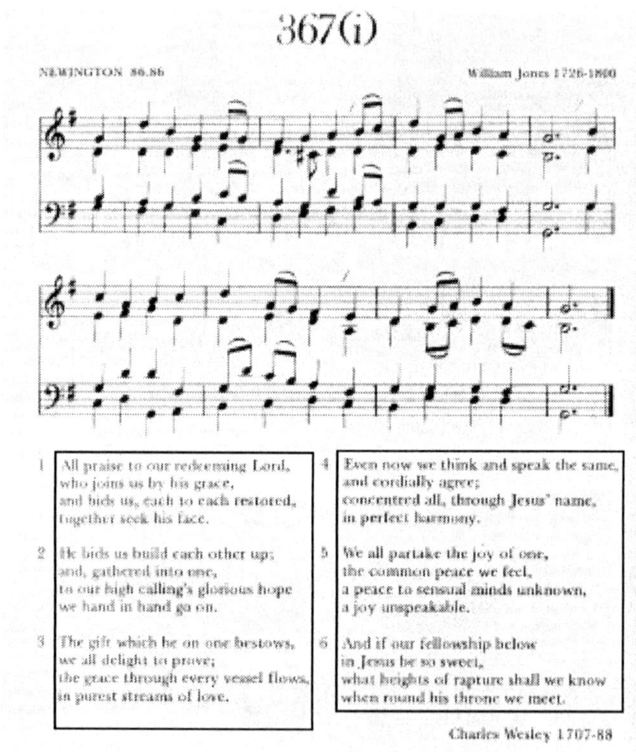

Figure 5 illustrates some typical problems of separating those markings that are lyrics from those that are performance directives or other markings. The boxed areas indicated the text that should be considered lyrics. The figure illustrates (a) choir directives/bar numbers/initial directives, (b) guitar chords, (c) lyrics (above and below) from title information, (d) lyrics from other directives, and (e) lyrics removed form the music. The hymns of church music particularly exemplify this segmentation problem where lyrics are removed from the music line entirely, but still need to be associated with the music while accounting for the rhythm and possible repetition of the first verse both within the staff and within the removed text block.

Aligning Words with Other Symbols on the Page

Another task that is crucial for lyric recognition is the task of aligning words or characters with other symbols on the page. There are two aspects to this task. The first step involves aligning the lyrics with the notes. The lyrics may be directly beneath (or above) or contain syllables that stretch across the page (as illustrated in Figure 2). There may also be different parts in the music (as illustrated in Figure 1 or 3) with varying notes that have to be matched to the lyrics — or even different musical arrangements for different verses, as illustrated in Figure 6 where the rhythm is dependant upon a particular verse, but alignment has to be made between the words/syllables and the note in a way that is quite unique to lyric recognition.

Figure 6: Examples of Alignment Between Verses (No 551)

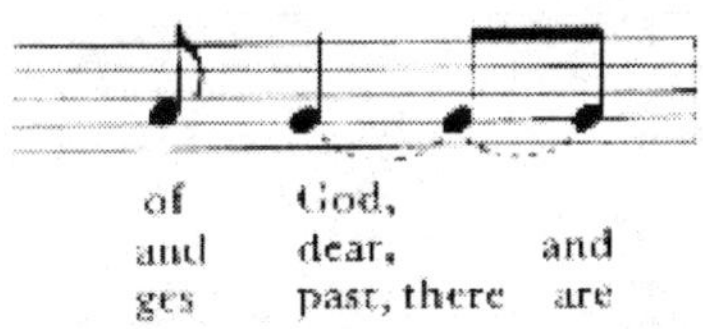

Associated with this task is the task of aligning distant verse text (as illustrated in Figure 5e) with music notation. Performing the task successfully requires not only recognising the characters within the words, but also recognising the syllables and how these might be mapped to the rhythm of the music. For a given set of lyrics there may be many different rhythms that fit the syllables within the lyrics — indeed this is what makes certain hymn lyrics interchangeable with a variety of tunes. The tunes are classified according to a scheme that marks the syllables on each line. For example, 88.88 indicates the music lyrics have eight syllables per line as does the following verse:

Creator of the earth and skies
To whom all truth and power belong
Grant us your truth to make us wise
Grant us your power to make us strong.

The music that fits this verse would also fit the verse of a totally different hymn that similarly had the same number of syllables per line:

Give to our God immortal praise,
mercy and truth are all his ways:
wonders of grace to God belong,
repeat his mercies in your song.

Handwritten Music

Naturally there are a few examples of handwritten music that also include lyrics, or (less commonly) handwritten lyrics inserted to typeset music, as illustrated in Figure 7.

Figure 7: Examples of Handwritten Lyrics

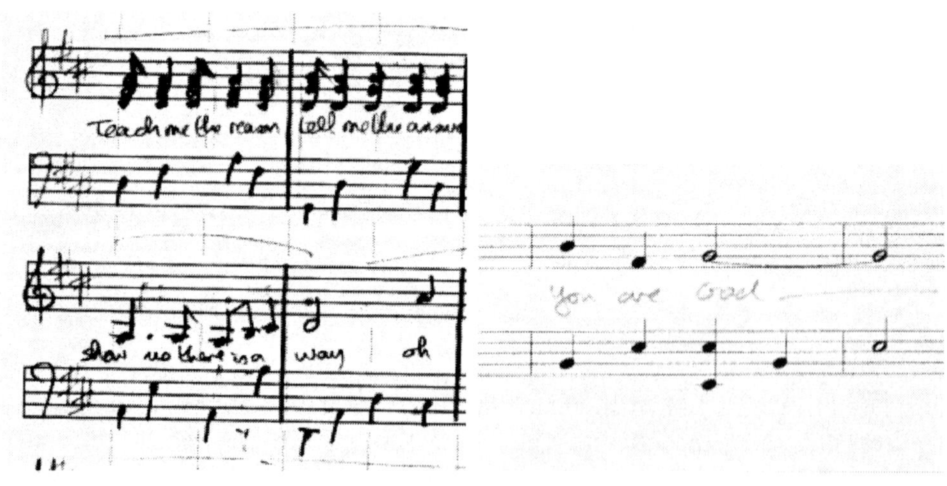

Unconstrained handwriting recognition is another challenge that could potentially be faced within lyric recognition. This is especially true within archived musical material such that composed before printing and typesetting were available.

Examples of Lyric Recognition in Current OMR Software

The chapter on evaluation elsewhere in this volume illustrates the scope of music-scanning software and the general issue of evaluation with music recognition. Here we focus especially on the recognition of lyrics and notice some of the problems that exist with an example taken from Rossini's "Cinderella in Salerno" using Smartscore to recognise the music. There have occasionally been some errors, but in general the recognition is reasonable, although this is hard to quantify.

One difficulty, even with a good recognition of the original score, is the subsequent re-aligning of the notes and lyric text. Figure 8a illustrates the original scanned image and 8b the interpretation.

Most of the lyrics have actually been identified, but they are not re-aligned with the correct notes with the precision of the original typesetting. For example, the end of the first line contains the phrase "Oh how you ..." and this is correctly recognised, but the alignment between note and lyric is not reinstated in the interpreted recognised image. However, the software has recognised hyphenated words and correctly aligned the phrase "startled me" with the notes on the next line. The title text has generally been recognised and typeset in an approximately similar position, although there is no way of telling how this has been "interpreted"; while the title is displayed separate

Figure 8a: Original Image

Figure 8b: Interpreted Recognised Image

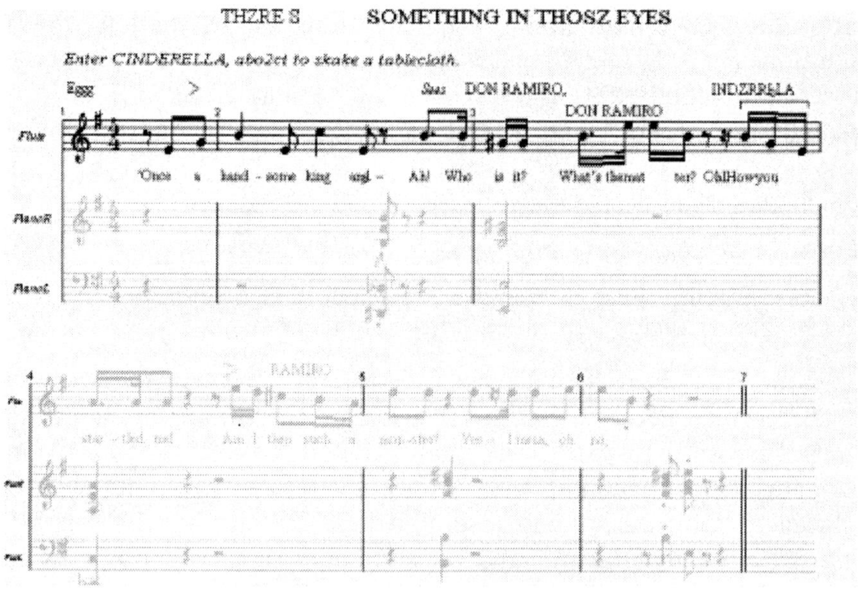

from the directives for actors, there is no indication of whether this is really "understood" as a title, as opposed to a directive. Similarly, identifying whether the part indications for "Don Ramiro" and "Cinderella" really have been understood, indicating lyrics for separate people, cannot be identified.

Figures 9a and 9b illustrate another example from Lloyd Webber's "Joseph's Amazing Techni-colour Dream Coat." They show the original image (Figure 9a) and its interpretation (Figure 9b), illustrating the same kind of alignment problems with the phrase "Won't you tell poor old," as well as a new type of confusion between the performance directive "very slow" and the lyrics, where it is impossible to tell from the output whether a correct interpretation has been made or not.

Evaluation is always going to be an issue whenever the results are visually inspected as opposed to being formally verified by some means. Of course formal verification is really only possible when the scanned image is translated into a logical representation language and this compared with some "truth representation" of the original music. As we shall see, a standard logical representation language for music is not really in existence and one that is suitable for representing information about lyrics is even harder to come by.

Figure 9a: Original Image

Figure 9b: Interpreted Recognised Image

Toward a Solution for Lyric Recognition

We have catalogued a number of problems that lyric recognition must solve and have demonstrated some of the capabilities of a typical commercial music OMR software package (Smartscore) in recognising music with lyrics. Clearly, the lyric-recognition problem has been partially solved, but we identify various requirements that are still outstanding and unaddressed in the solutions considered. These include (i) the page segmentation and character recognition capabilities, as well as (ii) the representation language suitable of capturing music with lyrics. This section outlines some approaches that may be taken to both page segmentation/character recognition and requirements of the representation language for music with lyrics.

Page Segmentation

Page segmentation divides a scanned document into appropriate regions. Identifying those areas of the page that are to be understood as text and those that are other is the natural first stage in lyric recognition. Layout analysis may be (a) structural — requiring isolation of structural units: columns, paragraphs, lines; or (b) functional — typically domain dependent and based upon syntactic criteria to which the page adheres. Additionally, approaches can be divided into top-down and bottom-up methods.

The bottom-up (data driven) techniques progressively refine the data by layered grouping of operations. It typically involves the grouping of pixels as connected components that are merged into small blocks based on local evidence and then merged into successively larger blocks. This approach is more time consuming compared to the top-down approach, but, on the other hand, it is useful for the cases where a priori knowledge about document nature is lacking. Typical bottom-up algorithms include: the Docstrum algorithm (Gorman), the Voronoi diagram-based algorithm (Kise), the run-length smearing algorithm (Wahl, Wong and Casey), the segmentation algorithm (Jain and Yu) and the text-string separation algorithm (Fletcher and Kasturi).

The top-down (goal-driven) approaches split a document into major blocks, which are further split into sub-blocks until the desired result is achieved. These methods use a prior knowledge about processed documents. These methods are very effective for processing pages with a specific format, for instance diverse types of forms. The third class of methods combines both mentioned approaches. Top-down approaches include the X-Y cut (Nagy) and the shape-directed covers-based algorithm (Baird).

Mao and Kanungo note that there is a lack of comparative evaluation — empirical or theoretical — for page-recognition algorithms (2001). They investigate five page-segmentation algorithms. It is found that the performance indices (average textline accuracy) of the Voronoi, Docstrum, and Caere segmentation algorithms are not significantly different from each other, but they are significantly better than that of ScanSoft's segmentation algorithm, which, in turn, is significantly better than that of the X-Y cut.

Printed Character Recognition

Mori, Suen and Yamamoto provide a historical review of OCR research (1992). There have been a variety of approaches to recognising characters. Two essential components in a character-recognition algorithm are the feature extractor and the classifier. Feature analysis determines the descriptors, or feature set, used to describe all characters. Given a character image, the feature extractor derives the features that the character possesses. The derived features are then used as input to the character classifier.

Template matching, or matrix matching, is one of the most common classification methods. In template matching, individual image pixels are used as features. Classification is performed by comparing an input character image with a set of templates (or prototypes) from each character class. Each comparison results in a similarity measure between the input character and the template. One measure increases the amount of similarity when a pixel in the observed character is identical to the same pixel in the template image. If the pixels differ, the measure of similarity may be decreased. After all templates have been compared with the observed character image, the character's identity is assigned as the identity of the most similar template.

Structural classification methods utilize structural features and decision rules to classify characters. Structural features may be defined in terms of character strokes, character holes, or other character attributes such as concavities. For instance, the letter P may be described as a vertical stroke with a hole attached on the upper-right side. For a character image input, the structural features are extracted and a rule-based system is applied to classify the character. Many character recognisers are based on mathematical formalisms that minimize a measure of misclassification. These recognisers may use pixel-based features or structural features.

Handwritten Character Recognition

The issues and methods of recognising handwritten characters are similar to the issues for recognising printed characters, except the task is harder due to the greater variation that may be found between individuals' writing. Even with the same person there is not guaranteed consistency, at least within general writing (although frequently written signatures designed for identification purposes contain a stronger signal that enables recognition and identification). A variety of methods have been designed to deal with general unconstrained handwriting and the most successful involve a classifier that learns, using writing samples from a particular person, and then goes on and generalises to recognise new unseen writing from the same person. Plamondon and Srihari (2000) give a comprehensive review of off-line (and also on-line) handwriting.

There are two main approaches to recognition. A global approach entails the recognition of the whole word by the use of identifying features. The segmentation approach requires that the word be first segmented into letters. The letters are then recognised individually and can be used to match up against particular words. With the segmentation approach, the recognition performance of handwriting depends crucially upon the segmentation process. Generally strategies for cursive word recognition can be roughly subdivided into two different categories: segmentation-explicit and segmentation-implicit approaches. Many researchers have focused on identifying gaps using only geometric distances between connected components. Because recognition is not involved during the segmentation process, it is difficult to mine the word gaps from a line of text image. It is assumed that gaps between words are bigger than the gaps between characters; however, in handwriting, exceptions are commonplace.

Suen et al. (1993) mention that the key to high recognition rates is feature extraction. However, this in itself is a very difficult problem, which has led researchers to use more complex methods for preprocessing, feature extraction and classification. Challenges faced for preprocessing deal with the choice of whether to convert raw handwriting into a more efficient form, i.e., whether to binarise the handwriting or keep it in grey-scale form. Other researchers are disputing whether the handwriting should be thinned or should remain the way it is to preserve features. Feature extraction poses the problem of choosing the right features to extract and the right technique to perform the task.

The CEDAR group has developed the PENMAN system for reading unconstrained handwritten text-page images. Favada and Srihari (1992) have developed an intelligent word-segmentation algorithm. The algorithm incorporates cues that humans use and does not rely on using only the simple one-dimensional distance information. There are five functional sub-modules in the system: (i) pre-processing of images, (ii) line separation, (iii) word segmentation, (iv)word recognition, and (v) post-processing.

Misclassification

Character misclassifications stem from two main sources: poor quality character images and poor discriminatory ability. Poor document quality, image scanning, and pre-processing can all degrade performance by yielding poor quality characters. On the other hand, the character recognition method may not have been trained for a proper response on the character causing the error. This type of error source is difficult to overcome because the recognition method may have limitations and all possible character images can not possibly be considered in training the classifier. Recognition rates for machine-printed characters can reach over 99%, but handwritten character recognition rates are typically lower because every person writes differently. This random nature often manifests itself by resulting in misclassifications.

Multi-Lingual Lyrics

Within an area of the page designated as text, there is the issue that more than one language may be present. Hochberg, Cannon, Kelly and White (1997) have explored the analysis of multi-lingual documents using script-identification vectors. A script-identification vector is calculated for each connected component in a document. The vector expresses the closest distance between the component and templates developed for each of thirteen scripts, including Arabic, Chinese, Cyrillic, and Roman. They calculate the first three principal components and map these components to red, green, and blue to visualize the information contained in the script vectors. Results are best for documents containing highly dissimilar scripts such as Roman and Japanese. Documents containing similar scripts, such as Roman and Cyrillic, will require further investigation.

Integrating Semantics

In many domains semantic information is integrated with recognition in order to aid syntactic interpretation. For example, recognisers of handwritten postcodes may be armed with semantic knowledge of permissible postcodes (such as where letters and numerals should occur). This knowledge can be used to disambiguate written symbols. Away from the pure image processing aspect of recognition, we find a higher level of recognition that can also aid interpretation. For example, a natural language understanding system may contain knowledge of the likely props that are found in a restaurant and this knowledge may help produce the sentence structure and, hence, meaning of sentences about events in restaurants.

In a similar way domain semantics within music may assist the task of lyric recognition in Christian music. There are a variety of levels at which this might occur in either specific or general terms at the image processing level. At a specific level, the knowledge envisioned is information relevant to a particular piece of music, or particular typesetting choice from a given publisher. In general terms the knowledge would be more widely applicable including general facts about valid music notation, or syllable information about words.

In specific terms, page-layout information may guide image processing with information about the page layout of the music — for example, specifying whether verses are above/below/removed from the stave, the presence and location of guitar chord markings, and other. Naturally, such information is either specific to a piece of music or music from a given typeset source (e.g., book or publisher). For interpretation of other music, information about the expected performer names (e.g., characters in a musical) or parts (e.g., choir, solo1, women) may assist in locating directives specific to certain performers, and subsequently associating lyrics and music with that musical part.

Knowledge about permissible numbers of notes in bars given a time signature, or pitches given accidentals and key signatures, may also be able to help not only with the recognition of music notation, but also with assigning lyrics to the (correctly identified) notes. Words of more than one syllable may need to be spread over bar lines or condensed onto one note depending upon the final form of the line/piece. Knowledge of word-syllable information would be invaluable in determining how to spread out or condense the words according to rhythm. General knowledge such as a list of likely performance directives (especially those that are textual and occur as markups in other languages such as Italian or French) would also help identify "stray" text as either lyric or part of the performance markings.

Review of Logical Representation Language for Lyrics

Finally we consider the outstanding difficulty in lyric recognition of having a suitable logical representation language that captures the various associations between music and lyric. A representation language is needed that is capable of isolating the performance directives from lyrics; of representing different parts, or voices, within the music that may have the same lyric but different pitched notes (and even notes of different rhythm); as well as indicating other directives, such as the singer for a particular section.

Logical representation languages have been reviewed elsewhere in this volume. Here we simply note that there are various levels of representation language extending from the basic midi (musical instrument digital interface) format, through the text, to XML-based. Several initiatives have addressed the need for a standardized markup-based music notation, although no standard has been chosen. In the muddle of representation languages that exist, identifying those that adequately represent lyrics and music parts is even more of a challenge. While languages do exist that tag words to music notes, there is no comprehensive definition of the scope of what they can represent in terms of voices, parts or other. Here we consider a few languages that have been used to express lyrics and then highlight the requirements of a language that can represent the association between lyrics and music notation.

MuseData is a text-based logical description language (Hewlett, 1987) described in Selfridge-Field (1997). It is optimized for data entry and storage, not for user applications. Each MuseData file represents the encoding of one musical part from a movement of a composition. A file has a set of time-ordered, variable-length ASCII records and the meaning of many elements are inferred from column placement, assuming an 80-column row. Naturally, the order of the records is essential to the representation. The fragment of a Telemann aria in Figure 10 illustrates the language and MuseData handling lyrics associated with notes.

Figure 10: Illustration of MuseData Description Language

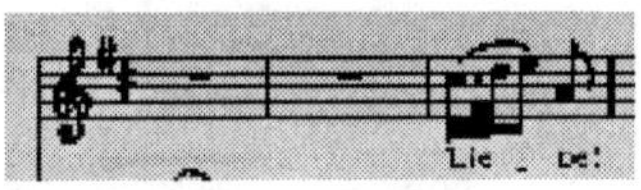


```
measure 13
rest 12
measure 14
rest 12
measure 15
C#5   3     s.   d [[   (        Lie-
D5    1     t    d =]\           -
E5    4     e    d ]    )        -
A4    4     e    u               be!
```

It is not clear how multiple lyrics could be associated with a single musical note. If the parts represented four-part harmony it is likely that MuseData would require a separate file for each part of the composition. If, however, the lyrics represented different verses for the same part, then the verses may have to be "expanded" out and the description of music repeated with the new lyrics for other verses.

MusicXML (Caston, Good & Roland, 2001) is an XML-based logical description language. An example of a fragment from Schumann's Op. 35 setting of Kerner's "Frage," can be found at http://www.musicxml.org/xml/frage.html. As with other HTML languages there are a number of tags (e.g., <note) and end tags (e.g., </note>) that introduce and end new conceptual items, such as part, key or time. Figure 11 illustrates the introduction of the lyric for the first note. The note fragment in turn belongs to a measure, a part, and a score-wise part. Basically, if a concept can be represented hierarchically, it can be represented in XML. With MusicXML, while it is possible to associate syllable information with the notes, it is not clear how phonemes could be included. Music Markup Language (MML) addresses this requirement.

Figure 11: Illustration of MusicXML Description Language

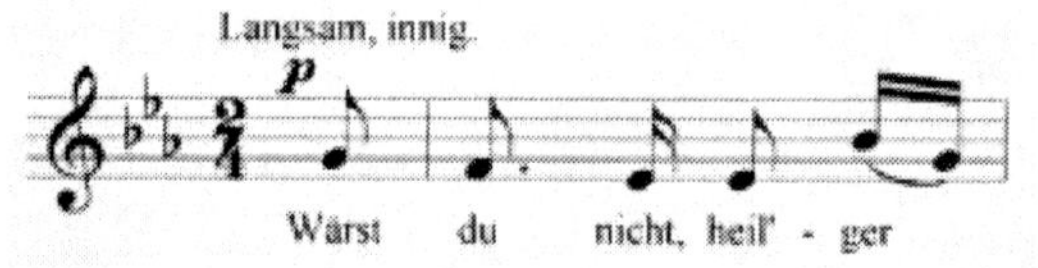


```
<note>
      <pitch>
        <step>G</step>
        <octave>4</octave>
      </pitch>
      <duration>2</duration>
      <type>eighth</type>
      <stem>up</stem>
      <notations>
        <dynamics>
          <p/>
        </dynamics>
      </notations>
      <lyric>
        <syllabic>single</syllabic>
        <text>Wärst</text>
      </lyric>
</note>
```

MML, developed by Steyn (2000), also makes it possible to relate sound events through the use of XML markup. MML was specifically designed for simplicity and has a number of modules responsible for different aspects of the music, such as time, notation, lyrics, performance and midi. An application only uses those modules it needs. The "squash" and "stretch" tags of MML are currently being implemented and without these it is not possible to bind a single syllable to multiple notes. The "div" and "match" tags also make it possible to bind different lyrics to the same music. Again the underlying approach is an XML one, with an extendible language that can integrate text data within the wider context of how the music is performed, as well as the actual music pitch/ rhythm that needs to be performed.

Requirements of a Logical Representation Language for Lyric and Music Notation

There is already a proliferation of logical representation languages for music, even those that are capable of representing the lyrics associated with the music. The most successful ones reviewed are XML-based. Such a language is capable of high-level expression of musical content, it is extendible, and it separates the markup (the tags that describe the text they encapsulate) from the actual data. A Document Type Definition (DTD) can be used to syntactically parse a representation of music, since it defines, among other things, the tags that can be used and where they can occur, the attributes within each tag, and how all the tags fit together — if syntactically correct music was required.

The representation language for music notation with lyrics should basically capture the meaning of the piece of music. The language should be capable of capturing the intrinsic meaning of the music notations, including the notes, the rhythm and the performance directives — and should also include the association of lyrics with parts. From such a language we would like to (a) be able to produce various typesetting variations for the music according to the vocal parts within it, (b) isolate note and syllable information such that a singing synthesiser could be able to compute the appropriate phonemes to generate for each note and (c) correctly represent the logical relationship between the music notation and text annotations, such that lyric text was represented as such and all other markings interpreted appropriately (for example, where part indications are given for different performers above a staffline, simply treating these as a textual additions above a staff does not add to the meaning that this has — there is no way of telling whether it is a performance directive, guitar chord, performance indication or other).

When synthesised singing is a goal, one important issue would be how the correct phonemes could be produced for given syllables and matched to the right note in pitch and time. While the basic word-syllable information and note would be necessary to include, the language would have to represent more than just a syllable; in fact, it would have to identify the correct phoneme in order that the right sound was produced.

Conclusion

This chapter has considered lyric recognition — an often-omitted aspect of OMR. It has considered lyrics particularly in the context of Christian music, where the lyric is integral to the genre and cannot be ignored. While lyrics are found within other music types they are so integral to Christian music that they should be considered as much part of the musical manuscript as are the notation symbols. Hence, there is a serious need to incorporate adequate lyric recognition into OMR procedures — lyric recognition that not only identifies the characters, but also their correct association with notes and melodic parts given the two-dimensional information implicitly present upon the manuscript page.

A summary of some of the phenomena that may be found when lyrics are present with music was made — contributing a greater understanding to the range of problems that must be tackled. Some of these include the hyphenation that may be found within words, the presence of several lyric lines for one melodic line, or several "musical parts." All this is complicated by such an unconstrained page layout where there may be other character symbols that could easily be confused with lyrics. Typical commercial OMR software was applied to some of the more challenging lyric recognition tasks and the results illustrate that there is a long way to go before a satisfactory integration (suitable for synthesis of song) is achieved for word and music.

Finally, an approach to a solution for lyric recognition within OMR was made, identifying the representation language as particularly important — once low level procedures for page-segmentation and character/word recognition have isolated symbols from the manuscript. An XML-based language is a promising format in which to capture the lyric and music information. Ideally it would also capture the phoneme information relevant to a speech synthesiser, such that the "sung word" could be generated at the appropriate pitch and rhythm.

References

Caston, G., Good, M. & Roland, P. (2001). Extensible markup language (XML) for music applications: An introduction. In W.B. Hewlett & E. Selfridge-Field (Eds.), *The Virtual Score: Representation, Retrieval, Restoration* (pp. 95-102). Cambridge, MA: MIT Press.

Favada, J. T. & Srihari, S. N. (1992). Off-line recognition of handwritten cursive words. *Proceedings of the SPIE Symposium on Electronic Imaging Science and Technology*. San Jose, CA.

Hayburn, R.F. (1961). *Digest of Regulations and Rubrics of Catholic Church Music (4th rev.)*.

Hewlett, W. B. (1987). The representation of musical information in machine-readable format. Directory of Computer Assisted Research in Musicology, 3, 1-22.

Hochberg, J., Cannon, M., Kelly, P. & White, J. (1997). Page segmentation using script identification vectors: A first look. In *Proceedings of the 1997 Symposium on Document Image Understanding Technology* (pp. 258-264). College Park, MD: University of Maryland Institute for Advanced Computer Studies.

Holy Bible, New International Version (NIV). (1991). Grand Rapids, MI: Zondervan Publishing House.

Mao, S. & Kanungo, T. (2001, March). Empirical performance evaluation methodology and its application to page segmentation algorithms. *IEEE Transactions on Pattern Analysis and Machine Intelligence*, 23(3), 242-256.

Mori S., Suen, C.Y. & Yamamoto, K. (1992). Historical review of OCR research and development. In O'Gorman, L. & Kasturi, R. (Eds.), *Document Image Analysis Systems – Guest Editors' Introduction to the Special Issue,* (pp. 244-273). IEEE Computer, 25(7), 5-8.

Murray, L.R. (1999). DECtalk – Some fun things we've done with it! Retrieved April 17, 2003 http://www.computing.dundee.ac.uk/staff/irmurray/dectalkf.asp.

Plamondon, R. & Srihari, S.N. (2000, January). On-line and off-line handwriting recognition: A comprehensive survey. *IEEE Transactions on Pattern Analysis and Machine Intelligence*, 22(1), 63-84.

Selfridge-Field, E. (ed.). (1997). *Beyond MIDI: The Handbook of Musical Codes*. Cambridge, MA: MIT Press. Retrieved April 17, 2003 from http://www.ccarh.org/publications/.

Steyn. (2000). Music Markup Language. Retrieved April 17, 2003 from http://is.up.ac.za/mml.

Suen, C.Y. et al. (1993). Building a new generation of handwriting recognition systems. *Pattern Recognition Letters*, 14, 303-315.

Section 4: Music Description and its Applications

Chapter 8

Towards Constructing Emotional Landscapes with Music

Dave Billinge
University of Portsmouth, United Kingdom

Tom Addis
University of Portsmouth, United Kingdom and
University of Bath, United Kingdom

Abstract

This chapter describes how the authors arrived at a new paradigm for human-computer interaction that they call tropic mediation. They describe the origins of the research in a wish to provide a concert planner with an expert system.

Some consideration is given to how music might have arisen within human culture and, in particular, why it presents unique problems of verbal description. An initial investigation into a discrete, stable lexicon of musical effect is summarised and the authors explain how and why they reached their current work on a computable model of word connotation rather than reference. It is concluded that machines, in order to communicate with people, will need to work with a model of emotional implication to approach the "human" sense of words.

> I will now, ladies and gentlemen, give you my celebrated "analysis" of Hamlet's soliloquy on suicide . . .
>
> "Shakespeare,[1] dispensing with the customary exordium, announces his subject at once in the infinitive, in which mood it is presently repeated after a short connecting passage in which, brief as it is, we recognize the alternative and negative forms on which so much of the significance of repetition depends. Here we reach a colon; and a pointed pository phrase, in which the accent falls decisively on the relative pronoun, brings us to the first full stop."
>
> I break off here, because, to confess the truth, my grammar is giving out. But I want to know whether it is just that a literary critic should be forbidden to make his living in this way on pain of being interviewed by two doctors and a magistrate, and haled off to Bedlam forthwith; while the more a music critic does it, the deeper the veneration he inspires.
>
> George Bernard Shaw (Form and Design in Music. The World, 31 May 1893)

Introduction

In the context of a book about the visual representation of music, a chapter on language may seem out of place. This is far from the case. Our work on the vocabulary of musical effect is focused primarily on the written word and that is as much a notation as is the written score. Most audiences, and not a few musicians, are not score readers and their primary mode of communication is their written, and spoken, natural language. The TV advertising director of a wholemeal bread manufacturer e-mails his researcher not for "a passage in Dorian mode scored for oboe and strings," but "a passage redolent of rural life in a time of peace and plenty." This is the user's "visual perception of music;"

no other communication mode is available to the non-technical musician. We need to understand that description almost as much as we need (for quite other purposes) the musical score. The words may also connote visual images. These too need to be understood; these too are visual perceptions of music. Just as other chapters consider the difficulty of representing the musical source code: the score, we consider the difficulty of representing its effect. Music has its audience, its users, as well as its practitioners. They both communicate by notation and all such communications are of interest to the researcher.

Before proceeding to the detailed account of our work it is worth noting also that the need for this written representation of musical effect goes beyond the concerts planner with whom the journey begins below. Acousticians need a vocabulary to describe acoustic spaces; those charged with selecting music for advertising, or for film accompaniment, would benefit from stable written descriptions in their databases; even those utilising music for therapeutic work need categorical descriptions of musical effect.

This paper tells the story of our journey from what one might call the computer science paradigm to another, very different paradigm. At the core of computer science there is the assumption that referential semantics is a given. This takes the view that the world consists of immutable objects that can be referenced from within a computer program[2]. This is seen in the world of databases where items are categorised according to attributes that have names. These names link the internal representation with the external objects. This gives these internal signs an external meaning (Addis & Addis, 2001). We believed, at the beginning of our research, that the key to making a decision support system for classical concert planning was to identify the words that described the music. It was assumed that the words would identify or name some real concept. These words would be put into our system and then, with the application of a few basic rules of juxtaposition, the system could produce concert programmes. We fell at the first fence, for the words turned out not to function as required. They had little, if any, referential power. What follows describes how and why we reached our present position where our search is for a computable model of how words connote rather than refer. We conclude that our machines, in order to communicate with people, will need to work with a model of emotions rather than objects in order to approach the "human" sense of words.

Billinge, one of the authors, has spent 40 years of his life listening to, reading, writing and talking about classical music. Many hours of those 40 years have also involved listening to others talk, formally and informally, about the subject. It is clear that something is being communicated between people and it was hoped that the words they used would be sufficient to correlate with the messages being passed. These messages are about the experiences people have while auditioning musical compositions. Any musical composition, whether it is *Aida*, *Wozzeck*, a Brahms Symphony, or the *Mass in B minor*, takes us on a journey. Our impression is that at the end of a performance, one has arrived at a different location within some kind of "emotional landscape." Just as a text-based composition like an opera or an oratorio takes a listener on such a journey, a well-structured concert programme should take account of differing landscapes and provide the audience with an experience that they will wish to talk about. The performing musicians have created this landscape from a visual symbolic code called a score. The audience, the writer of programme booklets, and the journalist-reviewer then utilise their symbolic lexicon, their natural language, in an attempt to preview or review something of the journey. The musician's code is guaranteed to make music, the analyst-critic's writings, as George Bernard Shaw notes above, are in danger of missing the effectual point entirely, and the reviewer's writings and audience's talk seem to be overburdened with an excess of inconsequent description. Why should this be? What purpose do such descriptions serve? This is what we want to understand.

Concert Planning by Machine

The Original Thesis

The language used by art lovers to describe their experience of artistic objects was assumed to communicate facts about that experience which could be uncovered by close analysis of their discourse. If evidence could be found that we can unambiguously communicate our artistic judgments and experiences to others and thus by implication explain the rules we are following in reaching our judgements, then it would become theoretically possible to build an "artistic decision support system." Once identified, this language could be used in future attempts to apply machine intelligence to artistic decisions such as, "Shall we programme Bax along with Schnittke in this concert?", "Is it appropriate to use this Mozart aria to advertise our credit card?", or indeed, "Can we hang this Manet next to this Bacon?" Currently such a system would only be able to act on the technical or factual issues such as the words being sung, the length or the size, and would thus fail to emulate artistic decisions made by people. These would appear to have aesthetic and emotional roots seeming to be derived from some non-factual data.

Human artistic judgements are generally expressed verbally, and if a machine were to be built to handle such, it would have to handle the language. As Wittgenstein might have said, "it would be able to play our language game."

It was necessary, therefore, to discover evidence that people actually do communicate their musical experience using verbal descriptions. It was not necessarily an attempt to explain the meaning of individual descriptions, but only to show that these communicate as a class of statements. This clarification should be extensible to all artistic descriptions even though they may differ in detail. If there were to be a successful application of machine intelligence to the handling of artistic decision-making, as there has been, for example, to medical decision-making (e.g., Buchanan & Shortliffe, 1984), then the machine must be given a clear set of rules about the use of this language. It is the authors' expectation that this mode of expression is different from the mode used in medical, and thus scientific and technological, discourse. Previous research[3] has hinted at this, but no attempt has been made, so far as the authors are aware, to place users in an experimental environment such that their language usage could be inspected closely.

The Questions

There is a long history of non-technical description of music, amusingly (and negatively) exemplified by Slonimsky (1953) which must always have played some role in telling a somewhat smaller public than today's what had transpired at the concert the night before and might have encouraged attendance at further events in a series. It is not the current purpose to analyse distant cultural milieu like the 18th and 19th centuries, but it is tempting to think that the marketing men had their own agenda then as now. What is different in our day is that musical performance per se has moved closer to centre stage[4] as the subject for critical discourse because recording technology has allowed the audience to easily compare performances.

There are three questions to be answered.

1. *The general:* can artistic objects be described formally in terms that will communicate the experience of a particular object to both the knowledgeable art-lover and the professionals of that art? In other words, is the language of musical effect stable?
2. *The particular:* can the compositions of classical music be described in ways that both the experienced audience and the concert-planner will accept? Neither the structural categories of classical music such as symphony and concerto, nor the technical language of harmony and rhythm convey what the music is like to listen to.

3. *A meta-question:* what was and is the role of this musical language?

The Beginning of the Research

Some years ago Billinge published an article in the magazine Classical Music (1992) about the potential uses of Information Technology (IT) in concerts management. In the course of that article and its follow up (Billinge, 1996a, 1996b) he considered how a database of musical information might help a concerts planner to plan more imaginative, less predictable, programmes. The suggestion was that the average concert-planner has a restricted subset of the repertoire in his mind. When faced with a gap in a programme he is quite likely to think of the same gap filler he thought of before. Thus we get yet another performance of Wagner's 17-minute *Siegfried Idyll* instead of something equally feasible by Martinu or Spohr.

With this purpose in mind, considerations turned to more fundamental questions about the nature of musical discourse. The reason being that the imaginary concert-planner, if he were to use his database effectively, must have some accepted means of categorising and describing the musical experience with which he deals. If he seeks something "romantic" or "powerful" then his decision support system must be able to classify music as romantic or powerful. Clearly someone must have imposed the classification to begin with.

So we arrived at this question: can we find agreement not only between concert-planners, but also concert goers, critics, recording company executives, on what our common musical discourse actually denotes? For example, what are we referring to when we talk of music as good, beautiful, romantic, exciting or fascinating, and, vitally, *can we agree on the words we use?*

A very similar problem would exist in categorising any "art" object for whatever reason. A film producer or a marketing executive seeking appropriate music may require similar solutions to the concerts director of a symphony orchestra. The director of an art gallery and a producer of multimedia software may also have parallel needs.

A Futuristic Scenario

The general manager of a symphony orchestra plans the season himself[5]. He knows how many concerts he wants and may know at least a few of the works that are to be performed and those that have been demanded by soloists or conductors. He instructs his Artistic Decision Support System to provide suggestions for so many concerts with a maximum performance time of one hundred minutes and within the orchestral strength he has at his disposal. Matters such as the calculation of costs for score extras, the restrictions of platform size at certain venues etc. are technically trivial and are automatically taken into consideration.

The creative input from the concerts planner is an overall programme design. He has a concert booked for Exonbury Town Hall. The audience in Exonbury is fairly conservative but has a significant number of people from the university nearby whom he knows like to be challenged. So his instruction to the system, including common descriptive vocabulary (italicised) is:

First half:
short gentle and tuneful piece
piano concerto *lyrical and passionate*
short piano concerto *demanding and spiky*

Second half:
warm and romantic symphony

This particular "emotional landscape" starts by easing the audience into listening, presenting increasing challenges, then finally allowing them to relax with a familiar genre so as to go home happy. Over the next few minutes while the manager gets on with other work the computer system produces a short list of programme items, with alternatives:

First half:
short gentle and tuneful piece
Delius: La Calinda or Gluck: Dance of the Blessed Spirits
piano concerto *lyrical and passionate*
Liszt: Concerto No.1 or Korngold Concerto for the Left Hand
short piano concerto *demanding and spiky*
Prokofiev: Concerto No.1 or Stravinsky: Movements for Piano and Orchestra

Second half:
warm and Romantic symphony
Sibelius: No.2 or Hanson: No.2

All suggestions are within the various constraints of time and budget[6] and the manager simply has to go through them, amending or accepting. He finds himself complimenting the system on its imaginative choices of repertoire. He would never have considered the Delius, Stravinsky or the Hanson because he has not heard them recently and they have slipped his memory. He has never even heard of the Korngold, thinking he only wrote film music, and is pleased to have it brought to his attention by the system.

Of course the system is not being imaginative at all — it is simply not suffering from the human failing of blinkered thinking. It does not assume that the best gap filler is always Siegfried Idyll because it has a perfect "memory" of a large repertoire.

There would seem to be no technological reasons why this cannot be done. The problems, as shown in this chapter, lie elsewhere.

If musical experience grows by a gradual accumulation of intellectual understanding, and by the application of appropriate labels, then the "knowledge" displayed by machine intelligence would presumably have to be similarly based on a lot of rules. If a machine is ever to understand why the juxtaposition of, say, the Beethoven Piano Sonata Op.111 and the Mahler 10th Symphony in a concert programme (as was done some years ago by the BBC National Orchestra of Wales promotions team) is a remarkably "right" and imaginative piece of programming, then it will need a great deal of established knowledge. That knowledge must be incorporated in something like a rule base of considerable size and sophistication because we are going to have to teach the machine to play our language game.

Explorations

Music and Language: An Evolutionary View

It is reasonable to ask how music gained such a significant place in our culture. Why should something apparently useless be ubiquitous? It "appears" to have no survival value and yet no culture has ever been discovered without music. The explanations and suggestions offered by anthropological studies are interesting for the light they cast on our difficulty verbalising musical effect.

Darwin, with, as we now believe, great prescience, speculated that music was derived from ancestral mating calls. Commenting on this, Pinker makes an intriguing extrapolation.

> ". . . his suggestion may make sense if it is broadened to include all emotional calls. Whimpering, whining, crying, weeping, moaning . . . and other ejaculations have acoustic signatures. Perhaps melodies evoke strong emotions because their skeletons resemble digitised templates of our species' emotional calls" (Pinker, 1997, p. 537).

He goes on to make a statement that goes to the core of the present problem.

> "When people try to describe passages of music in words, they use these emotional calls as metaphors . . . Ersatz emotion is a common goal for art . . ." (p. 537).

Robin Dunbar (1996), though attracted to the idea that language evolved from music, believes it not wholly right because the two processes occupy different brain hemispheres. Language is primarily a left-hemispherical process, music primarily right. He reports a study by Bever and Chiarello (1974) which demonstrated that subjects recognised tunes played into their left ears more quickly than when played into their right. Input to the left ear is processed by the right brain. Trained musicians, those who have applied more thought to the business of music, showed less tendency towards this. It has also been shown that poetry is processed in a similar way — the poetic music, rhythms, stress, and intonation, being processed in the right brain while the words themselves are processed in the left. Dunbar will only go so far as to admit that the music centres in the right brain may have hi-jacked some language processing because of the power musical expression has on the emotions. He admits "one of the more curious aspects of language, namely its complete inadequacy at the emotional level" (pp. 139-140).

Nevertheless, Dunbar cannot let music go in his discussion without noting the extremely suggestive fact that music stimulates the production of opiates, as does "nothing else" and that the possible existence of music before language as a part of ancient bonding ritual cannot be overlooked. The idea that we may have vocalised and danced together even before we spoke words is highly attractive[7]. There is support for the male selective advantages of a big voice to assist in yelling and thus settling mating rivalries. Indeed, Dunbar sees this as a good reason for the evolution of deeper voices for men because deep sounds travel better and are more impressive (imagine the music of the film *Jaws* played on a triangle!).

Susan Blackmore (1999) in her highly speculative consideration of the role of memes also points out the difficulty of explaining the evolution of language before we had anything to say to each other on a symbolic level, and suggests that it derived from our proneness to copy behaviours. She speaks of musical fragments as having the power to impress themselves on our memories and sees such musical fragments as the motto of Beethoven's 5th Symphony as examples of her "second replicator" the meme. Perhaps (a huge perhaps) that too is a reason for our difficulty in describing music; it is derived from pre-symbolic abilities of *homo sapiens* and our languages are at a loss to apply themselves to it. Perhaps the only medium for emotional description is art.

The idea is not new. Cranston (in Storr, 1992, p. 12) quotes Rousseau's Essai sur l'origine des langues:

> "men first spoke to each other in order to express their passions, and that at the early stages of human society there was no distinct speech apart from song . . . primitive men sing to one another in order to express their feelings before they come to speak to one another in order to express thoughts."

The great French philosopher is not the only proposer of such ideas. Ethnomusicologist John Blacking (1995, p. 33) even goes so far as to claim,

> "there is evidence that early human species were able to dance and sing several hundred thousand years before homo sapiens sapiens (sic) emerged with the capacity for speech as we now know it."

Extraordinarily thorough though Blacking was as an investigator, he too makes emotional statements like "the sound of the music conveyed as clear a message as the words of the songs" (1995, p. 35) for which he presents no evidence and which we will show is untrue. We are similarly doubtful about the content of statements like "Music cannot express anything extramusical unless the experience to which it refers already exists in the mind of the listener." In common with Pinker and Dunbar they too find the link between music and words suggestive and note work by Silberman (1963) who says that after "thousands of specimens from the music of all countries and all centuries" had been "listened to and evaluated" it was found that "when there are no words to give help, there are as many different meanings for the same musical messages as there are different people." Blacking comments that "such tests were administered to subjects in artificial and unsocial settings never envisaged by the creators of music, so that the sounds were divorced from their cultural environment and were unlikely to communicate with any consistency." As an ethnomusicologist, Blacking spent much of his time with Southern African tribes whose music was (and is) part of their lives in a way inapplicable to even the most fanatical concert goer in the West. Overall this is seen as support for the present idea that sung words provide an anticipatory set for the listener. Given no sung words, there cannot be precise communication. The best that can be achieved is the conveyance of a generalised emotion and even that may be claiming too much.

Since music does not convey information in the same way as words, there are no musical propositions; it does pose a problem for language theorists. Even the foremost among them are forced to fall back on rhetoric. As an example of such, Steven Pinker (1997) is clearly nonplussed and sees music as an enigma. In a lengthy discussion of art in general, how it fails to narrate and is non-adaptive ("it shows no signs of design for attaining grandchildren"[8]), he reserves for music these questions:

> "Perhaps [it is] a resonance in the brain between neurons firing in synchrony with a sound wave and a natural oscillation in the emotion circuits? An unused counterpart in the right hemisphere of the speech areas in the left? Some kind of spandrel or crawl space or short-circuit or coupling that came along as an accident of the way that auditory, emotional, language, and motor circuits are packed together in the brain?" (p. 538)

What is striking about this passage is the uncharacteristic rhetoric of the writing in the context of discussions that are normally consequent.

Turning now to the music being described, we must note that it is only in the past three centuries that music without accompanying words has become normal. Previous to this the role of music was always to accompany words or, at most, to preface or succeed them. Music accompanying words is not a problem to describe because the words being accompanied are conveyors of the "correct" meaning. It is only with the rise of purely instrumental music that this difficulty has presented itself. Of course dance music has always existed, often purely instrumental, but this has not been the subject of such discussions since it did not attain the status of "art" music. No one listened to dance music; they danced to it, (though even here some dances became stylised and were more for listening than dancing). The process of divorce between music and the word has only reached *decree nisi* in the current era with the rise of an entire, though small, industry devoted to the description of music. For the first time in the history of the art we are genuinely lost for words while struggling in a sea of them spouting from the mouths of reviewers and musical journalists. Whether we treat the words as helping us to think the "correct" thoughts about the music, or, as the present study does, treat them as the raw material of a search for commonality of understanding, we are faced with a whole category of musical descriptions that are with certainty descriptive only in the grammatical sense of being adjectival or adverbial.

Our research suggests that this new language of musical description has returned to its primeval roots and become an affirmation or denial of pleasure. In parallel with this we find that instrumental music itself has become more structured. The rise of the voiceless composition is accompanied by the rise of sonata form, rondo form, symphonic form and all manner of other forms, including the essentially inaudible forms of serialism. These provide the musical technician with plenty to discuss while the musical amateur has been cast adrift. We are now so uncertain that we need programme notes and experts to tell us what we "ought" to be thinking. We have indeed moved far away from word-centred composition where, even as recently as the 18th Century, music was still sometimes subservient to the text to the extent of being a coded description of it. (On this see Cameron, 2001.)

Music and Emotions

To return to more directly semantic issues, Budd (1992, p. 36) makes reference to several theories in which the emotions apparently described by music are described using certain words, for example "sad." He is right to ask whether there are musical characteristics, which can be identified, in a particular musical passage that can be labelled "sad," such that any piece of music exhibiting the same characteristics would also be called sad.

> " . . . a theory that maintains that emotion terms are applied to music in a properly musical way only if they designate purely

> audible features of the music would become attractive if it could be shown that the purely audible features in question were such that it was understandable why there should be such a strong and widespread inclination, on the part of composers and listeners alike, to characterise music by using words drawn from the language of emotions."(p. 36)

It seems to us that this is not the only thing that would make such a theory attractive. It would surely also strengthen the theory if it could be shown that two people discussing the music and utilising such terms had actually used the same terms with the same meaning prior to their discussion. If the term "sad" were applied consistently, under controlled conditions, it would imply that, even without any identification of the audible musical characteristic that made it "sad," that music was "sad." There is no requirement in this circumstance to identify the meaning of the words or the audible musical attribute. Consistent agreement as to word use alone would strongly imply that consistent message communication is taking place between listeners and between each listener individually and the music extract. The possibility that each listener is identifying a different audible characteristic but using the same label to describe it cannot be reduced unless several musical extracts are used. Even then it is possible that different things are being described, but the likelihood falls.

The complexity of this is increased by our findings that there is low agreement between users of musical predicates, but that the grouping of predicates increases this agreement significantly. This gives a set of words that can be used without quality of communication being reduced. For example, a set of words (a, b, c, d) is much more likely to be consistently applied to an audible musical feature than any one of the words a, b, c, d used alone. This would fit the thesis that audible musical features do not easily lend themselves to natural language description, using emotional or any other vocabulary. It is, of course, even more difficult to label the audible feature if one is going to have to apply an n-length compound name to it to allow reference[9]. Further, as already noted, as a result of applying word-sets there are going to be plenty of individual words that are members of many sets.

Tropic Mediation

Part of the reason for our difficulty with linking our descriptions of music with the music itself may well lie in the mediatory role of tropic (or figurative) language, metaphor, metonymy and synecdoche. The vocabulary under consideration functions largely as tropes and the intended referents for these tropic descriptions are secondary qualities of the music. The qualities of tunefulness, rhythm, mood, tempo and aesthetic value that the vocabulary describes are not part of the physical description of sound, the primary qualities that might be used by a scientist. Some qualities are actually possessed by an entity. For example, grass is actually green insofar as it reflects light of the frequency we describe as green. Glass is hard; it actually possesses a solid surface. Music, by contrast is just a sequence of sounds. It is we who describe a particular sequence as a tune. Tunefulness is a quality we impose upon the note sequence, in its context, as a consequence of mental processing, but which we imagine is inherent. (It is a moot point as to whether the word tuneful does not carry connotations of approval, which would thus make it a tertiary quality.) Likewise, rhythm is just a sequence of notes. We impose pattern on the sequence, again in context, and call it rhythm. These are known as secondary qualities (Scruton, 1997).

All the descriptive words we apply to these secondary qualities must be seen as tropic because music cannot actually be, for example, frenzied. Frenzied is a description of the behaviour of a person or an animal when that person or animal behaves in a certain way. The action is unusual and, therefore, to be considered within its context. Perhaps they move around very quickly, with uncoordinated limb movements. They probably act with some violence against objects, animate and inanimate, which are within reach. They make a lot of noise and perhaps, if human, use profanities. Other activities can doubtless be added. In describing a piece of music as frenzied we do not suggest that the music itself is moving around, waving its arms and swearing at the people around it. Similarly, as Scruton (1997) points out, a sad piece of music is not itself sad. Goodman (1976, pp. 50-51) is more explicit: "a picture is only figuratively sad. A picture [which] literally possesses a [for example] gray colour, really belongs to the class of gray things; but only metaphorically does it possess sadness or belong to the class of things that feel sad."

Scruton sees as one of the difficulties of giving clear definitions of terms used to characterise art that most of the terms deployed are transferred from another context; in other words, they are tropes. He believes that if one attempts to explain the meaning of a term as applied to the artistic object then one has to sever the link to the tropical referent and thus destroy the reason that the term is used. If we attempt to explain why a piece of music is sad by saying that it moves slowly, like a man who is sad would move slowly, we are committing just this error. He goes on to point out that if we take a different course and explain terms by making them attributes of the artistic object we are then ascribing, say, "passion" to a piece of "passionate" music, which quite clearly can have no such emotion since it is neither human nor even animate.

Scruton believes that the intention of describing music with such tropes is to draw some sort of parallel with the central examples of, for example, frenzy. Thus, several possibilities present themselves. Music that is frenzied has the same effect on the listener as a frenzied person; it shocks them, it causes them to worry about that person's state of mind, and it makes them want to do something with a calming effect. However, this suggestion does not wholly convince because no listener believes that they can do anything to calm down a piece of music, nor do we worry about its state of mind. Another possibility is that the music generates in the listener the symptoms of frenzy, thus when listening to it he wants to move violently and swear at his fellow concertgoers. Further possibilities are that it describes the state of the composer when he composed it or that the composer wishes to engender such a state in his listener. A realistic possibility is that it describes the emotions one feels when faced with a frenzied person.

Such aesthetic concerns as these of Scruton are further reason to reaffirm that the focus of this lexical search should not be on the meaning of music, however described, but on a pursuit for evidence that the language is commonly understood. Any discussion of trope can easily move into discussion of meaning because tropes try to ascribe qualities to art objects by analogy. A search for communicative stability would rest content if it finds evidence that a group of listeners are in agreement that a tropic description of musical work X is one with which they can all agree.

Let us look ahead at the vocabulary used by our investigation to confirm that it is tropic and that the central exemplar is generally not music itself. For ease of reference the vocabulary list is reproduced in the following.

angular	brilliant	compelling	directionless
ardent	bubbling	contrived	distinguished
attractive	buoyant	cool	dogged
balletic	busy	crisp	dramatic
beautiful	catchy	crude	dreary
bellicose	charming	crystalline	dull
bold	commanding	descriptive	dynamic

easy
eccentric
effervescent
elegant
elemental
engaging
enjoyable
entertaining
epic
exciting
exhibitionist
exhilarating
expressive
extraordinary
faceless
facile
ferocious
fierce
fine
flamboyant
flowing
fluent
forceful
formal
free
frenzied
fresh
full
genial
gentle
glacial
gleeful
gloomy
glowing
graceful
grand
graphic
grieving
heavy
humorous
icy
imaginative
impassioned
imposing
impressive
impulsive
intricate
inventive
involved
inward
joyous
lacklustre
light
lively
luminous
lurid
lusty
lyrical
magnificent
manic
mannered
marvellous
mechanistic
mellifluous
mellow
noble
novel
opulent
ornate
outrageous
outstanding
passionate
pastoral
pedestrian
picturesque
plain
plaintive
plodding
poignant
polished
potent
powerful
primitive
purposeful
radiant
rapt
relaxed
relentless
resonant
restrained
reticent
rich
rollicking
rugged
rumbustious
rustic
searching
sentimental
serene
shadowy
silken
simple
sinuous
sober
solemn
solid
spacious
sparkly
spirited
spontaneous
static
strong
surging
sustained
sweet
sympathetic
tasteful
tense
theatrical
thrilling
tragic
tranquil
turbulent
unsentimental
vivacious
vivid
warm
weighty
witty
wonderful
worthy
zestful

A close study of the items shows that they all fall most convincingly into the class of evaluative words like *magnificent* or *dull*, or the class of words lacking a conventional connection with the subject, like *bellicose* or *reticent*. One or two could, with a little effort, be seen as descriptors that denote (*balletic* perhaps?), and those connoting degree (*plodding*?), but they are more easily placed elsewhere. Indeed, there is almost no word that does not have a stronger non-musical exemplification than musical. Even *catchy*, often applied to tunes and an abbreviation of *catches the attention*, is only an adjectival derivation of *catch* which is far more commonly applied to ball games. Of course the vocabulary we are discussing excludes the simplest musical descriptions, like: *that is a high note*, or *that is a low note*, or like: *the sound sinks to the bottom of the orchestra*, all definitely descriptors of degree. [These also exhibit the "persistent spatial metaphors without which," says Scruton, "we would be silenced on the subject of music" (1997, pp. 80-96).] Thus, the whole set utilised for experimentation largely excludes descriptors that denote and those that reference by comparison. This outcome is both fortuitous, and easily explicable, for in seeking evidence for communication there is less value in considering words that explicitly denote and those for which an accepted comparative exists. Though there is some space for disagreement over *loud* and *soft*, it is much less valuable, and less interesting, to discover whether two listeners agree on this than whether they agree on *epic* and *exciting*, because no artistic decision-support system is going to help our concert planner by describing Barber's *Adagio for Strings* as *soft*. This is not the aspect of listener experience to which we need refer when juxtaposing musical compositions in a concert programme.

If, therefore, we are dealing with a vocabulary that is entirely tropical, then it follows that the vocabulary is, literally, false. For example, in the phrase "the pianist gives a warmly sympathetic performance," it is false that the performance is warm because firstly this would suggest that a performance is a type of entity to which a temperature can be attributed, secondly that the attribute sympathetic can be warm, and thirdly that a performance can be sympathetic to the idiom, implying that a performance has the characteristic of being able to empathise with a human being, or an idiom. None of these statements can be seen as true and yet the phrase is felt by its writer to convey information to the reader. There is clearly a difficulty distinguishing tropical from literal truth and either of them from falsity.

If the power of a figurative description can be conveyed to another person, this implies that both parties share both aspects of the experience, central examples as well as musical references. Lakoff and Johnson (1980) go very much further in their discussion in suggesting that "our conceptual system, in terms of which we both think and act, is fundamentally metaphorical" (p. 3). It may be that a coherent structure of musical description could be revealed from a thoroughgoing analysis of the categories to which tropes refer: spatial, experiential or structural, to derive indeed, in Scruton's nice adaptation (1997, p. 52) of Lakoff and Johnson, "the metaphors we hear by." Any attempt to answer the question "what do our musical descriptions mean?" or to model the ontology of this artistic predication would be wise to follow through such a line of enquiry. It is to this we now turn.

Fundamental Limits

It is clear from the above discussion that there is an emotional landscape and that words are used to mark out its territory. Although the landscape is not "in" any shared world, it is a virtual landscape we can (and do) assume we share. The words and phrases we use should (via the tropic connection) link with this landscape in the same way that they link with world objects. It would seem that all we have to do is connect these words through music to our shared experiences.

Further, we ought to be able to extend the linking process to be dependent upon the more subtle techniques of weighted-measurements as well as applying rules for the more concrete notions of time and rhythm. Mechanisms such as Baye's Rule, Neural Nets or Production Systems might be considered to relate the abstract ideas of emotion to the measurable elements of works of art. Both musical rhythm and the Golden Section[10] in visual art, for example, are related to subjective experiences, but have a measurable (objective) aspect. However, an aesthetic decision, such as whether three pieces of music should comprise a program, is not obviously based on any factual measures.

It may be that such assessments could be derived from the perception of the music that is reflected in the experiential predications used by music listeners. Experience indicates that phrases such as "every note weighted to perfection" are used to express the subjective experiences of a music listener. These phrases are found in specialist magazines and the art sections of newspapers where critics analyse music, concerts, performances or exhibitions in terms of their subjective experiences. Readers of such writings will recognise the range of subjective experience and make judgements from these descriptions that will guide them into some action such as attending a concert or exhibition or buying a record or picture.

It is evident that the assumption made by writers about music and other artistic endeavours is that we can communicate our artistic judgements and experiences to others. Unravelling this assumption requires that we make explicit the rules of such artistic judgements. We can start to do this by identifying the stable subjective concepts that relate to the objective artistic object, such as a performance or exhibition. In the case of music, we need to relate descriptive words and phrases to musical experiences.

Experiments into the Stability of Musical Descriptions [11]

Deriving a Vocabulary Set

The provisional musical vocabulary, listed above, was identified by combining experienced-user inputs with items from the professional and critical vocabulary. Given that this vocabulary is used by a specialist group, classical concertgoers, and that it was their intercommunication that was to be investigated, it was appropriate that all participants in the experiments were from this group, a group which is well above the average age and which regards this language use as normal.

The purpose of the first experiment was to identify a lexicon of descriptive words used by music lovers. For this experiment a questionnaire was designed to include a list of 50 compositions, an invitation to attach three words to each piece, and a list of some 250 words drawn from a well-known review magazine. Returns from volunteers at a music appreciation day school, six female, five male, resulted in a vocabulary set that was partly derived from these listeners and partly from professional writers. This list was then used in subsequent experiments.

The list of works was of pieces that many music enthusiasts would know without being too popular. The reason for avoiding overmuch popularity being the rather unvarying nature of the popular repertoire, much of which is mid to late 19th Century Romantic and Nationalist music and not seen as likely to elicit sufficient range of verbal response.

A sample of the summarised results for one of these pieces is shown in Table 1. If a word is used more than once it is listed with a number in parenthesis. It was stated on the questionnaire that the position of the words, one, two or three, was not important. This was to avoid people consciously imposing an evaluative sequence. However, words were recorded strictly in position because the order in which people entered the words was thought worth preserving. In the example following, some respondents submitted only two words.

Table 1: Initial Questionnaire, Sample Response

Work	Word 1	Word 2	Word 3
Mussorgsky/Ravel:	commanding	colourful	descriptive
Pictures at an Exhibition	descriptive (2)	imaginative	powerful
	outstanding	vivid	thrilling
	dramatic (2)	varied	radiant
	colourful (2)	descriptive	
	majestic	imaginative	
	powerful	energetic	
		dramatic	

Overall, for all pieces of music the most common word appeared to be *exciting*, followed by *evocative* and *descriptive*. The most frequent duplication of words came for Mussorgsky's *Pictures at an Exhibition* (above) where four words got repeated (one, *powerful,* only across columns), a notable number in this preliminary survey involving only eleven participants.

Though the aim of this preliminary exercise was to generate a usable vocabulary for later, much more detailed exercises, this first set of data is worthy of comment. The word sets do not seem to have much, if anything, by way of consistent characteristics and no musical work gains a large number of duplications. This suggests that, for this group, there is no agreed set of primary descriptors, by which is meant the words that come immediately to the respondent's mind. The closest we came to this was Ravel's *Bolero* that had a set of words dominated by *boring*, *repetitive* and *rhythmic* plus their synonyms.

The frequency lists show that only a few words, 40 out of the 1,032 submitted, are used repeatedly. Each word is preceded by the number of times it appears. Words appearing less than six times are not listed because in common with all word-usage distributions (Zipf, 1949; Pareto, 1897) the range of words appearing from five times downwards is huge.

30 tuneful
29 exciting
26 descriptive
20 rhythmic
20 dramatic
18 lyrical
17 powerful
16 evocative
14 beautiful
13 colourful
12 flowing
10 brilliant
10 virtuoso
10 imaginative
10 uplifting
10 expressive
9 great
9 bright
9 emotional
8 impressive
8 pleasant
8 poetic
7 thrilling
7 clever
7 boring
7 listenable
7 magnificent
7 enjoyable
7 intense
7 romantic
7 melodic
7 repetitive
6 delightful
6 elegant
6 memorable
6 accessible
6 skilful
6 varied
6 superb
6 nationalistic

The second phase in the analysis of the vocabulary was a categorisation of words with usage frequencies of three or more[12] into two dimensions[13] (Table 2). The first dimension is the binary division into emotional descriptors and non-emotional descriptors, nominated simply "emotional" and "descriptive" respectively. The second dimension was a ternary division, words being grouped as "approving," "neutral" and "disapproving." This categorisation is proposed by the authors and not derived from the participants' responses because at this stage no attempt had been made to ask for evaluative connotations.

Table 2: Emotional/Descriptive Matrix

	Emotional	Descriptive
Approval	exciting, dramatic, lyrical, powerful, evocative, beautiful, colourful, flowing, brilliant, expressive, imaginative, uplifting, great, impressive, poetic, enjoyable, intense, magnificent, romantic, thrilling, delightful, memorable, super, amusing, entertaining, exhilarating, haunting, inspiring, sensitive, spirited, charming, fun, impassioned, joyful, moving, passionate, vibrant, awesome, compelling, gentle, poignant, radiant, triumphant, wonderful	tuneful, melodic, elegant, lively, grand, majestic, catchy, vigorous, vivid, atmospheric, buoyant, forceful, peaceful, sonorous
Neutral	descriptive, bright, emotional, pleasant, clever, listenable, accessible, stimulating, clear, crafted, inventive, approachable, balanced, graphic, interesting, pure, relaxing, restful, robust, sombre, theatrical	rhythmic, virtuoso, repetitive, nationalistic, skilful, varied, classical, balletic, impressionistic, smooth, compact, English, precise, reflective
Disapproval	boring, worthy, acceptable, sentimental	spiky

The result gave what was, at the time, an unexpectedly heavy bias towards words connoting emotional approval, to the extent that only one word seemed to deserve placement at the opposite corner of the matrix under descriptive/disapproval. Only much later on did the significance of this become clear, but it suggested the need to create an experiment to test for evaluative connotation.

In conclusion, this initial analysis showed that the vocabulary lacked any clear consistency. However, it did lend itself to the above two-dimensional emotional-descriptive/evaluative matrix where the majority of the words fell into the category of emotional approval as opposed to an extremely small number being specifically descriptive and disapproving.

Three further experiments took place, two exploring the extent of user agreement and the third investigating the connotations of the words themselves.

The First Group Experiment

The first group experiment explored the extent of user agreement as to the commonality of musical predication by taking both individual and group predications and analysing them for agreement. Educational background, listening experience, and age were also taken into consideration. No consistency was found. However, the experiment did reveal the typical behaviour of people to concur with the opinion of the group against their own professed judgement (Asch, 1955; Kiesler, 1967).

Nineteen people participated in three groups on different dates. A preliminary questionnaire noted personal details having a direct bearing on the research, like sex (presumed to be significant, but not so shown) and age. There was no evidence to support the prediction that older and younger people would choose from different vocabulary sets, but it could not be excluded. The third question concerned a grading of listening experience from "occasional" to "frequent" listener. Any differences emerging here might have derived from the extent of the participants' reading of music literature, including popular journalism. Finally, it was asked if the participant played an instrument. Since the aim of this research was the investigation of non-technical language it seemed sensible to assume that knowledge of the technical vocabulary might be influential. Also noted, but not relevant for the present purpose, was the age of participants.

The first two tests used the same ten very short (circa two minutes) extracts. These were played from tape once for each test. Participants did not have the opportunity to request a repeat playing. The first test was designed to capture the single word that best fitted their subjective experience of a piece of music. In this test the participants were given as long as they needed to decide on, and write down, a word, before the next extract was played. Little duplication of vocabulary occurred for any of the ten items.

Mindful of the initial vocabulary exercise, the overall lack of duplication was predicted, and was the reason for designing Test 2 where the choices, though wide, were restricted to a given list. The attempt here was to increase the likelihood of duplication; the subjects used, once again, hardly any duplicate vocabulary.

Test 3 was different in that it was attempting to assess the expressiveness of a reduced set of words for the task of music description[14]. Here the participants were given a single word and asked to note the extent of their agreement as to its appropriateness. A different set of 10 short extracts from pieces of music had been chosen to produce strong agreement. For six of the extracts the word was judged to be appropriate by most participants; for three it was judged inappropriate. One word only, *fierce,* divided participants between agreement and no opinion.

Thus, if the freedom to choose a descriptive word is removed and people are only asked to judge the suitability of a given predicate, they do show commonality, whether of agreement or disagreement, with the prescribed choice.

Test 4 in this set explored the nature of group opinion. In this way it was hoped to identify a common reduced lexicon that could be employed to describe the subjective experience of music. It was predicted that this would tend to generate conventional descriptions and so improve the chances of producing this common vocabulary set. The participants were asked to listen to five extracts, all around two minutes long, and then to unanimously agree on a set of three descriptive words. The discussions were recorded. Agreement within discussion groups was reached fairly easily, but the agreed sets (5 extracts x 3 groups x 3 words = 45 words) showed only five common words (11%) and none of them were across more than two groups, once again showing the absence of common usage.

The Main Vocabulary Analysis

If the vocabulary is to be shown to be meaningful and communicative then the words must be susceptible to categorisation. It should be possible to show that, for example, the word *powerful* tends to refer to matters of loudness. If a measurable reference cannot be identified then at least a consistent response would indicate a subjective referent that was commonly experienced. These are the categories into which it was decided the words must be placed as specifically musical descriptions, with the proviso that words can be placed in more than one category: The categories are chosen to encompass fully all the characteristics of music which may be described: rhythm, melodic characteristics, aesthetic appreciation, tempo, quality.

Additionally each word should be placed on an evaluative scale (Likert, 1932): very positive, positive, neutral, negative, and very negative. This is described as measuring the import of the word.

It was decided to ask the maximum possible number of volunteers to complete a large survey of 160 words. Fifty-eight did so. For each word there was a set of eleven categories (A to K), five of them the set above, rhythm to value, five representing the Likert scale and one for those who were unable to decide how to place the word. Words were allowed in multiple domains. Table 3 is extracted from the issued questionnaire, which, be it noted, took participants close to two hours to complete.

Table 3: The Structure of the Main Vocabulary Survey

Word	**A**	**B**	**C**	**D**	**E**	**F**	**G**	**H**	**I**	**J**	**K**
category of word ➔	rhythm	tunefulness	mood	speed	value	don't know	very positive	positive	neutral	negative	very negative
sympathetic											
fluent											
forceful											
polished											
pastoral											
lacklustre											
light											

The objective of this experiment was, independently both from particular pieces of music and from other members of the test group, to assign classes of use to descriptive words. The experiment sought to analyse first the usage of the vocabulary to describe distinct categories of musical experience, and second to assess the vocabulary in its capacity to convey a range of positive to negative evaluations. This confirmed the largely positive nature of the vocabulary as well as its use primarily to describe indistinct categories like the emotional mood created by the music rather than firm categories like rhythm.

The results of the questionnaire can be subjected to analysis by listing the words that gain over 50% agreement, 30 or more out of 58 respondents — a simple majority. The number of words is noted for each category: rhythm 41, tunefulness 21, mood 66, speed 17, value 18; for the import category: very positive 6, positive 41, neutral 5, negative 0, very negative 1. This confirms the tendency to use the language for primarily positive predication and more for description of mood and rhythm than any other category.

A second analysis sought to assess combinations of categories on the assumption that neither the word nor the category necessarily represented any distinct dimension of the subjective experience. This analysis is derived from the horizontal patterns of response across Table 3 above. An example of such a pattern is *nnCnnnnHnnn* where the n shows a null and the capital letters show an affirmative response within the categories A to K shown in Table 3.

The distribution of pattern-use frequencies again followed Zipf's Law[15] in that a very small proportion of them occurred far more than the rest. Out of 304 different patterns submitted, 26 received more than 100 uses, and of those a small handful stood out:

nnCnnnnHnnn	533	meaning that the word best described mood and was fairly positive
nnCnnnnnInn	434	meaning that the word best described mood but was basically neutral as to the value placed on the description
nnnnnFnnnnn	369	meaning that the word could not be categorised in any way by the participants
nnnnEnnHnnn	295	meaning that the word best described the absolute value of the piece of music and was, unsurprisingly, positive
nBnnnnnHnnn	244	meaning that the word best described the quality of tunefulness and, once again, implied a positive assessment.

A note of caution must be sounded. The highest scoring pattern still represents less than 6% of the responses, just 533 out of 9,280 chosen patterns.

In the context of such persistent disagreement over descriptions, it was interesting to note that a very small number of words showed signs of reliable connotation for these survey participants. Full agreement would mean that with 58 participants a word achieving 58 identical patterns could be designated a carrier of meaning. None achieved close to this. But if the criteria of agreement are relaxed by accepting as the same all those patterns where there are clear common categories, then a few words do emerge as interesting candidates for a critic's lexicon.

As an illustration and clarification here are the results for sympathetic:

Pattern 1	nnCnnnnHnnn	18
Pattern 2	nnCnnnnnInn	9
Pattern 3	nBCnnnnHnnn	4
Pattern 4	nnCnEnnHnnn	4
Pattern 5	nnCnnnnnnn	4

It will be noted that this represents the top pattern and has achieved over 30% exact agreement. The agreement being that it is a positive word describing mood. Inspecting the pattern details reveals that the only differences are in the neutral rather than positive rating for pattern 2, the addition of extra usages as a tunefulness and value category word in patterns 3 and 4, and the absence of a value rating in pattern 5. Taken together this totals 39 responses, which is 67% of the set and thus provides some evidence that at least part of this vocabulary is commonly understood.

The only other words to achieve similar results are:

outstanding	35	60%
warm	41	71%
(subsidiary sets here contain higher counts than above)		
polished	27	47%
shadowy	22	38%
marvellous	32	55%
cool	22	38%
magnificent	33	57%

Once again we found the typical Zipf's Law distribution with a long tail off of results.

The Second Group Experiment

Agreement on Word Sets

The final experiment sought to find agreement between people when the language was restricted and the music was kept within prescribed categories. The extent of disagreement was extreme and led to the conclusion that, in essence, listeners do not agree in their predications.

Participants in this experiment were drawn from those used before and consisted of seventeen participants in three groups of five, six and six.

The aim was to match musical extracts to prescribed word sets — individually and by agreement. A list of items was played to the participants as individuals and each attached a choice of vocabulary set. In a second exercise the same extracts were discussed as a group and agreement on one vocabulary set was required. The length of the extracts was dictated by musical paragraphs, but with a time limit of about two minutes. Participants did not know the identity of the music, which is shown in column two, but were given the word sets. Here is a small sample by way of illustration:

Table 4: Sample Data for the Second Group Experiment

1	Prokofiev: Alexander Nevsky; The Battle on the Ice (opening)	icy, tense, crystalline, glacial, graphic
2	Milhaud: Scaramouche (3rd movt.)	vivacious, lively, joyous, rollicking, spirited
3	Weill: Surabaya Jonny (opening) (Happy End)	grieving, poignant, sentimental, passionate, theatrical

The individual responses showed the (by now) expected wide range of response with agreement on neither the words appropriate to the music, or the music appropriate to the words.

The responses to group agreement were only a little more encouraging. Overall, the predicted choices were discussed as possibilities 41 times out of 45, over 90%. However they were not as frequently chosen. They were the final agreed set just 42% of the time, 19 out of 45 agreements. The predicted choices, the actual word sets used to guide the experimenter to his musical extracts, are as much matters of personal opinion as are the group decisions. Thus, the fact that they figured highly in discussion shows a certain commonality of instinct about such descriptions. If it were the case that descriptions are applied randomly then this result would be remarkable. Equally, if such descriptors were normally applied consistently then the result would be a great disappointment. What seems the best-supported outcome is that we appear largely consistent in our decisions, but are prepared to accept wide variations. Accuracy is not what is sought. This can be seen as support for the multi-adjectival sentences often used in the musical press, e.g. a warmly sympathetic performance. It also points ahead to the use of metaphor.

Participant Comments

At the end of the exercises the general discussion was tape-recorded. Several interesting comments were made. One participant noted that knowing what the items were would have influenced their decisions. Another, that this comment raises a very interesting question about whether you should look at the caption of a picture when you go into a gallery. A third said, "if you had given us the titles we would have been much more superficial in our attitude in thinking about the sounds." Finally, a suggestion was made that this sort of language did not belong in musical description anyway, programme notes should not use any words like these; they should say "the third movement is a scherzo, a three part movement which goes into C# minor, sort of thing;" which brought the response "I wouldn't get anything from (such) a technical description." Even after negotiating agreed sets there was plenty of other disagreement.

The Puzzle

There is something very odd happening here. What has been shown is that the words used to describe music are too inconsistently used to allow the formulation of usage rules. There appears to be no stable relationship between a piece of music and its description. What is being communicated between music listeners and how people make coherent decisions based upon such descriptions has not been identified. Yet, there is a community actively participating in what seems to be nonsense interactions. So if people are not simply making random choices what are they doing?

Further, concert programmes demand, apart from technical feasibility, an appropriate juxtaposition of compositions. It was that appropriateness which still resisted any formal statement or even the identification of a stable language. We were puzzled and perplexed by these results, particularly since they suggest it is not the conventional referential semantics that express the aesthetic experience. There seemed to be some kind of meta-semantics yet undefined.

One possible reason for the instability is that what we are observing is a process that has no fixed ontology, but is dynamic in response to the participation of the listener (or observer). We are dealing with a subjective world that is not tied to any stable semantic structure. Such an internal world has the capacity to infer new features or categories, not quite at will, for that is to imply wilfullness, but certainly with a great range and flexibility, from the stimulus of the artistic object and in response to some (say) instinct towards pleasure.

Possible Explanatory Models

To start the process of understanding what might be happening we need to summarise our results within the framework of our primary concept. This is the notion that an artistic object stimulates a range of subjective experiences. The artistic objects considered are music and music descriptions. Three possible models might be considered to explain what is occurring. Initially let us consider the total range of possible subjective experiences that might be uniquely felt and identified by any individual on hearing a piece of music. For a particular piece of music, that person will experience a true subset of these experiences. Of these felt experiences, there will be a further subset. This further subset will relate to objective measures such as rhythm. Figure 1 describes this version.

It is assumed that every perceivable objective measure has its subjective counterpart for every person. *We are still assuming that we share a similar emotional landscape* that contains these subjective experiences, but that the music will be related differently. Now, whatever the *actual* subjective experience felt by (say) two people, A and B, when they are subjected to the same objectively measurable stimulus, these two (possibly different) sets of subjective experiences for each person will be referenced by the same description. This is the central part of the mechanism of language acquisition. Both Results Summaries (Figures 1 and 2) contain this common set.

Figure 1: The Emotional Landscape and a Piece of Music

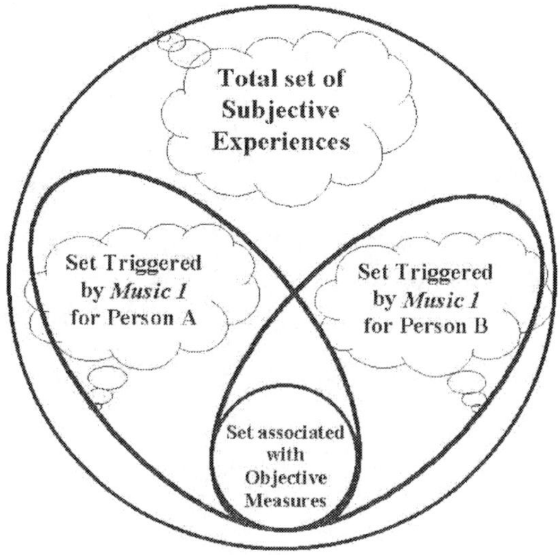

For the other subjective experiences that are not bounded by an objective measure then there is no direct mechanism for ensuring that any description can be properly associated with them. Figure 2 represents this interpretation of our results.

Figure 2: The Emotional Landscape and a Single Description

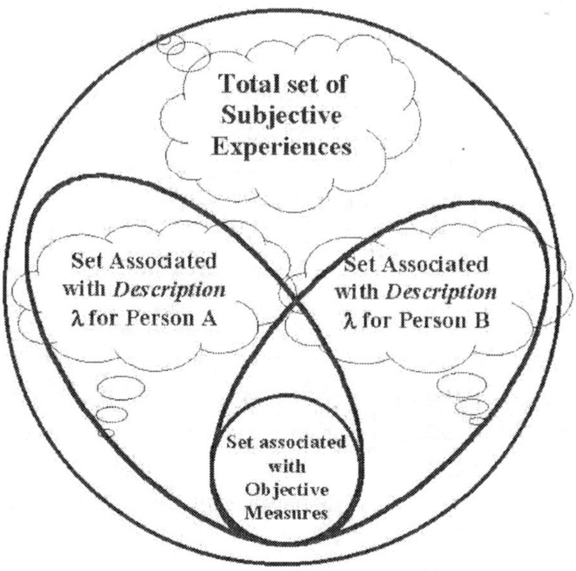

There are also no guarantees that a particular subjective experience of person A has any similarity to that of person B in the presence of the same artistic object. It is not even clear what could be meant by two subjective experiences being the same or even similar. *Worse still, and contrary to our original assumption, there is no mechanism through which even the ontology of subjective experiences can be presumed the same.* This variance of ontology between people can occur even when there are external objective measures. An example is the way in which colour in distinct languages can be divided along the physical spectrum, saturation, and hue very differently to a point where simple translations are impossible (Lyons, 1968, pp. 56-59).

Thus, the three possible models that account for this lack of communication are:

1. The *subjective experiences* for people *are different* as shown in summary I,
2. The *descriptions assigned to a subjective experience is different* as shown in summary II,
3. That *both* summary I and II are the case.

Our results support all three possibilities — a result that almost seems inevitable given the considerations above.

Metaphor and Artistic Description

These results would suggest that unless we can derive a new form of a system based upon a dynamic external referential semantic that can be translated into computer processes, we will be condemned to implementing incomplete and simplistic artistic decision-making systems. A possible solution is to find other objective measures in a different domain that reference the same subjective experience stimulated by the artistic object under consideration. This, in effect, extends the set of objective measures shown in Figures 1 and 2. This is the use of tropic language, especially metaphor (Lakoff & Johnson, 1980).

Two results support this possibility if we assume that subjective experiences, in line with objective measures, are subject to inheritable qualities. For example, we may "like" both the *Moonlight Sonata* and eating ice cream on a hot day. The subjective experiences may well be different, but they both share the property of "pleasure"; a subjective experience that is firmly related to objective measures in other fields. Metaphor is not a complete answer since there may well be subjective experiences that remain unique to music. The poetic, creative and clever use of words, which spin descriptions through metaphoric associations, can always refine the identification of subjective experiences, but such descriptions, a priori, can never identify that which is unique to music for an individual except perhaps at a very abstract level (e.g., approval or disapproval, emotional or descriptive). Such descriptions will always remain indistinct and unrecognised until the experience to which they refer is encountered and where, with luck, a uniqueness comes into focus. However, this uniqueness will remain a private affair and a personal experience that may be unlike anything intended by the writer of the description. This could be the role of the critic or aficionado: to publicly explore descriptions rich in trope, the connotations of which help people to enhance their own subjective responses to an art object. Communication as such does not occur. Consequent upon that, the process of concert planning remains a private and creative act. However, we might still be able to provide a tool to aid such an act by extending our studies to relating tropical descriptions to musical experience.

Fundamental Limits

We now have some evidence that subjective experiences, like objective experiences, can be set in an inheritance hierarchy of categories of which the parent level features are of value (e.g., approval, neutral or disapproval). Some parent categories span the range of domains (e.g., visual art, music and dance) and thus their related experiences. It is this range that is important at this level; the subjective experiences are stable to description provided there is some objective measure in one of the domains. Such descriptions open the path of communication about the subjective experiences of individuals by using trope. However, *if there are not any objective measures in a related domain then there cannot be communication*. We can suggest that an artistic support decision system needs to have access to a wide range of well founded human experiences that go beyond that of the subject domain to which it refers.

Modelling the Role of Metaphor

The Concert Plan as an Artistic Object

Planning a classical concert programme is a creative act. The product is an artistic object, a concert programme. Some parts of the activity are compromises with realities such as availability of musicians, hall space, wishes of maestros, economics, and so on. However at its core the act is creative.

Two issues have emerged so far.

(i) Experimental evidence showed unambiguously that there was no agreement on musical descriptors, either single or multi-adjectival. Because no user agreement could be identified, the problem of isolating consistent, direct musical descriptions will be insoluble. Indeed, taking the simplistic view of referential semantics, the conclusion was that such musical descriptors were essentially useless as tools of communication. As noted above, this was puzzling. Given that direct reference was inconsistent with observations it was decided to investigate indirect reference; thus, metaphor.

(ii) Coincidentally it became apparent at this point in our investigations that a solution to the problem of music and sound description, and thus of this investigation, is of wider concern. Parallels can be drawn with the problems encountered by acousticians in describing the general sound, and in particular the reverberative characteristics of their auditoria (Blesser, 2001), plus the problem was recognised many years ago by Langford-Smith (1953) that a restricted set of descriptors was required by audio system designers. We might speculate that there are other domains, such as pictorial art and architecture, which will also require a solution to this descriptor problem[16].

A Redefinition of the Model

The seminal work on metaphor by Lakoff and Johnson (1980) suggests a redefinition of the model. The old model was very simple: the solution to the problem of building artistic decision-support systems lies in creating combinatorial rules derived from a common descriptive vocabulary which is there to be uncovered. The new model needs only to explain two characteristics:

1. Why the language of artistic description is so unstable (i.e., has no consistent meaning)

and

2. Why, despite that, it is in such widespread use.

The new model can be most simply stated thus. Artistic descriptions consist of tropes. These tropes belong to trope sets (for example spatial metaphors).

These sets have a complex semantics that is an amalgam of the connotation of all the members of the set.

The notion of trope sets draws together certain relationships that relate to that set. For example, in spatial metaphors the general direction of *up* connotes positive emotions such as:

I am feeling high, or *The economy is on the rise.*

Alternatively, the direction of *down* connotes negative emotions such as:

He dropped dead, or *I am feeling low.*

Further, while the semantics will ultimately reference the *real* world, as do all tropes, it is possible, indeed probable, that a certain proportion of the tropes will reference, say, literary works, and are thus referencing a secondary level of trope. These secondary-level tropes may bring into play new emotional referents. Consequently, the model must be able to cope with the generation of new *primitive* descriptors from existing descriptors using, for example, some meta-linguistic relationships.

For example, it may be that a description of a late Beethoven string quartet might include the statement that it seems to imply "such things as dreams are made of" and thus relate the music to an example of figurative language which itself connotes much. Because the set has a complex semantic reference (e.g., the material content of dreams or of wishes) the use of even a single trope may imply a very large set of references (e.g., nightmares or fears). Those *real* references in turn may reference at a still deeper level by implying emotional states that are not intended to be referenced by the original statement. The reference to dreams in the context of a Beethoven quartet is presumably restricted to certain positive emotions.

This leads to the problem of change. *Common usage is not stable,* particularly with the use of trope. Since the user of the initial trope may have different feelings about an aesthetic artefact at different times, the description is dynamic and any communicative value of the description must be constantly negotiated between the transmitter-user and the receiver-user. This leads to the state of affairs shown above that the vocabulary is unstable. This results in the meaning of statements changing over time. This we have called *predicate instability*. We suggest, because it is the only observable mechanism, that this instability is controlled through feedback in the form of public use. Thus, the model predicts that there should be frequent public recording of the language that allows its manifestations to be inspected and tested against individual usage. That public manifestation is primarily the writing and broadcasting via the media of radio, television and the Internet of *professional* users like critics and reviewers.

The artistic object *concert plan*, the output of the creative act of planning, might also turn out to have close affinities with the trope sets. It is not clear what makes a good concert programme, in terms of the aesthetico-emotional impact on the audience member. Since the planner never places musical works together randomly, but operates within a mixture of practical and aesthetic constraints as noted above, it may be that the programme that satisfies aesthetically consists of musical works that may be described by tropes from, for example, the same set or contrasting sets. If this could be shown to be true then the machine can be programmed with rules aimed at aligning economic, timing and other practical constraints with concert works to which are attributed appropriate trope sets. Though such speculation is far from testable with our current knowledge, it does present a basis for a testable model for the future.

Predicate Instability

A particularly telling example of predicate instability (the changing of meaning of a statement) over time was shown in Billinge (2001) where the conventional description of a particular opus by Mozart (the G minor Symphony K550) as *tragic*, a description affirmed over time, was tested. In this experiment participants were able to choose from a set of words those that they felt to be most appropriate for that work. Despite the presence in the test group of a proportion of people who recognised the particular opus, the word *tragic* was specifically rejected as inappropriate by no less than 74%; the description had changed. There are two possible reasons for this change. Either the semiotics of *tragic* had altered or the associated emotional response to the music had changed. Pertinent to this example, because the appellation *tragic* is affirmed as a consequence of the use of G minor key, are the investigations of Steblin (1996). She shows how key characteristics were subjected to quite radical descriptive changes as far back as the 18th Century. Such instability continues. In this case, the instability over time would seem to relate to the emotional association of the key rather than the word, since *tragic* is a very specific word relating to an emotion.

Instability of musical predication between users was also shown in the group experiments described earlier, where we found almost no agreement between groups or between groups and the experimental predictions, despite the fact that groups were able to agree among themselves. Note again that in some cases the set considered by the experimenter to be the best was not even discussed. This illustrates the significance of the group setting up its own associations irrespective of external norms.

What mechanism(s) might be active within such groups is still a matter of speculation. A clue lies in the work by Robert Gordon (1987) where he suggests that emotional descriptors are *explanations* and useful summaries of human behaviour. He supports his argument through the Hebb experiment (1946) where anthropomorphic descriptions were banned during animal studies. The result was a collection of almost useless observations that told little about how particular animals should be treated or controlled.

Another consequence of our proposed model is that words drawn from different domains (the mixed metaphor) can be used freely since their semantic reference is subordinate to their semiotic value. The mixing of metaphor in music-critical figurative language continues to be so common that a single glance at a recent edition of a review magazine yields a pair of rich examples.

(i) She sings Aida without either sounding or feeling like her

and

(ii) . . . the frequent interaction of Aida and Amneris is sometimes clouded by [her] baleful rather than sultry low register

The combination of metaphors from different domains make for semantically meaningless statements, but which can have semiotically emotional coherence in that the writer has conveyed his feelings to the reader well enough. In (i) it is clearly impossible to sing anything without sounding, and hard to descry the mode of feeling, either active or passive, let alone understand how anyone can feel like a fictional character; yet this statement most probably means that in the opinion of the writer the singer does not convey the character of Aida. In (ii) the metaphors are more obvious (*clouded* as in *foggy*, hard to see; *sultry* as in *sexual* and so on) but their reference is to at least three different senses. *Clouded* is a visual reference, *baleful* is purely emotional, and *sultry* is a reference to air temperature and humidity. Without going into detail, (ii) very probably intends to suggest that the voices do not go together well. Both statements connote much more than this, that connotation being carried by the terms briefly discussed.

Conclusion: Metaphoric Form

Reconsideration of the Issues

At the beginning we had three questions related to the non-technical aspects of music. Is there a stable language of musical effect? Can music have acceptable descriptions? What is the role of such a language of music? Our review of the literature indicates a clear consensus that an emotional landscape exists in us all and that such a landscape is more fundamental or primitive than language. It can be further inferred that we all share an emotional landscape in the same way that we all share the same physical morphology. We would expect a wide range of individual differences in people, some born with a psychopathology and others traumatised by experience. We would also expect to find refinements that have been influenced by training, culture, and the act of living. These differences create the problem and the result is a language that is indirect and requires constant reaffirmation.

We have confirmed through controlled experiments that there is no simple stable language, principally because the landscape is not a shared world, as is the physical world about us. However, the simple observation that social discourse occurs implies that there is communication. If there is no communication then we are at a loss to account for such interaction[17]. The question arises as to how this communication can happen if there is no common objective reference.

Figure 3: The Emotional Landscapes for Two People and the Effect of Two Metaphors

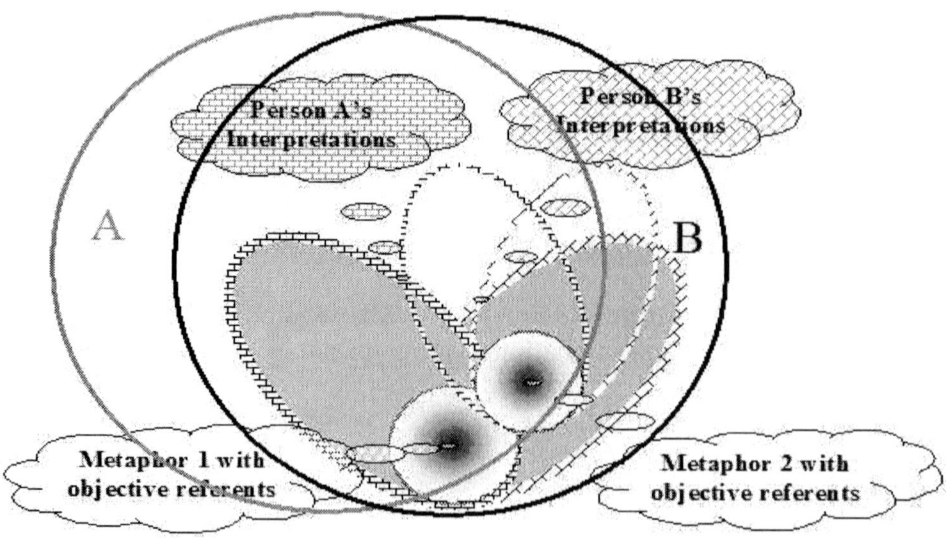

For communication to occur, the landscape has to be shared. This sharing is necessary because there has to be the possibility of validation of the use of language so that there is no mistake as to what is meant by an utterance or display of symbols. We thus extend the idea of validation by reference to validation by inference. We concluded above that this is only possible if the internal landscape possessed by each individual is essentially the same. However, this is not sufficient since we also have to insist that external objective experiences will trigger approximately the same internal emotional response in each individual. Figure 3 summarises these requirements. Here we have two landscapes belonging to persons A and B. Both are reading a description written by critic C. If it were possible to take a god-like view then we would expect to find that much of A's and B's landscapes would overlap in that each individual would have mostly the same emotional elements. Given C's two descriptions (say as metaphors describing a piece of music) then there will hopefully be a clear identification of the same emotions through the blending of A's and B's shared objective experiences. C's descriptions mark out two territories that can combine with or subtract from each other over time. It is the resulting construct and the path marked out during its construction that describes the emotional reaction that C is trying to communicate.

For example, the authors, acting as A and B, read from a critical review the following: "I was struck by the composer's ability to create a constantly changing and seemingly inevitable musical trajectory."[18] Reader A envisaged an abstraction of a drunkard's walk towards a goal. The path taken was jagged in detail, but broadly traversed a space. Reader B envisaged a rainbow in a green landscape arching over the sky, again towards a goal. The goal was on the ground. The generic characteristics of these two readings are that both trajectories have a goal and have a certain breadth overall in that the rainbow is wide but changes colour. The drunk's path, on the other hand, has a width brought about by his stagger. Both have goal, width and change and much more importantly, both visions carry an emotional payload which neither have stated nor can state. However, A brings in a drunk who might be singing and carrying a bottle, whereas B brings in a pastoral landscape and seven colours. These interpretations are not shared. The author C is assumed to have shared A and B's generic components, but may have had yet another scenario in his mind's eye. C writes in the belief that his readers will all get the generic characteristics along with the emotional elements of direction to a goal and some variety in the route. These are the only components of the description that can be validated through external observation. Everything else, including the emotional elements, must be either validated indirectly through inference or remain indeterminate and, hence, meaningless.

This analysis explains why words used in metaphorical description cannot be directly associated with an emotional element. To identify an area is to draw upon many different domains where words have their own specific role. Since the choice of domains and their combination is dependent upon the individual speaker then there can be no stable lexicon.

An inspection of Figure 3 will also show that because of the slight differences in each person's landscape there will be some elements of the description that will remain meaningless. We would also expect that these elements would be unlikely to overlap. A question that arises from this analysis is how those relying upon this process of communication can validate meanings.

The Influence of Culture

We know people within our lifetime who have experienced war at first hand and others that have never seen death. It would be obvious that a metaphor involving the very real events of war would have a much richer and intense effect on individuals who have experienced it. For those lucky enough not to have been involved in war, the metaphor would only be supported through cultural perceptions and exposure to rather abstract ideas. These abstractions tie this disparate range of experiences together for the individuals. Validation, and, thus, precision of meaning, can only cope with the metaphors at this abstract level. This explains why the ranges of descriptions seem to be so primitive (Table 2) and the window into another landscape so opaque.

Inferred Meaning

Our original aim was to provide a computational description of music. We have had to move away from a simple keyword association mechanism towards one that can cope with using tropes. Fauconnier and Turner (2002) describe such a mechanism. They call it *conceptual blending*. They give this name to the human ability to integrate superficially disparate ideas to make a new structure. This new cognitive structure carries many of the connotations of its parts, but expands and enhances them to illuminate an often wholly different referential framework. They call the parts *input spaces*, which derive some common characteristics from a so-called *generic space*. The product they call the *blended space*. This *blended space* has *emergent structure*. What they have effectively done is to flesh out the old saying that "the sum is greater than the parts." This ability is seen as a "fundamental mental operation." We suggest that this idea may provide the key to unlocking the mechanism that allows us to communicate using figurative language; it is a mechanism of inferred meaning. If that mechanism can be made explicit in a computational model we may be able to move one large step closer to understanding the role of metaphor and maybe automating artistic decisions. The act of implementation will certainly lead to a new way of communicating emotions through a machine.

Endnotes

[1] Shaw's spelling

[2] We note in particular the tremendous success of the current object-oriented approach.

[3] A paper (derived from Billinge, 2001) reviewing this earlier research, some of it going back to the 1930s, is under preparation. The work of Allen Newell and Herbert Simon (Newell & Simon 1972) on discourse analysis is key in the history of AI, but they did not concern themselves with artistic discourse.

[4] Though as long ago as the late 18th Century the Berlin paper *Vossische Zeitung* emphasised performance in its reviews [Sadic & Tyrrell (eds.), 2001) New Grove Dictionary of Music and Musicians, (2nd ed.) http://www.grovemusic.com/grovemusic//article/ section/4/405/40589.1.2.html accessed 27/02/01], the point still holds that the current era has a level of access to music undreamed of then.

[5] Concerts managers may, of course, be female or male. It just so happens that the authors have only spoken to the male ones. No gender bias is implied.

[6] The authors should admit that they are not able easily to check the orchestral requirements for these examples. The reader is asked to bear with this for the sake of the scenario.

[7] Miller (2001), in his startling exposition of sexual selection theory, offers the very best explanation the authors have yet encountered, laying out a strong case for viewing human Culture (with a capital C) as a derivative of mating display. His ideas deserve much more consideration and might provide a key to many mysteries. There are many emotional situations in which we use animal noises rather than words: one thinks of football crowds, but there are plenty of other examples. The need for pre-linguistic expression is still with us and what this has to contribute to the main thread can be put as a question. Is it surprising that we find it hard to make ourselves clear about our

right-brained reactions to music when we are forced, for lack of anything else, to make use of a left-brain derived communication system?

[8] Miller (2001) would disagree most profoundly

[9] This refers particularly to English, but other languages, such as German, depend upon such concatenated structures.

[10] The proportion of the two divisions of a straight line or two dimensions of a plane figure such that the smaller is to the larger as the larger is to the sum of the two. The Golden Section has been known since at least Euclid and has been thought to possess aesthetic virtue of itself (Murray & Murray, 1960).

[11] A full account of these experiments is in Billinge (2001) with further considerations in Billinge and Addis (2001).

[12] Three was arbitrarily chosen in order to reduce the number of words considered to a manageable set. Also we are only interested in the common lexicon that is shared by more than two people.

[13] This was triggered by Lehrer (1983), who, in a search for lexical structure in wine vocabulary, imposed a similar structure.

[14] There is evidence that an imposed, reduced set of words for communicating between people to achieve a practical task has very little effect on performance (Chapanis, 1975; Kelly & Chapanis, 1977).

[15] The reason why this law is valuable is that it shows that the object of communication (the word or the phrase) follows the expected pattern. It was conjectured by Scarrott (see Addis, 1985) that such a distribution can be explained by the use of recursive grammars as found in many natural phenomena.

[16] We would like to thank an anonymous reviewer for drawing our attention to Stephen Malinowski's Music Animation Machine (see http://www.well.com/user/smalin/samindex.html accessed 02/12/02). This invention makes sophisticated visual patterns from musical performances and is thus another way of "constructing emotional landscapes." It is not a solution to the verbal descriptor problem, because it is another modality. However it does point the way to an alternative resolution.

[17] Miller (2001) would appear to be suggesting that the whole of human culture is an epiphenomenon of sexual signalling. However, it is the internal structure of the epiphenomenon we

are investigating and we still need communication to take place.

[18] Gramophone (2002), 80, (959), 58.

References

Addis, T. R. (1985). Designing Knowledge-Base Systems. London: Kogan Page.

Addis, T. R. & Addis, Townsend J. J. (2001). Avoiding knotty structures in design: Schematic functional programming. *International Journal of Visual Languages & Computers*, 12, 689-715.

Asch, S. (1955). Opinion and Social Pressure. Scientific American, 193(5), 31-35.

Bever, G. & Chiarello, R.J. (1974). Cerebral dominance in musicians and non-musicians. *Science*, 185, 137-139.

Billinge, D. (1992, August 22). The Soft Option. *Classical Music*, 460, 16.

Billinge, D. (1996a, February 17). Chips with Everything. *Classical Music*, 549, 14.

Billinge, D. (1996b, March 2). A Matter of Opinion. *Classical Music*, 550, 14.

Billinge, D. (2001). *An Analysis of the Communicability of Musical Predication*. Unpublished Ph.D. Thesis. University of Portsmouth, UK.

Billinge, D. & Addis, T. (2001). Some fundamental limits of artistic decision making. *Proceeding of the AISB'01 Symposium on Artificial Intelligence and Creativity in Arts and Science. The Society for the Study of Artificial Intelligence and the Simulation of Behaviour*. University of York, UK.

Blacking, J. (1995). Music, culture and experience. In R. Byron (Ed.), *Selected Papers of John Blacking*. Chicago, IL: University of Chicago Press, USA.

Blackmore, S. (1999). *The Meme Machine*. Oxford, UK: Oxford University Press.

Blesser, B. (2001, October). An interdisciplinary synthesis of reverberation viewpoints. *J. Audio Eng. Soc.*, 49, 867-903.

Buchanan, B. G. & Shortliffe, E. H. (1984). *Rule-Based Expert Systems: The MYCIN Experiments of the Stanford Heuristic Programming Project*. Reading, MA: Addison-Wesley.

Budd, M. (1992). *Music and the Emotions*. London, UK: Routledge.

Cameron, J. (2001). *The Crucifixion in Music: An Analytical Study of Setting of the Crucifixus in the Eighteenth Century*. Unpublished Ph.D. Thesis. Liverpool University, UK.

Chapanis, A. (1975, March). Interactive human communication. *Scientific American*, 36-42.

Dunbar, R. (1996). *Grooming, Gossip and the Evolution of Language*. London, UK: Faber and Faber.

Fauconnier, G. & Turner, M. (2002). *The Way We Think: Conceptual Blending and the Mind's Hidden Complexities*. New York: Basic Books.

Goodman, N. (1976). *Languages of Art: An Approach to a Theory of Symbols*. Cambridge: Hackett Publishing Company.

Gordon, R. M. (1987). *The structure of Emotions: Investigations in Cognitive Philosophy*. Cambridge, UK: Cambridge University Press.

Hebb, D. O. (1946). Emotion in man and animal: An analysis of intuitive process of recognition. *Psychological Review*, 53, 88-106.

Kelly, K. J. & Chapanis, A. (1977). Limited vocabulary natural language dialogue. *International Journal of Man-Machine Studies*, 9, 479-501.

Kiesler, C.A. (1967). *Conformity and Commitment*. Trans-Action. In E.W. Stewart (1978). *Sociology : The Human Science*. (p. 129). New York: McGraw-Hill.

Lakoff, J. & Johnson, M. (1980). *Metaphors We Live By*. Chicago, IL: University of Chicago Press.

Langford-Smith, F. (1953). Radiotron Designer's Handbook (4th ed.). Wireless Press for Amalgamated Wireless Valve Company Pty. Ltd. Reproduced and distributed by RCA in America. Available on CD-ROM from Radio Era Archives 2043 Empire Central, Dallas, TX.

Lehrer, A. (1983). *Wine and Conversation*. Bloomington, IN: Indiana University Press.

Likert, R. (1932). A technique for the measurement of attitudes. *Archives of Psychology,* 140, 55.

Lyons, J. (1968). *Introduction to Theoretical Linguistics*. Cambridge, UK: Cambridge University Press.

Miller, G. (2001). *The Mating Mind*. London, UK: Vintage.

Murray, P. & Murray, L. (1960). *A Dictionary of Art and Artists*. Harmondworth, UK: Penguin Books.

New Grove Dictionary of Music and Musicians (2nd ed.). Retrieved February 2, 2001, from http://www.grovemusic.com/grovemusic//article/ section/4/405/40589.1.2.html.

Newell, A. & Simon, H. A. (1972). *Human Problem Solving*. Englewood Cliffs, NJ : Prentice-Hall.

Pareto, V. (1897). *Cours d'Economic Politique* (vol. 2, Section 3). Lausanne.

Pinker, S. (1997). *How the Mind Works. Allen Lane.* The Penguin Press.

Scruton, R. (1997). *The Aesthetics of Music OUP.* Oxford, UK: Oxford University Press.

Silberman, A. (1963). *The Sociology of Music.* London: Routledge & Kegan Paul.

Slonimsky, N. (1953). *Lexicon of Musical Invective: Critical Assaults on Composers Since Beethove's Time.* Washington: University of Washington Press.

Steblin, R. (1996). *A History of Key Characteristics in the Eighteenth and Early Nineteenth Centuries.* Rochester, NY: University of Rochester Press.

Storr, A. (1992). *Music and the Mind.* London, UK: Harper Collins.

Zipf, G.K. (1949). *Human Behaviour and the Principle of Least Effort.* London: Addison Wesley.

Chapter 9

Modeling Music Notation in the Internet Multimedia Age

Pierfrancesco Bellini and Paolo Nesi
University of Florence, Italy

Abstract

Music notation modeling is entering the new multimedia Internet age. In this era new interactive applications are appearing on the market, such as software tools for music tuition and distance learning, for showing historical perspective of music pieces, for musical content fruition in libraries, etc. For these innovative applications several aspects have to be integrated with the model of music notation and several new functionalities have to be implemented, such as automatic formatting, music notation navigation, synchronization of music notation with real audio, etc. In this chapter, the WEDELMUSIC XML format for multimedia music applications of music notation is pre-

sented. It includes a music notation format in XML and a format for modeling multimedia element, their relationships and synchronization with a support for digital right management (DRM). In addition, a comparison of this new model with the most important and emerging models is reported. The taxonomy used can be useful for assessing and comparing suitability of music notation models and format for their adoption in new emerging applications and for their usage in classical music editors.

Introduction

The modeling of music notation is an extremely complex problem. Music notation is a complex piece of information that may be used for several different purposes: audio coding, music sheet production, music teaching, entertainment, music analysis, content query, etc. In the Internet multimedia age, music notation and associated applications are being left behind. Many other applications are getting the market and most of them will become more diffuse in a short time. A unique and comprehensive format for music incorporating other media is required. In order to satisfy diverse applications several aspects have to be considered, ranging from problems of information modeling to integrate the music notation. The main problems are related to the organization of music notation symbols in a suitable and acceptable form. Such a set of rules has never been formalized, although they are informally used in several books and considered part of the experience of professional copy editors (engravers) of music sheets. Other problems include adoption of classical music notation in applications subject to DRM (digital right management), versioning, multimedia integration, and navigation, etc.

The evolution of information technology (IT) has recently produced changes in the usage of music notation, transforming the visual language of music from a simple coding model for music sheet to a tool for modeling music in computer programs. Enabling cooperative work on music and other information integration tasks is also necessary. More recently, users have discovered the multimedia experience, and thus, the traditional music notation model is likely to be replaced with something much more suitable for multimedia representation of music. The improved capabilities of computer programs are going to solve also early music notation formatting problems with powerful tools based on artificial intelligence technologies.

In this chapter, the main problems and the most promising evolution trends of music notation are reported. To this end, a comparison of the most representative music notation formats is included. The comparison has been performed on the basis of a set of aspects, which has been related to major problems mentioned in the first part of the chapter.

The chapter also introduces the WEDELMUSIC (WEB Delivering of Music) (Bellini, Della Santa & Nesi, 2001; Bellini, Bethelemy, Bruno, Nesi & Spinu, 2003) model and language. WEDELMUSIC does not claim to solve all problems related to music notation modeling, but it provides an effective framework that includes a comprehensive music notation and many innovative aspects suitable for multimedia and future applications in a XML-based format. On such basis, several problems highlighted in Byrd (1984) are solved. Other object-oriented music models (e.g., Taube, 1998; Pope, 1991) do not model relationships among symbols with the standard of accuracy required. They adopt a different object-oriented model, since they are mainly focused on producing sounds instead of visually presenting music to musicians. The WEDELMUSIC model allows the organization of rules for positioning notation elements on the staff, while considering their multiple representations and giving the possibility of including instrumental symbols and enabling their distribution in the network. In addition, WEDELMUSIC is a strongly improved version of MOODS (Music Object Oriented Distributed System), a cooperative model for editing music notation (Bellini, Nesi & Spinu, 2002).

Background

The problems of notation modeling and visualization of music scores have been addressed in computer systems several times (see Anderson & Kuivila, 1991; Blostein & Haken, 1991; Dannenberg, 1993; Dannenberg, 1990; Rader, 1996; Gourlay, 1986; Selfridge-Field, 1997; Blostein & Baird, 1992; Pennycook, 1985).

Among many possible computer-based applications of music, the notation editing for professional publishing and visualization is one of the most complex for the intrinsic complexity of music notation itself (Ross, 1987; Heussenstamm, 1987; Wood, 1989; Byrd, 1984). Music publishing requires the production of high quality music scores in terms of number of symbols and their precise placement on the staff. Music scores have to be presented to professional users (musicians) with specific relationships and proportions among symbols. The formal relationships among symbols are often neglected or misused by most commercial computer-based editors. Their aims consist of producing music by means of MIDI (Music Instrument Digital Interface) interfaces or sound-boards, or in acquiring music by means of a MIDI interface, or simply in editing music on the computer so as to manage sound-boards, etc.

In such events, a limited number of music notation symbols is needed (e.g., notes, rests, accidentals, clefs and points — approximately 50 symbols), which makes it impossible to reproduce through a MIDI interface the different effects specified by many other music notation symbols.

Sometimes the sets of music symbols available in professional editors (e.g., Score, Finale, Sibelius, etc.) for publishing music include also *instrumental and execution symbols* (symbols for describing the behavior of the musicians while playing a specific instrument — e.g., up or down bow, with mute, without mute, fingering, string numbers, accents, etc.) for strings, harps, drums, flutes, etc.; and *orchestral and repeat symbols*, etc. These symbols, together with many others, are needed when main scores and parts for classical music, operas, and ballets have to be produced, and they are mandatory when scores are used in music schools to train students to perform specific executions and interpretations of music. The number of elementary symbols is close to 300 in the commercial editors that are commonly used to prepare music scores for publishing. Such symbols are frequently treated as components to implement more complex symbols. Typically, musicians have to personalize/prepare a score for the execution; therefore, even this great number of symbols is not powerful enough to meet all their needs. On these grounds, some music editors provide a font editor to help the user in adding/creating symbols, which, unfortunately, are treated as simple graphic entities.

Commercial music editors for publishing are mainly inclined to place music symbols on the score page rather than to collect relationships among symbols and then organize the visual information accordingly. They are orientated towards printing music, since this is what they consider their most important application. They provide a complete set of symbols, which a user skilled enough in both music notation and computer graphic interface can use in order to produce professional music sheets. In music editors of this kind, the arrangement of many music notation symbols is often left to the users' competence. Music editors mainly consider music symbols (excluding notes, rests and a very few other symbols) as graphic elements to be placed in any position on a score page without feeling bound to address any problems related to the music notation like, for instance, the visual and syntactic relationships among symbols. This results in many music editors allowing several notation symbols to be placed in incorrect positions, thus producing strange and incorrect music scores. Eventually it follows that users are left with no technical support on how to place symbols.

For these reasons, professional music editors are powerful, but at the same time they are difficult to handle for non-expert users in music notation. Typically, musicians can read music, but they are pretty unfamiliar with rules for arranging symbols (e.g., when a symbol is associated with symbol B, symbol C has to be moved up one-half unit). Musicians have no problem when asked to read a correctly annotated score, but can be puzzled when they are faced with non-perfect visual constructs. Musicians are, in fact, artists, not music engravers nor notation technicians. It often occurs that conductors and composers are more sensitive to problems of music notation and visual expressiveness, while archivists in music theaters, music engravers, and music notation teachers are the experts of music notation problems.

Emerging New Applications

Recently, with the spread of computer technology into the artistic fields, new needs for computer-based applications of music have been identified: (i) cooperative music editing in orchestras and music schools, as with the project MOODS ESPRIT (Bellini, Fioravanti & Nesi, 1999; Bellini, Nesi & Spinu, 2002); (ii) music score distribution via the Internet, as with many Web sites distributing music scores or MIDI files; and (iii) multimedia music for music tuition systems: edutainment and infotainment. We have started to investigate these three new fields since 1994. MOODS consists of an integrated system of computer-based lecterns/stands for cooperative editing and visualization of music. MOODS is an innovative solution for automating and managing large amounts of information used by (i) orchestras during rehearsals and public performance of concerts, operas, ballets, etc.; (ii) students of music during lessons in conservatories and music schools; and (iii) publishers during massive editing of music.

The targeted MOODS end-users are theatres, itinerant orchestras, groups of musicians, music schools, television network orchestras, and publishers of scores. MOODS can be used to: (i) reduce the time needed for modifying main scores and parts during rehearsals in a cooperative way; (ii) manage (load, modify, and save) instrumental and personal symbols on main scores and parts; (iii) manage and reproduce the exact execution rate at which each measure of a score has been performed; (iv) automate page turning during rehearsals and final performances; (v) change music pieces quickly or restart from marked points; and (vi) manipulate the main score and all instrument parts together with the full music score in real time. Computerized music lecterns can be used by musicians to avoid transporting heavy paper music scores, to save their work, to manage versions, etc. A distributed system with the above features must be capable of showing music in different formats, and at the same time must support cooperative editing of music in different formats, which means showing the changes of one operator to the other ones in real time. A public demonstration of MOODS functionalities was given at La Scala Theatre in Milan. The main difference between the classical music editor and MOODS is the availability of cooperative work on music and the presence of integrated multimedia aspects. When cooperative work is relevant and the music has to be visualized at several resolutions regardless of the visualization support features — for example, low/high resolution monitors and printers — the following two main functionalities have to be available:

1. A clear distinction between the music notation model and the visualization rules: automatic reformatting while taking into account the user's needs, transposition, page dimension, etc.
2. Music notation model has to be abstract enough to allow the *interactivity with music at a symbolic level*: adding and deleting symbols, changing symbols features and making those changes available regardless of the visualization details without any reloading of the music score. To this end, the music notation and model has to support an indexing model (Bellini, Nesi & Spinu, 2002). This makes it possible to define policies of versioning, selective and un-linear undo, navigation among music notation symbols, etc.

This feature seems to be very far from being a reality in present Internet applications, even though it is of great interest for cooperative applications — e.g., virtual orchestras. It is noteworthy thinking of cooperative applications as something that will undergo a strong implementation among Internet applications in the very near future.

For the second type of application, music can be distributed by using images, audio and symbolic files. At present, the distribution of music via the Internet consists only of images of music scores or simple symbolic files, while audio files are widespread and better distributed. The music received from the Internet can be either *interactive or not*. For interactive music we intend music that can be manipulated in a certain measure: addition/deletion of symbols, transposition, reformatting, etc., without violation of the copyright law. Images of music sheets do not allow the music manipulation, while the MIDI model is too coarse to meet the needs of professionals, because MIDI provides a reduced set of music notation symbols.

In the past, the language called NIFF (Notation Interchange File Format) was supported by editing/publishing and scanning programs for creating an interchange format for music notation (NIFF, 1995). In the following years, the NIFF format has been abandoned as an interchange format by several companies and publishers. Recently, MusicXML has been proposed with the same aim (Good, 2001).

The Internet is at present dominated by the distribution of documents through the so-called mark-up languages derived from SGML, HyTime, XML (Extensible Markup Language), etc. (Sloan, 1997). A mark-up language consists of a set of constructs to express how text has to be processed with the main aim of text visualization. Generalized mark-up languages specify only what you have, rather than how to visualize it. The visual aspects are specified by using standard tags that state the typographic features: spacing, font change, etc. For example, when using XSL (Extensible Stylesheet Language) a formatting style should be defined. This means that a clear distinction has to be made between the content and the formatting aspects. These languages are mainly conceived for describing monodimensional pieces of information, like texts, and fail to model relationships among symbols at a logical level. For this reason, mark-up languages do not fit for any direct support to cooperative work, since they are not structured enough to be independent of the formatting aspects. In fact, mark-up languages were created for formatting textual documents and not for defining relationships among document symbols. This is one of the main problems, which prevents from an unreserved adoption/acceptance of SMDL (Standard Music Description Language) or other mark-up languages. Recently, several other XML-compliant mark-up languages for music modeling have been proposed, among them: MNML (Musical Notation Markup Language), MusicML, MML (Music Markup Language), MusicXML, etc. The MNML is a simplified version of SMDL. In MNML, it is possible to describe completely the basic melody and the lyrics of a music piece; on the other hand, it fails to describe all the needed details of real music scores (annotations, publishing aspects, etc.). MusicML can only represent notes and rests. Even staccato points and slurs are missing.

The adoption of a symbolic model totally separate from the visualization issues makes the distribution of interactive music a very complex task. In MOODS (Bellini, Fioravanti & Nesi, 1999), a cooperative editor of music has been proposed. It was built on a non-XML-based format. The solution was the definition of a specific language called MILLA (Music Intelligent Formatting Language), able to define rules for a formatting engine while letting users also have the possibility of forcing exceptional conditions. WEDELMUSIC model and language can be considered the XML evolution of MOODS format. With WEDELMUSIC several of MOODS' early problems for music modeling have been solved; in addition, WEDELMUSIC is a multimedia model. WEDELMUSIC provides an effective framework, which includes most music symbols and their relationships. On such basis, several new and innovative applications can be built and some exceptions and several modeling problems already highlighted in Selfridge-Field (1997) and Gourlay (1986). WEDELMUSIC format presents multimedia capabilities and includes identification, classification, symbolic, visual, protection, animations, image score, image, document, performance, video, lyric, aspects, synchronization, etc. It keeps separate visual/formatting from symbolic aspects. WEDELMUSIC format can be profitably used for new applications and as a format for interchanging symbolic description of music scores. Formatting rules and the corresponding MILLA engine of WEDELMUSIC can be found in Bellini, Della Santa and Nesi (2001).

The distribution of music sheets via the Internet can be considered one of the emerging new applications of music notation. Presently, a great part of the music sheets distributed via the Internet is in the form of PDF or Image files. In both cases, the music delivered is not interactive, since no transposition or annotation can be performed. Other more interactive solutions have been produced by Coda/Finale, Sibelius, and Noteheads. They distribute music notation in their proprietary formats, and this can be viewed and played in an Internet browser via MIDI by using specific plug-ins or ActiveX. For these applications, the DRM capabilities are particularly relevant to protect the distributed content. Typically, the models permit printing the music sheet only a limited number of times. In this field, WEDELMUSIC propose an integrated solution for distributing multimedia content. It may include files in any format and also files containing music scores. The obtained WEDELMUSIC objects can be protected and shared among archives and from these delivered to their attendees (Bellini et al., 2003).

Music Notation Problems vs. New Applications

This section deals with the most important modeling problems adopting the perspective of the emerging applications of music notation. As stated by several authors in the past, the modeling of music notation presents several problems: (i) the intrinsic complexity of formalizing both *music notation and the relationships* among music symbols; (ii) the necessity of providing different visualizations/views of the same music as it occurs with the main score and parts; (iii) the complexity of any automatic formatting of music symbols; (iv) the necessity of adding new symbols in order to expand the music notation model and make it fit for modern music and users' needs; (v) the necessity of presenting new functionalities for multimedia applications; (vi) the necessity of producing high quality music sheets in terms of tiny adjustments of symbols so as to avoid collisions and produce very clearly written and well recognizable music sheets at a first glance; and (vii) the formatting of music around the page end.

The modeling of all possible relationships among notation symbols is a complex task. As the number of symbols grows, the number of relationships among them grows with a ratio more than proportional. The syntax and semantics of music are strictly related and cannot simply be modeled by using only *non-visual* (relationships among symbols) or *visual* (positions with respect to the staff) aspects of music. The modeling of music symbol **relationships** is not enough to describe the music notation: for example, a *diminuendo* starting between two notes (and ending on the second) depicts the instant in which it has to be applied. The description of music as a collection of **graphical symbols** on the page regardless of their relationships relies too much on the visualization device (automatic reformatting is really complex). In most commercial music editors, the music notation symbols are simply managed as graphical symbols that can be placed on the screen.

The automatic generation of the main score from the different parts and the extraction of parts from a main score are complex tasks for real music, since the conductor's main score is typically formatted in a different way from the musicians' scores. Parts are obtained by using compressed versions of music notation symbols, and also present are several *instrumental, personal symbols*, which are typically omitted in the main score. The main score may present some specific textual notes or symbols for the conductor. The main score may show more than one part on a unique staff; in this case, parts are treated as distinct voices/layers. Other indications are added in the parts, so as to make the coordination among musicians easier — for instance, the so-called grace/cue notes. The main score and parts present different justifications, line breaking and page breaking. In some music editors, even the insertion of a measure in a part results in a huge manual work of reformatting in order to provide the replication of the performed changes on the main score, or vice versa. In Dannenberg (1990) a solution was given, suggesting the adoption of a unique model and distinct views for showing music on the basis of each specific need and context.

The positioning of music elements on the score presents many critical conditions. A music editor should help the users to produce well-formatted music scores. In most of the music editors, this task is addressed by considering only the visual representation of music symbols and not their relationships. As above highlighted, some visual aspects of music scores cannot be formalized in terms of symbol relationships. For this reason, the visual arrangement of music notation symbols makes the description of the music scores complete.

Music can be considered a visual language with its own rules. On this ground, the modeling of visual rules for formatting music is a requisite step to the completion of the model (Bellini, Della Santa & Nesi, 2001).

Typically, there is the need of adding new symbols for stating specific instrument aspects, and/or expanding the music notation model to take in modern music as well. The addition of new symbols means to add fonts, relationships among other symbols, execution rules, and formatting rules. For example, the addition of a symbol modeling a special figure (such as a cloud of notes) implies a deep change in the music notation model, whereas the addition of a new marker for notes can be performed by adding positioning rules and fonts, since the relationship with the note is already established. Several other symbols must be added to fulfill the needs of all instruments of a large orchestra (specific accents, jargon symbols, heel, toe, bridge, etc.). Most of them put on different visual representations depending on the instrument they are used for.

At a first glance, the new applications related to Internet distribution of music scores seem to be not too much different from the music editors currently on the market. The applications of the next few years will be mainly based on: (i) cooperative work on music notation; (ii) interactivity of music notation in the respect of the owner rights; (iii) the availability of different integrated information associated with the music piece; and (iv) music as support for tuition systems. In all these instances, music has to be independent from any visualization support features, formatting features, and resolution aspects. Then, the following functionalities have to be available:

- a clear distinction between the music notation model and the visualization rules: automatic reformatting on the account of the user's needs, etc.
- music notation model has to be abstract enough to allow interactivity with music at the symbolic level: adding and deleting symbols, changing symbols features, selective and unlinear undo, versioning, etc.
- music model has to integrate several aspects: audio, symbolic music notation, images of music score, documents, video, animations, Web pages, multilingual lyric, etc.
- mechanisms for distributing music by using shops, libraries, conservatories, etc., as local distributors.
- a refined protection model for DRM.

The first two problems may be managed by formal models supported by a separate engine for the automatic formatting of music according to precise rules. Ideally, this work is infeasible (Bellini, Della Santa & Nesi, 2001), but positive and promising compromises can be obtained. The new multimedia applications are bringing music into a new era. Simple audio files or music sheets are undergoing important changes in order to be included in more complex multimedia objects.

Music Notation Models and Languages

During our work for defining MOODS and WEDELMUSIC models and languages, several other music notation languages and tools were reviewed and analyzed; among them: MIDI, Finale, Score, MusiXTEX, NIFF, MusicXML, and SMDL. In this section, a short discussion and comparison among these formats is reported. The comparison does not claim to be exhaustive; it is focused on the aspects relevant for the adoption of these languages and models in the new applications. Please note that the WEDELMUSIC model and format is discussed in the next section and thus its description is not summarized in this section.

MIDI

MIDI is a sound-oriented language. It is unsuitable for modeling the relationships among symbols and for coding professional music scores. In MIDI, accents, ornaments, slurs, etc. are missing or very difficult to recognize. MIDI is the most widespread coding format among those that can be found on the Internet since (i) it can be easily generated by keyboards; (ii) it has been adopted by the electronic music industry for representing sounds in a computers form; and (iii) MIDI music can be played and manipulated with different synthesizers. A very large percentage of these files have been generated without the intention of recovering the music score and, therefore, they do not fit as music scores due to the presence of several small rests or notes. There is also a limited space for customizing the format. This space has been used for defining several versions of enhanced MIDI formats (Selfridge-Field, 1997). In the literature several extensions of MIDI have been proposed, but no one has really got the large diffusion to substitute the classical MIDI format. MIDI format is mainly used as an interchange format; on the other hand, its capability in modeling music notation is very limited. Most of the music editors are capable of loading and saving music notation in MIDI.

SCORE

SCORE is probably the most widespread notation editor among publishers for the high quality and professional Postscript printing (Smith, 1997). In SCORE, each symbol can be precisely arranged on the page according the engravers' needs. Complex symbols can be produced by using graphic elements on the music sheet. Several minor accompanying symbols of the note can be placed on the staff in any position; thus, the relationships with the note are non-defined. This means that a movement of the note or its deletion does not influence the life of these symbols. SCORE presents no distinction between slur and ties and no automatic conversion of sequences of rests into generic rests. SCORE is a page-oriented editor, in the sense that music information is collected only related to the preparing page: the editor is capable of managing only a printable page at time. Since the music is created page-by-page, parts (each page a file), are very hard to automatically extract because the match is based on part numbering and the numbering of staffs may be different in successive pages (some parts can be missing, the numbering is not ordered from top to bottom). When symbols are managed in the middle of a line or page break, they are drawn with two distinct graphic lines. This makes complex the extraction of parts and the reorganization of music measures along the main score and parts. The insertion of some measures in a page or the changing of the page dimensions may need the manual manipulation of all pages. This is totally unacceptable for music that has to be distributed via the Internet and that has to be viewable on several different devices for both size and resolution, with changes to be performed in real time.

MusiXTEX

MusiXTEX is a set of macros for LaTEX and/or TEX for producing music sheets (Taupin, Mitchell & Egler, 1997; Icking, 1997). The language is interesting since its structure is substantially symbolic, while graphic commands can be added to provide precise positioning. The relationships among symbols depend on the order symbols appear in the code. The language is printer-oriented; thus, it allows the placement of graphics symbols anywhere on the page.

Some simple rules for the insertion of symbols are available (definition of up and down of the stems for notes). With MusiXTEX, specific rules for the visual organization of symbols on the page could be defined exploiting the power of LaTEX and TEX. Classification features could be implemented by using a similar technique. In the past we developed a simple music editor based on an early version of MusiXTEX; it was called LIOO (Lectern Interactive Object Oriented). It has been the early version of the MOODS system.

In MusiXTEX, the work has to be manually performed during the score coding. MusiXTEX does not support: (i) the automatic beaming (identification of the groups of notes to be beamed together in the measure); (ii) the automatic definition of stem direction of notes in beams; or (iii) the automatic management of positioning for accents.

NIFF

NIFF was developed with the perspective of defining an interchange format for music notation among music notation editing/publishing and scanning programs (NIFF, 1995). Its present version if 6b. NIFF was derived from design rules of the Resource Interchange File Format (RIFF). NIFF design resulted from a quite large group of commercial music software developers, researchers, publishers and professionals. For this reason, the model was defined with the aim of supporting the most relevant aspects of several models. This represented a great limit in the expressiveness of the languages and models for describing exceptions. The main features of NIFF are: (i) a feature set based on SCORE; (ii) division of visual information in page and non-page layout information; (iii) extensible, flexible and compact design; and (iv) inclusion of MIDI data and format. Since 1995, the notation has not been improved. It is currently supported by LIME editor and few others. Since 1996, a kit for implementing a loading module for NIFF files is available.

NIFF language includes in a unique model of both visual and logical aspects. This makes it difficult to deliver music regardless of the visualization details, which is a feature needed in cooperative applications. Relationships among symbols are defined via specific links (anchorage). They can be set according to default rules, but specific actions can be performed for managing some changes in the editors. In NIFF, no support is provided for either versioning or cooperative work, since each logical element in the format cannot be univocally identified. NIFF presents a limited number of symbols, but grants the possibility of defining new symbols.

SMDL

SMDL is a mark-up language built on SGML (Standard Generalized Markup Language) and HyTime standards (SMDL, 1995). The aim was the definition of an interchange abstract model. The SMDL model includes the following aspects:

logical, gestural, visual and analytical. The logical aspect includes the music content (pitches, rhythms, dynamics, articulations, etc.), that is, the abstract information common to both gestural and visual domains. The gestural domain describes specific performances of the logical domain. It includes dynamic symbols, etc., and MIDI information. In MOODS, these aspects are collected in logical parts. The different versions due to the gestural aspects can be managed in MOODS via the versioning mechanism.

In SMDL, the visual domain describes the musical typographic details of scores (the symbol, placing, fonts, etc.). This is quite similar to the concept of MOODS, but SMDL does not include mechanisms for defining visualization rules for symbols. The analytical domain consists of music analyses for classification purpose and a support for defining more sophisticated analysis in the logical and gestural parts. SMDL was analyzed in depth in the CANTATE project (CANTATE, 1994). The result of the analysis was as follows: SMDL cannot be used for modeling scores. It can only produce visually visible scores by using other formats such as FINALE, SCORE, NIFF, etc., or images of music sheets. SMDL cannot be used as a standard interchange format for the visual aspect, but only for the logical aspects of music: a sort of container in which several different music formats and related information can be collected and organized (NIFF, MIDI, animations, textual descriptions, etc.) Currently there is no commercial SMDL software for editing music or producing music digital objects. In the CANTATE project, an application of SMDL for the distribution of music for libraries was developed.

SMDL presents a neat distinction between the visual and the logical parts that should be modeled by different languages and formalisms. For this lack of integration among music aspects, SMDL cannot be used for either distributing interactive music via the Internet or as a basis of cooperative work on music scores like in MOODS. More recently, several other mark-up languages for music modeling have been proposed. Unfortunately, they are weakened by the lack of managing slurs, accents, etc. The adoption of a structural model totally separate from the visualization issues makes the production of professional music a very complex task. In MOODS, the solution was the definition of MILLA (Music Intelligent Language) meaning a specific language for defining visualization rules and giving users the possibility of forcing exceptional conditions.

MusicXML

MusicXML is a XML format for music notation interchange developed by Recordare (Good, 2001). It is based on two other textual formats for music notation representation: the MuseData and the Humdrum formats (Selfridge-

Field, 1997). It represents the music in a time-wise (parts nested within measures) or part-wise (measures nested within parts) manner; a XSLT (Extensible Stylesheet Language Transformation) allows the transformation from one to the other format. The format covers the Western musical notation from the 17th Century onward; it is mainly oriented to describing the logical structure of music even if some graphical detail could be added. A plug-in for Finale allows it to load and save files using this format; the Sharpeye OMR application uses it as an interchange format with Finale. It includes a subset of the most commonly used formats. It can be useful for interchanging music notation, but is far from being a good format for new multimedia applications. At the XML level, MusicXML is strongly based on Tag rather than on Attributes. This limits the flexibility of defining new symbols that are considered values of attributes. The addition of a different value is simpler that the production of a new rule for managing a new tag of the XML.

FINALE, Enigma Format

Music produced by the FINALE program is coded in Enigma format. This format is partially documented. The editor and format are mainly oriented towards page preparation rather than defining relationships among symbols. Clear evidence of this is found in several symbols being non-linked to figures and simply placed on the page, assuming any position without any bound to follow the sort of the note whenever moving or deleting. The format has been recently improved and allows the definition of some relationships among music notation symbols. This is not its internal philosophy, but it is left to the users. The Finale model does not present a clear trace for voices that pass from one staff to the other in multi-staff parts, such as those for piano, harp and organ. In several cases, the arrangement of music notation symbols is quite hard since the automatic mechanism for completing the measure is quite disturbing.

GUIDO Format and Tools

GUIDO is a textual format (human readable) for symbolic music description. The description is extremely compact and it seems to be optimized for direct user entry rather than to have an editor produce it (like MusiXTex). A set of tools are present to transform this description to MIDI and to render it as PostScript or GIF, or to convert to it MIDI and FINALE files to GUIDO. GUIDO language has been designed in three layers: Basic GUIDO describes the basic musical symbols of Western music notation (notes, rests, slurs, etc.) and their structure (staffs, voices, chords); Advanced GUIDO extends the Basic GUIDO to support exact score formatting and more sophisticated musical concepts; Extended GUIDO introduce concepts beyond conventional music notation. The tools currently support Basic GUIDO and Advanced GUIDO. However the specification of Advanced GUIDO and Extended GUIDO are not available. Automatic formatting rules are encoded in the renderer and automatic beaming are supported; however, precise positioning and beaming can be specified forcing the position. The symbols supported in the Basic GUIDO are few and cover only the most important expressive indication (staccato, tenuto, accento, marcato...) and ornaments (trillo, mordente, gruppetto, tremolo, glissando), and no symbols for specific instrument are present (violin, piano, arpa, etc.). Moreover GUIDO lacks in the possibility to introduce new user-defined symbols.

The Basic Aspects of WEDELMUSIC Model and Format

WEDELMUSIC is an XML-compliant format, which includes constructs for the description of integrated music objects. Digital music objects compliant with the WEDELMUSIC format are called WEDELMUSIC or simply WEDEL objects. The model is supported by a full set of tools for multimedia music packaging and distribution. They are focused on a specific music piece or concept. Each WEDEL object presents sections about its identification, classification, protection, printing, symbolic music (fonts, formatting rules, versions), image score, performance, documents, animations, lyric, audio, video, and color image. Hereafter, these aspects are discussed with the rationale for their inclusion.

- **Identification** section allows the identification of the music piece. Typical identification codes such as ISMN, ISBN, etc., are included. Each WEDEL object has a unique identification (ID) called WDFID, while each of its components has its own code called WDFCID.
- **Classification** section allows the classification of the music piece according to multilingual archive mechanisms, integrating both the most well known standards Z39.50 and UNIMARK fields, plus other fields. Distinct classification records may be set up for the whole object and for its components.
- **Protection** section models details about the encryption of the WEDEL object and the watermarking of music (audio files and music sheets). According to a sophisticated DRM module, each operation that can be performed on the WEDEL object can be either permitted or inhibited; more than 150 different multime-

dia functionalities are managed. A permission table is available to define DRM. This model allows analysis of the end-users' needs with statistic tools, since each exploited functionalities can be tracked by the distributor.

- **Symbolic Music** section describes the scoring information, musical notation symbols, and their relationships. Symbolic music can include the main score and parts. The symbolic description includes specific sections for classification and identification of the music score (main score and parts). Formatting rules are formalized in MILLA language, like in MOODS (Bellini, Della Santa & Nesi, 2001), for positioning symbols, deciding the stem length, deciding where to place symbols (whether up or down the staff), orienting the beam and ordering to place notation symbols (slurs, accents, ornaments, etc.) around the notes. The user may decide to apply different rules for the automatic reformatting of the music piece. Files in other music notation formats can also be included, for example Finale, Sibelius, Score, MuseDATA, MusicXML, etc. With additional tools it is possible to convert MIDI, Finale, SCORE and Sibelius formats into WEDELMUSIC, and from this to save music notation in MIDI and Finale.
- **Image of Music Sheets** section allows to integrate images of music scores into the WEDEL object without converting them into symbolic format. Therefore, in the same WEDEL object, both symbolic notation and original images can be present. The same WEDEL object may contain images of the main score and the related parts, even in more versions. This makes it possible to build WEDEL objects to compare the original music score with revised and currently used symbolic versions. It is a good support for revitalizing and recovering cultural heritage.
- **Audio** section may contain none or one or more audio files in any format. Audio files can be watermarked according to the WEDEL object's parameters.
- **Performance** section describes the synchronization aspects between each audio file and the music score of the WEDEL object. The synchronization of audio files allows the contemporaneous visualization of the score and listening to the music with the selected audio and execution rate. This can be done by using symbolic music notation or simple images of the music

score. A performance can also be a sequence of slides associated with an audio file.

- **Documents** section may include documents in any format. Documents may be author biography, critical description of the piece, description of the music piece, etc. — any document related to the music score of the WEDEL object. This section could include also a document version of the music score. It can be in PDF or PostScript as well. Documents may have special HTTP links to other elements in the WEDEL object. PDF documents included in WEDELMUSIC present a very high level of protection, since WEDELMUSIC permits the full control of the number of printouts produced by PDF files.
- **Lyric** section includes multilingual lyrics associated with the music score and, therefore, with the WEDEL object. Several multilingual lyrics can be associated with the same symbolic part. This is performed by using the symbolic indexing of each music notation symbol.
- **Video** section may contain video files in any format. Video files in the WEDEL object turns out to be of great help for (i) showing the hands of the musician while playing music, which is very useful for didactical purposes (hands can be visualized while the music score appears on the screen); (ii) including/showing the video of a live performance and the songs text; etc.
- **Animations** can be in Flash included in HTML pages, or in PPT, or video, etc.
- **Image** section may include color images in any format. For example, the portrait of the author/performer, the picture related to the music or opera, or performer, the home/city of the author/performer, a picture of the instrument, a picture of the live performance, the CD cover, etc.

In each WEDEL object, several relationships among its components can be established as depicted in Figure 1.

For example, the following relationships can be established:

- Symbolic-lyric: different lyric files can be referred to the same symbolic file.

Figure 1: An Integrated Multimedia Music Object

- Symbolic-image score: relationship performed thanks to the specific number associated with each measure.
- Image score to symbolic: relationship performed thanks to the specific number associated with each measure.
- From Symbolic to video, images, documents, audio files: relationships performed via http links, which can be assigned to music notation elements.
- Images of music score to lyric.
- From symbolic or images of music score to the audio via performance section: each audio file can be synchronized with the music score.

Music Notation Aspects

The relationships among visual notation constructs can only be formalized considering syntax and semantic aspects. As far as music is concerned, the definition of a visual grammar is a highly complex task. To create the WEDELMUSIC formal model, we first modeled music notation components with a unified object-oriented formal model and language. In WEDELMUSIC and MOODS, the object-oriented model has been used as a music representation model and coding language, and also as the network message interchange protocol among lecterns. In WEDELMUSIC, the logical structure of music notation is modeled in XML, while the graphic details are generated in real time by using the style coded in MILLA (Bellini, Della Santa & Nesi, 2001).

MILLA can be used for defining default and exceptions rules in order to manage the already described two kinds of problems. Simple conditions can be also forced. Several symbols strictly related to notes are managed: accidentals, ornaments, fingering, accents, instrumental symbols, etc. In several instances, the mere presence of more than one of such symbols around figures changes the figures' order, orientation, and position. For instance, accents must be placed on the opposite side of the stem (if any). In the event of a slur on the same note, some accents must leave space close to the note at the slur; thus, they have to be placed just a bit farther from the notehead than usual (Ross, 1987; Heussenstamm, 1987). The slur itself has to make room for other symbols when they are contemporaneously present on the same note.

In MILLA, the users can specify the following types of rules for the:

- Insertion of symbols, such as the estimation of the direction (up/down with respect to the staff or with respect to the notehead) of stems, beam, slurs, etc. (they can be manually imposed if needed).
- Positioning of symbols, such as the estimation of stem length, distance with respect to staff lines, beam angle, position of the ornaments, expressions, etc., with respect to the notehead.
- Ordering symbols while considering the presence of neighboring symbols, ensuring precedence among symbols with respect to the notehead when depicting slurs, accents, markers, etc.
- Justification of measures according to specific algorithms, such as linear, logarithmic, and different scales; to consider alignment among voices and parts in main scores, line breaking and page breaking.

- Beaming rules for beaming notes on the basis of time signature, etc.
- Compressing symbols for the activation and deactivation of rules which display symbols in a compressed format, including generic rests and repeat symbols.

The set of MILLA rules associated with a music piece is a sort of formatting style, like the styles usually adopted in word processors. It is more sophisticated than those styles since MILLA rules can be activated according to the conditions estimated when considering local and/or general visualization contexts. Such rules typically change on the basis of the context: presence of other voices or parts, presence of other symbols, up/down the staff, etc. Most of the defined rules prevent the generation of collisions; others may permit the production of a specific collision under certain conditions (stems and beams, beams and barlines, stems and slurs, etc.). Once a new visual problem is detected, a specific rule can be added or the change can be manually performed.

Figure 2: An Example

In Figure 2, an example, which has been automatically formatted by WEDELMUSIC taking into account specific rules, is reported.

The slope of the two beams is determined by the following MILLA rule:

```
RULEPOS BeamInt BEAM RELNOTES ANYWHERE ANGLE=[0.15;0.3];

posIF STAFFNUMBER=1.0 AND STAFFLINES=5.0 AND DELTA<2.5 AND DELTA>0.5 THEN BeamInt;
```

The DELTA value is defined as (highest – lowest)/(number of notes -1), where highest-lowest is the distance in spaces (the distance between two staff lines) from the highest note to the lowest note of the beam.

The value of DELTA for the first beam is (11-10)/(2-1) = 1, and for the second one is (10-8)/(3-2) = 1; then both beams satisfy the condition of being greater than 0.5 and less than 2.5. This leads to the appliance of rule BeamInt. According to the former, the slope of the line connecting the higher and the lower note is calculated as follows: if this slope is between 0.15 and 0.3, this slope is applied; otherwise, when less than 0.15, slope 0.15 is assumed and 0.3 when greater.

The rules used to determine the length of the stem for a chord are as follows:

```
RULEPOS Stem3_5 STEM RELNOTA LENGHT=3.5;
RULEPOS Stem4 STEM RELNOTA LENGHT=4;
RULEPOS Stem4_5 STEM RELNOTA LENGHT=4.5;
RULEPOS Stem5 STEM RELNOTA LENGHT=5.0;
RULEPOS Stem5_5 STEM RELNOTA LENGHT=5.5;
RULEPOS Stem6 STEM RELNOTA LENGHT=6.0;
RULEPOS Stem6_5 STEM RELNOTA LENGHT=6.5;
...
RULEPOS StemHeight STEM RELNOTA LENGHT=STEMHEIGHT;

posIF NOTE CROMA AND INCHORD AND NUMUP>0.0 AND NUMDOWN>0.0 THEN Stem3_5;
posIF NOTE SEMICROMA AND INCHORD AND NUMUP>0.0 AND NUMDOWN>0.0  THEN Stem4;
posIF NOTE BISCROMA AND INCHORD AND NUMUP>0.0 AND NUMDOWN>0.0  THEN Stem4_5;
posIF NOTE SEMIBISCROMA AND INCHORD AND NUMUP>0.0 AND NUMDOWN>0.0  THEN Stem5_5;
posIF NOTE FUSA AND INCHORD AND NUMUP>0.0 AND NUMDOWN>0.0  THEN Stem6_5;
posIF INCHORD AND NUMUP>0.0 AND NUMDOWN>0.0 THEN Stem3_5;

posIF INCHORD AND NOTE STEMUP AND UPPERD>7.0 THEN StemHeight;
posIF INCHORD AND NOTE STEMDOWN AND LOWERD>7.0 THEN StemHeight;

posIF NOTE CROMA AND INCHORD THEN Stem3_5;
posIF NOTE SEMICROMA AND INCHORD THEN Stem4;
posIF NOTE BISCROMA AND INCHORD THEN Stem4_5;
posIF NOTE SEMIBISCROMA AND INCHORD THEN Stem5_5;
posIF NOTE FUSA AND INCHORD THEN Stem6_5;
posIF INCHORD THEN Stem3_5;
```

The rule applied to the chord of the example is the one evidenced, since other rules do not apply. The UPPERD and LOWERD values are the distance from the center line of the staff in spaces of the upper and the lower note of the chord. The NUMUP and the NUMDOWN values are the number of notes of the chord above and below the center line of staff.

In this case, the rule applied establishes that the stem has to be 3.5 spaces.

The XML encoding of the example reported in Figure 2 is the following (some details are missing, though):

```
<?xml version="1.0" encoding="UTF-8"?>
<SWF_Part>
   <WDFCID>00000100000K</WDFCID>
   <Identification>
      <WDFID>00020000H</WDFID>
      <Publisher PUBLISHING_STATUS="OTHER">Test</Publisher>
      <Preparation_date MAJOR_VERSION="0"
MINOR_VERSION="1">20021015</Preparation_date>
      <Music_Geographic_Area>Europe</Music_Geographic_Area>
   </Identification>
   <Classification xml:lang="en" Description="English">
      <Author>N/A</Author>
      <Unique_Short_Name>Example</Unique_Short_Name>
      <Title>Example</Title>
      <Genre>Classical</Genre>
      <Style>Classical</Style>
      <Original_language/>
      <Composition_date>00000000</Composition_date>
      <Epoque>
         <Start_year>0</Start_year>
         <End_year>0</End_year>
      </Epoque>
   </Classification>
   <score ID="1" TYPE="NORMAL" INSTRUMENT="Vln.I">
      <origin FROM="WEDELED"/>
      ...
      <measure PROGRESSIVE="1" ID="1">
         <justification MAINTYPE="LOG" MAINJUST="2.0" PMAINTYPE="LOG"
PMAINJUST="2.0"/>
         <header>
            <clef TYPE="TREBLE"/>
            <keysignature TYPE="DOM"/>
         </header>
         <timesignature TYPE="FRACTION" NUMERATOR="4" DENOMINATOR="4"/>
         <layer NUMBER="1">
            <beam ID="10" STEMS="DOWN">
               <note ID="1" DURATION="D1_8" HEIGHT="11">
                  <ornament TYPE="TRILL" UPDOWN="UP" ACCSUP="SHARP"/>
               </note>
               <note ID="2" DURATION="D1_8" HEIGHT="10"/>
            </beam>
            <rest ID="3" DURATION="D1_4" HEIGHT="1"/>
            <chord ID="5" DURATION="D1_4" STEM="DOWN">
               <chordnote ID="5" HEIGHT="4"/>
               <chordnote ID="6" HEIGHT="11"/>
               <augmentation DOTS="1"/>
               <dynamictext DYNAMIC="F" UPDOWN="DOWN"/>
            </chord>
            <beam ID="11" STEMS="DOWN">
               <note ID="7" DURATION="D1_16" HEIGHT="10"/>
               <note ID="8" DURATION="D1_16" HEIGHT="9"/>
               <note ID="9" DURATION="D1_16" HEIGHT="8"/>
            </beam>
         </layer>
         <barline TYPE="END"/>
      </measure>
      <horizontal ID="1" TYPE="TUPLE" UPDOWN="DOWN" TUPLENUMBER="3"
TUPLELINE="FALSE">
         <address MEASURE="1" LAYER="1" FIGURE="11" CHORD.OR.BEAM="7"/>
         <address MEASURE="1" LAYER="1" FIGURE="11" CHORD.OR.BEAM="9"/>
      </horizontal>
      <horizontal ID="2" TYPE="SLUR" UPDOWN="UP">
         <address MEASURE="1" LAYER="1" FIGURE="10" CHORD.OR.BEAM="1"/>
         <address MEASURE="1" LAYER="1" FIGURE="10" CHORD.OR.BEAM="2"/>
      </horizontal>
   </score>
</SWF_Part>
```

The symbolic description of a part (the score tag) is decomposed in a sequence of measures, followed by the sequence of horizontal symbols (slurs, tuples, crescendo, diminuendo, etc.). Each single measure contains the header information as clef, key signature and the time signature, followed by one or more layers with figures (notes, rests, beams, chords, etc.).

It should be observed that horizontal symbols refer to the starting/ending figure using a path of identifiers (measureID/layer/figureID/figureID...); for example, the second note of the first beam is identified by path:1/1/10/2.

It should be observed that the HEIGHT attribute of notes/rests refers to the line/space where the note has to be positioned: 0 is the first line of the staff, 1 the first space, 2 the second line, 3 the second space, etc.

WEDELMUSIC presents several innovative features that will be extremely useful for the new generation of music notation applications:

- Symbolic indexing of music notation. This makes it possible to implement selective and non-linear undo, symbolic navigation among symbols and multimedia documents (Bellini, Nesi & Spinu, 2002), management of versioning, or mounting multi-lingual lyric.
- DRM support, including rules and watermarking support of music sheets and audio/video files. It is very important to integrate this aspect into the music model since it allows to define specific rules for versioning, music fruition, music notation printing, multimedia integration and fruition, etc.
- Integration with multimedia components such as described above. Multimedia integration can be very useful for creating relationships among music notation symbols and multimedia content for educational purpose and content valorization.
- Definition of custom and new symbols with their formatting rules, starting from 500 symbols.
- Management of information related to formatting the music in two different cases/views. For instance, use computer view for music score reading on the computer screen during tuition and edutainment and print view as a graphic user interface for producing professional music sheets. This is performed for both the main score and each single part. This makes it possible to have, in a unique format, both the main score and parts with their formatting information.

Music Notation Models and Language Comparison

Table 1 is a scheme summary for the comparison of the above-mentioned languages and models, considering the aspects discussed in previous sections. In the table, (Y) means that the answer is not completely true or satisfactory, since these features are potentially available and their presence depends on the visual/graphic editor used. In most cases, the positioning of symbols is made a bit more complex by using a set of visualization parameters. This approach results in imposing a single rule for the positioning of the whole score, and turns out to be a coarse simple and unsuitable solution for managing automatic positioning.

Table 1: Coverage of Music Aspects (Y and N represent if a Given Feature is supported or not, when they are in Round Brackets means that Incomplete or Non-Satisfactory Coverage is provided)

	WEDEL MUSIC	MIDI	SCORE	MusiX TEX	NIFF	SMDL	Music XML	FINALE	GUIDO
Logic model	Y	N	Y	Y	Y	Y	Y	Y	Y
Classification	Y	N	N	(Y)	(Y)	Y	(Y)	(Y)	N
Identification	Y	N	N	(Y)	(Y)	Y	(Y)	(Y)	N
Visual	Y	N	Y	Y (print)	(Y)	N	Y	Y	Y
Visualization Rules	Y (Milla)	N	N	N	N	N	N	(N)	N
Visualization Parameters	Y	N	Y	N	Y	N	N	Y	(Y)
Performance or MIDI play in real time	Y	Y	N (SCORE MIDI)	N	Y	(Y)	N	Y	Y
Synchronization with real audio	Y	N	N	N	N	N	N	N	N
Images of music scores	Y	N	N	N	N	N	N	N	N
Animations	Y	N	N	N	N	N	N	N	N
Versioning support	Y	N	N	N	N	(Y)	N	N	N
Selective and un-linear undo	Y	N	N	N	N	N	N	N	N
DRM support	Y	N	N	N	N	N	N	N	N
Multimedia Integration (video, etc.)	Y	N	N	N	N	(Y)	N	N	N
Symbolic indexing of music notation	Y	N	N	N	N	N	N	N	N
Multilingual Lyric	Y	N	N	N	N	N	N	N	N
Graphic Lyric	Y	N	Y	Y	Y	Y	Y	Y	N
Stream Lyric	Y	N	N	N	N	Y	N	Y	(Y)

In Table 2, the results of the comparison are reported. The information has been obtained by reviewing tools related to the languages. When a number is given, it was obtained by means of questionnaires distributed to musicians and computer scientists. In the table, Interactive Music Editing states the availability of a visual editor; Adding/Editing Graphic Entities is the possibility of using graphic primitives (like lines) superimposed on the score; Print support, Extraction of Parts, Extensibility of Symbols, and Fusion of Parts do not need any comment; Main Score editing full length is the possibility of editing the main score as continuous information not interrupted by page breaks; Music Distribution for Cooperative work is the possibility of cooperative working during music editing or execution; Number Notation Symbols is a vote about the number and the relevance of the available notation symbols; Logic and Visual Independence is a vote about the independence of logic and visual aspects. This last vote has been obtained by analyzing the music formats and models and observing the behavior of symbols on the editors (when available) during insertion, moving, and deletion.

Table 2: Editor, Languages and Model Comparison (Y and N represent if a Given Feature is supported or not, when they are in Round Brackets means that Incomplete or Non-Satisfactory Coverage is provided)

	WEDEL MUSIC	MIDI	SCORE	MusiX TEX	NIFF	SMDL	Music XML	FINALE	GUIDO
Interactive Music Editing	Y	Y	Y	N	Y	N	(N)	Y	(Y)
Adding/Editing Graphic Entities	(N)	N	Y	Y	N	N	N	Y	Y
Print support	Y	Y	Y	Y	Y	N	N	Y	Y
Extraction of Parts	Y	N	Y	N	Y	N	Y	Y	N
Fusion of Parts	Y	Y	Y	N	(Y)	N	N	(N)	N
Main Score editing full length	Y	Y	N	Y	Y	N	Y	Y	N
Automatic formatting of music, symbol positioning	Y	N	Y	Y	N	N	N	Y	(Y)
Automatic line breaking	Y	N	Y	Y	N	N	N	Y	Y
Managing Formatting information for main score and parts in the same model and file	Y	N	N	N	N	N	N	N	N
Music Distribution for Cooperative work	Y	N	N	N	N	N	N	N	N
Music Distribution tools	Y	Y	N	N	N	N	N	Y	(Y)
Music Analysis	Y	N	N	N	N	N	N	Y	N
Braille Music	Y	N	N	N	N	N	N	Y	N
Vote on the number of notation symbols: from 1 to 10 (very good)	9	4	10	8	4	4	6	9	5
Extensibility of Symbols	Y	--	Y	Y	Y	Y	N	Y	N
Logic and Visual Independence	Y	N	N	N	Y	Y	N	N	N
Code editor availability	Tool Kit	Y	N	N	N	N	N	N	Y
Liveness of editor	Monthly	stable	none	none	none	none	monthly	yearly	none

The main problems of the considered languages in meeting the requirements of the new application are mainly due to the lack of formalization in the language and in the model for storing/coding music. Concerning the definition of relationships among symbols, the most flexible and complete language is NIFF. Even this language is not fully satisfactory since it does not model all the relationships. The real problem of these languages is the lack of versioning support and the management of visualization rules. These two aspects are also missing in the several new mark-up languages that have been recently proposed on the Web. They are presently strongly limited compared with the above models. Most of them do not present slurs, accents, instrumental symbols, justification, etc. There are also several other types of languages for coding music, as described in Selfridge-Field (1997), but, unfortunately, none of them can be held as a complete support for the requirements of the new incoming applications.

On the account of the work performed on several projects and products, some tools for operating the conversion among these formats have been produced. Table 3 summarizes the available converters among the considered languages. Some of them exist only at a hypothetical level because they are, for instance, based on claimed prototypes, but the converter is not distributed or the conversion has been only studied and analyzed. In all these conversions,

Table 3: Available Format Converters (Y and N represent if a Given Feature is supported or not, when they are in Round Brackets means that Incomplete or Non-Satisfactory Coverage is provided)

From\ to	WEDEL MUSIC	MIDI	SCORE	MusiX Tex	NIFF	SMDL	Music XML	FINALE	GUIDO
WEDELMUSIC	--	Y	N	N	N	N	N	Y	N
MIDI	Y	--	Y (MIDISCORE)	N	Y (Lime)	Y	Y	Y	Y
SCORE	Y via Sibelius	Y	--	N	N	N	N	N	N
MusiXTEX	N	N	N	--	N	N	N	N	N
NIFF	N	Y (Lime)	N	N	--	(N) (Cantate)	Y	N	N
SMDL	N	N	N	N	(N) (Cantate)	---	N	N	N
MusicXML	N	Y	N	N	N	N	...	Y	N
FINALE	Y	Y	Y (Final SCORE)	N	N	N	Y	...	(Y) only few symbols
GUIDO	N	Y	N	N	N	N	N	N	....

several details are lost since different formats treat the information in a different manner; others present a limited number of symbols and relationships, thus being forced to eliminate information during the transformation.

From the above comparison it evident that WEDELMUSIC is the best candidate for managing innovative and new emerging multimedia applications. It contains several innovative aspects at the level of music notation such as symbolic indexing, strong distinction between logic and graphics, MILLA formatting engine, multilingual lyric, etc.

Future Trends of Music Notation

Music notation and music notation programs are at present passing through the same evolution that text and text editors went through several years ago. Music publishers are still focused on obtaining good quality (in terms of visual formatting) of music scores. On the other hand, the market would like to have lower prices and considers the quality not so important. Publishers state that they sell only high quality music scores, which is quite obvious when prices are so high. Musicians are used to reading very poor music scores in terms of both formatting and visual resolution. To grasp this, it is enough to observe the quality of music sheets used by musicians in the conservatories and music schools. Their quality is really poor; they are frequently photocopies of photocopies of old originals. Sometimes it can even occur that the music is unreadable in some very ancient pieces.

The market is ready for massive production of music sheets, while publishers are not ready for it. The profit margins are in the high quality since the numbers are small. At the same time, students and music lovers prefer to make photocopies. This is the same story as it happens with books. Publishers have recovered their market only by producing cheap books with low quality paper and formatting shapes.

For these reasons, the future of this field is in the automatic formatting of music sheets and in the delivering of this via the Internet. Huge problems have to be solved for modeling music and for integrating this with the multimedia aspects of music. In Europe a special project and service has been set up by the European Commission to stimulate this integration. This project is the MUSICNETWORK, www.interactivemusicnetwork.org.

Conclusions

The WEDELMUSIC model and language has been defined after an analysis of several other coding approaches to look for a model to cover the needs of some new emerging applications, like the cooperative editing of music in theatres/ music schools and the distribution of music via the Internet, versioning, selective and non-linear undo, educational tool. The WEDELMUSIC presents a clear distinction between logic and visual parts. The latter is defined by means of MILLA rules. An early version of the WEDELMUSIC format was MOODS format. In its early version it was provided without MILLA, and that experience has convinced us to work on a separate and independent engine for music formatting with the aim of: (i) providing different rules that can be applied in different visual conditions along the same score and (ii) making possible the definition of formatting styles.

We do not claim to have solved all the problems related with music automatic formatting. On the other hand, MILLA can be used for defining rules for the automatic formatting of music scores with similar problems and conflicts. WEDELMUSIC editor is freely distributed on the Web site www.wedelmusic.org. The WEDELMUSIC development kit (WTK) is also freely distributed for loading and saving music in WEDEL format, including audio, image and symbolic aspects integrated together. An annual International Conference on WEB Delivery of Music is being organized. WEDELMUSIC format is royalty free; the format is public and available in DTD at the Web site www.WEDELMUSIC.org.

Acknowledgments

The authors thank all partners, members, experts and participants of the MOODS, the WEDELMUSIC (www.wedelmusic.org), and the MUSICNETWORK (www.interactivemusicnetwork.org) projects. A special thanks to Gerd Castan for his valuable comments that have permitted us to better explain the comparison model and its motivation. A sincere thanks to the constructive comments provided by the reviewers of this chapter.

References

Anderson, D. P. & Kuivila, R. (1991). Formula: A programming language for expressive computer music. *IEEE Computer*, (July), 12-21.

Bellini, P. & Nesi, P. (2001). WEDELMUSIC FORMAT: An XML music notation format for emerging applications. *Proceedings of the 1st International Conference of Web Delivering of Music* (November 23-24, pp. 79-86). Florence, Italy: IEEE Press.

Bellini, P., Bethelemy, J., Bruno, I., Nesi, P. & Spinu, M. B. (2003). Multimedia music sharing among mediateques, archives and distribution to their attendees. *Journal on Applied Artificial Intelligence*. Taylor and Francis, in press.

Bellini, P., Della Santa, R. & Nesi, P. (2001). Automatic formatting of music sheet. *Proceedings of the First International Conference on WEB Delivering of Music, WEDELMUSIC-2001* (November 23-24, pp. 170-177). Florence, Italy: IEEE Press.

Bellini, P., Fioravanti, F. & Nesi, P. (1999). Managing music in orchestras. *IEEE Computer*, (September), 26-34. Bellini, P., Nesi, P. & Spinu, M. B. (2002, September). Cooperative visual manipulation of music notation. *ACM Transactions on Computer-Human Interaction*, 9(3), 194-237.

Blostein, D. & Baird, H. S. (1992). A critical survey of music image analysis. In H.S. Baird, H. Bunke & K. Yamamoto (Eds.), *Structured Document Image Analysis* (pp. 405-434). New York: Springer Verlag.

Blostein, D. & Haken, L. (1991, March). Justification of printed music. *Communications of the ACM*, 34(3), 88-99.

Byrd, D. A. (1984). *Music Notation by Computer*. Dissertation, Indiana University, USA. Retrieved from UMI Dissertation Service, http://www.umi.com.

CANTATE project. (1994). Deliverable 3.3: Report on SMDL evaluation, WP3.

Dannenberg, R. B. (1990, February). A structure for efficient update, incremental redisplay and undo in graphical editors. *Software Practice and Experience*, 20(2), 109-132.

Dannenberg, R. B. (1993). A brief survey of music representation issues, techniques, and systems. *Computer Music Journal*, 17(3), 20-30.

Good, M. (2001). MusicXML for notation and analysis. In W. B. Hewlett & E. Selfridge-Field (Eds.), *The Virtual Score Representation, Retrieval, Restoration* (pp. 113-124). Cambridge, MA: The MIT Press.

Gourlay, J. S. (1986, May). A language for music printing. *Communications of the ACM,* 29(5), 388-401.

Heussenstamm, G. (1987). *The Norton Manual of Music Notation.* New York: Norton & Company.

Icking, I. (1997). MuTEX, MusicTEX, and MusiXTEX. In E. Selfridge-Field (Ed.), *Beyond MIDI - The Handbook of Musical Codes* (pp. 222-231). London: The MIT Press.

NIFF Consortium. (1995). NIFF 6a: Notation Interchange File Format.

Pennycook, B. W. (1985, June). Computer-music interfaces: a survey. *ACM Computing Surveys,* 17(2), 267-289.

Pope, S. T. (1991). *The Well-Tempered Object: Musical Applications of Object-Oriented Software Technology.* Cambridge, MA: MIT Press.

Rader, G. M. (1996). Creating printed music automatically. IEEE Computer, (June), 61-68.

Ross, T. (1987). *Teach Yourself. The Art of Music Engraving.* Miami, FL: Hansen Books.

Selfridge-Field, E. (ed.). (1997). *Beyond MIDI - The Handbook of Musical Codes.* London: The MIT Press.

Sloan, D. (1997). HyTime and standard music description language: A document-description approach. In E. Selfridge-Field (Ed.), *Beyond MIDI - The Handbook of Musical Codes* (pp. 469-490). London: The MIT Press.

SMDL ISO/IEC. (1995). Standard Music Description Language. ISO/IEC DIS 10743.

Smith, L. (1997). SCORE. In E. Selfridge-Field (Ed.), *Beyond MIDI - The Handbook of Musical Codes* (pp. 252-282). London: The MIT Press, London.

Taube, R. (1998). CCRMA, Common Music. CCRMA, Stanford University, California.

Taupin, D., Mitchell, R. & Egler, A. (1997). Using TEX to Write Polyphonic or Instrumental Music ver T.77,'hprib.lps.u-psud.fr.

Wood, D. (1989). *Hemidemisemiquavers...and Other Such Things. A Concise Guide to Music Notation.* Dayton, OH: The Heritage Music Press.

Section 5: Evaluation

Chapter 10

Evaluation in the Visual Perception of Music

Susan E. George
University of South Australia, Australia

Abstract

This chapter is about the need to evaluate the recognition performed by (i) Optical Music Recognition (OMR) systems, and also by (ii) counterpart on-line systems that directly recognise handwritten music input through a pen-based interface. It presents a summary of reviews that have been performed for commercial OMR systems and addresses some of the issues in evaluation that must be taken into account to enable adequate comparison of recognition performance. A representation language [HEART (HiErARchical Text-Based Representation)] is suggested, such that the semantics of music is captured (including the dynamics of handwritten music) and, hence, a target representation provided for recognition processes. Initial consideration of the range of test data that is needed (MusicBase I and II) is also made. The chapter is motivated by the outstanding need for (i) a greater understanding of how to evaluate the accuracy of music recognition systems, (ii) a widely available database of music test data (potentially automatically generated), (iii) an expression of this test data in a format that permits evaluation (for OMR and on-line systems) and (iv) the proliferation of representation languages — none of which captures the dynamics of handwritten music.

Introduction

There are a number of commercial systems, as well as research systems, that are designed to perform recognition of music notation, chiefly from a scanned image of music notation (OMR). There are also developmental systems that seek to recognise handwritten music input directly to a computer from a pen-based interface. In both these instances the need for evaluation arises so that the system can be assessed for its recognition performance. However, the subject of evaluation has been hardly addressed in the music recognition literature and it is difficult to asses the success, or otherwise, of music recognition systems.

This chapter begins by providing a summary of some commercial OMR systems, reviewing their scope and providing examples of the recognition that was attained with a system called Smartscore. Since there are currently no commercial systems for recognising handwritten notation dynamically input with a pen, we cannot make a review of these systems here, but focus on the off-line OMR situation. The examples of recognition obtained from the Smartscore system highlights some of the difficulties in evaluation — pointing to the need for a deeper consideration of evaluation and how it might be made in music recognition.

The chapter continues with a general review of the issues in evaluation considering the different criteria with which a system may be evaluated — in its accuracy, useability, efficiency, and other. A consideration is given of the specific challenges of music recognition compared with other document processing tasks and pen-based recognition endeavours. A special focus is made on the issues concerning measuring the accuracy of recognition in music, culminating in a discussion of the need for an adequate range of test data and truth representation for that data (ideally automatically generated) so that accuracy can be evaluated.

The chapter then contributes discussion of a representation language [HEART (HiErARchical Text-Based Representation)] that seeks to represent both (i) the semantics of music, as do a proliferation of other languages from MIDI (Musical Instrument Digital Interface) to MusicXML and (ii) the dynamics with which symbols were constructed (in the handwritten instance), seeking to capture the temporal information as do representation languages like the UniPen format for text-based handwritten data. Music representation examples are provided in HEART for expressing a static page of music and also dynamically constructed symbols.

Finally, the chapter considers the need for test data in music recognition. A review is made of some existing music notation repositories, noting their limitations due to an absence of truth representation for the examples. Legal issues in creating repositories of music are considered, focusing upon copyright considerations for both the music and the typesetting. Finally, consideration is given to the range of music notation phenomenon that should be considered in benchmark data sets. Version 1.0 of MusicBase I and II is introduced; these databases aim to provide data for static and dynamic music recognition respectively. A need to automate the generation of music examples in the databases is emphasised due to the amount of music data that would ideally be available for benchmarking.

The remainder of this introduction considers the motivation for the chapter. Primarily we observe the absence of benchmark music data with which recognition systems might be evaluated. This is regarded as an unnecessary limitation of the field that hampers research and makes choosing a commercial OMR system difficult. Most other pattern recognition fields have benchmark data sets — whether postcodes, signatures, handwritten numerals, or other — and there is no reason why there should not exist such a dataset of music.

Blostein was one of the first to recognise the need for music test data in the 1990s (Blostein & Carter, 1992). Later, Bainbridge created a small restricted dataset for (off-line) OMR (Bainbridge & Bell, 1997). This data also contained a "truth representation" that was created by hand for each image example. There the field rested without giving further consideration either to the range of data required, the means by which generation of a dataset might be automated, or an appropriate truth representation.

Further to the state-of-art observations made in off-line OMR, the emergence of the field of on-line, pen-based music notation recognition further prompts a consideration of benchmark data. Other handwriting recognition tasks enjoy the existence of a number of data sets — for signatures and numerals, characters and words, and even oriental writings — using the Unipen format to capture the temporal dynamics of construction. A repository of dynamically constructed handwritten music data is also needed for researchers to evaluate the accuracy of recognition methods.

Review of Commercial OMR Software

This section makes a review of commercial OMR software, noting how they have been "evaluated." We consider the systems Smartscore, Photoscore, SharpEye and OMeR and the range of recognition facilities they possess. Very few reviews of music recognition software (commercial or other) have actually been made and attempts to evaluate such systems generally draw upon informal "opinion." We present some examples of the current state-of-art in recognition music notation. This enables a subjective and informal understanding of both the scope of such systems and their limitations and highlights the difficulties in evaluating their performance.

Summary of Reviews

Very few reviews of music recognition software (commercial or other) have actually been made. One exception is the review presented in March 2001 in the German magazine C'T. This magazine reviewed the music scanning and notation programs Finale/MIDIScan, Sibelius/Photoscore, SmartScore, Capella-Scan, SharpEye and MIDI Connections Scan. They reported accuracy for all the music scanning programs on just three scores (of increasing "difficulty"). Their results are presented in (http://floti.bell.ac.uk/engapps/electronics_magazines.htm) where they find Sharp Eye 1.22 and Photoscore to be the top two performers across the three scores achieving recognition rates of 100%, 92% and 88% and 100%, 95% and 87% on the scores respectively. There is no mention of how these "accuracy" figures were obtained — whether it was symbol level or other, and indeed such "evaluation" is the crux of the problem in comparing and assessing scanning systems for recognition of music notation. The review is limited in its range of phenomena investigated and does not explain the criteria for evaluation.

We undertake an additional review of some existing music scanning software focusing upon the scope of their recognition facility. Unfortunately, information on some products do not appear in English (e.g., Capella at www.whc.de, and MIDI-Connections Scan at http://www.midi-connections.com/Index.htm) and we are unable to comment upon them. All the products reviewed contain favourable comments from the various users and stakeholders.

Smartscore by Musitek

The Musitek Corporation was founded in May 1991 by Christopher Newell of Ojai, California. *"Musitek's mission is to provide innovative and useful music software that significantly enhances user productivity"* (http://www.musitek.com/musitek.html). Christopher Newell, President, Musitek. Collaborating with Dr. Wladyslaw Homenda of Warsaw, claims that MIDISCAN for Windows, released in August of 1993, was the world's first commercial music-scanning software. MIDISCAN was essentially "Scan-and-Play." Subsequent to that, in 1995 music-scanning technology was integrated with computer-based music scoring, engraving, and MIDI sequencing in the release of SmartScore. SmartScore has evolved to become an indispensable tool for transcribing, part extraction/merging, as well as playback and reprinting of optically captured sheet music.

Table 1: Summary of SmartScore Editions Comparison Chart

LIMITED FEATURE SET	SmartScore Pro	Songbook Edition	Piano Edition	Guitar Edition	MIDI Edition
ENF Editing	Yes	Yes	Yes	Yes	Yes
Number of Staves Recognized	32 Staves max.	3 Staves max.	2 Staves max.	1 Staff max.	4 Staves max.
Text & Lyric Recognition / Editing	Yes	Yes	No	No	No
Score Structure	32 Parts	Limit to 3 Parts	No	No	No
Bracketing	Yes	Yes	Yes	No	No
Guitar and Chord Symbols	Yes	Yes	No	Yes	No
MIDI Editing / Step Rec. / Virtual Drums	Yes	Yes	No	No	Yes
MIDI Recording	Yes	Yes	No	No	Yes
Hidden Symbols	Yes	Yes	Yes	No	No
MIDI to ENF	32 Parts	3 Parts max.	2 Parts max.	1 Part max.	No
Instrument Templates / Master System	Yes	Yes	Yes	No	No
ENF Printing	Yes	Yes	Yes	Yes	No
ENF Transposition	Yes	Yes	Yes	Yes	No
File Export	ENF / NIFF MIDI / FIN	ENF / NIFF MIDI / FIN	ENF / NIFF MIDI / FIN	ENF / NIFF MIDI / FIN	ENF / MIDI

There are various editions of the Musitek recognition software as described at http://www.musitek.com/, including Smartscore Pro, Songbook edition, piano edition, guitar edition and midi (MIDIScan) edition. The software is Windows and Macintosh compatible. The differences between them are summarised in Table 1.

Among other things, Smartscore version 2 includes in its recognition facilities precision text and lyric recognition, optimised page scanning and recognition. They claim improved notation recognition with up to 99% accuracy and an optimised scanner resolution system that ensures highest possible accuracy. There are naturally a number of other features connected with the mouse-based music-editor (including smart beaming and repositioning objects) and intelligent facilities (including transposition), but these do not directly concern the OMR interest we have in this product.

Photoscore by Neuratron

Neuratron emerged in the British Acorn market and aimed to concentrate on what had not been done before. Starting with "Optical Professional" for Optical Character Recognition, the idea of sheet music recognition followed naturally, with "Optical Manuscript," released in winter, 1997, by software author Martin Dawe. Collaboration was made with Sibelius Software, who updated Sibelius 7 to import Optical Manuscript files and a Windows version, "Neuratron PhotoScore," appeared (with Sibelius) in late 1998 with the full Windows version of PhotoScore released in late 1999. The first Mac version appeared in the second half of 1999, followed by a full version at the beginning of 2000. A lower priced MIDI-saving only version was added to the family in the spring of 2000. Photoscore is used for accompaniment and guidance when practicing instruments, creating MIDI files to put on Web pages for others to hear, and for scanning music for use in sequencers or other editing programs — for re-arranging, transposing (e.g., to bring a vocal part into range), extracting parts and printing.

The various editions of Neuratron's products are described at http://www.neuratron.com/photoscore.htm and they include PhotoScore Professional, PhotoScore MIDI and PhotoScore MIDI Lite. PhotoScore Professional and PhotoScore MIDI are virtually identical — the main difference is that PhotoScore MIDI only saves MIDI files, although it has a realistic MIDI playback option. PhotoScore MIDI Lite is a reduced version of PhotoScore MIDI. PhotoScore Professional is designed to scan and read printed music with results that can be used in Sibelius and MIDI editing software. It claims to be fast and accurate in reading a wide range of musical markings, and is available in both Windows and Mac versions. PhotoScore MIDI Lite reads notes and chords (including ties, tail direction, beams and flags), rests, flats, sharps and naturals, treble and bass clefs, key signatures, time signatures, five-line staves (normal and small), standard barlines, and the format of the page, including the page size, staff size, margins, and where systems end.

SharpEye

The SharpEye music recognition software was developed by British mathematician Graham Jones, who started writing commercial programs for Acorn RISC OS machines in 1991. Development of SharpEye began in 1996 — initially part time, now full time. A Linux version exists, although little interest was expressed in this platform. SharpEye does not work on Apple Macs, but some people are using it successfully with Virtual PC, and another company is planning a Mac version. SharpEye outputs in MIDI, NIFF (Notation Interchange File Format), and its own format. SharpEye 2 also exports MusicXML format. MIDI is very popular and well-known, but it is limited, especially for printed output. NIFF and MusicXML can represent much more information about the score.

There are two versions of SharpEye as described at http://www.visiv.co.uk/about.htm. Version 1 does not support direct scanning, but will accept BMP and TIFF files produced via scanner software. Version 2 allows direct scanning from TWAIN-compatible scanners. When used, an image file is dragged into a window, and recognition is initiated at the click of a button. The output is shown in conventional music notation in another window, or can be saved as a MIDI file. Outputs can be edited for interpretation errors, and warnings are shown for each bar that does not make musical sense. For printing and other facilities such as transposing, another program is required. On average there are about half as many recognition errors in version 1 as there are in version 2, though this will depend on the type and quality of the sheet music. A summary of the recognition enhancements in version 2 are summarised in the following list:

- Greater accuracy: improved performance on broken stems, better recognition of flags, especially 1/16 versus 1/8 errors, improved performance on long rests and augmentation dots that touch a staff line, text recognition improved using digram and trigram frequencies, better interpretation when notes in different voices have stems that join one another (or nearly) and better recognition of slurs and ties, and better erasure of these.

- Symbols with old or unusual shapes: recognition of more old-style symbols such as crotchet (1/4) rests like a reversed quaver rest and old-style semibreves (whole notes), recognition of unusual styles of open heads and recognition of thin beams.
- New symbols recognised: dynamics (ppp...fff), hairpins, grace notes, chords and beamed groups that cross two or more staves (they are split into one-stave objects), and foreign language lyrics. The version recognises all ISO-88591 characters (which covers nearly all West European languages), recognises text other than lyrics (e.g., musical directions such as "Andante" or "cresc.") and guitar chords ("G," "Am7," etc.).

OMeR (Optical Music easy Reader)

OMeR Optical Music easy Reader, version 1.5 was released in September 2001 as a shareware program capable of converting a printed musical score to a music file that can be used with Melody Assistant or Harmony Assistant (Melody Assistant is a shareware program for writing and composing music; it has a friendly interface and many powerful features). OMeR is useful when there is a need to copy printed scores (e.g., for transposing). OMeR will drive the scanner, collect one or several pages, and analyze them to generate a musical document useable directly under Melody (4.0 or more) or Harmony (6.0 or more). OMeR can be run as an independent program, but Melody or Harmony Assistant is needed to view documents generated by OMeR. It is PC and Mac compatible.

The scope of the current version of OMeR is described at http://www.myriad-online.com/docs/omer/english/index.htm, and includes capability to process the following range of music phenomena: treble and bass keys, simple and complex time signatures (2/1, 3/1, 4/1, 2/2 or crossed C, 3/2, 4/2, 2/4, 3/4, 4/4 or C, 2/8, 3/8,4/8, 12/2, 12/4, 12/8), key signature, notes (from whole note to 64th) size, location and direction of note stems, rests, dotted and double dotted notes, tuplets en 2, 3, 4, 6, note accidentals (natural, sharp and flat), note hitching with value and graphical look, grace notes (appoggiatura), accidentals on grace notes, mordent, trill and staccato effects, repeat start and end, score start and end, notes tie/slur symbol when outside the staff, braces before a group of staff, first staff group indenting, relative bar (measure) sizes, staves' relative spacing, note fine spacing.

However, mistakes will occur on scores in poor condition, handwritten, or those using ancient typography. Since there are likely to be recognition errors, it is used to assist rather than replace the editing process. OMeR specifically does not claim to recognise the following: C clefs, square, diamond or other note heads, lyrics linked to the tune and miscellaneous comments, tablatures, chord diagrams, double sharp or double flat accidentals, coda jump or part break symbols, accent and dynamics notation, notes tie/slur when inside the staff lines, and other effects than those quoted above.

Examples of Recognition

Clearly there are a number of systems with a range of different recognition facilities and no standard way of comparing the systems for recognition performance. Thus, we focus upon one system, SmartScore, and present some examples of the recognition facilities of this system. We present a sample image and the "interpreted" result displayed in a music editor. Evaluation is based upon an informal visual inspection of the original bitmap with the interpreted result. From the results, we see some of the complexities of determining and evaluating accuracy in music recognition

The first test given to SmartScore is intended to demonstrate the system performing at its best, recognising virtually all of the music fragment presented as well as lyrics.

Figure 1a illustrates the original bitmap image and Figure 1b presents the result of recognition. Evaluation can proceed informally by inspecting the interpreted result and comparing it with the bitmap image. The fact that the results of recognition have been typeset in a similar manner as the original assists this comparison (since there are many ways that a note of a given duration can be expressed).

Figure 1a: Original Bitmap Image from "Worship from the Heart," Randy and Fred Meeks, 1986, p. 18

Figure 1b: Interpreted Result from "Worship from the Heart," Randy and Fred Meeks, 1986, p. 18

After visual inspection, the results are impressive since the interpretation has only one natural symbol missing (first bar in third line), two missing notes in the last bat (bottom line), a note missing in the first bar top line, and an extended phrase mark in the top line. An extra phrase marking has also been included in the last bar of the fragment. All other music notation symbols have been recognised. Importantly, the lyrics have also been correctly interpreted.

Figure 2a represents another bitmap image containing some more complex musical events, including parts and accidentals as grace notes, and Figure 2b is its interpretation. The example illustrates how it becomes harder to make a comparison between the original and the interpreted result due to typesetting differences.

Figure 2a: Original Bitmap Image from Liszt Rhapsodies Hongroises (Rhapsodie 8)

Figure 2b: Interpreted Result from Liszt Rhapsodies Hongroises (Rhapsodie 8)

The initial error in the grace note that is not recognised, together with an absence of bar lines gives the informal impression that this was not recognised as well, although a fairly impressive job has been done of isolating the parts in the top line with the beamed notes (that in the original spans the bar lines). However, it is not possible to quantify the accuracy. Making a count of all the correctly recognised symbols would be tedious and error prone. The test data in Figures 3a and 3b contains some initial text directives for players in a musical as well as some performance directives (Moderato).

Figure 3a: Original Bitmap Image from Cinderella in Salerno, Rossini

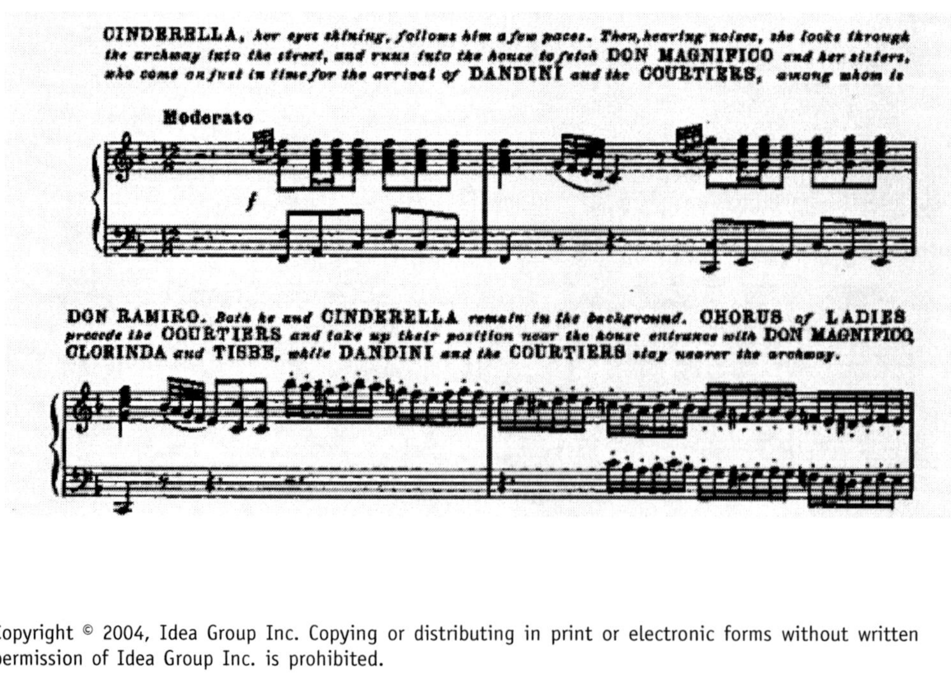

Figure 3b: Interpreted Result from Cinderella in Salerno, Rossini

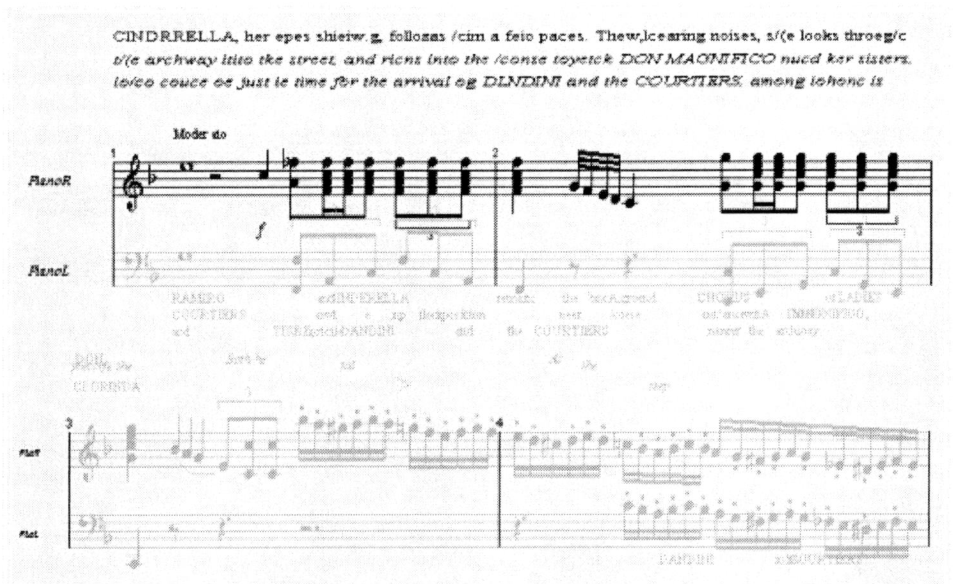

The main difficulty with the music recognition comes in the bottom and top line, where the deci-semiquavers have not been identified (neither has the time signature in the first line). The text recognition has also proved more problematic since the directives have been interpreted as lyrics, and among many of the correctly recognised words there are errors contributing to general confusion in the recognised data. Figures 4a and 4b continue to test the text/ lyric recognition.

Figure 4a: Original Bitmap Image from "A Selection of Collected Folk Songs," Cecil Sharp and Vaughan Williams, London, 1912

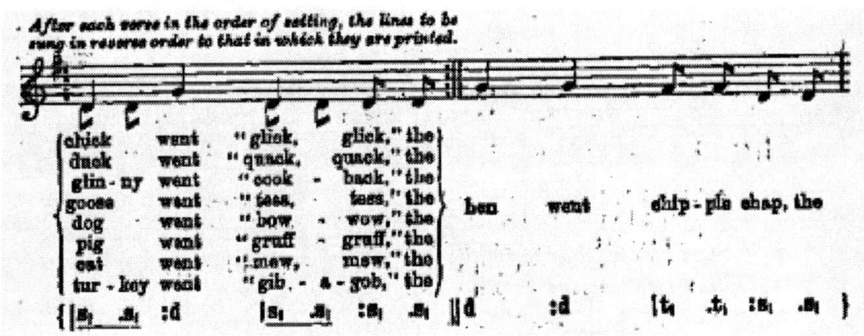

Figure 4b: Interpreted Result from "A Selection of Collected Folk Songs," Cecil Sharp and Vaughan Williams, London, 1912

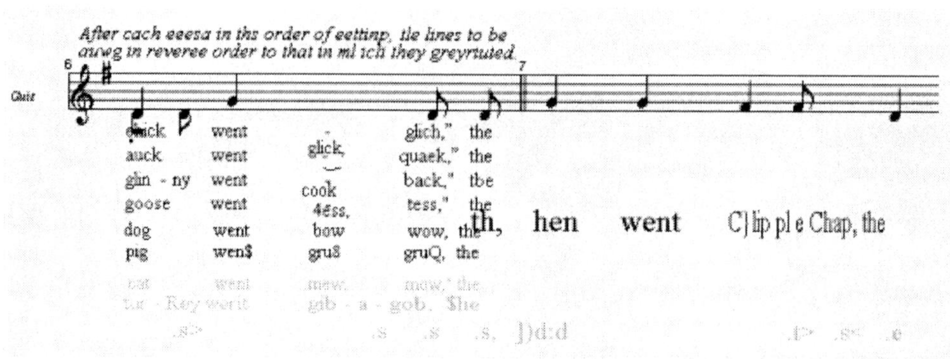

In this instance the way that the interpreted result is typeset does not add to the impression that this has been recognised accurately, although the ability to cope with the several lines of alternatives of lyrics for the first bar is impressive. Returning to focus upon the ability to recognise music, the data in Figures 5a and 5b explores the ability to cope with inserted stavelines. While this insert is recognised, there has been confusion with the smaller font used for the notes in this insert, and with the bar lines across the whole fragment. Only one or two of the ledger notes have presented problems in interpretation.

Figure 5a: Original Bitmap Image from Country Gardens Piano, Percy Grainger, Schott and Co., 1919

Figure 5b: Interpreted Result from Country Gardens Piano, Percy Grainger, Schott and Co., 1919

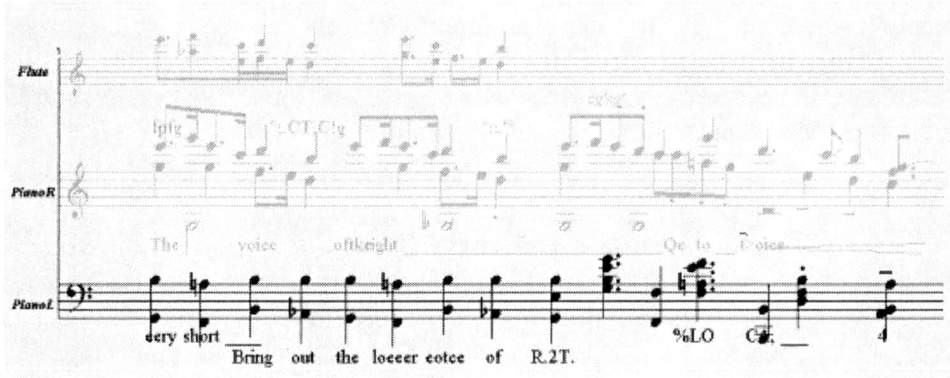

The data from Figures 6a and 6b presents some more complex music symbols, again some different sized fonts, pedal markings and a double flat. Unfortunately recognition did not identify the key signature, nor the bar lines, nor the semi-quaver triplets although it did correctly recognise some elements of the bitmap. Such examples demonstrate the difficulty of basing accuracy evaluation on visual inspection alone, yet some sense of the performance is attained.

Figure 6a: Original Bitmap Image from Chopin Complete Piano Works (Polonaise Fantaise op 61), Chopin

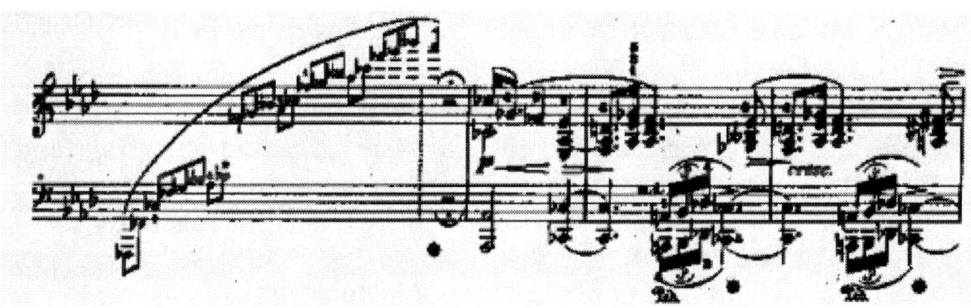

Figure 6b: Interpreted Result from Chopin Complete Piano Works (Polonaise Fantaise op 61), Chopin

Finally, this informal evaluation presented a scanned bitmap image of some handwritten music. Unfortunately, the Smartscore program was unable to recognise anything from the image. While all these examples re-iterate the necessity for some way to formally evaluate the accuracy of recognition, they also raise some more interesting questions about how evaluation should proceed in visual perception of music notation.

Difficulties in Evaluating the Accuracy of Recognition

From the preceding examples it is obvious that there are a number of difficulties in evaluating the accuracy music recognition. These include the fact that:

(i) there may be typesetting differences between the original scanned image and the representation of the music that has been "recognised." This prohibits a simple visual inspection being sufficient for evaluation — since music of the same semantics may be represented in different ways, or the typesetting itself may be the key feature of the music the OMR software is required to recognise;

(ii) musical forms are often composite objects (e.g., a beamed group of notes, a dotted pair or a key signature of several symbols) rather than individual symbols. This prohibits making a simple count of the number of symbols recognised — since recognition of isolated symbols does not necessarily mean that the composite form has been correctly recognised;

(iii) the music may contain textual information (e.g., be interspersed with lyrics or elaborate performance directives). Even if this is text recognised it needs to be tagged in some way to demonstrate that it is identified as lyric, composer, performance indicator, or other. It is not enough to simply recognise characters and display these with the recognised typeset music;

(iv) the music may contain a wide variety of symbols whose relative spatial placement is crucial, not in a typesetting sense, but in the association with other symbols that is necessary to give a correct semantics (e.g., an accidental modifying the pitch of a note). This relative spatial placement is related to the variable forms identified by Blostein and Baird (1992). They noted music contains forms that are variable, such as beams, phrase markings, slurs, the octave (8ve) marking, the crescendo/

> decrescendo marking (< / >), and a tie across notes — all presenting challenges for recognition methods; and we observe they present difficulties for evaluation procedures also.

Having opened up the issue of evaluation and how difficult it is to evaluate the accuracy of OMR systems we continue to examine the evaluation issue and present some solutions.

Evaluation

This section considers the nature of evaluation, acknowledging that there are many criteria by which a system might be evaluated — in its accuracy, useability, efficiency and other. Accuracy is primarily of interest and there are some specific challenges that recognising music must address in evaluating accuracy. We suggest some solutions, including (i) modifications of standard symbol-based metrics, such as the confusion matrix, to capture the extent to which musical forms and their combinations are recognised. This measure would be particularly useful to capture typesetting features that are not real "semantic" elements of the music, but are, nevertheless, components we desired to capture in the recognition process. (ii) A means of capturing the information within music data in a "truth representation," such that it is possible to verify the semantic truth of the recognition made via the actual "meaning" of the music; and (iii) the need for an adequate range of test data.

Criteria of Evaluation

Generally, evaluation is tied up with the user and intimately bound with the context of use. During evaluation the questions asked of a system depend upon why the system needs to be evaluated. For example, a company may evaluate new software because they are interested in the efficiency improvements it may promise, or a customer may evaluate a graphics package to inspect the range of features offered. Similarly, users of music recognition systems may have different criteria by which they want to evaluate the system.

The useability of a system comprises many different aspects. It may concern the interface – and whether this is natural for novice and experts alike; whether inputs can be made using mouse, pen-stylus or other. Useability may be related to the efficiency, especially if a real-time response is required, and it may even extend to the range of computer platforms with which the system works (e.g., PC, Mac, Linux or other) or whether it is Web-based. The amount of memory, additional software facilities required, the price, user-support availability, and compatibility with other programs may all also influence how useable is a system. In the context of music recognition systems, efficiency and accuracy of recognition are likely to be the main factors that influence useability, followed by interface issues (as considered elsewhere in this volume in on-line pen-based music input systems).

However, a highly accurate system is not necessarily more useable, in a given application context, than a less accurate one. For example, some retrieval applications may need to discriminate between keywords and irrelevant stop-words (such as "the" and "but") and correct recognition of keywords may be far more vital than stop-words. Thus, a system that is able to recognise a few keywords with high accuracy (at the expense of other words) may be more useable than one that can recognise all words with less accuracy. If the purpose of OMR is to scan a music repository and identify all manuscripts in a particular musical key, then recognising the key signature correctly in a music image determines the useability of the system, above recognising any other musical notation. We might develop a metric specifically to measure the accuracy of detecting this particular component of the music in order to evaluate the system.

Accuracy in Symbol Recognition

When considering accuracy in character recognition we are basically interested in how many characters were correctly recognised and how many were not. One popular way of measuring the performance is the confusion matrix, which records the number of mis-recognised, correctly recognised and unrecognised characters. Figure 7 illustrates a confusion matrix for just four character symbols, showing how nine examples of the character "a" were correctly recognised, and one was mis-recognised. With character "b" eight were correctly recognised and two were not identified at all.

Figure 7: Character-Based Confusion Matrix

		Recognized as					
		a	b	c	d	Reject	Error
True ID	a	9			1		1
	b		8			2	0
	c	2		6	1	1	3
	d	1			9		1
		3	0	0	2	3	5

From such a summary we can compute the character accuracy as a ratio for the recognised characters and the input characters. We may be interested in examining the source of error, and sometimes the confusion matrix can reveal whether there are structured errors within the recogniser (for example, are all mis-classifications occurring with the same character, or between given characters). However, recognition is not always as simple as consulting a confusion matrix. Document constructs that go beyond characters and words — for example music — are harder to assess as "correctly" recognised or not via a confusion matrix.

The confusion matrix may be adequate if the music contained a certain number of isolated symbols — such as notes, clefs, ties and rests. The isolated symbols could be treated in the same way as textual characters and a confusion matrix may very well capture the extent to which the music was recognised. However, music does not consist of isolated, fixed-size symbols, unrelated in spatial terms. Rather, it contains composite musical forms (e.g., beamed groups) made from many symbols (notes, stems, accidentals, etc.) that are not always fixed size (e.g., phrase marks) where the relative position of elements is as important as the elements themselves. This complicates the use of the simple single symbol-based confusion matrix to evaluate the recognised forms.

Assessing the accuracy with which a composite object where spatial information is vital may require a more sophisticated version of the confusion matrix that captures the additional semantics. At this level, we think it is useful to regard the additional semantics as largely typesetting; for example, whether quavers are grouped in pairs or a larger construct would be reflected by the composite form. Although we recognise that there is overlap in the meaning and typesetting choices — since a variable form, such as phrase mark, is both a feature of typesetting and has a semantic meaning.

We suggest the confusion matrix be developed into a fuzzy confusion matrix — where instead of a single symbol there is a composite with various (typesetting-related) properties, and the matrix records how many of those properties were correctly identified or not. There would be a difference between having four correctly recognised symbols in a group of five compared to having none recognised, and the fuzzy confusion matrix would be able to capture this concept of "partial correctness of composite symbols."

Capturing the Meaning — Truth Representation

The most abstract representation of the music data would capture the meaning of the manuscript, ignoring typesetting differences that were irrelevant to the meaning. However, we recognise that trying to distinguish the "meaning" of music from typesetting choices is a little like trying to separate syntax and semantics in natural language; they are both tied together in a unique way. In language, as with music, there may be several syntactic forms with the same meaning. For example, four quavers may be grouped in two lots of two, or as a single group of four. A minim note may be composed of two tied crotchet notes, or be a single minim symbol. While the music may be typeset in different ways it can express the same information. If we are primarily interested in the meaning we can use a truth representation to capture this separately from the typesetting.

Many other computer-based document recognition areas make use of a truth representation. This representation makes the attributes of the input image explicit and becomes the point of reference for evaluating recognition capacity. For example, in OCR (Optical Character Recognition) systems the "truth" representation will contain all the characters and symbols that appear within the image of the document. Document understanding systems that process the images can then verify their results against the text-based "truth" representation of the document, which becomes the means of evaluating the accuracy of different systems. The University of Washington has a database (UW-I) with 1,147 page images from scientific and technical journals with the corresponding *truth* representation containing the text found within the images, making it a highly useful resource for OCR researchers. As yet, no such repository exists for OMR researchers.

We suggest that a logical representation language for music (the final target of many commercial OMR systems) may be regarded as the highest level "semantic" description of the music and is the truth representation. Now there is already a proliferation of languages for describing music, ranging from MIDI to MusicXML, and a representation standard cannot be agreed upon. However, such a high-level representation of the music would constitute an expression that could be utilised by OMR systems as the "target" representation. The system would aim to output its recognition in terms of the high-level language. System accuracy could then be evaluated by how much overlap there was between the output of an OMR system and the target representation.

Often the truth representation has to be derived by hand from the original data and this is far from ideal, being a time-consuming, error-prone, and expensive process. Ideally, preparation of the truth representation is automated. We envisage the high-level language capturing the meaning of the music, and from this representation various typeset image forms would be generated. The automated generation of typeset forms may also include an element of image "noise" to create realistic test data (such as image skew and dirty backgrounds), as well as a variety of music "fonts" to challenge the recognition facility. Having generated a corpus of image data from the high-level representation, the results of any OMR process (expressed in terms of the high-level language) could be directly evaluated against the initial "truth representation."

Test Data

The field of pattern recognition has long since recognised the necessity for test data in both developing and evaluating systems. Large, publicly available corpora of training and test data make it possible for developers to benchmark recognition algorithms and commercial systems can be evaluated. The field of OCR is fortunate in having a number of character-based databases containing a range of data — from hand-printed segmented Japanese characters to U.S. postal addresses. Similar data repositories exist for audio speech data. The absence of such a benchmark suite in off-line or on-line music recognition is glaring and this chapter will address this limitation.

Even the field of on-line handwriting recognition has a large repository of training and test data for handwritten characters and words since the UNIPEN format was developed (Guyon, Schomaker, Plamondon, Liberman & Janet, 1994). The developers, Isabelle Guyon and Lambert Schomaker, noted that a large corpora of training and test data for on-line writing was needed, and in summer 1993 the UNIPEN format was released, incorporating features of the internal formats of several institutions. No such format exists for on-line handwritten music with its spatially significant components.

We perceive that it is necessary to take into account various criteria when considering the construction of a database of music test data. These criteria revolve around the need to be able to automate the generation of test data and to ultimately have a point of reference for evaluating the accuracy of OMR methods and systems. We suggest that a database of music test data (i) be stated in a high-level language such that the semantics are captured separate from the typesetting choices of that music, and (ii) from this high-level statement it is possible to generate music test data — as both images, and as dynamically constructed handwritten music. This would automate the creation of large databases of test data. To this end we suggest a representation language be used that is able to capture the meaning of music isolated from the typesetting choices. Additionally, this language must be capable of expressing the particular dynamics of handwritten music, such that recognition systems can test algorithms for not just off-line OMR processes, but also dynamic pen-based interfaces.

The Evaluation Process

Figure 8 illustrates how we envisage the high-level language representing the semantics of music being used. There is a given piece of music used as test data (illustrated in the top document box) expressed in the given high-level representation language. This is converted by a process (illustrated by the rectangular box) to produce an image of either a particular printed typeset version or simulated handwritten data. We require a typesetting model — expressing how music will be laid out — and also a user-writing model — simulating the dynamics of how people write music (illustrated by the ovals). The image or handwritten form is the input data to an OMR program or pen-based interface respectively (illustrated by shaded box). The results of the OMR process, and also the pen-based recognition, can then be compared during the accuracy evaluation. We may want to evaluate both the basic semantic content of the music and also the typesetting (to verify that we could reproduce the particular typeset form from the recognised music). The figure also shows how the simulated handwritten data could be converted by another

Figure 8: Using a Semantic Representation of Music in the Evaluation Process

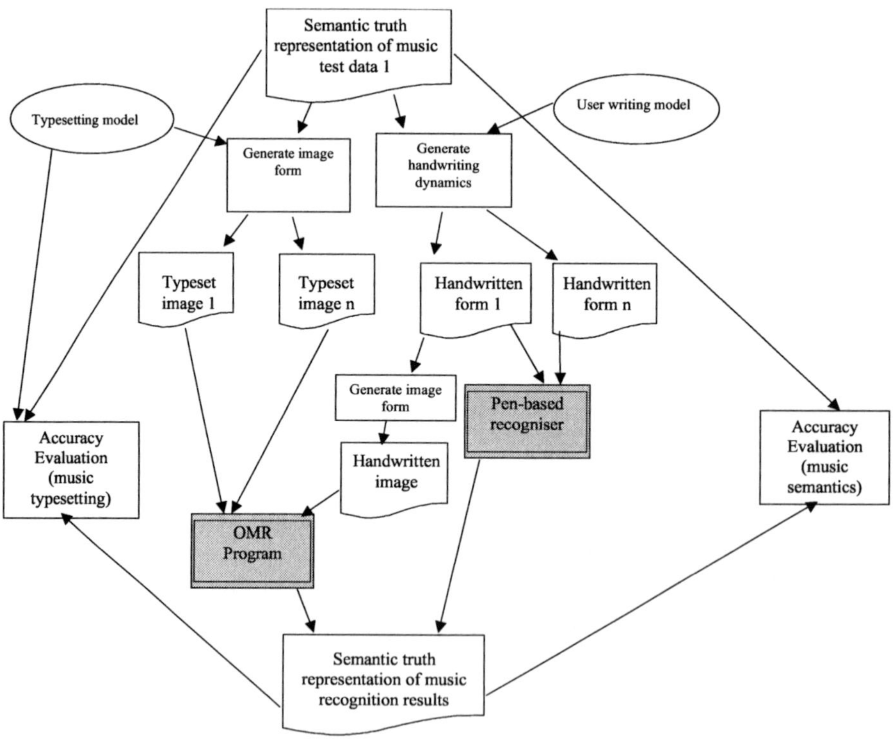

process to produce an image of handwritten music used as test data for an OMR program in the same way as the simulated printed image data.

The process to generate the image form (printed typeset version) could use methods for music display currently used by music editors associated with OMR packages. From a given rendering, an image file would have to be generated — perhaps with image perturbations to test for skew and rotation and other image noise. Such a process would avoid the need to scan in test data, and would also enable many different variations in image quality for a given piece of data. The automation would enable large quantities of data to be verified, and wide variations in the image quality to be made.

Producing the handwritten form is a task that would require modelling the writing characteristics of a particular writer with respect to symbol shape, pressure, writing dynamics, and even the spatio-temporal order with which musical forms are written. The simulated data would be in the same form as that produced from a pen-based input device, and would enable pen-based interface solutions to evaluate how accurate the recognition was for a particular piece of test data written in a particular way.

Obviously, within such a scenario for test data and evaluation, there are many complex processes that need to be worked out. However, at the heart of the concept is a high-level representation language that is able to model the semantics of music and, vitally, represent the dynamics of how that music might have been constructed (this is naturally closely related to the user model). While there is a proliferation of representation languages, there are none that are capable of capturing music dynamics. This chapter makes a contribution to such a language in the proposed language HEART.

Representation Languages for static and Dynamic Music

In this section we review music representation languages with a view to developing a suitable representation language, particularly for dynamic handwritten music data, that captures the semantics of music. We see that the earliest representation languages were orientated towards printing music, and only later moved on to representations suitable for more general tasks such as editing and composing music. We also consider the basic elements of pitch and rhythm that need to be represented (and as far as possible focus on how the "meaning" may be isolated from the typesetting choices). The range of music representation languages from binary (MIDI) to XML-based are briefly reviewed, outlining some of the choices before presenting the HEART standard as a novel representation language capable of expressing the on-line, dynamic elements of music data and the underlying "meaning" of the music in a truth representation.

Music Printing, Composing and Editing

The earliest work on a representation language to represent music notation was done by Leland C. Smith at Stanford University (at the Center for Computer Research in Music and Acoustics, or CCRMA), where the SCORE PC-based program was developed to create complex music on an X-Y plotter. The language requires text-based entry and it is not possible to see what the music looks like until after it prints out, but it is now the standard program in use by the music publishing industry.

Page layout under operating systems such as Unix is done using TeX. Over the years several sets of macros for TeX, such as muTeX and musicTeX, have expanded its capabilities to include music. There is an open-source Linux development group working along the same lines as TeX. Their program is called Lillypond. It is still text-based entry, but various developers are adding graphical features. One promising one is KooBase, now known as Brahms. The first Mac program that printed music from a graphics screen was ConcertWare, by Chad Mitchell. Chad set up a company called Great Wave software to market ConcertWare. Chad designed the first font of music symbols. The font layout included "q" for the whole note, "w" for the half note, and so on.

Around 1990, serious attempts at commercial music software for editing and composing began appearing. The first was Finale, which now includes a good range of features and an improved interface ensuring that it competes with Finale from Mosaic. More recently, languages such as Sibelius have added features for music distribution over the Internet. Most publishing houses accept work in Finale format and pay someone to convert to SCORE. High-quality MIDI playback can be achieved from programs such as Overture, originally by OpCode, now sold by Cakewalk. While Lime is an editor that contains a licence particularly for distribution within a music laboratory.

However, the different programs listed above cannot work on the same file, and the only level at which data can be exchanged is Standard MIDI Files. As we shall see this format leaves out most of the notation since MIDI only deals with when the notes go on and off; adding performance directives is impossible. An excellent standard has been developed, called the Notation Interchange File Format (NIFF), but only one product supports it.

Representing Music Pitch

Common musical notation of pitch requires two elements: (i) the letter name of the note together with its octave range, and (ii) the accidentals that are applied to that note. From these elements the absolute pitch may be calculated. Representation of musical pitch by absolute pitch alone, as is done in the MIDI protocol and in other sound applications, is not a complete representation of the pitch's notation and its attributes. For instance, C#4 and Db4 have the same absolute pitch, but they have different note names and different accidentals. This difference becomes apparent when we try to print the note or when we seek to calculate musical intervals. The interval between C#4 and Bb4 is a diminished seventh, whereas the interval between Db4 and Bb4 is a major sixth.

Several numerical systems have been proposed for representing pitch notation in the computer. The most successful systems to be proposed thus far have been those that recognize the two-dimensional nature of pitch notation, i.e., that the unambiguous representation of pitch notation requires two independent parameters. Norbert Böker-Heil and Alexander Brinkman independently have proposed systems based on the parameters of note name and absolute pitch or pitch class. Each system includes simple algorithms for the computation of accidentals and musical interval sizes. From the standpoint of data storage and retrieval, however, the representation of musical pitch by a single numerical parameter would be superior to any system using two parameters. While any single-parameter system will have inherent ambiguities, it can be shown that for any finite set of pitch names, a single-parameter system can be constructed that is unambiguous over that set.

The construction of a single-parameter representation system, or encoding scheme, i.e., the mapping of all musically relevant pitches onto the number line, is easily accomplished. For example, we could assign the numbers 10, 20, 30, ... to the pitch names C, D, E, etc., within an octave, and then increment the basic number for each sharp, or decrement the number for each flat attached to the pitch. There are several solutions to the problem of interval-invariant, number-line representations that are suitable notations for data entry, music printing, and search including the Base-40 system (http://www.music-notation.info/en/compmus/index.html).

Representation Languages

Music's complexity has led to this proliferation of languages and formats used to express the logical content of music notation independent from any two-dimensional typesetting of the notation. No language is perfect and, other than MIDI, none has been widely adopted. The languages are broadly divided into three classes: (a) binary based (e.g., MIDI/NIFF), (b) ascii based (e.g., Humdrum/MuseData), or (c) XML based (e.g., SMDL) that represents structured data in text on the World Wide Web. These, and some twenty other formats, are described by Selfridge-Field (1997) and a comprehensive summary of the different languages can be found at http://www.music-notation.info/en/compmus/notationformats.html.

Generally, logical representation languages do not seek to encode the exact position of every note on the page, since this would contain more information than the composer intended to convey. Also, encoding a specific graphic representation is not seen as the aim of the logical description of music, although languages such as Humdrum explicitly represents the two-dimensional nature of musical scores by a 2-D layout notation. Logical representation languages enable interchange between various descriptions to generate descriptions that are suitable for playing, typesetting, searching, analysing or other.

The limitations of MIDI for notation, analysis, and retrieval include the fact that it stores little more than the sound of the music (for example, information from the printed page about stem direction, beaming, expression marks such as staccato and accent, ties and slurs are all lost and text inclusions are not standard). It is also limited in representing musical concepts such as rests and enharmonic pitches (distinguishing Db from C#). Text-based languages were the next development, but it is the XML-based languages that hold the most promise for the future.

MusicXML, by Recordare, (Caston, Good & Roland, 2001) can represent scores either part-wise (measures within parts) or time-wise (parts within measures), with a description of the language at http://www.musicxml.org/xml.html. MusicXML was specifically designed as an Internet-friendly method of publishing musical scores, enabling musicians and music fans to get more out of their on-line music, but has other uses as well, including musical analysis and interchange between formats.

It would be desirable to select a logical description language and use this as a high-level representation of the music from which images could be generated, and recognition and interpretation methods could then re-generate the high-level description. There would also be scope to produce intermediate representations that were targets for the recognition process. But clearly, it is not an easy task selecting one of these formats over another as a high-level representation of the logical structure of music, and also there is the necessity to translate the music notation into the logical language in the first place. This itself would be a time consuming process and an efficient, accurate OMR system would be necessary!

Musical Grammars

A formal language can be defined using "grammar" (Aho, Sethi & Ullman, 1986). Such a grammar consists of a set of terminals, non-terminals, a start symbol, and productions. Terminals are the basic symbols from which strings are formed. Non-terminals are syntactic variables that denote sets of strings. The start symbol is a special non-terminal denoting the language defined by the grammar. The production rules of the grammar specify the manner in which the terminals and non-terminals may be combined to form strings. Productions are identified by the "—>" symbol, indicating that the left-hand side can be replaced by the right-hand side. Alternatives among the productions may be introduced by the "|" symbol. The rules may be written in the form of a regular expression that captures alternatives and repetition of symbols.

Kopec, Chou and Maltz (1995) have developed a message grammar that describes a music message (a page of printed music). The relative horizontal alignment of consecutive lines is specified using a backspace, and a string of 0s and 1s that specify in binary the horizontal displacement in pixels from the end of a line to the beginning of the following line. Glyphs that appear on the page are accurately specified in terms of their position on the page using the Sonata font design specification (Adobe, 1992). A fragment of this grammar using regular expressions is presented in Figure 9.

However, very quickly we realise that such a one-dimensional grammar does not intuitively describe the two-dimensional placement of music notation symbols. An alternative way to capture the relative placement of symbols and regions upon the page would be to use a shape grammar. Shape grammars were

Figure 9: Example of Regular Expressions to Describe a Page of Music (from Kopec, Chou & Maltz, 1995)

```
message --> (music_line[backspace])* music_line

backspace --> <1(0/1)*

music_line -->

       clef[key_signature][time-signature][chord|blank_staff|bar_mark)+$

clef --> ...
```

invented by Stiny (1976) and are a set of shape rules that are applied in a step-by-step way to generate a set, or language, of designs. The rules of a shape grammar generate designs, and the rules themselves are descriptions of the forms of the generated designs. Shape grammar theory has advanced over the years to include complexities of shapes and shape computations, including parametric shape grammars that compute designs with variable or parametric shapes, and colour grammars that compute designs with shapes and properties of shapes (such as colour, material and function).

A Representation Language for Dynamic Data

One important aspect of representation languages — so far omitted from their features — is a representation language for dynamic, on-line music data. The representation languages considered above have largely been developed with a view to obtain a logical representation of the music — perhaps to enable exchange between music editors, or to render electronic performance possible, or some other. No language has been developed solely to capture the dynamic aspects of handwritten data. Such a format is ultimately necessary to make a repository of data, such that recognition algorithms for on-line music data can be developed.

Representation standards have still to emerge with data retrieved from graphics tablets and pen-input devices. There are dozens of binary and ASCII file types used by manufacturers of digitizer tablets and by researchers. It is necessary to capture much information (not just the X and Y coordinate information). This information would include the sampling rate, resolution, time of sample point, origin, and even pressure with which the pen was utilised.

JOT is one standard that has evolved to represent electronic ink and to share this between users, applications, and machines — especially on PDAs (Personal Digital Assistant) and pen-based notebook computers (Slate, 1993). JOT grew out of the insight that ink, that is, sequences of two-dimensional vectors, is a data type not very well covered in existing data standards for applications. The *ink* data type combines the graphical aspects of line drawing functions with the temporal aspects of media like sound or video. JOT is similar in intent to existing computer format specifications such as TIFF (Tag Image File Format), GIF (Graphics Interchange Format), and PCX. However, JOT specifies the richness and depth of attributes required for ink that are not provided by existing data formats.

The UNIPEN format is another standard designed specifically to represent dynamic handwritten data. It is particularly useful for researchers investigating handwriting recognition algorithms since it captures the basic pen-input information. It contains fields tagged with ASCII (American Standard Code for Information Interchange) keywords, and although there is no provision for representing ink width or ink colour, the format could be extended by adding additional tags for this purpose. Databases in the UNIPEN format include isolated digits, characters (upper and lower case), symbols (punctuation), mixed-case characters, characters in context of words, isolated printed words (mixed and with digits and symbols and isolated), isolated and mixed cursive words and general text.

UNIPEN is very useful for capturing the basic pen strokes made by a stylus. It is hierarchical in that pages of data are composed of paragraphs and lines and words and characters. One deficiency with the format is that the tags are designed to capture textual information rather than the symbols of music notation. With music notation symbols there is an almost unlimited scope for variation in how the symbols are constructed — in a way that is not found to such an extent with handwritten data. Pen strokes may be temporally distant but related in characters such as "i" and "t", where a component of the character is added later. The scope for such temporally distant but related strokes is far greater with music notation. Thus, more knowledge about the constructs of music is necessary to correctly group and tag symbols that are spatially related.

HEART: Music Regions

In proposing the HEART representation format we are aiming to capture (i) the spatial relations between music components upon a page, as well as (ii) the (spatio-temporal) relations between individual music symbols using a spatial grammar. The language takes a hierarchical view of the manuscript and components within it and utilises tagging. Identifying which region (the tag) a given set of points belongs to is important to aid recognition. For example, during temporal construction lyrics might be added after the music notation has been completed, and being able to identify the set of points as lyrics (as opposed to a part of the staff- would make it possible to structure the data gathered from the digitiser/pen tablet — regardless of the timestamp with which the data was entered.

First we consider the high-level spatial relations between music components in the different regions that may be present upon a page. We identify tags, including page, staff line, bar, lyric text, title text, dynamic marking, and chord marking. These are hierarchical since a page is composed of title area(s), lyric area(s) and staves. Staves are composed of lines; lines are composed of phrases and/or bars. While Figure 10 illustrates some of these regions on a printed page, the same principles would apply to handwritten music.

Figure 10: Illustration of Hierarchical Regions of a Music Page

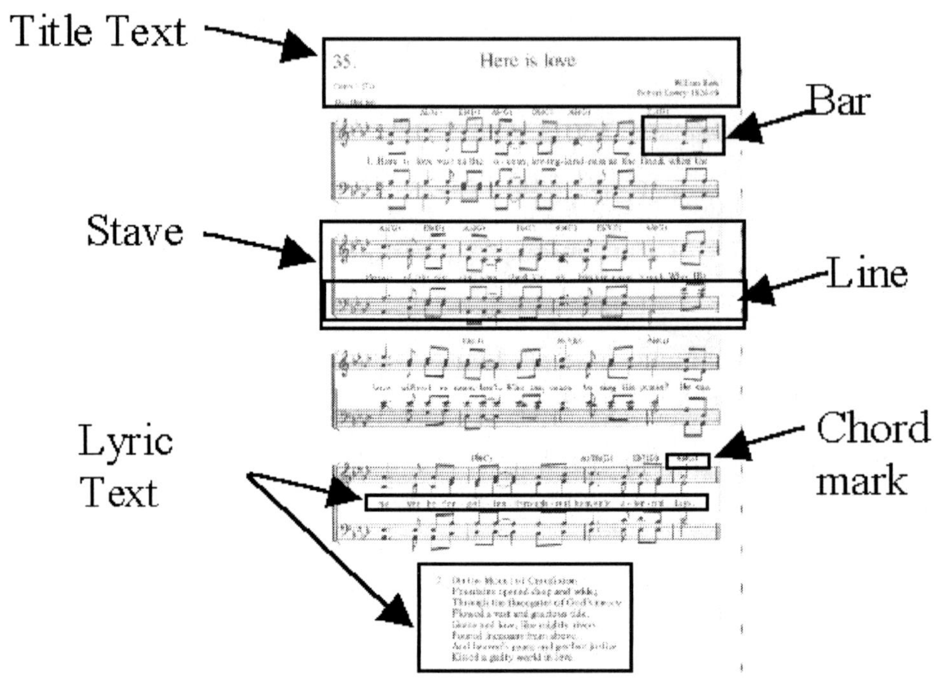

To capture the hierarchy within a page we use a shape grammar to describe the hierarchical arrangement of regions upon a score as the relative placement of two-dimensional items. The production rules explain how pages and variations may be constructed. Figure 11 presents a fragment of such a grammar that starts to describe a page of music in terms of a title area (heading the page) and a music area. The main point about the rules of such a two-dimensional grammar is that they capture the relative placement of region items that may be found upon the staff.

The first rule indicates that the 'title text' area may be repeated ("*"), either in the horizontal (H) or vertical (V) direction. Some leeway has to be permitted here for the precise placement of the repeated "title text" units since there is no attempt to specify a precise bearing direction from the given start symbol of where the repeated element may occur! Rather there is a general indication

Figure 11: Fragment of a Two-Dimensional Grammar to Specify the Relative Placement of Music Regions on a Page

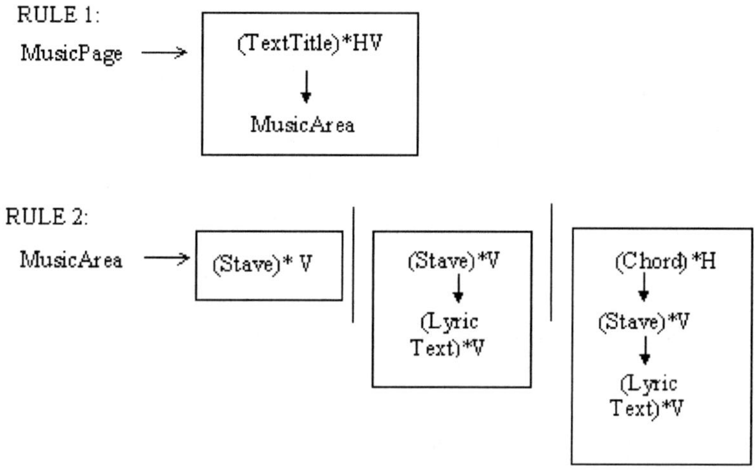

that a repeated element may occur below or adjacent to the original. There is also an indication that below the "title text" a "music area" is to be found. The second rule specifies the form of this "music area," giving three alternatives (separated by "|"). There may be one or more staves repeated vertically, one or more staves repeated vertically with a "lyric" text unit, or a "chord" symbol marking heading the one or more staves repeated vertically with a "lyric" text unit.

HEART: Music Primitives and Units

Capturing the basic relations between regions of a page is obviously not unrelated to capturing the basic spatial relations between the symbols of music notation themselves. These are particular pen-strokes that correspond to music "primitives" (such as stem lines, or note heads) and units (composite objects). Distinguishing a unit from a primitive is not a trivial task, and what is a unit and what is a primitive may depend upon the music being written. For example, primitives might correspond to individual crotchet and quaver notes (with stem up), or (if the music warranted it) the primitives might extend to include beamed dotted pairs of quavers and semi-quavers.

The description of music primitives is again hierarchical and will include the set of points from which the primitive is composed. These may have been written in one pen-down movement, or more likely are a combination of a few pen-up/down movements. Consider the points in Figure 12a corresponding to a chord triplet, the stem, beam, note heads and triplet marker that have been constructed with a series of pen-up/down movements. From the visual (bitmap) representation of these points there is no way of telling the order in which components were added. A static representation language may simply record four notes in a chord, beamed as triplets. But a representation suitable for capturing the dynamics must include how the unit was constructed.

Figure 12a: Music Unit (Triplet) Composed of Primitives

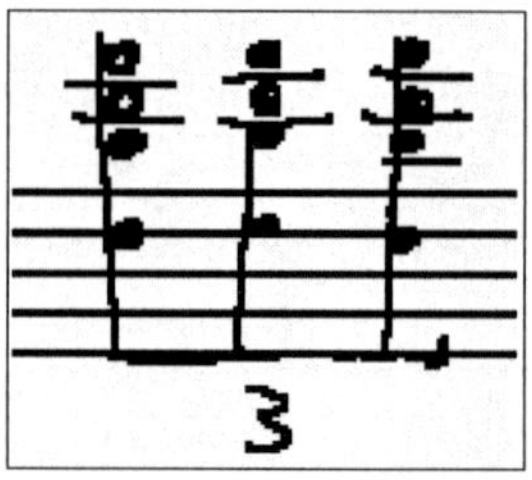

Figure 12b shows the temporal construction of the unit, starting at the top left and moving to the bottom right. Twenty-four different pen-down/up movements were required to construct the symbol. Also, the last step, the addition of the "3" triplet marker, was completed at a very distant temporal event (another such triplet unit having been constructed to its right in the meantime). Only when this was finished was the original unit re-visited and the "3" added to complete it. Capturing such distant spatio-temporal events is vital for the representation of dynamic on-line data.

We suggest a format based around pen-up/down movements where a catalogue is made maintaining the coordinate, pressure, and time information every time the pen comes into contact with the tablet. There may be several hundred of these movements, ranging from just a few points (e.g., for a dot) to several hundred (e.g., for a long line where there are many unique coordinate points, or a symbol constructed very slowly where there would be the same coordinates recorded at many repeat timestamps). The time when the

Figure 12b: The Temporal Construction of the Triplet Unit

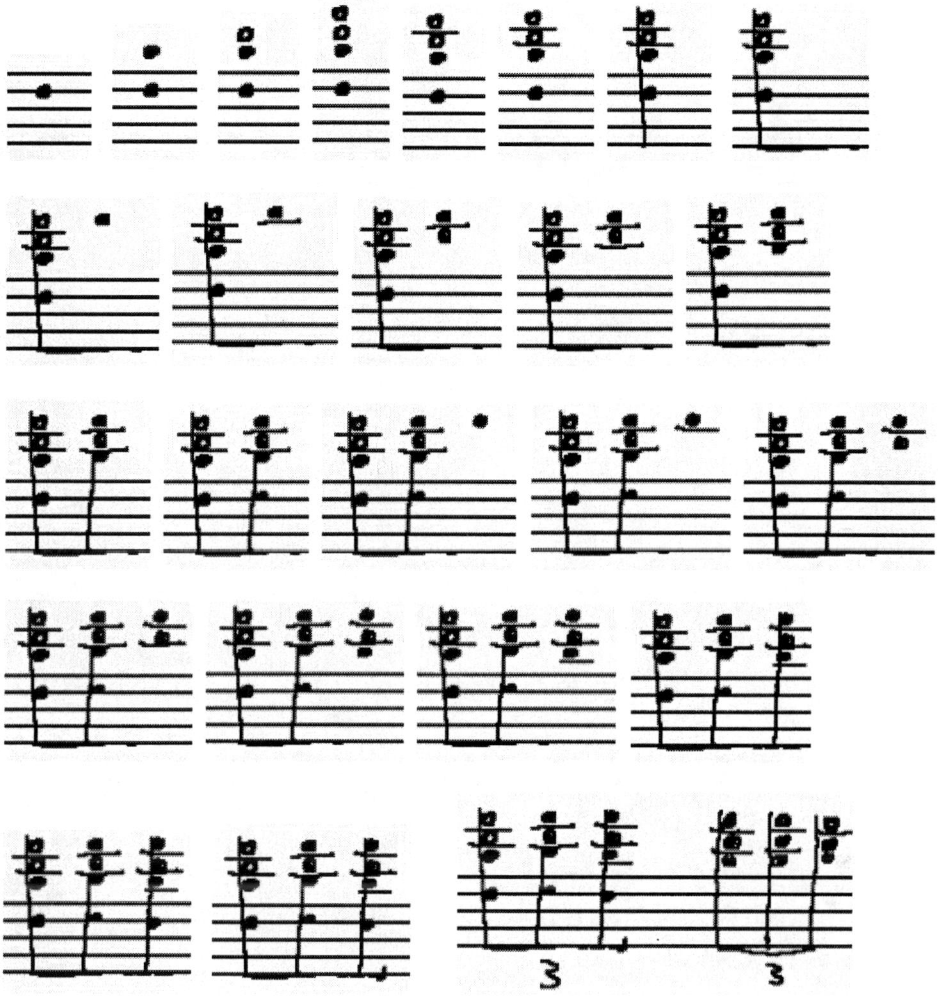

pen is in contact with the tablet is the smallest and most basic unit recorded, and from these groups of points higher level constructs are created — including the "units" and primitives previously mentioned and ultimately the lines and staves that compose the music page. Figure 13a illustrates a fragment of music and 13b the 42 basic pen-up/down movements used to construct it.

Figure 13a: Music Fragment

Figure 13b: 42 Pen-Up/Down Movements

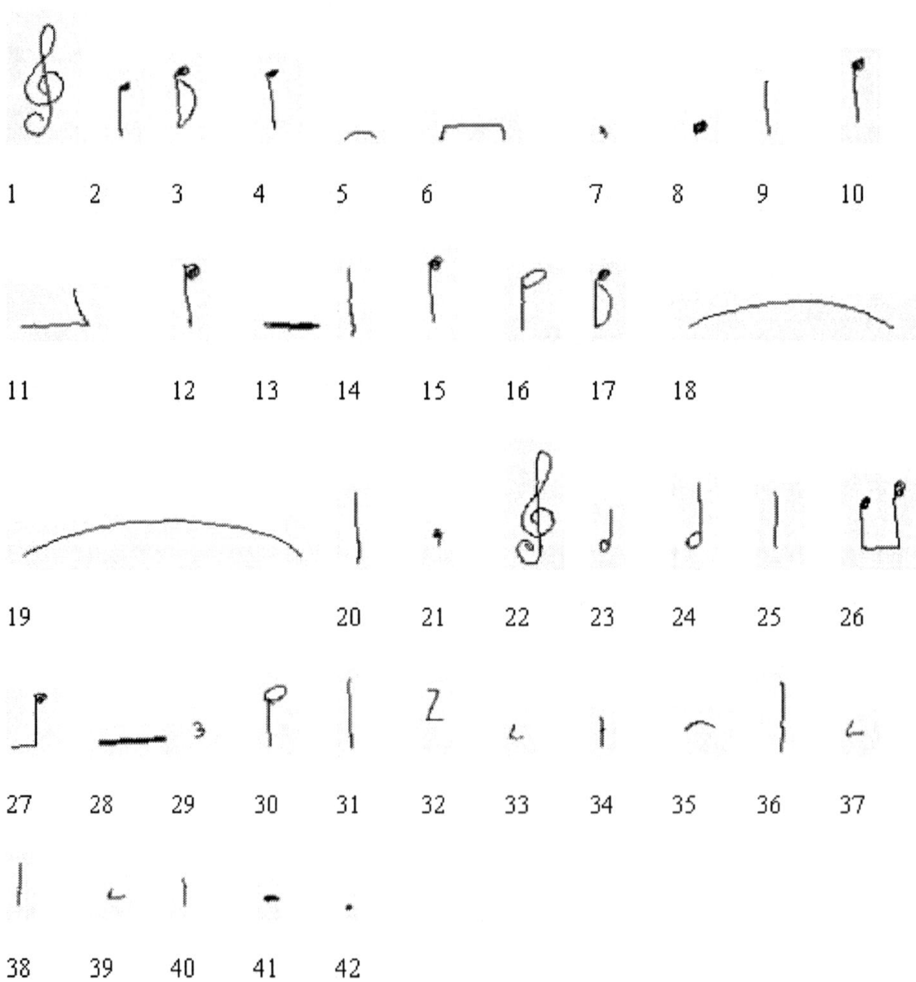

Naturally there are many different ways of composing these basic pen movements into higher level units and music notation primitives. Figure 14 illustrates one way in which the 42 movements may be grouped, starting with level 1, which combines some of these basic movements into note units (including triplets and quaver pairs) and also time signatures. Level 2 includes

Figure 14: Combining the Pen-Up/Down Movements into Higher Level Units

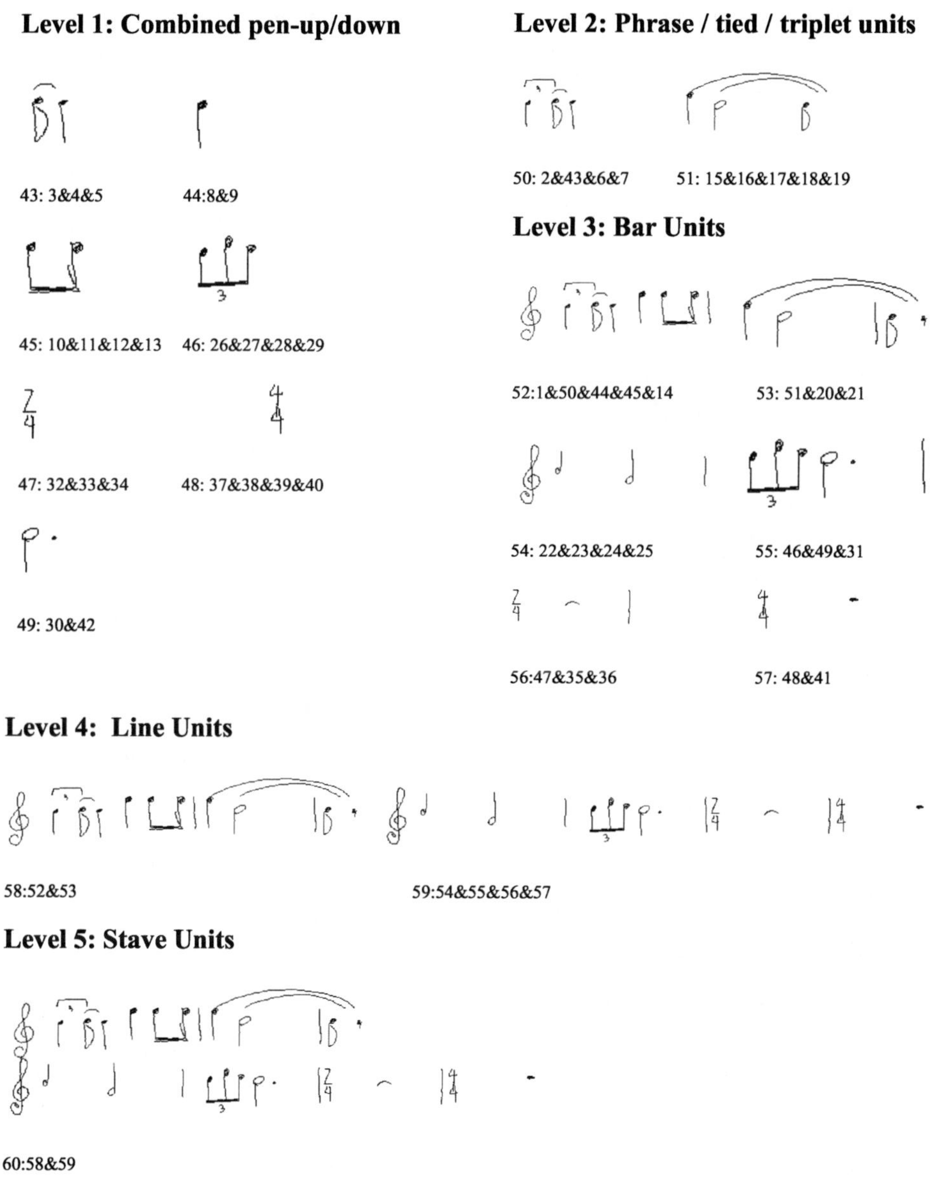

the phrase, tied and triplet units; level 3 includes bar units; level 4 includes lint units; and level 5 is staff units. This imposes 18 new "units" onto the raw data, including semantically meaningful ones (such as number 44, which combines the two pen movements required to make a crotchet note) as well as grouping the notes into bars and lines at the higher levels.

The primitives are arranged in a simple text file that organises the basic pen-down and pen-up movements separately, upon which a structure is imposed — putting them into groups and progressively higher level semantically meaningful units as illustrated in Figure 15. The basic tagged structure can be used

Figure 15: Schema of How the HEART File Organises the Raw Data into a Truth Representation

```
<Header>
<MusicRegions>
     <StaveLocations>
          <S1> Startx Starty Endx Endy </S1>
          <S2> Startx Starty Endx Endy </S2>
     </StaveLocations>
     <LyricLocations>
          <Word1> Startx Starty Endx Endy </Word1>
          <Word2> Startx Starty Endx Endy </Word2>
          <Word3> Startx Starty Endx Endy </Word3>
     </LyricLocations>
</MusicRegions>
<Title Locations></Title Locations>
</Header>
<PrimitivesandUnits>
<BasicPenDownUnits>
     <Level0> 1 2 …  42 </Level0>
          <Level0_p1_1> t1 x1 y1 p1 </Level0_p1_1>
          <Level0_p1_2> t1 x1 y1 p1 </Level0_p1_2>
          …
          <Level0_p42_1> t1 x1 y1 p1 </Level0_p42_1>

     <Level1> 43 …  49 </Level1>

     <Level2> 50 51 </Level2>
</BasicPenDownUnits>

<BasicPenUpUnits>
     <Level0_p1_1> t1 x1 y1 p1 </Level0_p1_1>

     <Level0_p2_1> t2 x1 y1 p1 x2 y2 p2 </Level0_p2_1>
</BasicPenUpUnits>
</PrimitivesandUnits>
```

to represent other information such as deleted pen strokes, strokes of a particular colour, the sampling rate, the writer, or any other information that is deemed necessary.

Note that the section "primitives and units" contains the basic data for pen-down and pen-up movements, and additionally the 42 primitive pen-down movements are each composed of a number of points. Hence, the tag <Level0_p1_2> indicates a level 0 definition for the first of 42 symbols, and this is the second piece of information for the pen-down movement and it includes time, x coordinate, y coordinate, and pressure. Where more than one reading was captured at a given time there would be no new time stamp, but rather the x, y and pressure values captured at that time. To this representation we also need to add region information, including the location of the stavelines and any title/lyrics that may be found.

Each basic pen-down unit contains a set of data points including time, x and y coordinate and pressure recording. The time in microseconds is relative to the current page on the tablet; the coordinates are absolute coordinates relative to the current page on the screen and the pressure is the absolute pressure recorded. We also include the pen-up information since this contains the pen movement pattern made when the pen was not in contact with the tablet. The region information includes the location of other elements that may be found upon the page after region analysis.

The HEART format can be applied to structure printed music data. Naturally the pen-up/down information will not include either time values, but rather a fixed set of coordinates corresponding to given music symbols. The pressure value can be used to indicate the thickness of pen with which the symbol would be printed. These primitives can still be composed in a unique hierarchical way to create the high-level representation of the data, specifying in a very detailed way the typesetting choices.

Benchmark Data

In this section we identify the need for a set of benchmark data to evaluate music recognition in both the off-line (OMR) and on-line (pen-based interface) contexts. Using a representation language such as HEART, it would be possible to capture the semantics of a piece of music as well as the typesetting/handwriting dynamics. First we review a few specific repositories of electronic music data that currently exist, and note that these are not totally suitable for a comprehensive benchmark data set in OMR, since they are generally developed for other purposes. We briefly consider the legal implications of establishing a database of music samples before outlining the range of test data that needs to be considered. We summarise databases designed to meet these purposes in MusicBase I, containing a range of off-line image data, and MusicBase II, containing some dynamic on-line data in the HEART described format.

Repositories of Music Data

Repositories of electronic music notation data are rare. There are some repositories of scanned music, chiefly printed, some handwritten, some from medieval notation standards and non-common music format. However, these databases are not explicitly set up for the evaluation of music recognition software! There is no "truth" representation (at any level) made available, since there is often a musicological or sociological slant to the collection that renders it less than adequate for a benchmark set of test data for OMR. Repositories for on-line dynamic data are non-existent. The absence of such a test database for music samples (with or without their truth representation) has already been noted (Blostein & Carter, 1992).

The Lester Levy Collection is one example of an electronic repository containing 29,000 pieces of American music from the 1780s onwards. Much of it is band music (levysheetmusic.mse.jhu.edu) found at the John Hopkins University. Another selection of digital music is a selection of band music from the American Civil War era (www.multcolib.org/ref/music.html). There are opera and lieder examples at clasicalmus.hispeed.com/operalinks.html, and some images of medieval music at LaTrobe University, Australia.

There also exist repositories such as MuseData (Selfridge-Field, 1997) that contain music expressed in a logical description language. The text-based language is currently being used in the construction of databases for composers, including J. S. Bach, Beethoven, Corelli, Handel, Haydn, Mozart, Telemann, and Vivaldi and could eventually be used for music printing, music analysis, and production of electronic sound files. MuseData code is designed to represent both notational and sound information, but is not complete in what is represented. The database currently consists of more than 7,000 MuseData files and when complete, could exceed 100,000 files. Each MuseData file represents the encoding of one musical part from a movement of a composition.

Indiana University has an electronic music collection including music sound recordings and print and handwritten musical compositions from the songwriter Hoagland "Hoagy" Carmichael (http://www.dlib.indiana.edu/collections/

hoagy/intro/index.html). The relatively recent music (of a composer who died only in 1981), naturally, has associated copyright issues.

In contrast, the Digital Image Archive of Medieval Music project at Harvard has collected images of medieval music in the Neume Notation Project. Included are samples of chant, sacred, and secular music (http://scribe.fas.harvard.edu/medieval/). The aim is to record in machine-readable and searchable form the corpus of medieval music, obtaining a "lossless" data representation that captures the semantic content of the source material in a way that will support all anticipated uses. They observe that there are about a dozen standards for digital representation of music, but encoding chant with any of them forces an interpretation in the modern musical idiom.

Legal Issues in a Music Repository

Naturally, there are legal issues to consider when making a repository of music data, particularly with respect to copyright that may involve both the composer and the publisher's rights on the music. In Australia the copyright law is contained in the Copyright Act 1968. Music is protected as soon as it is fixed in a material form (written or recorded). The copyright owner controls the right to reproduce or perform the work, as well as to transcribe or translate the lyrics. Copyright in music lasts for 50 years after the death of the composer. If the composer is alive or died less than 50 years ago the work is under copyright. Copyright in lyrics also lasts 50 years after the death of the lyricists. Copying music that includes lyrics must also consider the copyright life of the words. With collaboration the copyright lasts up to 50 years after the death of the last author. Arrangements of public domain work may also be protected, even though the original work is not. Again copyright lasts for the life of the arranger plus 50 years. The published edition or typesetting of a work is protected for 25 years from the date of publication. This does not apply to the copying of public domain works in educational institutions.

There are special exceptions where copying can be done without permission. The Australian Act allows copying of up to 10% (or one chapter of a work) for research and study. A musical work is a complete piece of music and each individual piece in the collection is a separate piece, so only 10% of an individual piece of music may be copied under these provisions. Copies of music and lyrics can be made by hand by a teacher or student, but multiple copies of this transcription cannot be made (Copyright Agency Limited, www.copyright.com.au).

Range of Test Data: MusicBase I and II

There are a variety of test cases to consider when it comes to recognising on-line or off-line data. We may broadly divide these into categories including (i) page segmentation issues (coping with title and staff and intervening text), (ii) range of music symbols covered (e.g., double sharps, clef symbols, various note durations), (iii) lyrics (alignment with words), and (iv) performance directives (within and at the start of music). There are also some specific issues to consider in the off-line case including the quality of the scanned image — the resolution, binary/greyscale format, whether skewed, or degraded by noise, even whether the image is in colour or not.

MusicBase I and II are proposed as repositories of data for on-line and off-line music recognition respectively. Appendix 1 illustrates some samples from MusicBase I, while Appendix 2 illustrates some bitmap images of handwritten data in MusicBase II. As the section below discusses these test cases, that we suggest are included in MusicBase are ideally present in a high-level format such as HEART. From such a "truth representation" it is possible to both (a) generate off-line data simulating the various typesetting possibilities that might exist to produce a bitmap image and (b) also automatically generate HEART files representing on-line data, representing small perturbations of the printed data as it is rendered in handwritten form.

Conclusion

In this chapter we have considered the evaluation of music recognition in both the off-line (OMR) and on-line (pen-based interface) contexts. We provided some examples of OMR recognition achieved by the SmartScore OMR system and noted that there is a general difficulty in quantifying the accuracy of music recognition systems — and, hence, assessing them. We considered the issues in evaluating accuracy and augmented the confusion matrix (for simple character-based recognition) to express "composite typeset elements," introducing the possibility of a degree of correctness for recognition of the composite, rather than an absolute measure. We also identified the need for a high-level representation of the music semantics in a language capable of capturing both the dynamic elements of handwritten music and particular typesetting choices, proposing the HEART language to do this. A review of music repositories revealed that there are few in existence and that they would benefit from including a wide range of examples and being automatically generated. Version 1.0 of MusicBase I and II were proposed containing some music data that might be included in an OMR/pen-based repository for music notation recognition.

References

Adobe Systems Incorporated. (1992, March 31). Sonata Font Design Specification, Technical Note 5045.

Aho, A., Sethi, R. & Ullman, J. (1986). *Compilers: Principles, Techniques and Tools.* Reading, MA: Addison-Wesley.

Bainbridge, D. & Bell, T.C. (1997, July). Dealing with superimposed objects in optical music recognition. *6th International Conference on Image Processing and Its Applications,* (vol. 2, pp. 756-760). Dublin, Ireland.

Blostein, D. & Baird, H.S. (1992). A critical survey of music image analysis. In H.S. Baird, H. Bunke & K. Yamamoto (Eds.), *Structured Document Image Analysis* (pp. 405-434). Berlin: Springer-Verlag.

Blostein, D. & Carter, N.P. (1992). Recognition of music notation, SSPR'90 working group report. In H.S. Baird, H. Bunke & K. Yamamoto (Eds.), *Structure Document Image Analysis* (pp. 573-574). Berlin: Springer-Verlag.

Caston, G., Good, M. & Roland, P. (2001). Extensible markup language (XML) for music applications: An introduction. In W. B. Hewlett & E. Selfridge-Field (Eds.), *The Virtual Score: Representation, Retrieval, Restoration* (pp. 95-102). Cambridge, MA: MIT Press.

Copyright Agency Limited. (n.d.). www.copyright.com.au. Last accessed April 17, 2003.

Guyon, I., Schomaker, L., Plamondon, R., Liberman, M. & Janet, S. (1994, October). UNIPEN project of on-line data exchange and recognizer benchmarks. *Proceedings of the 12th International Conference on Pattern Recognition, ICPR'94* (pp. 29-33). Jerusalem, Israel: IAPR-IEEE.

Kopec, G. E., Chou, P.A. & Maltz, D. A. (1995, February 5-10). Markov source model for printed music decoding. *IS&T, SPIE Intl, Symposium on Electronic Imaging.* San Jose, CA.

Selfridge-Field, E. (ed.). (1997). *Beyond MIDI - The Handbook of Musical Codes.* London: The MIT Press.

Slate Corporation. (1993). *JOT A Specification for an Ink Storage and Interchange Format, Version 1.0.* Scottsdale, AZ: Slate Corporation.

Stiny G. (1976). Two exercises in formal composition. *Environment and Planning,* B(3), 187-210.

Appendix 1: Example of Data From MusicBase I (Off-Line Data)

Example 1: Essential Scales and Arpeggios for Piano, Eileen Stainkamph, Allans, 2000

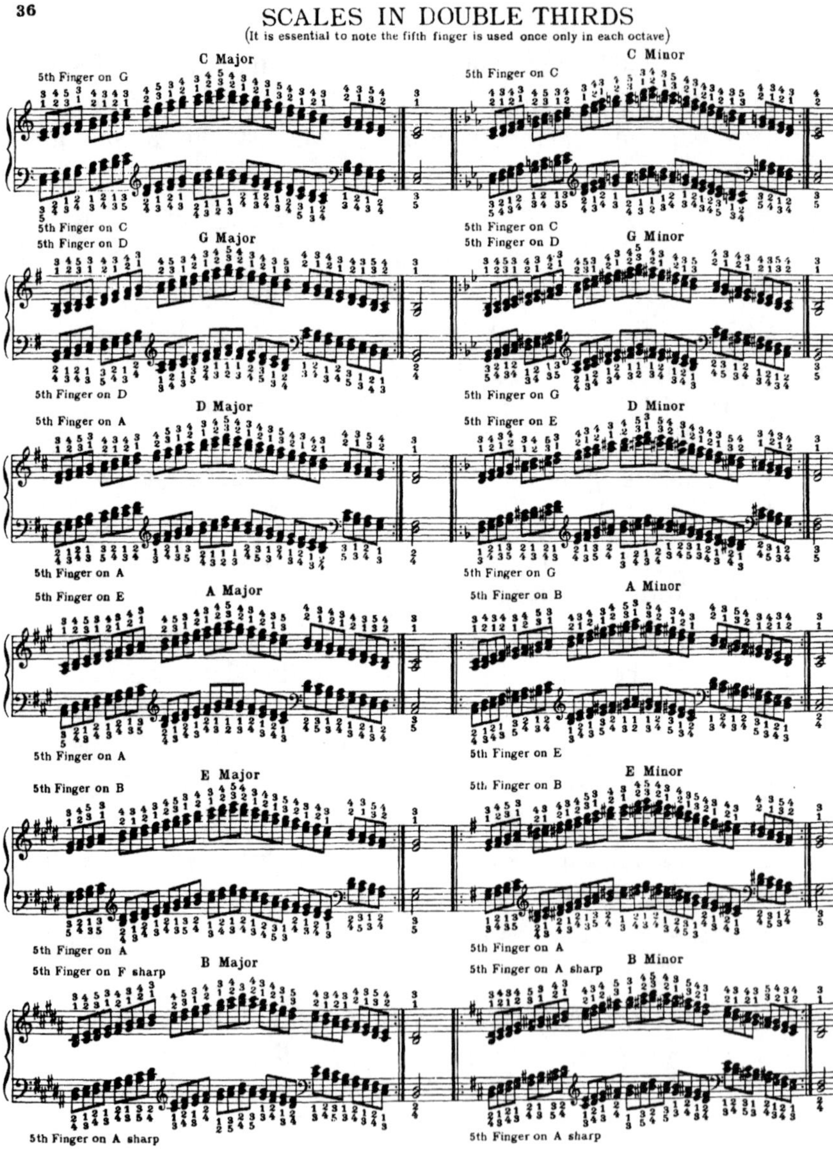

Example 2: Liszt Rhapsodies Hongroises (Rhapsodie 8), p. 85, London, Augener Ltd.

Example 3: Class and Romantic Pianoforte Pieces (Fur Elise, Beethoven), Associated Board of the Royal Schools of Music, 1929

Appendix 2: Example of Data From MusicBase II (on-line data)

Example 1

Example 2

Example 3

Example 4

Example 5

Example 6

Example 7

Example 8

Example 9

Example 10

Example 11

Example 12

About the Editor

Susan E. George received her B.Sc. and Ph.D. in computer science from the University of Reading, UK, and M.Sc. in knowledge-based systems from Edinburgh University, UK. Dr. George has undertaken post-doctoral research at both the Department of Optometry and Vision Sciences, University of Wales, and the School of Computer and Information Science (CIS), University of South Australia. She is currently a senior lecturer in computer and information science. Her research interests include artificial neural networks and pattern recognition with applications in biometrics, medicine, language learning, and music recognition.

About the Authors

Tom Addis leads the Intelligent Systems Research Group at Portsmouth University and is a visiting professor at the Science Studies Centre, Department of Psychology, University of Bath, UK. He has a regular technical exchange with the University of Delft involving postgraduate students. He is actively engaged in modelling the "discovery" process in science and engineering. He has developed an expert control system for oil tankers and is working on intelligent robot control. He is currently investigating the use of architectural and urban development theories to understand system evolution as well as exploring, with Dr. Billinge, metaphor as a mechanism for human computer interaction. He worked at the ICL Research and Advanced Development Centre on computer speech recognition and user behaviour. He lectured at Brunel University and then moved to the University of Reading as professor of computer science. He was a technical consultant to GEC Hirst Research. With Plessey, he evolved a wafer manufacturing scheduling system. He has more than 70 major technical and scientific publications. He is associate editor of the *International Journal of Human Computer Studies*.

Pierfrancesco Bellini is a contract professor at the University of Florence, Department of Systems and Informatics (Italy). His research interests include object-oriented technology, real-time systems, formal languages, and computer music. Bellini received a Ph.D. in electronic and informatics engineering from the University of Florence, and worked on MOODS, WEDELMUSIC, IMUTUS, and MUSICNETWORK projects of the European Commission.

Dave Billinge is director of computing undergraduate studies for the Faculty of Technology at the University of Portsmouth, UK. He is a qualified teacher, and holds degrees in philosophy from London and in information systems from Portsmouth. He taught grade school in the UK, Zambia, and Saudi Arabia through the 70s and 80s before moving to Portsmouth to take his higher degree and doctorate. He now lectures on information systems and databases. Dr. Billinge's research interests, on which he has published more than a dozen articles and papers, include the language of emotional effect, the potential of expert systems for artistic decision-making, and the links between language and music. He is a frequent concert goer and also lectures on music appreciation.

Ivan Bruno is a Ph.D. candidate in software engineering and telecommunication at the University of Florence, Italy. His research interests include optical music recognition, audio processing, computer music, object-oriented technologies, and software engineering. He worked on WEDELMUSIC, VISICON, IMUTUS, and MUSICNETWORK projects of the European Commission.

Ichiro Fujinaga is an assistant professor at Faculty of Music of McGill University (Canada) and the chair of the Music Technology Area. He has bachelor's degrees in music/percussion and mathematics from the University of Alberta, a master's degree in music theory, and a Ph.D. in music technology from McGill University. He was, until recently, a faculty member of the Computer Music Department at the Peabody Conservatory of Music of the Johns Hopkins University. His research interests include pattern recognition, machine learning, music information retrieval, software synthesis, virtual concert stage, vibrato analysis, music perception, and optical music recognition.

Paolo Nesi is a full professor at the University of Florence (Italy), Department of Systems and Informatics. His research interests include object-oriented technology, real-time systems, quality, system assessment, testing, formal languages, physical models, computer music, and parallel architectures. Dr. Nesi received a Ph.D. in electronic and informatics engineering from the University of Padova. He has been the general chair of the WEDELMUSIC conference and of several other internal conferences. He is the coordinator of the following research and development multipartner projects: MOODS (Music Object Oriented Distributed System, http://www.dsi.unifi.it/~moods/), WEDELMUSIC (WEB Delivering of Music Score, www.wedelmusic.org), and MUSICNETWORK (The Interactive Music Network, www.interactivemusicnet work.org).

Kia Ng is director of the Interdisciplinary Centre for Scientific Research in Music (ICSRiM) at the University of Leeds, UK. His research links together works in the Schools of Computing, Music, and Electronic and Electrical Engineering on multimedia, computer vision, computer music and digital media. Dr. Ng has been active in Optical Music Recognition (OMR) research since 1991, working on computer recognition, restoration and translation of printed and handwritten music manuscripts. His Music via Motion (MvM) system allows users to have real-time control of musical sound using their physical movement. It has been widely featured in the media, including the BBC's News 24 and Tomorrow's World Plus and Sky TV. His paper on 3D reconstruction of real environment won the prestigious U.V. Helava Award (Best Paper 1999, ISPRS Journal, Elsevier Science), and a Young Author's Award at the International Society for Photogrammetry and Remote Sensing Commission V Symposium on Real-Time Imaging and Dynamic Analysis. Dr. Ng is an editorial consultant of the *Computer Music Journal*, MIT Press, and chairman of the Music Imaging Ltd., UK.

INDEX